VERSITY OF
IGHAM

How Africa Works

Praise for this book

'This book, rich in well-grounded case studies on work and working in different parts of Africa, makes a sustained and compelling case for taking seriously the making of occupational identities, in ongoing scholarly efforts to theorize the construction of social identities on the continent.'

Francis B. Nyamnjoh, Professor of Social Anthropology,
University of Cape Town

'A valuable collection of reflective studies of occupational identity in Africa, hugely welcome in the context of a long overdue reassessment of what work is and should be, after a century of labourist distortion. Africa has much to teach the rest of the world.'

Guy Standing, Professor of Economic Security, University of Bath

'An important contribution to African studies, one which should be read by others interested in changing occupations, identities and moralities everywhere.'

Pat Caplan, Professor of Anthropology, Goldsmiths College,
University of London

'This book addresses a nagging question which I, like many other Africans, frequently encounter in these globalizing heydays of the livelihood discourse: "How do you earn a living?" From multiple vantage points, the book shows how the types of work we do in Africa shape and are shaped by our social identity and self-worth as individuals and as a community which is stereotypically viewed as being stuck in poverty. It is a must read for anyone who genuinely needs to understand how work is valued or perceived - and thus practised and diversified – in various African occupational settings.'

Chambi Chachage, independent researcher,
newspaper columnist and policy analyst

How Africa Works
Occupational Change, Identity and Morality

Edited by Deborah Fahy Bryceson

PRACTICAL ACTION
Publishing

Practical Action Publishing Ltd.
Schumacher Centre for Technology and Development
Bourton on Dunsmore, Rugby,
Warwickshire CV23 9QZ, UK
www.practicalactionpublishing.org

© Deborah Fahy Bryceson, 2010

ISBN 978 1 85339 691 5

A catalogue record for this book is available from the British Library.

Since 1974, Practical Action Publishing (formerly Intermediate Technology
Publications and ITDG Publishing) has published and disseminated books
and information in support of international development work throughout
the world. Practical Action Publishing is a trading name of Practical Action
Publishing Ltd (Company Reg. No. 1159018), the wholly owned publishing
company of Practical Action. Practical Action Publishing trades only in
support of its parent charity objectives and any profits are covenanted back
to Practical Action (Charity Reg. No. 247257, Group VAT Registration
No. 880 9924 76).

Cover photo: Pulling ropes, Tanzania, 2007, credit: D.F. Bryceson
Cover design by Practical Action Publishing
Indexed by Andrea Palmer
Typeset by S.J.I. Services
Printed by Hobbs the Printers Ltd

Contents

Figures

Tables

Acknowledgements

This book is a product of years of collaborative work in the fields of de-agrarianization and urban studies. Thanks go to Ann Reeves for her copy-editing work and to the Urban Studies journal and the Department of Geographical and Earth Sciences at the University of Glasgow for support during the final stages of preparing this collection for press.

SECTION I
Introduction

CHAPTER 1

Africa at work: transforming occupational identity and morality

Deborah Fahy Bryceson

Over the last decade, livelihood studies have documented the shifting contours of Africans' attempts to make ends meet and improve their household welfare, but the significance of work for social identity and sense of self worth has been largely disregarded in favour of concentration on ethnicity, gender and generational identities. This introductory chapter situates the subject matter of the volume's case study chapters by theorizing the occupational and sectoral transformation currently underway in the globalizing local economies of East, West and Southern Africa. Probing issues of work motivation, trust and ethics, the intricate bonds between occupational identity and public morality are revealed. Occupational upheaval has been an axis around which the African problematic, namely, the continent's present welfare predicament and political instability, have coalesced. Current occupational identity formation and the process of building trust at workplaces constitute profound moral realignments girding sub-Saharan Africa's national economies and cultures.

Introduction

In Africa,[1] more than any other continent, people are engaged in uncertain, poorly remunerated work for daily survival. Smallholder farming populations are diversifying into non-agricultural work activities from which they increasingly earn their livelihood. Meanwhile in the continent's expanding urban settlements, migration from the countryside and the contracting size of the formal sector has channelled millions into new informal occupational pursuits.

Over the last decade, livelihood studies have documented the shifting contours of Africans' attempts to make ends meet and improve their household welfare, but the significance of work for social identity has been nonetheless largely disregarded. Instead, social and political studies fixate on the role of ethnicity, gender and generational identities, ignoring their intricate bonds with occupational identity.

Occupational upheaval has been an axis around which the African problematic, namely, the continent's present welfare predicament and political instability, have coalesced. Rapid occupational and sectoral transformation and the profound moral realignments girding this process constitute the subject matter of the chapters that follow. This introductory chapter presents a conceptual overview focused on occupational mobility and forms of exchange in Africa's globalizing local economies. The case studies from East, West and Southern Africa that follow document the intricacies of the on-going social construction of work identities, motivation, trust and ethics.

Work's centrality to identity and the ethical foundations of national cultures

Exploring the multiple social identities of individuals, postmodernist theorists have revealed how knowledge of oneself and society can be highly illusory (Foucault, 1970; Harvey 1990). Much of postmodernist enquiry into the construction of African identity and self worth has centred on the reshaping of gender, generation and ethnicity, which were previously seen as inherently ascribed (Werbner and Ranger, 1996). Researchers have largely ignored occupational identities. And yet in everyday life an individual's habituation to specific work activities is pivotal to his or her sense of self worth and others' perceptions of the individual. Ironically the term 'occupation', which is one of the first questions asked in formal surveys, has been relegated to a background detail, rarely utilized as a pivot in the analysis of African social identity.

Social identity can be thought of as an individual's or group's claim to rights in social space, which encompasses an assemblage of attributes that the social environment avails to the individual within that environment. An occupational identity can be likened to a *laissez-passer* by which the individual finds a place in two-dimensional social space: a situational work location on the horizontal plane and a vertical position within the society's social hierarchy. In brief encounters, people tend to make snap judgements about each other on the basis of their respective occupational pursuits. In effect, occupation becomes a rule of thumb for estimating social status. However, increasingly over recent decades an individual's occupational identity has become chameleon in character and social status is accordingly malleable. Occupational manoeuvrability has been especially fluid in Africa. The past three decades have constituted a protracted period of work experimentation involving a transition from comparatively static to dynamic but insecure occupational patterns. For this reason, the term 'occupationality' is used here to highlight the transitional nature of occupational identity and work ethics in Africa today.

Occupationality and work

'Occupationality', the *process* of skill acquisition, economic exchange, psychological orientation and social positioning through which an individual becomes actively engaged in specific work and identifies with it as an extension of his or her social being, is rarely an exercise in free choice wherever it takes place in the world. At the outset, there is a bifurcation of male and female work trajectories and multiple class-based paths. In turn, these alignments pre-condition whether a person is uneducated or educated to a particular level thereby determining entry into manual or non-manual work and whether the person will engage in unpaid or paid, low or high status and legal or illegal work. Individuals gravitate towards work through a labyrinth of compelling or repelling options. The eventual outcome can be pleasing or disappointing to the individual. In periods of social, economic or technological flux, the trial and error search may be repeated time and again, channelling the individual towards growing affluence, impoverishment, fluctuating fortunes or homeostasis.

Before probing the significance of occupationality, it is useful to dwell on the meaning of 'work'. The Concise Oxford Dictionary defines work as 'expenditure of energy, striving, application of effort or exertion to a purpose'. Work, in the first instance, is composed of the material goal of livelihood to facilitate physical output for direct consumption, trade or contractually exchanged for a wage. There is however an intrinsic, psychological and social realm to work that has been studiously circumvented in economic analysis until recently.[2] Similarly, the livelihood literature has bypassed the multi-faceted psychosocial dimensions of work. It is for this reason that the concept of 'occupationality' is advanced to draw attention to how an individual's livelihood search is a process of both finding an economic livelihood and formulating their social identity as economically active members of society, especially in periods of sectoral restructuring.

People seek self-esteem and a sense of social worth through work. Ideally, work provides a feeling of personal confidence, enjoyment and belonging. In management-speak, this would be called 'job satisfaction', but a utilitarian management perspective fails to encompass the full psychological meaning of work. So too, economists' focus on wage incentives is far too delimited. Work is intrinsically bound up in striving for a sense of security, competence, mastery, and in many cases, the desire to contribute to society. An individual's work motivation is multi-faceted and changes in complex ways over his or her life cycle.

Ideally, individuals find work that makes them not just materially better off but also happy and socially fulfilled. Most adults acquire their core social identity through work, either through their own active projection of their work identities or, more passively, through the work identity that people ascribe to them. In other words, 'you are what you do'.

By contrast, in 'traditional' rural societies, as recorded by a barrage of social science literature, the dictum tended to be the reverse: 'you do what you are' (Mair, 1983). The progression of one's work life was ordained by gender, age and ethnicity. From birth to death, the individual was expected to progress through a well-trodden path of work tasks and changing status grounded in the community's agrarian, pastoralist or hunting-gathering modes of livelihood. Skills were transmitted relationally within the ethnic community, imparting a blended occupational and ethnic identity in the process. Ingold (2000) sees skill acquisition as an entwined process of relational interaction and learning rather than generational transmission *per se*. Colonial policies directed at encouraging monetization, peasant commodity production and wage labour began to erode both ethnic locality-specific skill transfer and identity formation, but it was not until the global oil crises of the 1970s, and post-colonial international financial institution-directed reform policies extending global market penetration, that ascriptive work and social status in Africa's ethnic-based local rural communities entered rapid freefall.

Work ascription in the African countryside has increasingly been displaced by the search for diversified income-earning activities aimed at material survival, improvement or prosperity (Bryceson, 2000). Now social status derives from the kind of work one does and its level of remuneration for both men and women. A man's success in life is less likely to be measured in terms of the size of his harvest, herd, land holdings or household membership. And the calculation of a woman's success is no longer restrictively based on the number of children she has. As localized plant and animal husbandry practices decline in income-earning potential, people gravitate towards occupations on the basis of self-selection or relegation rather than local community expectations. Furthermore, as the mobility of individuals extends beyond the confines of one's home area, wealth accumulation serves as the central means of claiming status wherever one resides.

Nonetheless, given the severely constrained employment opportunities of the continent, over the last three decades African occupationality at present spans traditional 'ascribed by birth' and modernist 'achieved by individual choice' registers. It occupies a primarily middle ground, a rugged terrain of work assignment involving individuals in livelihood experimentation without well-formed career expectations, promising remuneration trajectories or desired traditional fallback traditions. In this way, there is recourse to non-monetized subsistence-based household production when other work activities fail to yield a sufficient livelihood. Figure 1.1 diagrammatically distinguishes the trial and error approach of African experimental occupationality as opposed to more institutionally structured, specialized occupational career choice. The labour market is present and influential in the African case but it is not as well established nor a driving force to the same degree as in capitalized industrial economies.

In occupationally specialized work contexts, labour market incentives in the form of wages and terms and conditions of employment strongly influence people's work selection. Occupations are professionalized and formally regulated. State welfare measures provide a basic subsistence for the unemployed. Current African occupationality, by contrast, is characterized by the individual's experimental search for a material livelihood in the immediate sense. Over the longer term, risk-averse work diversification is inescapable, in view of the compulsive need for the individual to secure a means of subsistence from market or non-market sources and the lack of fixed career trajectories. The optimizing career dynamic of advanced capitalist societies is

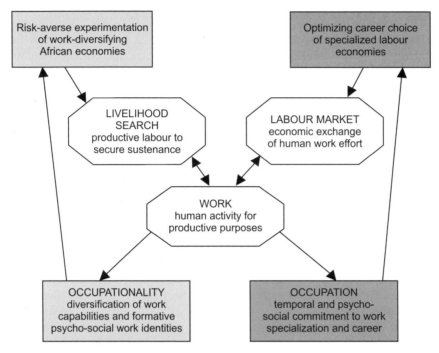

Figure 1.1 African diversified occupationality versus specialized occupational work contexts
Source: Author's representation

outlined in dark grey whereas African experimental occupationality is traced in lighter grey.

'Failed occupationality' in African experimental diversification has a similar psychological effect on the individual as the lack of occupational work has in a capitalist labour market context. In addition to material deprivation, people experience social disapproval and a personal lack of meaning and purpose in their lives. Those who cannot obtain 'suitable' work congruent with their expectations or who fail to find any work are likely to suffer from a lack of social status and respect and feelings of demoralization – a common occurrence in periods of occupational upheaval and uncertainty. Politicians in developed capitalist countries fear the adverse social welfare consequences and political unrest that can arise from a high rate of unemployment that prevents a significant segment of the populace from having an occupational identity. The negative implications of failed occupationality are more far-reaching. Not only are the unemployed devoid of a clear occupational identity and a basic material means of livelihood but at a collective level, high levels of unemployment and under-employment can result in the simultaneous creation of material need and an ethical vacuum in economic life. Not surprisingly, such societies are more liable to experience a breakdown in civil order and public morality as well as rising levels of crime and social indifference.

Ethical codes of work behaviour and accountability in national cultures

Livelihood imperatives, work performance and labour market parameters are entwined at both individual and societal levels. Meritocratic principles ordain that a worker has to deserve promotion through effort or favourable levels of quality or output achievement. The social status of the worker accrues from the society's general awareness of the occupational career ladder and the contributions that the occupation makes to society. Apart from the value placed on exerting oneself at work, the hierarchy between occupations pegs workers' social status relative to one another.

In diversifying economies, where work career trajectories are still in formation, professional codes of behaviour remain undefined formally. Individuals may gain success materially and socially but they are less likely to be publically acknowledged by their peers due to the relative absence of established traditions of professionalism, work target setting and promotion.

In African societies experiencing rapid labour diversification, career trajectories and indeed vertical organizational movement are far less in evidence. Informalization of the economy and *ad hoc* self-employment are the norm (Seppälä, Chapter 13). Individuals move horizontally in a labour market of uncertainty (Bryceson, 2002a; 2002b). Work ethics are present but are, like the material circumstances they are found in, uncertain and contestable. They mediate an individual's service towards clients and customers and collegial interaction, providing a sense of social and economic order to local communities. Scaling up, work ethics impart moral meaning to the country's division of labour and are thereby foundational to national cultures. As a basis and guide for monitoring work, they facilitate national production and are a vital component of a society's collectively held moral values and national identity. What is important to note is that work ethics can realistically only be imposed and enforced from within the society (Haidt, 2006). Attempts to impose external moral standards are likely to have the opposite effect to what is intended.

How do moral ethics evolve in labour-diversifying economies? In urban medieval Europe, occupation-based guilds functioned to codify work ethics to moderate naked self-interest and encourage trust against the background of a hegemonic Roman Catholic Church (Epstein, 1991). Specialized professional groups capable of establishing and enforcing occupational ethics emerged. While apprenticeship systems operate in some places in Africa, they are not widely prevalent continentally. Nor is there a dominant religion acting as a generalized moral authority. Occupational ethics in Africa are coalescing in a far more decentralized *ad hoc* 'on-the-job' manner. The case studies in this book document the moral qualms and dilemmas people face in their daily work lives and how they are resolving these in situations of flux where state and market institutions are weak.

The profound upheaval: African sectoral transformation

Over the latter part of the 20th century, African agrarian core values have been challenged by a number of economic and social trends, notably the drastic change in terms of trade initiated by the oil crises of 1973 and 1979, the steady decline in value of agricultural products in the world market, and urbanization. The former pushed most African countries into a severe debt crisis, setting in train the imposition of structural adjustment conditionality, which destabilized peasant farmers' commercial agriculture. The rural search for alternative sources of income to peasant commercial farming in the 1980s escalated in the 1990s and continues to the present (Bryceson, 2002a,b).

Economic, political, social and cultural processes of change have been deeply entwined in these trends, catalysing extremely rapid restructuring of existing rural households, communities, markets and the operation of the state at all levels. The case studies in this volume illustrate how economic shocks and restructuring have jolted social organization and cultural identities. In several instances world market prices were the first to catalyse large-scale sectoral change. Mohogu (Chapter 4) writes about the negative effect of the drop in the price of copper in Zaire. Jua (Chapter 7) dates the beginning of Cameroonian decline to 1986 as the country's oil wealth gave way to debt and structural adjustment was implemented to scale down the public sector. Lindell (Chapter 8) documents the surge in income diversification and urban traders, whereas Mbilinyi (Chapter 9), relates the effect of structural adjustment policies (SAP) on the Tanzanian peasant agricultural sector, notably the cutback in agricultural inputs and rising transport costs. Bank (Chapter 10) records the process of adjustment in the new South Africa during the 1990s – the steady progression of government programmes generating a bewildering number of acronyms amidst decreased industrial subsidies and rising urban unemployment. Similarly, Konings (Chapter 12) charts the implementation of SAP in Cameroon resulting in retrenchment of plantation labour and the undermining of rural trade unions. Seppälä (Chapter 13) observes the shrinkage of formal labour market and civil service employment in Tanzania, arguing that this engendered 'deprofessionalization' as formal wages ceased to be living wages and formal work became an adjunct to income-generating activities. In addition, introduction of user costs in education reduced school enrolments as foundational training for eventual professionalism.

The sectoral decline of agricultural output as a percentage of total GDP is most salient and is mirrored by a rise in service sector activity (Figure 1.2). These trends denote a long-term process of deagrarianization that involves occupational adjustment, income-earning reorientation, social re-identification and spatial relocation of rural dwellers away from agricultural-based modes of livelihood (Bryceson, 2000). Depeasantization is a specific form of deagrarianization in which peasantries lose their economic capacity and social coherence and demographically shrink in size. In Africa, smallholder farming households, which historically combined commodity and subsistence family farming, have

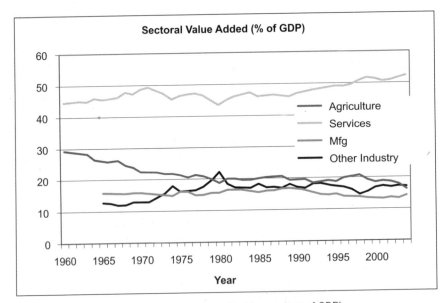

Figure 1.2 Sub-Saharan Africa sectoral value added (percentage of GDP)
Source: World Bank 2008, World Development Indicators

increasingly lost their commercial agricultural component. The African rural household is now less cohesive as a productive unit and members seek to diversify their livelihoods through a wide array of both on and off-farm activities. Peasant village communities are liable to shrinkage through population movement and lose their sense of moral community in the process.

The process of deagrarianization is not unique to Africa. The industrialized western world, Latin America and Asia have all experienced similar developmental trajectories but they have been more fortunate in being able to channel surplus rural labour into industry. With the exception of mining, most African countries have not been so inclined. While manufacturing has remained stagnant over the last 40 years, agriculture as a percentage of GDP has halved (Figure 1.2). Other industry, which represents all non-manufacturers including public utilities and mining, has a rather erratic pattern showing two sharp peaks at the time of the 1970s oil crises. Significantly, as both small and large-scale mining activities have increased in recent years, this category has now overtaken agriculture as a percentage of GDP. Manufacturing industry, on the other hand, fostered in the national independence era of the 1960s and early 1970s, has stalled. Sub-Saharan Africa has witnessed the decline of import substitution and industrial enclave production in South Africa to the extent that the term deindustrialization is applicable (Bryceson and Bank, 2001).

Services have recorded the most consistent upward trend after two noticeable dips at the time of the 1970s oil crises (Figure 1.2). Trade is a major component of services and has undoubtedly made a significant contribution to material welfare in the face of agricultural decline as well as fostering changes in occupational identities and public morality. In some parts of colonial Africa, trade was primarily the preserve of non-African minorities, notably Lebanese in West Africa and Asians in East and Southern Africa. Many of them left at the time of national independence or nationalization of key sectors of African national economies. In several countries, Africanization of the service sector took place in the context of parastatal expansion. Structural adjustment rolled back the state's involvement in the economy. Economic liberalization policies provided Africans with the opportunity to engage in a panoply of service activities. Under structural adjustment policies, the service sector was more protected from the rigours of world market competition compared to internationally traded agricultural and industrial commodity exports.

The most significant feature of the burgeoning service sectors of African countries at this time was their informal nature. The weakened state and economic liberalization policies reduced the degree of regulatory control on commerce and services and the ability to enforce what controls remained. The informal sector afforded *in situ* rural opportunities and an explosion of urban possibilities, growing to vast proportions in terms of the population who derived a livelihood from it and the array of goods and services it encompassed. The sector was highly uneven with respect to its employment composition, entry capital demands and levels of earnings.

Service expansion fuelled by rapid urbanization is, not surprisingly, the other major influence on social and cultural change. Africa's urban population rose from 15 to 37 per cent of sub-Saharan Africa's population (World Bank, 2008). This overall average, however, masks the marked variation between national urbanization levels.

Occupational identity construction in Africa

Amidst the economic upheaval of the last three decades of global market restructuring and the policy turnarounds of African states, African modes of livelihood have been shaken to their core. As labour diversification has proceeded, individuals throughout the continent have experimented with new occupational identities, reflexively interacting with one another, reconfiguring group identities to reflect the new realities of their work lives. Social science research cannot always capture the change. The mental constructs of former occupational identities as farmers or civil servants endure, leading survey respondents to answer social science questionnaires as if their work status was unambiguously that of a peasant farmer or white collar public sector worker glossing over the fact that their families are deeply involved in income diversification and their work lives and income streams are far more complicated. Not mentioning such activities suggests that they have, as yet, not been regularized nor accorded a desirable social status. In many cases, informal sector activities are still tinged with negative associations of marginality or illegality, whereas in other cases the wider public is simply unaware and unappreciative of the effort, ingenuity or skill involved in the activity.

People's diversified economic activities have required the acquisition of new work skills, economic attitudes, strategies and associational ties. The certainties and trusting relationships of former work lives as farmers or civil servants can no longer be counted on. Income diversification involves direct and indirect contact, cooperation and/or competition with hitherto unknown people in local, regional and national markets and other public forums. Amidst a gamut of economic and social uncertainties, income diversifiers must devise viable working relations to gain a basic livelihood at the very least. Since Africa's national economies started their downward descent during the late 1970s and early 1980s, networking and negotiating has proliferated, generating a wide array of iterative social outcomes. The next sub-sections, citing chapter case study material, explores to what extent they may be contributing to the spread of trust, empathy and professionalism in African economic life.

Trust, empathy and professionalism

In highly mobile, socially diverse societies where new relationships are constantly being initiated, trust is often at issue. Kohn (2008) writes of the confusion of no one knowing their station in life anymore. Trust, in these circumstances, hinges on inter-personal assessment. Social science literature on trust has moved beyond the instrumentalism of Putnam's (2000) concept of social capital to muse about a human predisposition for cooperation and trust. Experimental social psychologists (Haidt, 2006; Hauser, 2006) suggest that humans are inclined to trusting cooperative relations based on emotional intuition. This premise infers that people have an innate craving for trust and moral consensus.[3] Nonetheless, it is apparent that some material circumstances are more conducive than others to fostering trust. One of the central concerns of this book is to explore where and how trust is fostered in African work settings.

Single-person own-account enterprises dominate Africa's burgeoning informal sector, which may suggest that bonds of trust are difficult to achieve.[4] Adaptation to the high levels of risk inherent in income diversification experimentation and the general uncertainty and poor level of returns of most African national economies in circumstances in which the economic agents live so close to basic levels of survival may account for low levels of trust. Senegalese Mouride traders overcome this barrier through an extensive social security system in which they agree to share their earnings to cover the likelihood of individuals' failure to make sufficient earnings to cover their living costs on any one day. Along similar lines but still within the context of single own-account businesses, Lindell (Chapter 8) documents how urban women petty traders in Bissau have formed associational ties to insure themselves against the high risks of credit and earnings failure in their enterprises.

Beyond trust, the development of a common occupational group identity requires empathy. Through empathy one appreciates or even projects oneself into someone else's position, which, if reciprocated, can become mutual identification. A group of individuals doing the same kind of work can easily empathize with one another at the level of their shared work experience, progressing towards reflexive action in pursuit of common interests. Familiarity and understanding of others' difficulties amongst those with similar occupational activities may explain the somewhat anomalous cooperation that often takes place amongst market competitors in makeshift African contexts. The basis for empathy might centre on feelings of alienation, insecurity or poverty, or more positively on a shared sense of achievement or desire to safeguard gains. These efforts can be constructive and improve services or alternatively result in collusive practices at the expense of clientele and outside competitors.

De Waal (2005), from an evolutionary biology perspective, argues that humans are predisposed to empathy from early childhood but that such behaviour is scale-dependent and is most likely to arise in small, stable communities where people know each other on a face-to-face basis. Certainly work-related empathy of this nature is place-dependent and as such usually fulfils the scale criteria involving a limited range of people who physically encounter each other on a regular basis. To be effective, associational ties must be rooted in empathy as well as trust. Strong associational ties can lay the foundation for apprenticeship arrangements and other work relationships, capable of enduring over considerable periods of time. Durkheim (1964) argues that the social solidarity and moral character of such ties were the foundation of the medieval guilds in Europe, ultimately instrumental in establishing work standards and a sense of professionalism. In the African context, apprenticeship was a notable feature of urban West Africa amongst the Mande, Yoruba and Igbo but, as Meagher (Chapter 6) notes for the Igbo of Aba, recent trends have been undermining rather than strengthening existing apprenticeship systems.

Professionalization is defined here as nation-wide formal, self-governing associational ties of practitioners within a specialized work area who are committed to achieving collectively agreed work rules and product and service standards. There are several reasons why professionalization has yet to become a dominant social force in most African countries. First, an enormous portion of the labour force is not in a position to specialize in a specific area of work. Uncertainty of returns to labour in any one type of work necessitates work diversification. People have divided loyalties and many retain a link to subsistence agriculture as well in case their cash-earning income streams fail them. Hence they lack the requisite commitment to a single occupation.

Second, there is a relative lack of formalization of associational ties through written rules regarding work qualifications, work procedures and standards of service and products. People are likely to move in and out of specific work activities, without any regard for entry qualifications and largely incapable of achieving adequate work standards due to lack of training and skill. In other words, their work will be 'unprofessional' in the Weberian sense of labour specialization, work competence and ethical codes of conduct.

Seppälä (Chapter 13) argues, however, that the Weberian concept of professionalism is too western biased. He provides an alternative interpretation of professionalism relevant to the prevailing Tanzanian context of income diversification and clientelistic social networking premised on congeniality, politeness and human respect aimed at attracting and maintaining clients. Given the shared nature of this behavioural ideal, it can, in effect, be seen as an informal institution with an unwritten code of behaviour upon which social sanctions can be imposed for non-compliance. Seppälä's conceptualization accords with the earlier distinction between African diversified, experimental as opposed to western specialized careers (Figure 1.1). The occupational identities emerging from these distinct processes will, not surprisingly, be fundamentally different in nature.

Occupational identity formation

Western occupational identity formation ideally evolves amongst a professionalized citizenry engaged in specialized production. An occupational identity arises from membership of individuals in professional bodies sharing common productive objectives, skills training and ethical perspectives with the aim of ensuring good quality, reliable, impartial service and commodity delivery to consumers in a national context of rights and opportunities for citizens. Such professional bodies have tended to arise in cities where there is a wide array of specialized occupations, which afford urban inhabitants an identity that can be distinguished from personal characteristics of ethnicity, gender or age. The state has often intervened to codify and regulate occupational standards.

By contrast the African reality is mired in risky, diversified production. Occupational identity beyond familial circles coalesces around people negotiating amongst themselves on the basis of the need for trust to facilitate work practicalities in the first instance, and empathy arising from regular face-to-face encounters, common work experiences and shared problems. Nonetheless, given the lack of confidence in the infrastructural delivery capacity of the national economy and stability of national politics, work commitment to any one specialized area of work can be foolhardy. One's primary effort must necessarily be placed on ensuring family subsistence needs. At this fundamental level of material insecurity, family empathy is likely to prevail over collegial ties.

The case studies in this volume overwhelmingly relate to occupational identities negotiated and networked under conditions of risky diversified production. At the outset, it must be acknowledged that in some instances occupational identities are collapsing rather than coalescing. Bank (Chapter 10) documents the declining productive agency of male urban migrants in the Eastern Cape who left their rural home areas in preceding decades and gradually had been less able to send remittances to their rural-based households given declining income earnings or loss of formal employment. Suffering a loss of work identity and individual demoralization, many no longer were inclined to visit or resettle in their rural homes having lost face as family provisioners.

Building trust at work

Having outlined the negotiating dynamics that are giving shape to the emergence of new occupational identities in Africa, this section focuses on the necessary first step, the building of functional networks of trust. Before analysing the nature of these networks, attention is drawn to the relative absence of the African state in public economic life and the consequent lack of a stabilizing context for encouraging the formation of trust. These circumstances date back to the state's loss of its nation-building role during the implementation of structural adjustment cutbacks. State infrastructural provisioning began to unravel, posing severe obstacles to people's work lives.

State of distrust

Several of the case studies document the public's disregard for their national governments' performance. Dijkstra (Chapter 3) describes the Kenyan state as lacking parliamentary democracy, ethnically partial and normless. Mohogu (Chapter 4) traces the impact of Zaire-cum-DRC's civil unrest and deepening corruption largely amidst the introduction of multi-partyism in the early 1990s. Cameroon's outstanding economic performance during the heyday of its oil wealth was reversed in the early 1990s when its oil output tapered and a stringent structural adjustment programme was imposed. Jua (Chapter 7) discusses how civil service cutbacks triggered nepotistic hiring practices on the part of state officials for the more limited pool of jobs that remained.

Far from facilitating enterprise, public institutions were not offering the infrastructural services required in many African countries. In Kenya, traders had no faith in banking operations and carried large sacks of money to cover their costs (Chapter 3). Similarly, Kinshasa residents in the Democratic Republic of Congo (DRC) complained of unreliable banking services and sought their own ways of saving and investing their money (Chapter 4). All of these do-it-yourself banking solutions posed high risks especially since police crime prevention was negligible, except in South Africa's large crime-infested cities like Johannesburg where alternative security forces operated in addition to or in place of the police (Simone, Chapter 5). Police and security forces, however, realizing the strategic power they wield, were known to take advantage of their position. Dijkstra (Chapter 3) describes how Kenyan traders had to factor in the costs of bribing police at road checkpoints.

Government taxation was highly contested. In Cameroon, the introduction of 'global tax' subjected informal women traders to taxation for the first time (Niger-Thomas, Chapter 11). The women made strenuous efforts to avoid paying, viewing it as an arbitrarily enforced, unjustified regressive tax, with little ultimate benefit to them in terms of government service provisioning.

Their moral outrage was premised on the tax's incursions into their means of subsistence.

Problem-solving business negotiations

Over time, as infrastructural services and formal employment opportunities dwindled in urban areas and farmers' marketing margins narrowed in rural areas, people's resort to diversified informal income-earning activities posed enormous logistical problems. Beyond the illegality of many of these activities prior to economic liberalization, there were questions of how commodities were going to be transported and marketed over long distances and how money, foreign exchange and credit could be handled in the absence of trustworthy banks.

Commodities, credit and capital investment

Dijkstra (Chapter 3) details how several rural horticultural traders resolved these dilemmas. Bulky fruit and vegetable loads were particularly vulnerable at trans-shipment points where stocks had to be counted and confirmed by trusted family or friends. Financially incentivized checks and balances were designed to ensure that agents at those critical points in the marketing chain had a vested interest in the stock size as well. Travelling with large sums of money was hazardous, particularly for women traders. Produce traders had to find wholesalers they could trust with their commodities, extending commodity credit to them with the expectation of payback following commodity sale. The women market traders of Bissau established similar alliances to facilitate their trading operations and credit access based on clientelistic relations of kin, ethnicity or religion (Lindell, Chapter 8).

Kenyan horticultural traders' rotating credit circles consisted of both mixed tribe and single tribe credit groups. Often only traders with a sound business reputation were allowed to join. There was a tendency amongst members to spread the risk of default by being a member of a range of groups (Chapter 3). Mohogu (Chapter 4) documents the thorny problem of credit in the DRC. Decades of national economic mismanagement led residents of Kinshasa to devise a diverse array of local-level solutions. Rotating credit in the form of mutual lending groups composed of family, relatives, friends, neighbours or other frequent associates became common, which did not preclude some seeking loans on an individual basis for unanticipated needs. Local moneylenders charging exorbitant interest rates were to be avoided if possible. Then there was the *cambisme*, a multi-purpose financial institution of great renown dominated by women whose primary service was that of a *bureau de change*, buying and selling US dollars upon which the DRC's mineral-export dependent economy pivoted. Alongside Kinshasa residents' localized rotating credit activities, many harboured a gambling streak, which fuelled the financial scams and fraud that abounded in Mobotu's Zaire.

Rural women in Mooiplaas, South Africa, took advantage of growing non-governmental organizations' (NGOs) interest in women's activities to access credit. Bank (Chapter 10) describes how older women, facing the decline in remittance money from urban migrant members of their family and shrinking intra-household exchange relations, nonetheless, came into their own. They were highly adept at impressing NGO donors with their commitment to income-generating activities. Meanwhile the local men as 'domestic nomads' scratched around for income, resenting the women's growing power and influence over local resources.

In Aba, Nigeria, declining rather than expanding credit access was observed by Meagher (Chapter 6). During economic liberalization, increased competition amongst small-scale Igbo manufacturers of shoes and clothes in Aba, Nigeria eroded suppliers' credit and buyers' partial advance payments squeezing profit margins and propelling smaller, under-capitalized manufacturers to the margins of the industrial sector. They could not survive the rigours of 'cash and carry' transactions for inputs and outputs. Long-established trust between suppliers, manufacturers and wholesale buyers was undermined by *ad hoc* best-deal-of-the-moment arrangements making manufacturers very wary about offering advances lest the buyer abscond. Some of the increasingly marginalized manufacturers, however, retained elements of mutual credit support through equipment loans.

Igbo entrepreneurs cultivated strong ties of support, which facilitated Igbo expansion into new areas of investment in their homeland as well as internationally. The most salient example of the latter was the extremely rapid post-apartheid development of Nigerian syndicates specialized in the lucrative international drug trade passing through South Africa (Simone, Chapter 5). The rich pickings of this field of investment generated tensions and challenges to self-regulation with respect to agreement on territorial boundaries between syndicates rather than credit arrangements.

Securing labour

Several of the case study chapters reveal the profound restructuring that has taken place in peasant farming households as commercial agricultural production declines. The male head of household's monopoly on cash-earning through export crop production has eroded along with his patriarchal status (Therborn, 2004). Male household heads now accept and usually encourage their wives and children to earn cash, opening the door to negotiation over the intra-household division of labour. In a sugar-growing area of Tanzania, Mbilinyi (Chapter 9) observed women with a triple workload: as wage labourers on the sugar estate, as family farm labourers growing subsistence crops and sugar through an outgrowers' scheme and as housewives shouldering the burden of housework. Nonetheless, male household heads were exerting increasing pressure on family members' unpaid labour on the family farm and were known to contest control over their wives' wages. Many women were able to use their wage as leverage and increase their role in household decision-making. Overwhelmingly, they expended their wage on basic needs for the household.

Konings's (Chapter 12) Cameroonian rural case study traces how working on the Ndu tea estate became a habit for second and later-born sons within certain families enabling them to accumulate and gain status to compensate for not inheriting the family farm. Family well-being of this stratam was posited on the reliability of plantation earnings of the male heads of household. This situation was reversed during the late 1980s and 1990s. The estate was privatized and the labour force was subjected to increasing casualization.

Generally, as agriculture shed youthful labour, the trade sector ballooned throughout the continent. Unlike agriculture where climatically patterned labour peaks occurred, traders could operate on their own-account learning while doing. Traders, however, had to contend with an over-abundance of competitors (Simone, Chapter 5; Lindell, Chapter 8).

Weaving networks of trust

As the impact of global market trends and international financial institution conditionality catalysed income diversification and the necessity for the work-related negotiations outlined above, social networking structured the content of such negotiations. Through networking, people seek contacts to facilitate their work, gather relevant information, build mutuality and trust, and, in some cases, form alliances for sharing equipment, customers or credit, etc. Given the widening geographical reach and intensified competition of product and service markets in which income diversifiers operate, constructing networks is likely to proceed on an *ad hoc*, opportunistic basis with eclectic recruitment from a variety of different sources including: hometown/ethnic ties, neighbourhood, religion, gender, age, and workplace.

Ethnic links

The entrepreneurship of the Igbo surfaces in several chapters of this book. Chukwuezi and van den Bersselaar (Chapter 2) trace how and why Igbos, originally from rural settings gained their entrepreneurial reputation under colonialism, as members from other Nigerian ethnic groups had also long been active as traders. The story is complex but certainly adversity in the form of growing rural land shortages and the experience of being on the losing side of civil war imparted not only the necessity to seek livelihoods outside of agriculture and beyond their tribal boundaries, but also a sense of solidarity and mutual support that stood them in good stead in business ventures in 'strange' places in Nigeria, South Africa, Europe and North America. By retaining a hometown connection they affirmed their common identity. The hometown refers primarily to a person's community of origin denoted by their language dialect rather than their birthplace or Nigerian residence. Igbo hometown unions were self-help in nature to facilitate trade, credit management and migratory life. Strategically, they initiated transport enterprises that gave them an advantage in the transport of products over long-distances. The cultural stereotype attributed to the Igbo in Nigeria is now one of individualistic traders who form tight-knit clannish groups, embracing Western modernity.

Despite Kenya's reputation for tribalism in politics and land allocation, ethnicity did not dominate bonds of trust in the horticultural trade because the current ethnic diversity of regional towns lent itself to the formation of bonds of trust on the basis of a variety of social criteria (Dijkstra, Chapter 3). There was no single ethnic group dominating the trade. Horticultural markets with their highly perishable, bulky, low-value products were not attractive to highly ambitious entrepreneurs.

Quite the opposite prevailed amongst the *cambiste* network of women foreign exchange agents in Kinshasa who depended on extremely tight family clan or religious ties of trust to enforce strict group discipline over pricing (Mohogu, Chapter 4). Simone (Chapter 5) contrasts Hausa and Igbo business networks. While ethnic ties were capable of reducing transactional costs, the decorum of deal-making could be very time-consuming amongst the Hausa on Lagos Island. The Igbo entrepreneurs in Johannesburg moved into large hotels in the former white middle-class neighbourhoods in Johannesburg after the collapse of *apartheid* in the 1990s. The hotels served as Igbo business headquarters and provided ready accommodation for Igbo work recruits who owed their bosses unquestioning loyalty. Although the syndicate operators demanded loyalty from traders within their territories, the trader networks were not restrictively Igbo. Ten years later Nigerian syndicates disguised their activities and averted local criticism by trying to integrate illegal trade with normal legal trade in order to become less a target of police surveillance and local South African resentment. Trade collaboration veered towards more diffuse trade objectives and spatial operations that took place on-the-spot rather than being identified with specific localities in Johannesburg. Igbo migrants in Johannesburg became more transient and less visible (Chapter 5). Along somewhat similar lines Lindell found traders in Bissau trying to conform to local ethnic patterns. Especially ambitious traders there felt compelled to change their ethnic identity to Fula or Mandinga. The new identity was believed to offer the political and economic connections necessary to advance.

Gender and age bonds

Gender was a key source of network mobilization in Kenyan horticultural markets as well. Dijkstra (Chapter 2) notes that there was a gender divide, corresponding to status in the level of marketing one operates within. At the local level, women traders cooperated extensively in sending and receiving areas, trusting each other to operate in the interest of the other, despite being separated by large distances. Not surprisingly, gender solidarity had arisen amongst female local retailers relative to male regional wholesalers.

Lindell (Chapter 8) documents strong female solidarity amongst Bissau's women market traders who dealt in very similar products, cooperating with each other with respect to rotating credit, practical help with stall minding, and agreement about sale prices to obviate competition amongst themselves. The women bushmeat traders that Niger-Thomas (Chapter 11) describes were similarly situated, selling the same product and presenting a unified front against the market tax collectors. The solidarity amongst the women foreign exchange dealers in the DRC was rumoured to be heavily intersected by the women's sexual liaisons with powerful men who protected their illegal trading activities. As '*deuxieme* or *troisieme* bureau' mistresses, the women gained inside information at the same time as they could act as conduits for their lovers' on the side business deals (Mohogu, Chapter 4).

Cameroonian youth's shared disillusionment and resentment of declining job opportunities following the country's economic crisis in the 1990s accelerated their economic maturity and political awakening. The Cameroonian state was aware of the potential political threat posed by this youthful despondency and attempted to mobilize them politically into an official youth group as well as trying to undermine their solidarity through selectively offering jobs to certain youth (Jua, Chapter 7).

Religion and other social ties

Networks centred on religious ties are likely to overlap with ethnicity, as illustrated in the case of the Muslim Hausa, described by Simone (Chapter 5). Attitudes towards money, profit-making and labour relations were influenced by religious beliefs, so that traders and other entrepreneurs who shared the same religion, used it as a common platform for negotiating business. Weber (2001) stressed the influence of the Protestant work ethic in the development of capitalism in Europe. Pentecostal Christian religious conversion, although more limited in extent, exerts comparable influence on its mainly educated and youthful middle class converts. They embraced a body of beliefs that had the effect of weakening a person's identification with family and kin and cultural traditions in favour of 'liberating' the individual to pursue wealth and prosperity (van Dijk, 2002). Loyalties were transferred to the community of believers with rites of passage and markers of individual achievement shared amongst the new faith-based community rather than within traditional kin circles. Meagher (Chapter 6) observes that Aba traders embracing evangelical religion had grounds for escaping the rights, responsibilities and decorum of hometown associations. In Cameroon, prostitutes were lured to Pentecostalism in the belief that they would gain financial acumen and protection against AIDS (Jua, Chapter 7).

Sharing religious values can undoubtedly encourage network bonds of trust, but there are a raft of other associational ties which may catalyse trusting relations in the here-and-now. These include dance groups, sports associations and various other clubs in which people spend their leisure time. School links at secondary and university levels as well may provide enduring ties based on memorable shared experiences at an impressionable age (Mohogu Chapter 4).

Workplace relations

Increasingly, networked bonds of trust are developing at the workplace as people with mutual interests pragmatically resolve their daily work constraints for a number of reasons. First, in a work situation, repetitive contact over a considerable time period provides physical evidence of an individual's trustworthiness. Second, bonds of trust are necessary at strategic locations or in essential functions to enable the work process to progress. Third, there is the shared interest of 'making a living', which people continue to cherish as fundamental to their moral economy.

It can be argued that 'getting the job done' in the company of familiar colleagues in an atmosphere of mutual respect and cooperation represents embryonic professionalism. While formal contractual relations, standardized levels of performance and ethical codes are absent, there is nonetheless a general understanding that genial relations and a supportive attitude to one another and to one's clients is demanded. Moral reprobation from one's colleagues ensues if one fails to act accordingly.

Seppälä's (Chapter 13) concept of 'culturally-conditioned professionalization' refers to this phenomenon and relates to Tanzanian and indeed many other African cultures, where a high premium is placed on achieving basic survival and collective welfare. In these contexts, competitive tendencies within working groups may be denied or censured. Competition nonetheless surfaces, especially under the influence of economic liberalization, but the economic agents involved often devise measures to depress or hide competitive tendencies, as exemplified in the case study of Guinea Bissau women traders (Lindell, Chapter 8).

Nonetheless, having recognized the horizontal networking and bonds of trust forming throughout the continent as income diversification in the informal sector spreads, we cannot overlook that hierarchical dependency-linked 'forced trust' patterns are also being fostered. This is illustrated by the dependency of Igbo migrants and prostitutes on bosses in Johannesburg (Simone, Chapter 5), vicious cycles of debt in Kinshasa in which money-lenders who continually stay aware of the whereabouts of their debtors (Mohogu, Chapter 4), the defeatism of wage labourers on a Cameroonian tea estate subjected to forced wage deductions by labour leaders as the tea estate flounders (Konings, Chapter 12) and the political clientelism of Nigerian informal manufacturers in return for state support (Meagher, Chapter 6).

Inter-institutional dynamics of occupationality

Occupationality is a reflexive process in which individuals interact with one another through existing institutional structures. The vast majority of literature on African work life concentrates on the interactive influences of the market and state, without integrating the roles of the household and community in shaping occupationality. Fundamentally, household needs spur the search for viable livelihoods, while communities provide the collective cultural and social norms, which motivate the search. In effect, households *necessitate*, communities *motivate*, markets *incentivize* and states *regulate* occupational pursuits of individuals.

Every African country and indeed every locality within each country will have its own specific institutional interplay. Nonetheless at a general level of abstraction, and to distinguish this analysis from the corpus of state and market-centred analysis, it is worth stressing how occupational identities and work ethics are structured by the interaction of the household, community, market and state.

Figure 1.3 is a Venn diagram representing the inter-relationship between the four institutions with the household and community primarily occupying the informal realm of legally uncoded cultural and social guidelines while the market and the state represent more formalized realms theoretically subject to market regularity and rules of law. The overlapping pattern of the four circles would vary depending on the national society in question. In this diagram, the household and community are deliberately shown as subsuming rather than being subsumed to the state and market. This is intended to suggest that more informal cultural institutions dominate in African settings. Face-to-face, non-contractual exchanges on the basis of unwritten conventions and shared expectations often of a closed, confidential nature leave open the terms of actual interaction and are largely self-regulated within and between the parties and their wider communities. This contrasts with formal exchanges of an impersonal contractual nature subject to externally imposed written rules or laws, usually with clearly delineated schedules and terms of execution that facilitate transparency and accountability, and can be resolved by an independent third party in case of disagreement between the two contracting parties.

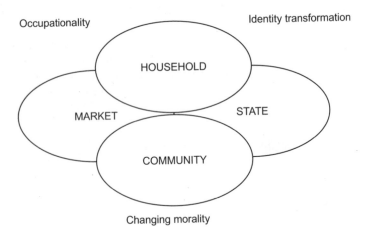

Figure 1.3 Institutional inter-relationship in occupational, identity and moral transformation

Leading markets and dragging states

The process of occupationality in Africa was triggered primarily by global market restructuring since the oil crises of the 1970s and the implementation of SAP in the 1980s. The undermining of market infrastructure and incentives for peasant agriculture, affecting tens of millions of small-scale farmers across Africa, engendered an enormous scramble for alternative livelihoods. Rural transformation encompassed the shrinkage of the agricultural sector with smallholders' tendency for declining agricultural production relative to non-agricultural pursuits, declining family farm production, and the switch to self-employment with the entry of family members across the age and gender spectrum into the cash-earning labour force.

In rural and urban areas regular wage labour became casualized. Vast numbers of people attempted to straddle a formal job with entrepreneurial self-employment on the side, multiple income sources and, if possible, reliance on a kinship fallback given the prevailing low, irregular earnings and uncertainty of paid work. Labour, commodity, service and financial markets fluctuated unpredictably (Chapters 4–6, 9). Increasing landlessness raised the stakes in the livelihood scramble if and when people lost recourse to own farm production (Chapters 9–10, 14).

As labour markets surged, state activities were rolled-back under western donor pressure and have only relatively recently been given scope to make a limited comeback. South Africa was exceptional in having a strong state both in the apartheid and post-apartheid era with taxation and social welfare provisioning capabilities. Nigeria's oil riches conferred power enabling it to modify various World Bank and IMF structural adjustment and economic liberalization policies but this independence did not translate into strong infrastructural support for national manufacturing and instead informal manufacturers were forced to rely on patronage ties to the state. Similarly, Niger-Thomas (Chapter 11) graphically describes the Cameroonian state's inability to effectively tax the informal sector and provide better infrastructural support. Jua (Chapter 7) writes of Cameroonian urban youth's disillusionment with their declining career prospects and the state's failure to chart direction. During the protracted debt crises of the 1980s and 1990s, most African nation-states relinquished their state policy-making autonomy to the international financial institutions. Weak African states were neither able to adhere to their own legal codes nor offer a clear sense of economic direction to their citizenries.

Households and communities in dynamic disarray

The world market has been the main catalyst for African deagrarianization, while households have been the launching pad for occupational change. In the absence of state guidance, individual family members' experimentation in previously untried economic activities has given content and form to occupationality.

The dominant role of male heads' family provisioning has been challenged by the involvement of women and youth household members' income earning with repercussions for the internal social coherence of the household. Mbilinyi (Chapter 9) documents the growing strife between husbands and wives over their respective cash earnings and youths' disinterest in marriage compounded by the insufficiency of land to start up their own households to the extent that women feared 'the costs of having a husband'. Bank (Chapter 10) finds a not dissimilar apathy towards conjugal relations amongst youth in the Eastern Cape. Paradoxically, the crisis in material survival of households, which engendered widespread livelihood diversification helped to resolve household material needs at the same time as it posed dilemmas for the collective identity and moral integrity of African households as social and cultural units. Tensions, in some cases, surfaced in the form of male violence and child abuse (Chapter 9).

The community should be the repository for moral consensus and norm enforcement based on a common community membership. However, in periods of rapid material and normative change, the community will inevitably reflect the economic upheaval around it. Community norms and authority figures will be challenged and the community, at best, can serve as a central arena for negotiating new norms and for the testing of the legitimacy of new authority figures and community efforts to construct a shared sense of coherence amongst its members. When there is little sense of collective identity, the community necessarily becomes the site of unease, distrust and contestation.

Finally, we come to the crux of this book's concern. What happens to social identity and morality when clearly delineated occupations are not in operation? Work patterns in Africa are now exceptionally malleable and clearly defined professional identities are only starting to congeal. By focusing on the concept of occupationality, this chapter has examined changing work patterns and explored evidence suggesting the development of trust in the work arena and hints of emerging occupational identities connected with non-traditional labour activities.

The following sections of this book provide detailed case study analysis, illustrating how occupational change and social identity formation and work morality mesh. Chapters in Section II examine how African informal trade and industry and work-related mobility patterns have been affected by economic liberalization and the global economy. Section III explores changing work patterns in relation to linkages between households, communities markets and nation-states. The last section discusses African occupational change and public policy. The concluding chapter of this book turns to the question of public morality discussing the transition from African moral economies based on cultural consensus and a shared localized social identity to a national civil society embedded in impersonal state and market forces where work identities and careers form the bulwark of the division of labour, social identity and work ethics for the population nationwide.

About the author

Deborah Bryceson is a reader in urban studies at the University of Glasgow and a member of The Policy Practice. As an economic and social geographer, she has been engaged in African rural and urban livelihood studies for over a decade. Her focus has been on the processes of deagrarianization and urbanization. Her books include *Farewell to Farms* (Ashgate 1997), *Disappearing Peasantries: Rural Labour in Africa, Asia and Latin America* (IT Publications 2000) and *African Urban Economies: Viability, Vitality or Vitiation?* (Palgrave Macmillan 2006). She is currently coordinating the Urban Growth and Poverty in Mining Africa research project with case studies in Angola, Ghana and Tanzania.

Notes

1. 'Africa' refers to sub-Saharan Africa throughout this edited collection.
2. Some of the economic literature has begun to question the fundamental assumption that profit maximization necessarily always drives economic activity (Layard, 2005; Bruni and Porta, 2005). Happiness is seen as an alternative goal, which embodies tangible and intangible rewards. Using proxies for measuring happiness is unwieldy and can be highly reductionist or misleading. Furthermore, focusing solely on the individual's happiness at work would make it impossible to disaggregate the multi-faceted psycho-social dimensions of work or appreciate that work enjoyment extends beyond the individual's psychological happiness to a sense of social contribution and recognition, which is reflexive in nature.
3. Recently some economists (see Zak, 2008) have become interested in the concept of moral markets, in effect rediscovering themes that Adam Smith outlined in his *Theory of Moral Sentiments* at the inception of the discipline of political economy (Smith, (2007) [1759].
4. Lack of trust may also be evidenced in the individual worker's avoidance of a family enterprise that, it is commonly believed, is over-taxed by family members' demands to spend the working capital on consumption.

References

Bruni, L. and Porta, P.L. (2005) *Economics and Happiness: Framing the Analysis*, Oxford University Press, Oxford.

Bryceson, D.F. (2000) 'Peasant theories and smallholder policies: past and present', in D.F. Bryceson,C. Kay and J. Mooij (eds), *Disappearing Peasantries: Rural Labour in Africa, Asia and Latin America*, pp. 1–36, Intermediate Technology Publications, London.

Bryceson, D.F. (2002a) 'The scramble in Africa: reorienting rural livelihoods', *World Development* 30(5): 725–39.

Bryceson, D.F. (2002b) 'Multiplex livelihoods in rural Africa: recasting the terms and conditions of gainful employment', *Journal of Modern African Studies* 40(1): 1–28.

Bryceson, D.F. and Bank, L. (2001) 'End of an era: Africa's development policy parallax', *Journal of Contemporary African Studies* 19(1): 5–24.

De Waal, F. (2005) *Our Inner Ape*, London, Granta Books.

Durkheim, E. (1964) [1933] *The Division of Labor in Society*, The Free Press, New York.

Epstein, S.A. (1991) *Wage Labor and Guilds in Medieval Europe*, University of North Carolina Press, Chapel Hill, NC.

Foucault, M. (1970) *The Order of Things: An Archaeology of the Human Sciences*, Tavistock Publications, London.

Haidt, J. (2006) *The Happiness Hypothesis*, Arrow Books, London.

Harvey, D. (1990) *The Condition of Postmodernity*, Blackwell Publishers, Oxford.

Hauser, M.D. (2006) *Moral Minds: How Nature Designed Our Universal Sense of Right and Wrong*, Harper Collins, New York.

Ingold, T. (2000) *The Perception of the Environment: Essays in Livelihood, Dwelling and Skill*, Routledge, Abingdon UK.

Kohn, M. (2008) *Trust: Self-Interest and the Common Good*, Oxford University Press, Oxford.

Layard, R. (2005) *Happiness: Lessons from a New Science*, Penguin Press, London.

Mair, L. (1983) *An Introduction to Social Anthropology*, 2nd edn, Oxford, Clarendon Press.

Putnam, R. (2000) *Bowling Alone: The Collapse and Revival of American Community*, Simon & Schuster, New York.

Smith, A. (2007) [1759] *The Theory of Moral Sentiments*, Cosimo Inc, New York.

Therborn, G. (2004) 'Introduction: globalization, Africa, and African family patterns', in G. Therborn (ed.), *African Families in a Global Context*, Nordiska Afrikainstitutet, Uppsala.

van Dijk, R. (2002) 'Religion, reciprocity and restructuring family responsibility in the Ghanaian Pentecostal diaspora', in D.F. Bryceson and U. Vuorela (eds), *The Transnational Family: New European Frontiers and Global Networks*, Berg, Oxford.

Weber, M. (2001) *The Protestant Ethic and the Spirit of Capitalism*, Routledge, London.

Werbner, R. and Ranger, T. (eds) (1996), *Postcolonial Identities in Africa*, London, Zed Books Ltd.

World Bank (2008) *World Development Indicators*, http://publications.worldbank.org/WDI/

Zak, P.J. (2008) *Moral Markets: The Critical Role of Values in the Economy*, Princeton, University Press Princeton.

SECTION II
New Occupational Mobility and Forms of Exchange in Globalizing Economies

CHAPTER 2

From farmers to traders: shifting identities in rural Igbo society, Nigeria

Barth Chukwuezi and Dmitri van den Bersselaar

This chapter explores the question of why, of all the Nigerian ethnic groups, the Igbo have become the group that is known for being astute traders. It traces how the Igbo acquired their identities as traders historically, and what impact this had on trade and identity in rural Igbo society. The colonial origins of Igbo trade networks and the identification of the Igbo as traders are discussed, tracing how the colonial period created a socio-economic situation allowing traders from southern Nigeria a specific niche in the Nigerian economy, thereby establishing the connection between 'Igbo' and 'trade'. The Nnewi traders, representing contemporary Igbo trade networks are the focus of an exploration of the impact of developments instigated by traders 'back home' in communities in the Igbo area. The case of the Osumenyi community in Nnewi (Nnewi South Local Government) is used to discuss changing perceptions of status, power, migration, and the process of deagrarianization.

Introduction

Throughout West Africa, the members of the Igbo ethnic group have gained a reputation for being successful traders. Of the approximately 300 ethnic groups in Nigeria, the Igbo are considered to be one of the three major groups. While the Hausa and the Yoruba dominate respectively the north and the west of the country, the Igbo are the major group in the east. From their ancestral towns in the east, many Igbo have migrated to cities and towns elsewhere in Nigeria and across Nigeria's borders to trade centres in West Africa and beyond. They have created effective trade networks, based often on kinship ties or town. Various groups specialize in certain goods and organize its trade from import or production through wholesale to retail. In most Nigerian cities, for instance, the trade in vehicle spare parts is dominated by Igbo trade networks. While the Igbo are famous for their entrepreneurial spirit, they are not the only West African group with such a reputation. Other groups in Nigeria such as the Hausa, and also some minority groups, have organized similar trading networks but without acquiring a similar occupational reputation (Cohen, 1969; Paden, 1971).

Why, of all the Nigerian ethnic groups, have the Igbo become the group that is known for being astute traders? How did they acquire their identity as traders historically? What impact did this development have on trade and identity in rural Igbo society? One way to approach these questions would be to look at older trading patterns and conclude that long-distance trade has been going on in the area for centuries. For two reasons, this observation cannot, however, explain why the Igbo are renowned traders. First, the area was not exceptional as non-Igbo areas were similarly involved in long-distance trade, and, second, only a limited number of specialized centres were involved in this trade, while most pre-colonial Igbo communities concerned themselves with food production for local consumption. We therefore propose that the roots of Igbo occupational identification as traders stem from a more recent past. It was the colonial period (1900–60) that created a socio-economic situation allowing traders from southern Nigeria a specific niche in the Nigerian economy, thereby establishing the connection between 'Igbo' and 'trade'. In the post-colonial era, the experience of the Biafra War (1967–70) and the following period of Igbo marginalization convinced Igbo individuals that neither the government nor major companies would help them, and that the only thing they could rely on was their own success as traders.

This chapter consists of three parts. The first section is a discussion of the colonial origins of Igbo trade networks and of the identification of the Igbo as traders, while the second section discusses contemporary Igbo trade networks, focusing on the case of Nnewi traders. The final section explores the impact of these developments 'back home' in the communities in the Igbo area. The case of the Osumenyi community in Nnewi (Nnewi South Local Government) is used to discuss changing perceptions of status, power, migration, and the process of de-agrarianization.

Igbo migration to colonial cities

Nigeria was a British colony between circa 1900 and 1960. Although aspects of the colonial set-up caused resentment among the population, the colonial society also provided social and economic opportunities. It allowed traders to widen the scope of their activities, it increased the market for agricultural products, and it offered employment opportunities for interpreters and clerks with the colonial service or with European firms, and also for labourers in the mines or in road or railway construction. There were many Igbo among those who operated in the new sectors of the economy. This dynamic response to new opportunities and change has often been explained as a result of the traditional Igbo way of life that was extremely competitive and allowed a great deal of social mobility.[1] However, there are other explanations too. One obvious reason for the large number of Igbo working as clerks for the colonial administration is the fact that missionary education in the south provided southerners with the necessary skills and, especially, a knowledge of English, which many northerners lacked. This explanation of course only applies to those who had had missionary education, while many others were simply un-skilled labourers. Therefore, another factor that was at least as important was the economic situation in the Igbo area.

The Igbo area extends from the coastal mangrove swamps through the rain-forest belt to the northern savannah. It is a heterogeneous area with one part being well-watered by rivers, while others are not. It is partly lowland and partly mountainous, partly forested and partly savannah. The region is densely populated by African standards. Nevertheless, and in contrast to other parts of Nigeria, it had no pre-colonial urban tradition. The pre-colonial eco-nomic structure was characterized by small-scale cultivation of mainly yams and other food crops, but also of palm products. As the climate was favourable to the tsetse fly, there was hardly any cattle breeding (only small livestock). Along with agriculture, trade has been important for a long time. At the lo-cal level, trade was usually conducted by women, some of whom managed to accumulate considerable wealth, and at the same time a long-distance trade existed, principally in cattle, slaves, food, salt and luxury items. There were a number of specialized communities in the area, which concentrated on metal-lurgical industries, religious rituals, or the administration of justice.

Trade with Europeans greatly affected the economy of the area long before the beginning of colonialism. First, there were centuries of transatlantic slav-ery. After 1840, the international slave trade started to decline and the price of slaves dropped considerably. At the same time, European demand for palm oil developed which led to increasing prices and a growth in the palm-oil trade until the 1880s (Northrup, 1976). The end of the transatlantic slave trade did not, however, stop the hunting and selling of people. On the contrary, lower prices led to a rapid increase in the already existing practice of domestic slav-ery (*ohu*). It provided a cheap labour force that worked in the production of palm oil and the cultivation of yams (Martin, 1995). The British administra-tion abolished domestic slavery, but the ban was only slowly enforced. Initial-ly, anti-slavery proclamations were released, in response to which thousands of slaves left the farms (although the proclamations forbade this). It was only in 1916, the year after the collapse of the palm-oil trade, that the colonial government passed a final law against domestic slavery (Ohadike, 1994). It is not clear what happened to the former slaves. Thousands remained in the communities that previously owned them, some moved away from the towns and formed new settlements several miles away, while in other cases the exist-ing slave villages were converted into autonomous settlements. Thousands of slaves simply walked away and were never heard of again. At least some of those working on the railways or who came to the urban centres as labourers were former slaves, just as there were many *osu* cult slaves who perceived mi-gration as a way to escape social discrimination in their hometowns (National Archives of Nigeria, 1936).

Partly in response to the abolition of slavery, a shift occurred in cultivation from yams to cassava. Not only was the cultivation of cassava less labour-intensive than that of yams, cassava could be planted on land that was too infertile for yams. Together with the lowering of transport costs through the construction of a road network and the introduction of lorries, this development allowed for the production of cheap food for urban dwellers. Cassava became a cash crop, but did not significantly increase the demand for labour in rural areas (Ohadike, 1994).

The population continued to increase, in spite of a drop around 1919 as a result of an influenza epidemic. In parts of the Igbo area the pressure on land became severe, resulting in soil degradation and erosion. In the 1930s, extra pressures were added due to the consequences of the world economic depression (Isichei, 1976), and the introduction of taxes and school fees by the colonial administration. These factors together provided an incentive for young people to look for opportunities outside their own communities and many ended up in the growing urban centres (Nnoli, 1978).

From around 1914, inhabitants from eastern Nigeria began to move north while working on the extension of the Port Harcourt-Enugu railway to Jos and Maiduguri. During and after World War II, many inhabitants from south-east Nigeria migrated to cities in the west and north of Nigeria, as well as to other West African territories. In 1921, only 3,000 Igbo were living in northern Nigeria while their number rose to 12,000 in 1931. In the 1950s, the number of Igbo in the north was estimated at 127,000, with over 57,000 living in the west, almost 32,000 in Lagos and 10,000 in neighbouring British Cameroon (administrated as part of Nigeria).[2] Not only was the actual number of Igbo migrants relatively large, they also came to constitute a large proportion of the total number of migrants in Nigerian cities. In the early 1950s, the Igbo constituted between 40 and 55 per cent of the total non-indigenous population in major Nigerian cities.[3]

In most cases, the new arrivals did not settle among the indigenous population, but in separate districts, known in northern Nigeria as *sabon gari*. In many Nigerian cities a division developed between the traditional part of town and the areas that the colonial government reserved for migrants, and even within these districts there often existed distinct ethnic areas (Hannerz, 1985). In Ibadan, where the Hausa lived in their own districts but the Igbo did not, some Igbo requested their own Igbo areas (NAI, 1938). Being considered 'new' and 'strange' elements to the cities, the migrants were not allowed to participate in the 'traditional town council' that governed the towns, as a result of which Igbo and other migrants often felt repressed and excluded from political activities and decisions. Occasionally, tensions rose between Igbo and other migrants (such as the Hausa-Igbo riot in Jos in 1945), or between Igbo migrants and the indigenous population of a town (for example, in the same year a confrontation took place in Oturkpo when Igbo migrants took over Idoma farmlands) (NAI, 1949). These tensions increased after World War II, when thousands of former soldiers were unemployed and many moved to the cities. The colonial administration noted the existence of a 'deep and growing antagonism between Hausa and Igbo' and blamed this in part on what it regarded as the arrogant and maladjusted behaviour of the Igbo migrants (NAI, 1945).

An ethnic division existed in the labour market. In northern Nigerian towns during the 1930s and 1940s, people from the south (often Igbo) predominated in administrative functions within the colonial administration as well as with foreign firms. These southerners also dominated skilled and semi-skilled functions in the modern sector and in trade, while unskilled work was left for the northerners. The character of the interaction between the groups was to a large extent determined by these factors. Nonetheless, there were also many southerners doing unskilled labour; initially most Igbo came to the north as railway workers.

The existence of ethnic unions and town unions was an important characteristic of life in Nigerian cities (Hodgkin, 1956; Gugler, 1991). Compared to the pre-colonial period, these unions were a new type of organization, reflecting a general tendency for modern urban dwellers to organize themselves into associations that defended the social and economic interests of the members. These ethnic unions were essentially self-help organizations which provided funds in case of death or illness of members, fought for educational facilities, and made grants available to promising youths. They also played a part in making or at least influencing political decisions concerning the migrants in urban centres (Osaghae, 1994). When organized by Igbo migrants, these organizations were often regarded as 'Igbo unions'. However, they were a general feature of West African urban life and not limited to the Igbo. Furthermore, most Igbo unions regarded themselves as unions representing a village or district within the Igbo area rather than as a union of all Igbo people. Other Nigerians nevertheless saw these unions as typically Igbo. In the context of this chapter, the unions are mainly important in their role as platforms facilitating trade and as ways of controlling bad debts among trading members.

The rise of Igbo traders

Colonial society provided the basis for the rise of Igbo traders from the 1930s onwards. The Igbo took over the position as the main traders from the Hausa, not because the Hausa stopped trading but because the Igbo managed to dominate the rapidly increasing modern trading sectors: motor transport, Western goods, and food for the expanding urban centres. This was the result of several factors. Firstly, as we have argued above, the high population pressure on a mainly agrarian economy resulted in a readiness among the Igbo to leave agriculture and also to (temporarily) leave their hometown in search of income. Secondly, the fact that many southerners, including many Igbo, were employed in government service or with European companies made it easier for them to start up a private enterprise. From their salaries they could save the starting capital required for a business venture, and they could use their contacts with European firms to win contracts or to acquire imported goods to sell locally. Thirdly, the Western-style education more widely available in the south made it easier for Igbo and other southerners to acquire permits and licences and to operate in the colonial bureaucratic system in general. Fourthly, education also resulted in the availability of a number of trained car mechanics who then either started their own transport enterprises or were hired by Igbo transport entrepreneurs. The existence of Igbo transport companies made it easier to transport products over long distances, and allowed for the development of trade networks. These networks were often made up of the members of one family, or people coming from the same town. It was thus possible to control the members of the network through their relatives, thereby reducing the risk of fraud. Igbo traders also developed a system in which they provided goods on credit to retailers from the same area, as they could use the town unions to collect bad debts.

While these factors explain the advantages southerners had over northerners in the modern business sector during the colonial period, two questions still remain. Why did the Igbo rather than other southern groups acquire an identity as traders? Second, why did the Igbo specialize in trade rather than in other opportunities provided by the modern sector?

The fact is that, initially, Igbo people *did* try other opportunities provided by the modern colonial sector. Many went into education and worked as teachers. Others worked with the colonial administration as clerks or in other functions including menial ones with the Public Works Department, while others worked in the mines in Enugu and Jos. There were also many Igbo among the staff of the railways. From the 1930s onwards, a number of Igbo went abroad to gain a university education and returned as lawyers, medical doctors or political scientists. However, none of these positions were as profitable as a successful trading or transport enterprise, and indeed many Igbo decided to combine a position in the modern sector with trading. While, initially, education enjoyed a high status in colonial Nigerian society, over time it was recognized that it was the traders, and not the educators or academics, who could best fulfil their obligations towards their kin and family and support the development of their hometown. V.C. Anene, a trader who became the vice-president of the Igbo State Union even claimed that his business ventures were to be regarded as 'development projects' (Anene, 1982). Even staunch promoters of university education and Western-style education in general, such as Dr Nnamdi Azikiwe, stressed the importance of business activities. Indeed, traders managed to acquire leading positions in Igbo society, as chairmen of local town unions, as leaders of the Igbo State Union, and as successful politicians. A well-known example is Z.C. Obi, a businessman from Nnewi, who founded his own enterprise after working with the UAC. He was the president of the Igbo State Union for fifteen years as well as the president of the Port Harcourt branch of the NCNC political party, and enjoyed great influence in Nnewi, his hometown.

Why is this typically Igbo? Many other southern groups had similar opportunities and some of them, such as the Yoruba, had a historical advantage in terms of education. Members of other southern groups were similarly involved in the modern sector of the economy and a town such as Benin City is as well known for its wealthy traders as the famous Igbo trading centres. However, in colonial society there was a strong tendency to put ethnic labels on groups and activities. Contacts between groups usually took place within certain, fixed patterns. This interaction, combined with existing linguistic and cultural differences between Nigerians from different parts of the country, resulted in a situation in which Hausa notions about Igbo, Igbo notions about Hausa, and Igbo notions about being Igbo became stereotyped. Hence the images that these groups developed of one another stressed the differences rather than the things they had in common. For example, although differences existed in preferred means or behavioural norms, Hausa and Igbo in towns had very similar values with regard to achievement, materialism and modernization (Paden, 1971).[4]

To ensure a better position in the competition for economic gains, but also for other gains such as friendship and mutual help away from home, individuals looked for support to those with whom they felt connected by family ties, by language, or by regional or ethnic origin. Since most families of migrants were living in rural areas and were therefore more likely to demand rather than provide support, origin and language, and thus ethnicity, became important for association. Traditional festivals, which used to be celebrated in the villages, were now celebrated in the cities by people who came from the same area. In the process, local cultural differences became less important, and emphasis was placed on the elements of the festivals that were shared. It was in the cities that the different local Igbo festivals celebrating the tasting of the new harvest were brought together into one 'New Yam Festival', supposedly attended by all Igbo people resident in the town.

Are twentieth century Igbo trade networks traditional?

In the context of colonial Nigeria, the Igbo gained a reputation for being obsessed with 'progress' and for adopting at least the outward signs of modernity and of Western civilization. Other Nigerians noted how Igbo dressed in Western styles, spoke English even amongst themselves, and worked in large numbers with the colonial administration and European firms. During the 1930s and 1940s the Igbo increasingly challenged the lead of the Yoruba and immigrants from Sierra Leone in education and Western professions such as law, medicine, and publishing. While educated members of the Yoruba and other groups felt threatened by the rapid rise of the Igbo in the modern sector, common Nigerian stereotypes described the Igbo as uncivilized, primitive people, slaves and cannibals. The paradox in all this is the recognition of the Igbo as both modern and traditional. They were seen as educated as well as primitive, they were hated as pushy and arrogant traders but also as slaves, they were accused of being selfish and individualistic but also of being clannish and always sticking together as a group.

This situation has become known in anthropological literature and also in local discourse as Igbo receptivity to change. In a series of influential articles based on research in Afikpo, a peripheral Igbo group in the extreme east of the Igbo area, Ottenberg argued that the Igbo, compared to other Nigerian groups, were quick to adopt Western education, economic culture, values and religion because Igbo traditional society was characterized by receptivity to innovation and a lot of social mobility. As a result, Ottenberg (1962: 130–43) argued: 'The Igbo have probably changed the least while changing the most'. Although outside appearances and actions give the impression that Igbo traditional culture has been replaced by Western culture and values, according to Ottenberg: 'Many of the basic patterns of social behaviour, such as the emphasis on alternative choices and goals, achievement and competition, and the lack of strong autocratic authority, have survived and are a part of the newly developing culture'.

The notion of Igbo receptivity to change made sense in the colonial context where the relative modernity of the Igbo had been noted frequently by Igbo and non-Igbo alike. A later psychological–anthropological study confirmed the view that the Igbo were more individualistic and achievement-oriented than the other major Nigerian ethnic groups (Levine, 1966). The idea that the Igbo were inherently modern has stuck and been used by Igbo in political discourse by the leaders of development unions and also by Igbo academics. As recently as 1990, John Njoku (1990: 1) noted that the Igbo were 'continuing their time-honoured tradition of modernity'.

One must be careful not to exaggerate the eagerness with which the Igbo accepted innovations. Often it took quite a long time, sometimes up to 30 years, before the Igbo population accepted the advantages of new modes of transport, communication and finance and started to use them (Afigbo, 1981). Despite the lasting power of the idea of Igbo receptivity to change as a part of Igbo identity, as a description of the actual situation it was wrong for two reasons. First, it implied that all Igbo groups were receptive to change, which was not the case. Second, it claimed that Igbo modernity was a reflection of basic Igbo culture and it ignored the relevance of socio-economic circumstances (Anyanwu, 1995). Mistaken or not, these two aspects of the notion were the very reason why Igbo receptivity to change became such a popular concept among the Igbo themselves.

The claim that modernity is inherent in Igbo culture has been criticized by Nnoli (1978: 220) who pointed out that, before the arrival of the Europeans, the Igbo were the least developed of the major Nigerian ethnic groups in material terms. He wondered why, if the Igbo had a tradition of modernity, it was possible then to explain: 'Why this assumed receptivity to change needed colonialism to express itself'. Part of the answer may be that modernity, achievement-orientation and competitiveness were central to the culture of Christian missions and colonialism in which many Igbo took part. Both mission Christianity and colonial rule used the claim that they introduced modernity and development to justify their presence. Since the

British discouraged Christian missions from operating in the north, and indirect rule in the north was much more indirect than in the south, the Igbo and other southerners were much more directly influenced by colonial interaction than northerners. Also, many Igbo were working with the colonial civil service and thus became part of a bureaucratic culture hoping for pay rises, promotions and pensions (Tonkin, 1990). The large number of Igbo among the colonial clerks and civil servants, on the one hand, supported the notion that the Igbo were more modern and more status-oriented than members from other Nigerian groups. On the other hand, as a consequence of their position in the colonial administration, these Igbo often managed to achieve considerable status in their hometowns which helped to spread the notion among a wider Igbo audience.

It may also be argued that the socio-economic circumstances, and not culture, were responsible for Igbo modernity. One only has to think of the large number of freed slaves and *osu* who turned to the colonial administration and labour markets to earn a living as well as to escape social discrimination in their hometowns. Not only the slaves and *osu* had reason to escape their hometowns. According to Nnoli, more than other Nigerian groups, the Igbo stood to gain from the new colonial situation because of the inefficient methods of production, the poor soil and the high population density in Igbo areas which drove out part of the population (Nnoli, 1978). While this certainly occurred in some areas, it is not true for every Igbo town. The colonial administration itself noticed that Igbo migrated away from some towns more than from others. For example, the 1934 intelligence report on Uguawkpu, after noting that the people were of an 'enterprising disposition', points out that: 'The poorness of the soil between the towns and the density of the population has forced numbers of them to seek their livelihood abroad, and some from this area can be found in every Government Department, while others have become travelling petty traders or craftsmen' (Archive Rhodes House, 1934). The demand for education differed throughout the area (Archive Church Missionary Society, 1939). There are considerable differences between a number of successful, progressive Igbo communities, and many relatively poor, 'underdeveloped' Igbo towns (Public Record Office, 1933: 40). Here it is not necessary to address the question of why this notion gained so much popularity,[5] it suffices to conclude that the emerging trade networks may have had their roots in Igbo community organization, but that they are not the result of inherent 'Igbo modernity'.

One has to be equally cautious with accepting the common perspective that describes Igbo traders as male, even though this is very much our own perspective in the Nnewi case presented in this chapter. Indeed, we mentioned above that trade was largely in the hands of women during the pre-colonial period. During the early colonial period, women dominated the trade in palm oil and foodstuffs in the Igbo area, and there are examples of very influential female traders (Ikejiuba, 1967; Ekechi, 1995). The important Onitsha market was not only dominated by women in terms of trade, it was also women who owned the stalls and supervised the market. When the market was moved in 1916, supervision of the market passed from the Omu's (queen's) council to Onitsha town council, which was dominated by men (Forrest, 1994). The position of the Onitsha women traders deteriorated further from the 1920s onwards, as a result of increasing competition from non-Onitsha male traders from towns such as Nnewi. Similar processes of male encroachment on a trade that was hitherto largely in the hands of women have been described for other parts of the Igbo area during the same period (Ekechi, 1995). This may reflect cultural constraints on women, which made it hard for them to adapt to the changing patterns of trade during the colonial period, which involved being away from home for a long time (ibid., 1995). It may also reflect male bias in the colonial administration, which made District Officers and other officials more sensitive to the demands of men, in line with what has been described as a general masculinization of Igbo culture during the colonial period (Amadiume, 1987). It appears, therefore, that the 'gender' aspect of Igbo trade is as much linked to developments and perceptions during the colonial period as its 'ethnic' and 'modern' aspects.

Igbo traders after Biafra

The role of Igbo migrant traders as it had emerged during the colonial period did not change when Nigeria gained independence in 1960. The real watershed was the Nigerian Civil War (1967–70) which shattered the existing pan-Nigerian networks of Igbo traders. Although a detailed discussion of the civil war is outside the scope of this chapter, we need to briefly discuss the consequences of this war for the Igbo traders. Before the war broke out, Igbo trade networks were already collapsing as a result of riots against Igbo in the cities in northern Nigeria when thousands of southerners (Igbo and others) were massacred. This resulted in a flow of hundreds of thousands of refugees from northern Nigeria towards their home communities in the south-east. The numerous refugees did not merely lose their source of income, they also left behind most of their property and capital invested in trade goods, while their arrival back in the south-east placed pressure on already weak local economies. When the civil war started, the result was severe: famine, the destruction of infrastructure, and the exhaustion of farming lands.

After the war, the then Nigerian head of state, General Yakubu Gowon, promised to reintegrate the Igbo into Nigerian society, following a policy of 'three Rs' (Reconstruction, Rehabilitation and Reconciliation). While the policy of Igbo reintegration was widely applauded at the time of its announcement, it is now generally regarded as having been an empty promise. A few attempts were made at the reconstruction of infrastructure in the Igbo area, but no serious attempt was made to bring the Igbo, as a group, back into the political and economic life of Nigerian society. Various authors have described this situation as a state of 'Igbo marginalization' (Ojukwu, 1989; Madiebo, 1980; Igbokwe, 1995).

Feeling that they had lost both political power to the northerners and positions of control in major companies and banks to the Yoruba, many Igbo resorted to their pre-war *forte*: trade. Soon after the war, various groups of Igbo people started to migrate away from their home communities to rebuild and expand their pre-war trade networks. They have been remarkably successful in doing so. Nowadays, Igbo traders are again found all over Nigeria and beyond the country's borders. Igbo traders occupy every street corner in Lagos pursuing their trading business (Nwosu, 1998), and are also preponderant in other major cities in western and northern Nigeria. Outside Nigeria, they are known in Cameroon, Gabon, and Ghana, and can also be found in other West African countries, South Africa, East Africa, Asia, North America and Europe.

Igbo traders living overseas concentrate on the importation of trade goods from their country of residence into Nigeria. These goods include electronics, processed foods, used clothes, second-hand cars and vehicle spare parts. There are also a few Igbo traders exporting products such as tropical timber and animal bones, while others have specialized in the transit trade of narcotics mainly from Asia to markets in Europe and North America.

Within Nigeria, the most notable aspect of the Igbo trade networks is the tendency of Igbo communities to specialize in certain trade items. In those cases, members of one community are involved in the entire trading chain, from production or importation into Nigeria through wholesale markets to retail selling in markets across Nigeria. One of the most well-known examples of this phenomenon is the town of Nnewi, whose inhabitants dominate the trade in vehicle spare parts. The spare-parts market in Nnewi is famous and attracts people from all over Nigeria and from other West African countries, while motor spare-parts traders from Nnewi are found in many Nigerian towns dominating the spare-parts trade.

Other examples of trade specialization include the Enugwu-Agidi people close to Awka (Anambra State capital) who are noted for their trade in building materials; the Nkanu Akagbe people in Enugu who trade in beef; the Orlu people who are carving a niche for themselves in the pharmaceutical drug market by manning pharmacies throughout Nigeria; the Abiriba people who specialize in the textile trade (both new and second-hand), stock fish and jewellery; and the Agulu people in Anambra State who dominate the bread trade.

Many Igbo are very successful traders but it should be noted that the notion of the Igbo as highly specialized traders who through their trade networks dominate the trade in most sectors is an exaggeration. In spite of trade specialization among traders from particular towns, many Igbo from various parts of the Igbo area continue to engage in very diverse types of trade. Furthermore, the Igbo are not the only group known for their entrepreneurial skills. Other such African groups include the Chagga in Tanzania, the Gurage in Ethiopia, and the Bamilike in Cameroon (Baker and Pedersen, 1992). Within Nigeria, Igbo traders face competition from traders from other ethnic groups, including Hausa, Edo, and Calabari traders. Nevertheless, it is the Igbo who have achieved the ethnic stereotype of being traders. This identification of 'Igbo' with 'trade' is not only by non-Igbo. It has also become an important part of Igbo self-identification, as many Igbo believe that it is through trade that the Igbo ethnic group has overcome the hardship of the civil war and the neglect that followed. In this sense, entrepreneurship has acquired a heroic dimension: post-war Igbo traders are perceived as heroes who fought like wounded lions to regain their lost markets, who succeeded as a result of their astute business acumen and doggedness, thereby saving the Igbo people from marginalization. Consequently, businessmen have become role models for Igbo youth, and a career in trade has become the goal in life of many young Igbo men. It is no surprise that Igbo ethnic identification has turned away from agriculture (yam farming) and towards trade.

Current trade, identity and social stratification in rural Igbo communities

Igbo migrants trading in cities throughout Nigeria have adopted a 'trader' identity but what needs to be explained is the impact trading has had on income and identification in rural Igbo communities. The impact of Igbo trading activities on their home communities forms part of a broader process of de-agrarianization, which has its roots in the early colonial period. Earlier in this chapter we discussed the process of migration away from rural Igbo communities during colonial times. This process has continued since the civil war. For example, Chukwuezi (1999) revealed that more than 65 per cent of the households in Osumenyi had migrants outside the town, while of those currently living in the area, 35 per cent were returned migrants. The migrants sent remittances to those at home to help to sustain them, but also to start up some form of non-farm activity. Some of the migrants had shops, taxis, filling stations, or other businesses in their hometowns, providing employment opportunities for their relatives. Small-scale manufacturing businesses had also been set up, a development partly inspired by experiences during the civil war when local substitutes had to be developed for imported goods. In 1998, about 75 per cent of the households surveyed in Osumenyi were involved in non-farm activities, while income from non-farm activities accounted for about 80 per cent of total incomes. A similar trend was discernible in many other Igbo villages and towns.

Alongside activities by individuals and families to diversify their incomes and become less dependent on agriculture, there have been attempts at community development. This is not a recent phenomenon as town development associations have been in existence since the 1930s. However, the experience of the Biafra war, when many Igbo migrants lost their property because they were not indigenous to the places where their property was situated, has shown migrants the value of having assets in their home villages. Hence, Igbo traders with additional money have decided not only to spread the tentacles of their trading businesses across the country, but also to have a branch in their hometown.

Nnewi traders were involved in the development of their community into a famous trading centre (Forrest, 1994). According to Dike (1979), the civil war marked something of a watershed in the economic and demographic development of Nnewi, with many Nnewi people returning to their hometown as refugees. These developments in Nnewi were part of a larger movement of Igbo migrants back to eastern Nigeria. After the war, Nnewi motor-parts specialists who were rebuilding their trade networks made Nnewi their headquarters. Their success led to a large commercial enterprise in motor spare parts, but also to considerable community development. Many of the wealthy businessmen started as traders and having acquired reasonable capital, moved into manufacturing and medium-scale industries. During the 1990s, the Structural Adjustment Programme resulted in high costs of imported materials and many Igbo traders – and especially Nnewi traders – regarded this as an opportunity for establishing local industries to engage in semi-manufacturing and packaging. Nnewi grew to have over 20 medium-sized manufacturing industries including the Ibeto group of companies manufacturing batteries; GOD industries for motor brake rubber pads; and John Whyte industries producing fan belts.

Snerch (1995) cited Nnewi's pace of community development as a good example of a bottom-up approach to development. Nnewi traders endeavoured to attract capital to their hometown as a way of developing the area, feeling that it was their responsibility to initiate development schemes since successive governments had failed to do so. Nnewi citizens, through their astute trading business, have developed Nnewi into a flourishing centre of commerce without the help of any external agency or government.

The growth in migration and trade has not only strengthened trade over agriculture, it has also made its mark on identification and social stratification within local communities, especially where income diversification and trade activities generated noticeable wealth. This was observable in the Osumenyi data collected by Chukwuezi (1999).

The inhabitants of Osumenyi attach a high premium and value to wealth. The level of wealth in Osumenyi community is apparent from the size of some of the big residential homes to be seen throughout the 10 villages that make up the community. Some have satellite dishes or other modern comforts such as a private electricity generating plant which can be used when the national supply fails (which is quite often). Generally, the Igbo place a great deal of value on owning a residential house in their hometown. Someone who has wealth but has no house in his hometown to show for it is not highly regarded. An imposing residence with modern furnishings tends to elevate one's social status. People with big cars, like a Mercedes Benz or a four-wheel drive, command influence and are respected and envied as they drive around the community.

Those who can afford the material symbols of wealth are honoured at social functions within the community and are invited to make donations to various social activities. Most young Osumenyi men dream of such accomplishments and are prepared to work hard to fulfil their ambitions. Their efforts are primarily directed to trade. Wholesale trading in various items after leaving primary school is especially popular. Youth start as apprentices.

Attending university is not a goal for many in Osumenyi. Nowadays, university graduates are regarded as people who are poorly paid and unable to generate reasonable material comfort for themselves. Some youths do not finish even their primary school career because they feel that getting an education is too time-consuming. They look for a shortcut to enable them to jump into business as soon as possible. This attitude towards education is strengthened by the example of the current wealthy people in the area, most of whom did not continue their education after primary school.

The influence of the rich on the rest of the community has also affected social ceremonies such as traditional weddings (*Igbankwu*) and burial ceremonies. The cost of these traditional ceremonies has risen because conspicuous displays of wealth are encouraged. The wealthy use these occasions to exhibit their wealth. People who are less well-off feel that in order to avoid public ridicule, they also should spend a lot of money on such ceremonies and try to impress the public. Although actual spending on public occasions has decreased during recent years as a result of the worsening economic situation and the government crackdown on those suspected of being '419' (involved in fraud), the pressure on individuals to spend lavishly is still enormous. Traders are the most likely occupational category to engage in these displays which reinforces the belief that to be really successful as an Igbo one has to become a trader.

Conclusion

Trade, although not peculiar to the Igbo, has become a central part of Igbo group identification and aspirations, and is important to many individuals' self-identity. During the 20th century, Igbo communities have moved from an almost entirely agricultural mode of production, through a continuing process of de-agrarianization, to a situation in which a large proportion of the community's income is generated from non-farming activities, notably trading. These developments have often been initiated by migrants who live away from the rural community and make their living in the modern sector of the Nigerian economy. With their income, often generated from trade, they have created trading businesses in the rural community and also invest in other non-farm activities, including light industry. These changing occupational patterns are also reflected in a shift in occupational identification away from agriculture. While, initially, Igbo migrants in the cities as well as Igbo in rural communities regarded Igbo identity and traditions as linked to the soil and to agriculture, modern Igbo identify themselves as traders more than as farmers.

Not only has the Igbo's group identity become linked to trade, being a trader has become an important aspect of individual identity too. Igbo individuals realize the importance of having links beyond their local communities, and see that these contacts are successfully managed by traders. They also see how, through trade, new goods and practices enter the rural community, and how these shape rural values and social practices. It seems clear that it is the traders who are best able to represent the community in the wider world, who invest in the community, and who, within the community through displays of wealth, manage to achieve a high status. As a man, it is now almost impossible to comply with the new social norm without being a trader and more than that, without being a trader who has moved away from the rural community. Young Igbo men have adopted trading *en masse* as their preferred career, thereby further strengthening the identification of the Igbo with trade, now and in the foreseeable future.

About the authors

Barth Chukwuezi is currently the Director for Educational Services and Training at the National Commission for Museums and Monuments in Abuja, Nigeria. Formerly he lectured in the sociology/anthropology department at the University of Nigeria Nsukka. He is author of *University of Education in a Liberalizing Economy: A Study of Nigerian Universities* (Social Science Academy of Nigeria, 2001).

Dmitri van den Bersselaar is senior lecturer in African history at the University of Liverpool, and director of the Centre for the Study of International Slavery. He works on the social and cultural history of 19th and 20th century West Africa. Recent publications include *The King of Drinks. Schnapps Gin from Modernity to Tradition* (Leiden: Brill, 2007), 'Slave-trade city revisited: moving beyond the triangle', in: J. K. Anquandah (ed.), *The Transatlantic Slave Trade: Landmarks, Legacies, Expectations* (Accra: Sub-Saharan Publishers, 2007) and 'Imagining home: migration and the Igbo village in colonial Nigeria' in the *Journal of African History* (2005). He is currently working on a project which explores the careers and experiences of Ghanaian and Nigerian employees of the United Africa Company between 1929 and 1987.

Notes

1. Ottenberg (1962) was one of the first scholars to write on this matter and continues to be influential as exemplified in work by Njoku (1990).
2. Care needs to be taken when quoting these figures. It is impossible to ascertain how they were constructed and what is meant precisely by the categories used. For example, the figure quoted for Cameroon almost certainly includes non-Igbo from south-east Nigeria. In any case, the figures suggest an enormous increase in labour migration during the 20th century (Paden, 1971; Amaazee, 1990).

3. Coleman (1958, reprinted 1971: 77) gives the following figures for Igbo as a percentage of the total non-indigenous populations: Lagos: 44.6 per cent, Benin 53.3 per cent, Sapele 46.0 per cent, Calabar 70.7 per cent, Kano 38.0 per cent, Zaria 39.0 per cent, and Kaduna 40.7 per cent.
4. Other authors have, however, laid much emphasis on the differences in behavioural norms. Levine (1966: 84), after concluding that Igbo are significantly more achievement-oriented than Yoruba or Hausa, remarks: 'Hausa traders are everywhere in West Africa. Their pattern of trade, however, is traditional, and no matter how long they stay in modern cities like Accra and Lagos, they remain conservative with regard to education, religion, and politics, and aloof from modern bureaucratic and industrial occupations. This does not seem to be an unreasonable adaptation, but it is very unlike that of the Igbo migrants to the same cities.'
5. This is discussed in van den Bersselaar (1998: 310–11).

References

Afigbo, A.E. (1981) 'Igboland under colonial rule', in A.E. Afigbo (ed.), *Ropes of Sand: Studies in Igbo History and Culture*, pp. 283–354, University Press, Ibadan.

Amaazee, V.B. (1990) 'The "Igbo Scare" in the British Cameroons, c. 1945–61', *Journal of African History* 31(2): 281–94.

Amadiume, I. (1987) *Male Daughters, Female Husbands: Gender and Sex in an African Society*, Zed Books, London and New Jersey.

Anene, V.C.I. (1982) 'An Aspect of Igbo History', presented to the first international seminar of the Society for Promoting Igbo Language and Culture at the University of Nigeria, Nsukka, 26 August–1 September, Unpublished Paper.

Anyanwu, U. (1995) 'Igbo Easy Receptivity to Change: Fact or Fallacy?', University of Nigeria, Nsukka, Unpublished Paper.

Archive Church Missionary Society (CMS) (1939) G3 A 3/1 'Memo Bishop Lasbrey on the position in the Niger Mission re supply and demand for teachers', Birmingham, CMS.

Archive Rhodes House (1934) Mss.Afr.s.699 Albert Francis Bridges, 'Intelligence Report on Uguawkpu Group', Oxford (RHO), Awka Division.

Baker, J. and Pedersen, O. (eds) (1992) *The Rural Urban Interface in African Expansion and Adaptation*, Nordiska African Institute, Uppsala.

Bersselaar, D. van den (1998) In Search of Igbo Identity: Language, Culture and Politics in Nigeria, 1900–1966, PhD, University of Leiden, Leiden.

Chukwuezi, B. (1999) 'De-agrarianisation and Rural Employment in South-eastern Nigeria', African Studies Centre, Working Paper 39, Leiden.

Cohen, A. (1969) *Custom and Politics in Urban Africa: A Study of Hausa Migrants in Yoruba Towns*, Routledge and Kegan Paul, London.

Coleman, J.S. (1958) [reprinted 1971], *Nigeria: Background to Nationalism*, University of California Press, Berkeley and Los Angeles.

Dike, A.A. (1979) 'Growth and development patterns of Awka and Nsukka, Nigeria', *Africa* 49(3): 235–45.

Ekechi, F. (1995) 'Gender and economic power: the case of Igbo market women of eastern Nigeria' in B. House-Midamba and F.K. Ekechi (eds), *African Market Women and Economic Power: The Role of Women in African Economic Development*, Greenwood Press, Westport, CT and London.

Forrest, T. (1994) *The Advance of African Capital. The Growth of Nigerian Private Enterprise*, Edinburgh University Press, Edinburgh.

Gugler, J. (1991) 'Life in a dual system revisited: urban-rural ties in Enugu, Nigeria, 1961–1987', *World Development* 19(5): 399–409.

Hannerz, U. (1985), 'Structures for strangers: ethnicity and institutions in a colonial Nigerian town', in A. Southall, P.J. Nas and C. Ansari (eds), *City and Society: Studies in Urban Ethnicity, Lifestyle and Class*, pp. 87–103, Institute of Cultural and Social Studies, University of Leiden, Leiden.

Hodgkin, T. (1956) *Nationalism in Colonial Africa*, Muller, London.

Igbokwe, J. (1995) *Igbos Twenty Five Years after Biafra*, Advent Communications, Lagos.

Ikejiuba, F. (1967) 'Omu Okwei, the Merchant Queen of Ossomari: a biographical sketch', *Journal of the Historical Society of Nigeria* 3(4): 633–46.

Isichei, E. (1976) *A History of the Igbo People*, Macmillan, London.

Levine, R.A. (1966) *Dreams and Deeds: Achievement Motivation in Nigeria*, University of Chicago Press, Chicago and London.

Madiebo, A.A. (1980) *The Nigerian Revolution and the Biafran War*, Fourth Dimension Publishers, Enugu.

Martin, S. (1995) 'Slaves, Igbo women and palm oil in the nineteenth century', in R. Law (ed.), *From Slave Trade to 'Legitimate' Commerce: The Commercial Transition in Nineteenth-Century West Africa*, pp. 172–94, Cambridge University Press, Cambridge.

National Archives of Nigeria, Ibadan Branch (NAI) (1936) CSO 26 27948 Secretary, S.P., 'Confidential Memorandum on the Osu System', Enugu, 8 April.

NAI (1938) OYO PROF.I 2156 J. G. Onwuka, Hon. Secretary Mother Ibo Union Ibadan to Senior Resident, Oyo, Ibadan, 23 August.

NAI (1945) CSO 26 45368 'Report on Disturbances in Jos by Resident, Plateau Province, Jos, 11 October.

NAI (1949) CSO 26 45368 Question by N. Azikiwe for the Legislative Council, Lagos, 16 February and prepared government reply to the question.

Njoku, J.E.E. (1990) *The Igbos of Nigeria: Ancient Rites, Changes and Survival*, E. Mellen Press, Lewiston, NY.

Nnoli, O. (1978) *Ethnic Politics in Nigeria*, Fourth Dimension, Enugu.

Northrup, D. (1976) 'The compatibility of the slave and palm oil trades in the Bight of Biafra', *Journal of African History* 17: 353–64.

Nwosu, N., (1998) 'Ukpor: a new horizon in community development', *Community News Magazine*, Ukpor, 50–3.

Ohadike, D. (1994) *Anioma: A Social History of the Western Igbo People*, Ohio University Press, Athens.

Ojukwu, E. (1989) *Because I am Involved*, Spectrum Books, Ibadan.

Osaghae, E.E. (1994) *Trends in Migrant Political Organizations in Nigeria: The Igbo in Kano*, IFRA, Ibadan.

Ottenberg, S. (1962) 'Ibo receptivity to change', in W.J. Bascom and M.J. Herskovitsj (eds), *Continuity and Change in African Cultures*, University of Chicago Press, Chicago.

Paden, J.N. (1971) 'Communal competition, conflict and violence in Kano', in R. Melson and H. Wolpe (eds), *Nigeria: Modernization and the Politics of Communalism*, Michigan State University Press, Michigan.

Public Record Office (1933) Annual Report on the Southern Provinces of Nigeria for the Year 1932, London (PRO); CO 583 193/1269, Lagos.

Snerch, G. (1995) 'Planning for the Future: A Vision of West Africa in the Year 2020' in 'West African Long Term Perspective Study', (WALTPS), Provisional Document, Paris SAD/D94, 439.

Tonkin, E. (1990) 'Zik's story: autobiography as political exemplar', in K. Barber and P.F. de Moraes Farias (eds), *Self-Assertion and Brokerage: Early Cultural Nationalism in West Africa*, University of Birmingham, Centre of West African Studies, Birmingham.

CHAPTER 3

Does trust travel? Horticultural trade in Kenya

*Tjalling Dijkstra**

Current literature suggests that lack of trust and absence of a generalized moral-ity impede stable business arrangements beyond the community space. How do entrepreneurs deal with this? Kenya is taken as an example of a low-trust society where limited-group morality prevails and the state and civil society fail to act as norm-enforcing agencies. A long tradition of private horticultural trade has resulted in well established and relatively efficient trade networks. Case studies reveal a lot of cheating and distrust in horticultural trading. Traders have reacted by developing systems that minimize risks. However, not all relations are based on distrust. Trust develops on the basis of face-to-face personal ties and endures due to common interests and occupational integrity. Ties do not necessarily originate from kinship or from place of birth or residence, but may also result from collegial interactions in the market place. The case studies show that professional ethics and integrity can begin to form in a low-trust society like Kenya.

Introduction

All over rural Africa people are looking for sources of income besides agricul-tural production. One of the most common options is going into trade. In the past, private trade had a negative connotation in many African countries but this changed in the era of neo-liberalism and the implementation of structural adjustment programmes (SAPs). African governments have largely dismantled their state control over agricultural marketing, which had previously been ex-ercised through state marketing boards and parastatals. They are now actively promoting private trade and private enterprise development. The blossoming of capitalism in Africa is not, however, always taking place as swiftly or as smoothly as had been anticipated. One hitch is that partnerships or com-panies involving a genuine pooling of finances have so far remained rare in most African economic sectors and their absence has had a negative impact on economic development.

Fukuyama (1995), amongst others, has tried to explain the pace of cor-porate development by looking at trust or, more generally, social capital, of which trust is an aspect. He compares what he calls 'high-trust' and 'low-trust' societies and concludes that there is a relationship between high-trust societies with an abundance of social capital, and the ability to create large business organizations. Germany, Japan and the United States, which in his view are all high-trust societies, were the first to develop large, modern, and professionally managed hierarchical corporations. By contrast, the economies of Taiwan, Hong Kong, France and Italy, which he considers as relatively low-trust societies, have traditionally centred around family businesses. 'In these countries the reluctance of non-kin to trust one another delayed and in some cases prevented the emergence of modern, professionally managed corporations' (30).

Fukuyama does not include African countries in his comparison. Kennedy (1988), taking a similar approach, argues that unwillingness among African entrepreneurs to establish corporate arrangements closes one of the most important potential avenues to business expansion. He identifies the main reason for this marked reluctance to establish pooling arrangements as 'widespread fear that partners will cheat in some way or fail to pull their weight' (166).

Platteau (1994a, b) reinforces this line of reasoning and points to a lack of trust as an impediment to stable business arrangements: 'If individuals do not trust others to fulfil their terms of an agreement, they will not wish to enter into exchanges with one another – except in so far as exchanges are constituted by spot transactions' (1994a: 545). Unlike Kennedy, Platteau suggests that the lack of trust in African economies results from the expansion of African economies 'beyond the community space' (ibid., 550). Within the community, bilateral and multilateral reputation mechanisms largely preclude the problem of trust. This is no longer the case when business takes place with genuine strangers with whom no personal ties have been woven. In other words, reputation mechanisms cannot cope adequately with mobility and long-distance transactions, which arise when capitalistic economies expand. Trust does not travel.

A 'generalized morality' is needed to fill the gap. The absence of such a morality hampers stable business arrangements beyond the community space. Platteau maintains that limited-group morality prevails in sub-Saharan Africa: 'People tend to remain entangled into all sorts of tightly-knit networks of personalized relationships encompassing the family, the clan, the religious sect, the ethnic group, the loyalty of birth and so on'. These entities contribute 'to compartmentalize the social space into rival factions which apply different standards of social conduct to inter- and intra-group relations' (1994b: 795–6).

To change this situation, two higher-level institutions should act as general-norm suppliers or norm-reinforcing agencies: the nation-state and the civil society (Platteau, 1993). Unfortunately, both fail to do so. Chabal and Daloz (1999) posit that the legitimacy of political systems in Africa depends on the ability to deliver goods, services or information to those who are linked with the political elites through micro-networks of patronage and clientelism. 'There is no scope with such a perspective for deferring to a larger but less immediate macro-rationality, most significantly to the greater good of the country as a whole' (161). Bayart *et al.* (1999) do not expect positive changes in this respect. On the contrary, they notice an unrestrained privatization of sovereignty and of the sovereign functions of the state. The power-holders reinforce the tendency to clientelism, co-optation and collaboration by violence and deception in 'the economy of dirty tricks'.

Both politicians and the judiciary fail to act as suppliers of general norms, with African courts tending to work less reliably than those elsewhere in the world (Collier and Gunning, 1997). Widner's (1997) interviews with members of the bar in Botswana, Tanzania and Uganda revealed that only about a quarter of lawyers considered the judiciary fully independent of the executive and 20 per cent admitted that they were occasionally put under political pressure. Collier and Gunning (1997) conclude that African courts fail as a check on opportunism.

If the political and judicial systems fail as norm-enforcing agencies, the potential role of civil society becomes especially significant in Platteau's eyes (1993). Civil societies in most sub-Saharan African countries are poorly developed because they lack a middle class with a strong interest in limiting bureaucratic power and ensuring some degree of rationality in bureaucratic performance. Chabal and Daloz state more explicitly that civil societies in Africa are not counter-hegemonic: 'Political actors within both "state" and "civil society" link up to sustain the vertical, infra-institutional and patrimonial networks which underpin politics on the continent' (1999: 22). The dilemma is clear: a civil society cannot be expected to act as a general-norm supplier as long as it is intertwined with a normless state.

The picture presented by these commentators is gloomy and their generalizations have been applied to the whole of sub-Saharan Africa. This chapter examines the relevance of their views in the context of one specific country, notably Kenya. Kenya's state of public morality is considered before tracing the problems of trust in one specific economic sub-sector, the country's horticultural trade. Relations between actors operating in the marketing channel and the role of trust and reputation in these relations are investigated. Platteau's (1994a) ideas on the difference between relations within and beyond the community space are also considered.

Public morality in Kenya

There is ample evidence from academics and journalists that Kenya could certainly use a dose of generalized morality, but Platteau's (1994b) suggestion that the Kenyan state should adopt the initiative would amuse many Kenyans. Successive Kenyan governments have actually cultivated limited-group morality by stimulating tribalism. The British colonial government was the first to contribute by creating bureaucratized tribes under indirect rule. They replaced systems of fluid voluntary clientage and loyalty by carefully designing and defining fixed tribal groupings. 'Tribe' came to be viewed as an exclusive category, influencing the conceptualizations of 'us' and 'them'.

The colonial government further widened the gap by introducing land registration for private titles. Shipton (1988) traced the registration process in Luoland back to its start in the 1950s, concluding that land registration raised tensions between autochtones and immigrants, and between labour migrants and native dwellers. It led to manipulation and double deals over title deeds that reinforced moral obligations towards limited groups, notably the homestead family and lineage segments, to the exclusion of strangers, banks and the government. In other words it enhanced limited-group morality at the expense of generalized morality.

After independence, Presidents Kenyatta and Moi carried on the colonial policy of land privatization. In a similar way they embraced the colonial inheritance of tribalism and created and institutionalized what Gibbon calls a 'manipulative political tribalism' (1995: 19). In the early 1990s, the Moi regime went one step further towards embedding tribalism in land transactions. With Moi's apparent approval, Kalenjin and Maasai politicians reintroduced the concept of regionalism, which had been proposed by the British Governor on the eve of independence. At the time, their call for *majimboism* (Kiswahili for 'regionalism') appeared to be nothing less than a call for ethnic cleansing.[1]

Ethnic clashes undermined Kenya's prospects for generalized morality and fuelled a culture of corruption. Looting of state resources took place with the approval, complicity or knowledge of the head of state (Gatheru and Shaw, 1998). Politicians utilized public resources to benefit themselves and their patron–client networks, thus serving as a rent-seeking role model for society.

In the 1960s and 1970s a growing number of parastatals offered numerous opportunities for predation. Ikiara *et al.* (1993) cite the example of the Agricultural Finance Corporation (AFC). Large unsecured loans were advanced to senior politicians who, using their connections, refused to repay them. Occasionally, district-wide write-offs of debts took place in parts of the country. Such write-offs tended to discourage farmers in other parts of the country from making repayments in anticipation that their loans would also be written off. They followed the example set by politicians.

In the 1980s, when the World Bank and the IMF started to demand economic reform, Kenyan politicians developed a new strategy. They sold off the valuable parts of parastatals to themselves. 'In the last decade many of the ADC[2] farms in Rift Valley, Eastern Province and in some other parts of the country have been sold at throw-away prices or even distributed free of charge to politicians, civil servants and senior military officers' (ibid.: 97). This resulted in a rapid reduction of the ADC's income and hence in its ability to carry out its core function, namely the production of hybrid and improved seeds and livestock breeds.

The frequency of these 'irregularities' calls into question Kenya's status as a democracy with a constitution and a parliament. Gatheru and Shaw (1998) show that the Kenyan constitution is inadequate as an instrument of governance. The judiciary is weak and under-capitalized, the parliament is hamstrung by its weak position *vis-à-vis* the executive, and the police and the Directorate of Security Intelligence behave as extensions of the executive, violating the constitutional requirement that they be politically neutral. All this has a negative impact on the Kenyan people's trust in their state institutions. A survey in 1997 among Kenyans with civic education showed that 86 per cent of the respondents had little confidence in the president and they did not believe that he was working in the interests of the people. The judiciary, parliament, county councils and police did not inspire any higher regard. Religious organizations were the only institutions that inspired confidence among the people.

Religious organizations, NGOs and self-help groups are all part of civil society and are expected as such to supply norms when the state fails. In the 1980s Kenyan self-help groups became redefined as channels for extending centralized state patronage networks to the grass-roots level. They were regulated through the security apparatus, or organized from above to obtain foreign funding and accumulate personal wealth (Gibbon, 1993).

Another potential source of counter-hegemonic power is the cooperatives. The tremendous growth of the cooperative movement since independence has been activated by heavy government support. Gatheru and Shaw (1998) argue that this has created problems related to what they call 'a dependency syndrome'. Direct intervention by the government in day-to-day management has compromised cooperative values such as self-help, self-reliance, democracy, equality, solidarity and mutual trust. Cooperatives have been infected by corruption and clientelism, which threaten their very existence.

The Kenyan churches seem to be the only civil institutions that have not been compromised and are still strong enough to articulate national interests, but even they are vulnerable. Holmquist and Ford (1994: 25) observe that 'church organizations may not be able to maintain a national presence as ethnic divisions tug away at the church as they have with all other organizations in society'.

In summarizing this section, it can be stated that the low level of public morality in Kenya is not unlike that described by earlier cited authors for Africa generally. This question will now be explored in relation to Kenya's horticultural trade. The analysis is based primarily on surveys among horticultural farmers and traders in Nyandarua, Taita Taveta, Kisii and Nakuru districts.[3] Mistrust characterizes economic intercourse at the national level, but how prevalent is it in the dealings of Kenyans in their local communities and regional economies? Are people in their everyday lives and livelihoods able to effect trust beyond community space?

History and characteristics of the Kenyan horticultural trade

At the outset of the 21st century Kenya had 29.5 million inhabitants, of which approximately only one in five lived in urban centres (Kenya, 2000). All these city-dwellers are potential buyers of horticultural commodities. About 60 per cent of all the fruit and vegetables produced in the country are consumed in urban areas (Gatheru and Shaw, 1998). Approximately 2 million metric tonnes of horticultural produce are brought to urban centres annually. Transport from the farms to the urban markets is physically challenging given the highly perishable nature of the commodities and the generally poor road conditions.

Smallholders produce the bulk of the horticultural commodities for the domestic market,[4] and private entrepreneurs are the main trading agents. This has been the case ever since the pre-colonial period. In the early days, exchange took place in *ad hoc* gatherings, and in rural periodic markets along inter-ethnic boundaries. Transactions could be safely carried out in these markets, even during tribal warfare. In western Kenya, for instance, 'a truce would be organized to enable the women folk to go to the market, the opposing warriors remaining at a distance at either side of the market' (Fearn, 1955: 29, as quoted by Obudho and Waller, 1976: 10). The trade often had a regional and inter-zonal character as cattle from the lowlands were exchanged for food crops grown upland (Cohen, 1983). Apart from exchanges in rural periodic markets, the food trade (including horticultural trade) took place in Muslim trading towns on the coast and in towns along caravan routes.[5]

During the colonial period horticultural production remained largely a smallholder business, and horticultural trade an African affair. African and non-African traders of food and non-food items were officially segregated. Non-African food traders were allowed to set up businesses only in urban areas, townships and trading centres, while African traders could establish themselves 'anywhere in the bush' (Rimmer, 1983, quoting a report of the East African Royal Commission). A growing number of periodic markets appeared in the fertile regions away from the white-settler areas and these markets functioned as collection centres for coffee and cotton (cash crops which were successfully promoted among Africans by the British colonial administration) and as centres of local food trade (Obudho and Waller, 1976). The collection of cash crops was in the hands of Indians and Arabs, while the local food trade remained primarily the domain of Africans.

After independence the Kenyan state monopolized the trade of food commodities such as grains and sugar, leaving vegetables and fruits to the free market. The horticultural commodities were not regarded as strategic, and their perishability made interventions risky. The horticultural trade developed relatively undisturbed. Demographic and physical changes rather than political and legal influences determined the horticultural trade process.

Market places still continue to be the centres of horticultural trade. The smallest markets are rural informal markets, which are not registered and have no facilities. The markets are periodic, with one or two market days a week and the number of traders is limited. Most are 'farmer-traders' selling produce cultivated on their own farms, which they display on a piece of cloth or plastic on the ground.

Next in the market hierarchy are the registered rural retail markets. They are also periodic, but at the bigger retail markets some trade may take place outside official market days. Farmer-traders and professional retailers are the main sellers, and local consumers the main buyers. Permanent stalls, toilets and a proper drainage system are often missing and traders display their produce on the ground as in the informal rural retail markets, or on wooden tables in ramshackle stalls. The market fees collected by the council are rarely used for improvements to the market place. Some rural retail markets develop into rural assembly markets to which wholesalers from large towns come to buy produce.[6]

Markets operate daily in the towns and in the biggest cities separate wholesale and retail markets can be found. Trade takes place on the ground, from wooden stalls, and in concrete structures built by the municipal council. The 'collecting wholesalers' buy their produce from farmers and traders in the production area, thus combining collection and distribution activities. Others specialize either on the collection or distribution side. 'Distributing wholesalers' stay in the wholesale market and buy from collecting wholesalers who sell to them from the back of their truck.

In terms of ethnic background, horticultural traders are normally a cross-section of the general population in the region they operate in (Dijkstra, 1997). In terms of gender, however, this is not the case. Over 95 per cent of the traders who sell horticultural commodities in rural market places and in small urban market places are women. Only in the daily markets of large urban centres are male traders more numerous.

The gender difference between markets in rural areas and small urban centres on the one hand and large urban centres on the other is most probably related to the incomes to be earned. In the first two, most female traders are so-called 'petty traders' who sell the surplus of a farm household or small quantities of bought produce, trying to earn a little money. For them trade is one of their rare opportunities to obtain cash. Capital requirements are low and a licence is not needed. The remuneration per hour is low but attractive when no other opportunities exist. Farm revenues from export crops such as coffee and tea are often controlled by their husbands, while trade revenues may provide the women with a personal income allowing some economic autonomy.

Husbands may be cultivating export crops, be absent because of jobs elsewhere, or have died or abandoned their wives. Those that are around and idle are often too proud (or, as some women say, too lazy) to work all day for such a small amount of money. According to men, cultural standards do not allow them to trade commodities while sitting on the ground (which is often necessary due to an absence of stalls). Selling clothing and cooking utensils in a similar way is, however, not a problem. Trading these commodities is usually more financially rewarding than retailing fruit and vegetables. The same is true for the wholesaling of horticultural commodities, and doing this without a stall is not a problem for men either.

Incomes are highest at the level of the collecting wholesale trade where women's involvement is most restricted (ibid.). This is at least partly related to unequal access to capital. The traders' capital requirements are high, especially when they hire a truck without sharing it with other traders. In addition to the rent of the truck, the load of some 70 bags of potatoes or 800 bunches of bananas also has to be financed. Fewer female than male traders are able to do this. Female traders do not have access to bank loans because they do not have title deeds to serve as collateral. Therefore, the majority of collecting wholesalers who handle truckloads of produce are men. Women are more often found among collecting wholesalers handling smaller quantities and sharing a hired truck.

Trust and distrust in the long-distance horticultural trade

The long tradition of private (African) horticultural trade has resulted in well established and relatively efficient trade networks with a high level of competition. The marketing system does not suffer from the infancy problems with which the recently liberalized maize market has had to deal (e.g. uncertainty because of a recurrent reversal of reforms). Nevertheless most horticultural traders run one-person businesses, and hardly any have established a corporate form. This supports Kennedy's (1988) observation about the lack of business partnerships in Africa. However, mutual cooperation and the use of agents and employees do occur as shown by the following case studies.

Our first case study concerns a woman collecting wholesaler, Priscilla, who lives in Ogembo, Kisii District, and trades cooking bananas between her home area and Nairobi, 400 km away. She is in her twenties, has two small children and no farm of her own. She started as a rural assembling trader, buying bananas from farmers who came to her house, and selling them to collecting wholesalers from Nairobi. When she had accumulated some capital she went into the collecting wholesale trade herself. At the time of the interview, Priscilla was taking one truckload of cooking bananas to Nairobi a week and each time she hired a 7-tonne truck from a transporter in the capital. The wholesale value of the load (800 bunches) was Ksh60,000 and the potential profit some Ksh10,000, the equivalent of a senior government official's monthly salary at that time. The exchange rate fluctuated considerably over the time period of the study: US$1 = Ksh24 (31/12/90) to US$1 = Ksh68 (31/12/93).

Whether the profit materialized or not was partly dependent on factors beyond the control of the trader. If the truck got stuck in the mud on its way out of the production area the bananas would go bad and the trader would get a very low price on arrival in the Nairobi wholesale market. If the truck was attacked by bandits while climbing the escarpment of the Rift Valley, the bananas would not reach Nairobi at all.

The success of the enterprise also depended on the experience and skills of the trader. It was especially important to know who could be trusted and who could not. As the trader explained, two steps in the marketing process were crucial in this respect, the loading in the production area and the unloading in the Nairobi wholesale market. Priscilla bought the bananas from farmers before they were harvested and hired casual labourers to harvest the bunches and carry them from the banana farm to a road where the truck would wait. Soon after starting her business she found out that she could not deal with the labourers on a basis of trust. Without careful supervision, the banana load that arrived in Nairobi contained fewer bananas than she had agreed to purchase. Some of the bunches had disappeared between the farm and the road because the labourers had hidden them in the bush. To solve this problem Priscilla employed two supervisors, one to count the bunches the moment they were cut from the trees and one to count them while they were being loaded. If fewer bunches were loaded than harvested the labourers were not paid until the lost bananas reappeared. The supervisors were people the trader trusted and knew well. She always worked with them, in contrast to the casual labourers who were hired on the spot.

The unloading of the bunches in the Nairobi wholesale market appeared to be another critical moment. The distributing wholesaler to whom she agreed to sell the bananas hired casual labourers to unload and carry the bunches to the wholesale store. In the beginning, the trader agreed that the buyer would count the bunches when they were brought into the store. Priscilla soon discovered, however, that some of the bunches did not reach the store, having been secreted to another part of the busy market place. She suspected the distributing wholesalers but could not prove their involvement. From then on, the bananas were sold by the truckload. She informed interested distributing wholesalers of the number of bunches in the truck and of their quality, and negotiated a lump-sum payment. In this way disappearing bunches were no longer a problem.

In addition to the physical handling, payments proved to be a headache. The overall supply of cooking bananas to the Nairobi market fluctuated greatly from one day to the next. When only a few trucks arrived, collecting wholesalers could ask for cash on delivery. When on the other hand many trucks arrived, distributing wholesalers would only be willing to buy cooking bananas on credit, promising to pay the following week. It took Priscilla some time to get to know the distributing wholesalers who indeed kept their promise, and to identify those who never intended to pay. It also took time to find out what to do if things went wrong. When rewarded properly, certain policemen were willing to render immediate assistance. They would threaten to take the defaulting distributing wholesaler to the police station for interrogation. The culprit would not want to leave his stall and would propose a settlement, which usually meant paying part of his debt immediately with an added payment the following week.

Having received the money, one final problem remained: how to get the money home safely. Priscilla did not trust the banking system. Several banks had branch offices in her home area of Ogembo but she was convinced that the money would get lost, or 'stolen' as she called it, while being transferred from the branch office in Nairobi to the Ogembo branch. Her views were supported by many Kenyans who had stories about money transfers that never reached their destination or only after a delay of several months. Priscilla decided to carry the money in her pocket. However, on one occasion some of her money was stolen when she fell asleep on the long-distance bus going home. To make sure that this would not happen again she called upon the help of specific bus drivers. She always travelled with the same bus company and had befriended the drivers. She trusted them and asked them to keep the money for her under the front seat during the trip.

The case study demonstrates something about trust and mistrust in the horticultural trade. Priscilla learned to mistrust casual labourers in the field and wholesalers in Nairobi, finding ways of minimizing the risks when dealing with them. She had to adapt to operating in a business environment in which financial institutions and law enforcement agencies were corrupt. She was able to operate without using banks, and got police officers on her side by bribing them.

However, she could not survive entirely without people who were trustworthy. She trusted the supervisors who checked on the casual labourers in the field, and the bus drivers who looked after her money. They were not recruited on the basis of ethnicity or gender but were founded on the collegial interest of doing a job properly and efficiently. This trust was based on personal ties that had been deliberately cultivated.

Our second horticultural trader is a businessman who lives in Tulaga, Nyandarua District, about 100 km from Nairobi. He is in his fifties, runs a sawmill and has a farm and tractor. He has been a collecting wholesaler of potatoes for several years. Initially, he used to hire a truck, but after making enough money was able to buy one. At the time of the interview, he owned a two-year-old 8-tonne truck with a replacement value of some Ksh1 million. He handled a maximum of 6 truckloads of potatoes a week, each load worth Ksh30,000 to Ksh40,000 in the Nairobi wholesale market. The estimated profit margin was around Ksh3,500 per trip.

Joseph had developed an efficient team of 10 purchasing agents. Each day he told the agents the maximum price he was willing to pay for a bag of potatoes. Each agent then negotiated with farmers on a bilateral basis about the buying price. After reaching an agreement the agent packed the potatoes in gunny bags. The negotiations took place early in the morning, and the packing during the rest of the morning and in the afternoon. Towards the end of the afternoon Joseph would turn up with his truck. The bags were loaded in the back, and Joseph asked each agent how much money he needed to pay the farmers. He handed over the money and a commission per bag for the work done. The agents paid the farmers after the truck had left for Nairobi.

Joseph was able to handle up to six truckloads a week because of his purchasing agents. If he had done the negotiating himself he would have lost a lot of time (and he would still have had to employ people to do the packing). He would also need time to look for produce. Ten purchasing agents were more efficient in finding potential sellers than one trader. They knew exactly where to look because of their day-to-day contacts with farmers and would try to come up with as many bags of potatoes as possible to maximize their commission. Even when produce was scarce and they needed 2 or 3 days to fill the truck with the required 80 to 90 bags, Joseph would have needed more time if he had undertaken the task himself.

When Joseph was younger he went with the truck to Nairobi, together with the driver and two assistants ('turnboys'). At the time of the interview, he was sending a relative in his place to whom he paid a monthly salary and a bonus for each trip made. The truck arrived at the Nairobi wholesale market during the night to queue up with other trucks in front of the market gate. After the market opened and it was the truck's turn to enter the market place, there were two selling options. The first was to sell the entire load to a residing distributing wholesaler (as the previously mentioned banana trader did). The second option was to bypass the distributing wholesalers and sell from the back of the truck to retailers. This was potentially more profitable but was also more risky, as our trader found out. There was a lot of competition in the market place and distributing wholesalers did not shy away from what he called 'dirty tricks'. The first time he entered the wholesale market, resident wholesalers sent a few of their people to the truck to act as 'retailers' who wanted to buy. They offered a low price and bargained endlessly. In the end our trader accepted their price only to find out later that he had been fooled. From then on he changed his tactics and obtained the assistance of a selling agent who knew the market very well and who sold on behalf of collecting wholesalers. On arrival in the market the trader told the agent the minimum selling price he could accept. The agent negotiated with potential customers and, after finalizing a transaction, handed over the money to the trader. When the entire truckload was sold, the agent received a commission for the work undertaken.

The activities of the purchasing agents in the field and the selling agent in Nairobi were monitored by Joseph and his relative. The weak spots in the supervision were the negotiated buying and selling prices. The purchasing agents might tell the trader that he had agreed to pay the farmers Ksh180 per bag while in reality paying them Ksh160 and putting Ksh20 in his own pocket. Similarly, the selling agent might relay that he had received Ksh300 per bag while in reality he had received Ksh320 and kept the difference. If the agents wanted to cheat they could. And indeed, Joseph knew they did. Nevertheless the relationship between Joseph and his agents worked, the reason being that the trader set a maximum buying price and a minimum selling price. On the basis of these prices he made a good profit. Whether the agents then made some extra money in addition to their commission was not really important to the trader. He had actually already anticipated this by keeping the commission low. In other words, the trader had already reckoned on his agents' lack of trustworthiness. The agents on the other hand knew that the trader would not punish them for making some extra money as long as his sales were secured.

Our third case study concerns collecting wholesalers who take high-value vegetables from the Taita Hills to Mombasa, some 200 km away. The traders, both men and women, deal with relatively small quantities of vegetables such

as French beans, baby marrow, cauliflower, tomatoes, lettuce, leek and cap-
sicums. They buy the products directly from farmers in the production area,
and sell them to distributing wholesalers in the wholesale market and retailers
in the retail markets of Mombasa. Each trader works on his/her own, negotiating on a bilateral basis with farmers in Taita and traders in Mombasa. The
turnover per trip is usually some three to ten baskets of produce.

Most of the traders started in business after the access road to the hills (the
Mwatate-Wundanyi road) was tarmacked in the 1980s. The upgrading of the
road reduced the travel time to Mombasa by half a day and increased the
number of transporters who operated in the hills. In addition to minibuses,
small (4-tonne) trucks started to commute between the hills and Mombasa.
The trucks offered traders the opportunity to carry more produce to Mombasa
than the few baskets that the minibus drivers allowed per passenger. On the
other hand, an individual trader did not have to fill an entire truck because
the truck drivers traversed the production area to collect produce from various
traders. The traders just had to wait along one of the main roads in the hills
until a truck passed. After loading the produce, he/she would take a minibus
to Mombasa to await the arrival of the truck.

In the beginning transport arrangements did not always work out as
planned. Not all truck drivers were trustworthy. After collecting their baskets
in Mombasa, traders might discover that some baby marrows or cauliflowers
were missing from their baskets. Most probably, the driver would have taken
them and sold them on his way to Mombasa, but this was difficult to prove.
Baskets did not have a standardized size, and one basket might contain three
or more different types of vegetables. How could the trader prove that one
cauliflower was missing?

Over time a system developed that was said to be more or less watertight.
The truck drivers used a logbook and before baskets were loaded onto a truck
they were marked, and weighed by means of a balance. The driver registered
the name of each trader in the logbook and the weight of each of his/her baskets and showed the trader the entry. The driver kept the logbook, with the
entries for all the traders, in his cabin. On arrival in Mombasa the baskets were
weighed again when unloading and the weights compared with the figures in
the logbook. If the weights had not changed during the journey, the trader
could be more or less sure that the driver had not tampered with the load.[7]

The truck driver still had one other means of stealing. He could disap-
pear with the truck and its entire load. This would be a financial disaster for
the traders concerned. The chances of this happening were small, however,
because most truck drivers did not own the trucks they were driving but were
hired to do the job. The truck owner who employed the driver knew where the
driver lived and would do everything he could to find both the driver and his
truck. Once the driver was found the traders could come forward with their
claims. The truck owner would probably fire the driver, and the traders would
take the driver to the police if he refused to pay. For the driver, it would not
be worth taking the risk. If he wanted to earn more than his driver's salary it

would be easier to take some produce from the production area to Mombasa on his own account. This is what indeed happened and the traders' business was not affected.

The case study shows that a transport arrangement initially based on trust would develop into one that worked even when the partners were not trustworthy. Checks were refined to such an extent that cheating by the truck driver could be immediately detected. Once discovered, the driver would be at the mercy of the trader. The latter could use the police and the truck owner to make the driver's life miserable.

Our fourth case study concerns four women who sold cabbages from stalls in the municipal market of Kisii Town. Like most retailers, the women used to work entirely on their own account. They bought produce from collecting wholesalers who came to the market, and from farmers in the production areas. The latter alternative was more attractive in terms of buying prices but less attractive in terms of time management. The women had to travel to the production areas very early in the morning and try to be back in the market in time or otherwise lose a selling day.

The women's stalls were near to each other and they had got to know each other. All four were of the Gusii ethnic group and lived near Kisii Town, though not in the same villages. One day they decided that it would be more profitable to join forces. From then on, each time cabbages were required, two of the women went to the production area to make purchases from farmers, while the other two looked after the sales from all four stalls. The traders who went out to buy cabbages had more time to find cheap but good quality produce, while the traders who stayed behind made sure that sales continued. At the end of the day all costs and benefits were shared equally.

At the time of the interview their joint business was doing very well. The women's cabbage prices were competitive and they attracted both consumers and retailers. The women had become the leading cabbage traders in the market, both in the wholesale and retail trade.

The women's cooperation was based on trust. At the same time, the risks were calculable and as the women worked in pairs, none of them could cheat the others unless she implicated her partner. The two that went out to purchase the cabbages could cheat the other two by stating that they had to pay more for the cabbages than they actually did, and the women who stayed behind could claim that they had received less for the cabbages than expected. Neither couple could exaggerate too much. Cabbages were bought and sold per piece, the price being a round figure, for example small ones bought at Ksh1.5 sold at Ksh3, and big ones bought at Ksh2 sold at Ksh4. Prices doubled over the seasons but not within a few days. Deception in prices would at most involve half a shilling per cabbage. Although the women handled hundreds of cabbages per day, half a shilling extra per cabbage was probably not worth the risk.

The case study shows that even in a society lacking a generalized morality, some traders cooperate successfully on the basis of trust. The women in the case study are from the same ethnic group, but not from the same village. They do not live in the same community. According to Platteau's (1994a) argumentation, their cooperation is doomed to fail because it goes 'beyond the community space'. There are two reasons why, in this case, Platteau is wrong. First, the women have built in safety measures against cheating (by working in pairs). Second, and probably more important, the women do not come from the same village but their personal ties have been woven on the basis of mutual business interests. When they started to cooperate they already knew each other quite well from having been together in the market place six days a week. They had formed, in a sense, a small community within the walls of the market place. In other words, community space is not only determined by one's residence but also by one's work place.

Our fifth and last case study deals with professional retailers who sell produce in the retail market of Njoro, a town with some 10,000 inhabitants in Nakuru District. In December 1992, 26 of these retailers were sampled from a total trader population of some 160 traders.[8] As many as 19 of the 26 interviewed traders (73%) participated in a savings and credit association. The associations were usually relatively small, one had 33 members, and all the others fewer than 15.

Most of the associations worked with a rotating fund whereby all members contributed a fixed amount of money and each member received the pool in turn.[9] The majority of the traders were in the market twice a week on official market days. Therefore most of the associations collected and paid out twice a week. The largest association, with 33 members, consisted of retailers with permanent stalls in the market. They were present 7 days a week, and their rotating fund also worked on a daily basis.

The contributions were relatively small with Ksh10 to Ksh30 being the most common. If traders wanted to save more they participated in more than one association. One third of the interviewed retailers actually did so. They were a member of two to five and, in one case, even ten associations.

The large majority of the retailers in the market belonged to the dominant ethnic group in the region, the Kikuyu. There were, however, also Luo, Luhya and Kalenjin traders. These minority groups had their own associations, but also participated in Kikuyu-led groups. The large association of retailers with permanent stalls, for instance, had a Kalenjin member. This did not seem to present problems, even while Kalenjin and Kikuyu were on opposing sides in the ethnic clashes that were racking the country at the time of the interview.

The credit system was based on trust. Members who received the pool last trusted members who received the pool first to keep on paying their contributions. Sometimes the confidence of members was betrayed, and early receivers turned into late defaulters. Not everybody appeared to be trustworthy in this respect and, to reduce potential losses, traders had learned to spread risks. They preferred to take part in several associations that each demanded small contributions rather than participating in only one that demanded a substantial contribution. Moreover, they preferred small associations in which the time lapse between the first and the last draw was shorter, and in which everybody knew each other better.

The chances of defaulting were reduced by only allowing people with a sound reputation to participate. Traders who had defaulted in earlier rounds or who were known to have defaulted in other groups were excluded. To be able to check reputations an applicant did not by definition have to come from the same town, village or ethnic group as existing members, but her business activities in the market place had to be known.

The case study confirms Platteau's (1994a) statement that reputation is an important tool in tackling the problem of trust. It also shows that horticultural retailers who join an association are from within the same community sphere. As in the Kisii case study, community is, however, not solely defined in terms of birthplace or geographical residence. It is also defined by one's place of work, i.e. the market, or a section of the market.

Conclusions

Fukuyama (1995) would classify Kenya as a low-trust society. Platteau (1994b) would add that limited-group morality rather than generalized morality prevails, and that the Kenyan state and civil society fail to act as norm-enforcing agencies. As a result people distrust 'non-kin' (Fukuyama) and those 'beyond the community space' (Platteau).

Our case studies of horticultural traders do indeed reveal a lot of cheating and distrust in horticultural trading. Priscilla, the Kisii woman trader, did not trust the casual labourers who harvested and loaded for her, and the wholesalers in Nairobi to whom she sold. Joseph, the Nyandarua trader, did not trust his purchasing agents in the field and his selling agent in Nairobi. The Taita wholesalers did not trust their transporters and the Njoro retailers did not completely trust their fellow traders with regard to rotating credit.

In all cases, the distrust of the studied traders was justified, arising from daily business experiences. The traders reacted by developing systems that minimized risks. Priscilla organized supervision of her casual labourers and sold to wholesalers before unloading. Joseph set maximum buying prices and minimum selling prices for his agents, and the Taita traders insisted that transporters keep log books to register their produce. The Njoro traders went for small savings and credit associations with limited contributions, and checked the reputation of potential members before allowing them to join.

The case studies amply demonstrate, however, that not all relations are based on distrust. Priscilla trusts the supervisors of her casual labourers, and Joseph relies on his relative who accompanies his produce to Nairobi. To a large extent they have no choice but to trust them because they cannot manage without them. The four cabbage-trading women in the Kisii municipal market do have a choice. They could buy their produce on an individual basis but have decided to join forces on the basis of trust. However, even these women have built in some safety measures, notably working in pairs.

Kenyan horticultural trade has developed relatively undisturbed ever since the pre-colonial period. Distrust among Kenyan horticultural traders does not therefore originate from short-term or transitional conditions. It is not limited to the horticultural trade. Nor is it a problem experienced only by Kenyan African traders. Successful Kenyan traders of Asian origin, who deal with anything from sugar to cars, also operate on the basis of distrust. The problem extends beyond Kenya. Van Donge (1992: 184) studied the Waluguru vegetable traders in Tanzania and concluded that partnerships 'are bound to fail as one cannot trust the other'.

If we accept Kennedy's proposition that Africa needs corporate forms of business, and that in order to pool resources traders have to trust each other, the question remains as to how this can be realized. It brings us back to Platteau's (1993) norm-enforcing agencies. As long as the government, the police, the judiciary, the cooperative movement, the banking system and other national institutions cannot be trusted there is little hope that trust can prevail in business beyond the community sphere of face-to-face contacts and enduring friendships.

The trust in the above-mentioned case studies was always based on face-to-face personal ties in the first instance. These ties do not necessarily have to originate from kinship or from place of birth or residence. The ties may result from collegial interactions in the market place. Traders cooperate on the basis of reputation in the market or on the basis of long-term friendship. The place of work (the market) replaces their home area as frame of reference. These ties often transcend gender, ethnic and age divisions. They are established on expediency but the fact that they last is what is most significant. They endure due to common interests and occupational integrity.

Beginning as early as 1986, UNIDO (1996: 24) stated that the goal of the Kenyan government was to create an 'enabling environment' in which development would flourish. This was in accordance with World Bank terminology of the time.[10] The government-sponsored ethnic clashes in the 1990s have, however, not 'enabled' the development of trust among Kenyan citizens, and nor have the devastating forms of corruption practised by the nation's ruling politicians. A kleptocracy is never enabling. Until the political environment changes, limited-group morality will prevail and trust will not travel far.

Nonetheless, the ingenuity with which ordinary Kenyan people contend with the constraints and the deliberate intervention of trust in relationships of the work place, in addition to those in residential neighbourhoods and amongst kin, has greatly facilitated the movement of goods and services on a daily basis over considerable distances. Furthermore it suggests that professional ethics and integrity can begin to form even in the presence of rampant national corruption and a seriously deficient 'enabling' environment. Trust tiptoes forward.

About the author

Tjalling Dijkstra is presently working as a senior policy advisor at the Directorate General for International Cooperation at the Ministry of Foreign Affairs in the Netherlands. He is dealing with trade issues, including market access negotiations (WTO, EPAs, EU CAP) and public–private partnerships in developing sustainable trade and fair trade. When writing the chapter of this book, he worked as a researcher at the African Studies Centre, Leiden, the Netherlands. He is a development economist who has done field research in Kenya, Uganda, Sudan and Sierra Leone. He wrote his PhD thesis on horticultural marketing in Kenya.

Notes

* The analysis of the author in this paper does not necessarily reflect the views of his present employer.
1. To ensure that this cleansing was indeed carried out, 'warriors' were hired to be transported by government vehicles and helicopters to the battlefields (Human Rights Watch, 1993; Kenya Human Rights Commission, 1996).
2. Agricultural Development Corporation.
3. The surveys were carried out between 1990 and 1992 as part of the Food and Nutrition Studies Programme at the African Studies Centre, Leiden (see Dijkstra and Magori, 1995; Dijkstra, 1997).
4. Horticultural exports are outside the scope of the present chapter.
5. Coastal ports began to develop in Kenya during the second millennium AD (Hrbek, 1992). Caravan towns appeared in the interior in the 18th century (Obudho and Waller, 1976).
6. For more details on the development of rural assembly markets see Dijkstra (1996, 1997).
7. A more precise alternative would have been to register the number of cauliflowers, leeks, etc. per basket but this would involve turning all baskets and boxes upside down before loading and after unloading to count the contents. This was not a feasible option.
8. When sampling, no distinction was made between farmer-traders and professional traders. The total random sample consisted of 31 traders, of which 5 appeared to be farmer-traders (only selling produce from their own farm), and 26 professional traders.
9. The alternative was an accumulating fund whereby members borrowed money.
10. More recently, the World Bank has also been advocating an 'attractive environment' (World Bank, 1995).

References

Bayart, J-F., Ellis, S.and Hibou, B. (1999) *The Criminalization of the State in Africa*, James Currey/Indiana University Press, London and Bloomington.

Chabal, P. and Daloz, J-P. (1999) *Africa Works: Disorder as Political Instrument*, James Currey/Indiana University Press, London and Bloomington.

Cohen, D.W. (1983) 'Food production and food exchange in the precolonial Lakes Plateau Region', in R.I. Rotberg (ed.), *Imperialism, Colonialism, and Hunger: East and Central Africa*, pp. 1–19, Lexington Books, Lexington, MA.

Collier, P. and Gunning J.W. (1997) 'Explaining Economic Performance', Centre for the Study of African Economies, University of Oxford, Working Paper Series 97–2, Oxford.

Dijkstra, T. (1996) 'Food assembly markets in Africa: lessons from the horticultural sector of Kenya', *British Food Journal* 98(9): 26–34.

Dijkstra, T. (1997) *Trading the Fruits of the Land: Horticultural Marketing Channels in Kenya*, Ashgate, Aldershot, UK.

Dijkstra, T. and Magori, T.D. (eds) (1995) *Horticultural Production and Marketing in Kenya; Part 5: Proceedings of a Dissemination Seminar at Nairobi, 16–17th November 1994*, Ministry of Planning and National Development & African Studies Centre, Food and Nutrition Studies Programme, Report no. 53, Nairobi and Leiden.

Fearn, H. (1955) 'The Problems of the African Trader', East Africa, Institute of Social Research Conference Papers, unpublished report.

Fukuyama, F. (1995) *Trust: The Social Virtues and the Creation of Prosperity*, Penguin Books, London.

Gatheru, W. and Shaw, R. (1998) *Our Problems, Our Solutions: An Economic and Public Policy Agenda for Kenya*, Institute of Economic Affairs, Nairobi.

Gibbon, P. (1993) 'Introduction: economic reform and social change in Africa', in P. Gibbon, P (ed.), *Social Change and Economic Reform in Africa*, pp. 11–27, The Scandinavian Institute of African Studies, Uppsala.

Gibbon, P. (1995) 'Markets, civil society and democracy in Kenya', in P. Gibbon (ed.), *Markets, Civil Society and Democracy in Kenya*, pp. 7–30, The Scandinavian Institute of African Studies, Uppsala.

Holmquist, F. and Ford, M. (1994) 'Kenya: state and civil society the first year after the election', *Africa Today* 91(4): 5–26.

Hrbek, I. (ed.) (1992) *General History of Africa III; Africa from the Seventh to the Eleventh Century*, Abridged edition, James Currey and UNESCO, London and Paris.

Human Rights Watch (1993) *Divide and Rule: State-Sponsored Ethnic Violence in Kenya*, Human Rights Watch/Africa Watch, New York.

Ikiara, G.K., Jama, M.A. and Amadi, J.O. (1993) 'Agricultural decline, politics and structural adjustment in Kenya', in P. Gibbon (ed.), *Social Change and Economic Reform in Africa*, pp. 78–105, The Scandinavian Institute of African Studies, Uppsala.

Kennedy, P. (1988) *African Capitalism: The Struggle for Ascendancy*, Cambridge University Press, Cambridge.

Kenya, Government of (2000) *Population Census 1999*, Central Bureau of Statistics, Nairobi.

Kenya Human Rights Commission (1996) *Our Rights, Their Mights: A Study on Land Clashes*, Kenya Human Rights Commission, Land Rights Program, Nairobi.

Obudho, R.A. and Waller, P.P. (1976) *Periodic Markets, Urbanization, and Regional Planning*, Contributions in Afro-American and African Studies, no. 22, Greenwood Press, Westport CT.

Platteau, J-P. (1993) 'The free market is not readily transferable: reflections on the links between market, social relations and moral norms', in J. Martinussen (ed.), *New Institutional Economics and Development Theory*, pp. 71–178, Occasional Paper no. 6, Institute of Development Studies, Roskilde University, Roskilde.

Platteau, J-P. (1994a) 'Behind the market stage where real societies exist – Part I: the role of public and private institutions', *Journal of Development Studies* 30(3): 533–77.

Platteau, J-P. (1994b) 'Behind the market stage where real societies exist – Part II: the role of moral norms', *Journal of Development Studies* 30(3), 753–817.

Rimmer, D. (1983) 'The economic imprint of colonialism and domestic food supplies in British tropical Africa', in R.I. Rotberg (ed.), *Imperialism, Colonialism, and Hunger: East and Central Africa*, pp. 141–66, Lexington Books, Lexington, MA.

Shipton, P. (1988) 'The Kenyan land tenure reform: misunderstandings in the public creation of private property', in R.E. Downs and S.P. Reyna (eds), *Land and Society in Contemporary Africa*, pp. 91–135, University Press of New England, London.

UNIDO (1996) *Kenya: Paving the Road to NIC Status*, United Nations Industrial Development Organization, Vienna.

van Donge, J.K. (1992) 'Waluguru traders in Dar es Salaam: an analysis of the social construction of economic life', *African Affairs* 91: 181–205.

Widner, J. A. (1997) 'The courts of restraints', in P. Collier and C. Pattillo (eds), *Risk and Agencies of Restraint: Reducing the Risks of African Investment*, Macmillan, London.

World Bank (1995) *Private Sector Development in Low-Income Countries*, The World Bank, Washington, DC.

CHAPTER 4

Calculated chaos or cooperation? Informal financial markets in Kinshasa

Mindanda Mohogu

This chapter argues that weak legal institutions in Congo-Kinshasa have led to the coexistence of two financial markets, the formal and the informal ones. Informal finance in Congo-Kinshasa has emerged as a reaction to the inability of the formal financial sectors to respond to the population's needs for access to formal finance. The informal activities are devised through social networking generally without regard for any government regulations and social legislation. They are often formed on the basis of strong linkages within particular areas and use various techniques to address problems related to information, transaction costs and risk. Through their services to households and micro businesses, they create new spaces of unregulated waged labour. Despite their importance in the country, the government has not yet decided to include them in any economic provisions.

Introduction

Kinshasa, home to roughly 7.5 million people, is the economic and political capital of the Democratic Republic of the Congo (formerly Zaire). This vast, resource-rich country derives its wealth primarily from mineral exports of diamonds, gold, uranium and copper. An export economy of this dimension necessitates reliable financial banking services. However, Zaire's lack of political accountability and stability has not been conducive to the provisioning of such services. During the final two decades of Mobutu's reign in Zaire, the formal banking system eroded and the informal financial sector in Kinshasa became ever more prominent to the point that it dwarfed formal banking services. The informal sector not only became an important vehicle for mobilizing household savings and financing small business but also accounted for an ever-increasing volume of foreign-exchange transactions. Regarded as the direct consequence of the economic crisis and the absence of the state, the activities of this sector successfully avoided control by the authorities.

This chapter examines how Kinshasa's residents resolved their need for credit and foreign exchange through informal inter-personal networking during the 1970s and 1980s and into the 1990s until the eclipse of Mobutu's regime. The first section reviews the context of the economic crisis and the development of informal activities in Kinshasa. The second section examines the anatomy of the pre-existing Congolese formal financial market and the events that triggered its implosion. Thereafter, the array of informal institutions that has evolved to cater to people's credit needs is considered, before turning to the informal foreign-exchange market, the *cambisme*. The emergence and centrality of women *cambistes* in the foreign-exchange market are highlighted. The penultimate section discusses the nature of inter-personal relations in financial services evaluating their effectiveness *vis-à-vis* credit and foreign exchange network participants and the national economy as a whole. The conclusion summarizes the argument and poses the question: when financial services are highly personalized, who wins and who loses?

Political patronage and the spread of the informal economy

The development of informal activities in Kinshasa paralleled Zaire's unfolding political and economic crisis. The crisis can be traced back to the mid-1970s when most of the companies and trade belonging to foreigners were nationalized. In 1973, Mobutu decreed that foreign-owned farms, plantations, commercial enterprises – mostly in the hands of Portuguese, Greek, Italian and Pakistani traders – should be turned over to nationals, the 'sons of the country'. This was followed by the confiscation of the largely Belgian-controlled industrial sector and the distribution of thousands of businesses to top officials in what could be termed the most comprehensive privatization exercise the African continent has ever witnessed. In its aftermath, the country's wealth was concentrated in the hands of a very small elite who were politicians and members of Mobutu's Gbandi clan from northern Congo.

Many of the new owners had neither the skills nor the interest to manage their businesses and some never even bothered. They pocketed savings and sold company equipment locally. The proceeds were spent on luxury items. The businesses took on the nature of corporate clans. Jobs were bestowed on family members and, in this way, the number of workers multiplied without a parallel increase in production.

As businesses closed, prices rose and the disastrous implications of what Mobutu had done began to sink in and prompted the government to make efforts to reverse the damage. Majority shares were offered to former owners and some compensation was finally paid. But few entrepreneurs were motivated to invest in the country. Zaire's industrial and commercial infrastructures rapidly collapsed.

Mobutu's nationalization plans coincided with the oil crisis, the deterioration of the terms of trade and the drop in the world price of copper, the country's principal source of export earnings. In 1974, copper prices plummeted by nearly two-thirds just as the oil crisis plunged the world into recession. The remedial structural adjustment policy proposed by the International Monetary Fund (IMF) and applied between 1978 and 1980 succeeded in rectifying the balance of payments temporarily, but it engendered perverse social effects by accelerating the impoverishment of the population (Ngondo, 1996). Life in Kinshasa became ever more difficult, with living standards declining in line with a gradual deterioration in the national economic situation.

The crisis however became further accentuated during the 1990s when the state lost control of its bureaucratic apparatus, triggering a political crisis and national economic disarray. The refusal by the authorities to attempt reform led in 1991 and 1993 to acts of frustration and despair by segments of the population who resorted to systematic plundering of shops and the destruction of many industrial factories. At the same time, the country became internationally isolated because of the state's wilful transgression of international human rights conventions.

The collapse of large enterprises, the decline in the administrative capacity of the state, the impossibly low real incomes of the Kinshasa population at all levels of society, spiralling inflation and the rampant shortages of goods contributed to an explosion of second-economy activities which people jokingly referred to as Article 15; *'debrouillez vous'* or *'fend for yourself'*. These were survival strategies that gave rise to a new urban economic order (MacGaffey, 1991, 1994, 1998).

Between 1984 and 1989, the number of enterprises in the informal sector expanded by roughly 50 per cent, amounting to an annual average increase of 3 per cent (Marijsse and De Herdt, 1996). More than 85 per cent of the working population were believed to be earning their living mainly in the informal sector.[1] This growth in informal activities spurred the development of a significant informal financial sector in Congo-Kinshasa.

Many factors explain the specific characteristics of the Congolese informal sector. First, the high rate of unemployment and the low level of salaries and wages in the formal economy forced people to seek refuge in the informal sector. However, during this period people working in the informal sector were loathe to give up their employment in the formal sector because a job in government gave them access to markets or supplies needed in their informal activities. Many found that the level of income they could earn in the informal sector in Congo-Kinshasa was higher than in the formal sector.

By 1997, Kinshasa's informal sector was not only a survival strategy for its participants but also a dynamic sector that represented about 80–85 per cent of economic activities (Lensink, 1993; Ngondo, 1996). It was estimated that only 5 per cent of the working population in Kinshasa had formal employment and the rest were assumed to be operating in the informal sector (Marijsse and De Herdt, 1996).

In April 1990, Mobutu, weakened by a series of domestic protests and international criticism of his regime's human rights practices, had agreed to the principle of a multi-party system with elections and a constitution. But the reform was delayed and civil unrest broke out in September 1991 and again in January 1993 resulting in looting and property loss. A wide range of classes in the Congolese population participated in the looting, including civil servants, soldiers, students and business people. Their destructive activities were open and unchecked robbery, functioning to transfer resources from the formal to the informal sector. This was not the first time such events had occurred. The theft of fixed capital had become a feature of the Zairean economy making it possible for individuals to establish themselves in the informal sector as independent producers who, in their minds, were being compensated for years of low-paid employment (MacGaffey, 1994). According to the Congolese newspaper *Le Phare* (1992), an estimated 924 companies were destroyed during the first plundering and 90,517 people lost their jobs. A significant amount of capital and foreign investors took flight. Some Congolese businessmen also escaped abroad, particularly to South Africa.

Collapse of the formal banking system

A formal financial system in Congo-Kinshasa has been almost non-existent. Serious problems prevent it from playing its role as an effective financial intermediary to support the emergence of efficient economic agents. There is no market for government bonds and the number of banks and the quality of financial products offered is relatively low compared to the size of the country. Almost all the banks are located in Kinshasa whereas in the rest of the country there are only 26 banks for a population estimated at 50 million inhabitants. Certain large provinces such as Bandundu, Maniema and Equateur are almost devoid of any banks (*Groupe l'Avenir*, 2000) while in the other provinces, the banks are restricted to the urban areas. Most bank capital is controlled by foreigners.

The crisis has affected the entire mechanism of financial payment, the collection of savings and the distribution of credits. Between 1975 and 1990, the deposits in Zaire currency in the banking system decreased from 14.5 to 6.4 per cent of the money supply (Aneza, 1991).

There has been a general tendency for the level of deposits to fall accompanied by a drain of credit in real terms and overall decline in the level of savings mobilized by the banks (Table 4.1). Several structural as well economic factors are at the root of this situation. The most salient are centred on the destruction of productive infrastructure during past looting, an increasing demand for liquidities in the banks following the pyramid schemes (see below) and the dollarization of the economy.

Despite monetary and economic instability from the mid-1970s, the dollarization of the economy was a relatively marginal phenomenon in Kinshasa

Table 4.1 Evolution of deposits and bank credits (million of Zaire)

	1990	1993	1996	1999
Deposits	122.8	65.4	63.9	68.4
Credit	54	57.1	25.1	53.8

Source: Groupe l'Avenir, 2000

until 1988. The regime of fixed exchange rates was abandoned on 12 September 1983. Between 1970 and 1988, the rate of dollarization in the strict sense of bank deposits oscillated between 1 and 4 per cent, while dollarization in the broader sense of total money supply was low, estimated to vary between 1 and 6.5 per cent.[2] From 1989, however, it became a force in the Zairean economy such that, by 1997, dollars accounted for an estimated 22 per cent and 44 per cent of bank deposits and total money supply respectively associated with trade liberalization especially with respect to diamonds (Ngonga et al., 1999).

Surprisingly, liberalization of foreign-exchange markets did not seem to have an impact on dollarization. Indeed it was the persistence of economic and monetary instability that spurred economic agents to acquire and trade in dollars. Dollar holdings gave individuals partial protection against the country's rampant inflation. It was only in September 1999 that President Kabila reintroduced restrictions under the new government.

During the 1990s, the country experienced protracted political upheaval and an explosion of government spending financed almost entirely by printing more of the national currency. Inflation skyrocketed from about 56 per cent in 1989 to 256 per cent in 1990, then soared in 1994 (World Bank, 1997). Thereafter, inflation fluctuated, declining to 370 per cent in 1995 but rising to 657 per cent in 1996. During this period, the Zaire exchange rate and consumer prices moved in synchrony. Dollarization subverted monetary policy, undermining the operational effectiveness of any attempts at regulating exchange rates, making it impossible for the authorities to control the overall money supply (Ngonga et al., 1999).

Increased demand for liquidities was another cause of the collapse of the Congolese banking system (De Herdt and Marijsse, 1999). Not only were people reacting to inflation and spending rather than saving, they were also diverting their savings into investment games. These games, generically known as pyramid schemes, were analogous to a reversed pyramid because payouts to early investors depended on ever-expanding numbers of later investors. All schemes promised to make investors instantly rich and people flocked to a proliferation of such games usually named after their entrepreneurial creators, notably: Bindo, Masamuna, Nguma. Mr. Bindo quickly became known through the *radio-trottoir* and the media as 'the new Messiah', Moses and the 'Doctor of Misery'. As Gondola (1997) affirms, all the inhabitants of Kinshasa swore by the name of Bindo.

Through the very high rates of return received by early investors, these games attracted thousands of Kinois (residents of Kinshasa) investors. Unlike the lottery, the games rested exclusively on the credulity of the subscribers since they are not founded on chance but on the promise of an exponential interest rate based on an inexhaustible supply of investors. Bindo-Promotion proposed rates of return of 800 per cent at the end of 45 days (ibid.). However, from the day they opened for business, the schemes were insolvent and liabilities exceeded assets. Nonetheless investors were drawn in by the observation of high payouts to early investors and ostentatious spending by the game's initiators. As more and more people became involved, the interest and principal promised to earlier investors grew larger than the money paid in by new investors. To attract new investors and generate more capital, the game's initiators raised interest rates thereby delaying but also exacerbating the game's ultimate financial crash.

> These games instigated significant cash outflows from formal Congolese financial institutions as very eager and gullible investors demanded liquidity to make their game investments. The games generated a monetary playground of activity which, apart from its perverse character, snatched money from people who could not afford the losses, deceiving them with the impression that their investments were experiencing astronomic growth. In reality, the money changed hands without generating any productive economic activity, often culminating in extravagant expenditure on the part of the game initiators. On top of all this, many persons in charge of formal banking institutions were implicated in these fraudulent schemes. (ibid.: 106)

Between 1990 and 1997, the looting of capital assets in Kinshasa, dollarization, fraudulent games and the associated bank liquidity crisis all contributed to the undermining of the internal management of the formal banking system. Undercapitalized and largely insolvent, the financial products and services of the formal banks were no longer attractive to the population of Kinshasa (Masangu, 1997). Formal banking was marginalized and in its place people and companies turned to informal institutions as financial intermediaries.

Informalization of credit and banking

The informal financial market can be defined as all financial transactions that take place beyond the functional scope of various country banking and financial regulations (Aryeetey and Hyuha, 1991). It includes associations such as rotating savings groups and credit associations, mutual assistance groups of neighbours, friends and/or family members, moneylenders and landlords. These institutions mobilize savings and disperse credit among people with small incomes in both rural and urban areas. They serve a broad spectrum of the African population, from the poorer segment of society to the middle classes (Miracle et al., 1980: 701). The credit system in the informal financial market takes various forms. Unlike the formal sector, informal financial transactions rarely involve legal documentation.

The ever-growing size of informal activities in Congo-Kinshasa encouraged the proliferation of informal financial activities, promoting the effectiveness of resource allocation by the mobilization of domestic savings and financing small-business activities that the formal system would not be interested in dealing with even if it had the capacity to do so (Adams, 1992). Informal financial services are characterized by high nominal interest rates, low transaction costs, and a willingness to cater to small-scale borrowers. They are present in Kinshasa's credit and foreign-exchange markets.

Information on informal financial markets is very scant. Virtually all funds in this market are locally mobilized. Therefore, it is hard to measure the extent to which credit funds are generated. However, recent studies confirm that the informal financial sector provides the bulk of financial intermediation in the country. Since banks and other credit institutions do not provide consumption loans, all credit needs for consumption are satisfied by informal lenders. The rural and urban poor borrow from relatives, friends and neighbours and if they are excluded from these sources of credit, they rely on moneylenders and traders in financial emergencies such as illnesses, funerals, as well as celebrations like weddings.

The informal financial sector in Kinshasa can be divided into four categories: first, mutual lending among family members, relatives, friends and neighbours; second, self-help groups, some organized with the help of an NGO or a formal credit institution, although the vast majority are organized by the participants themselves and operate as savings associations or rotating savings and credit associations (ROSCA); third, moneylenders; and fourth, the *cambisme*, the informal foreign-exchange market. The first three form an integral part of the credit market whereas the latter is clearly part of the money market. However, credit and savings schemes play an important role in all four categories.

The remainder of this section details how different informal financial credit institutions function and compares their rules and ways of operating *vis-à-vis* the conventional economic theory of credit markets. According to Schumpeter (1939), there is no evolution without innovation and no innovation without entrepreneurs. Entrepreneurs by the very nature of their activities need credit. Few can become entrepreneurs without initially incurring debt. Before commencing his/her economic activities, the entrepreneur needs purchasing power. The role of a banker is not only that of an intermediary but also a 'producer' of goods, namely credit, that provides an entrepreneur with the requisite purchasing power (Piettre, 1970). Not having this means, many Congolese entrepreneurs rely on the informal financial sector.

Informal loans from associates

Many day-to-day purchasing needs and emergencies are covered by non-commercial arrangements in the form of loans between parents, neighbours and friends. People in close proximity to one another or with family ties lend to each other at negotiated rates depending on social relationships and reputation. Interest rates are usually quite low for neighbours and in many cases free-of-charge for relatives and close friends. Loans are generally short term, of less than one year, and usually for only three to six months. However, terms of repayment are easy to reschedule if need be. A long tradition of mutual assistance in Zairean society underpins these loans. The number of loans granted in this way is impossible to estimate in the absence of reliable household budget surveys.

Savings associations

The participants of savings associations make periodic (monthly, weekly or even daily) payments to a treasurer. The group is often made up of people having something in common like their neighbourhood, place of work or ethnic origin. Most savings associations only accept members with a regular source of income. The treasurer has responsibility for safeguarding members' contributions, usually keeping the money in a secure place in his/her house rather than in a formal bank account. The money is on hand for members to use in emergencies like a burial or alternatively for personal advancement like marriage or further studies. Once a contribution to the association has been made, it is not refundable. In rural areas this money is used sometimes to build schools, health centres, etc. for public use.

The decision about the amount of contributions (subscriptions) is taken together. The amount is fixed only after the common agreement of all members. It is the same when a member needs help from the association or when the association wants to finance a public activity. Generally the proposal concerning the financing of a public activity comes from one or several members who suggest it during a meeting for approval. This proposal is often the subject of debates before being adopted. It is extremely unusual to proceed immediately to a vote to accept a proposal. The proposal is adopted only with the agreement of everyone in the association.

The fact of having something in common (neighbourhood, place of work, ethnic origin) generates a mutual confidence between members. This proximity often intervenes in the choice of members and allows an evaluation of the credibility of the members (Mayoukou, 1994).

Rotating savings and credit associations (ROSCAs)

Bouman (1977) defines a ROSCA as a group of people who on the basis of self-help make regular contributions to a fund, which is given, in whole or in part, to each member in turn. Credit generated in this manner is given exclusively to members and repayment is normally in instalments made in the form of future contributions to the group. The striking aspect of ROSCAs is that credit and savings processes are intertwined. Members save to obtain credit of a sizeable sum from the group. The first collector in the group receives an interest-free loan while the last collector extends credit to other members. Members of the group alternate between debtor and creditor positions.

These mutual help associations are the most widespread types of informal financial institutions in Congo-Kinshasa referred to locally as *likelemba* or *moziki*. Their prevalence has grown over the last 30 years of economic crisis. The guiding principles of *likelemba* or *moziki* are that a group of people agree to contribute to a common fund at regular intervals of time (weekly, monthly). The collected funds are given in their entirety to each member of the group in turn. The order of rotation is determined following negotiation or according to the degree of solvency of the participants. The prerequisite for a person to join a *likelemba* or *moziki* is a regular income. The amount of money received by a member, when his/her turn comes, and the duration of the cycle of rotation depends on the number of participants. Indeed, the small number of participants allows *likelemba* or *moziki* to have a short cycle, however the amount of money received by the member is less than if a *likelemba* or *moziki* applied to a broader circle.

Unlike the *likelemba*, the *moziki* is more organized and incorporates social aspects. The groups of *likelemba* in theory are limited to group financial obligations which cease after a full rotation. In the *moziki*, personal interaction involves members meeting periodically either at a member's house or at a neutral place (generally a refreshment bar) to discuss everyday problems like marital relationships, business activities, births and deaths (Tambwe 1983a). The member whose turn it is to benefit from the payments of the other members organizes the meeting and is obliged to offer something to eat and drink. Generally, all the members of the *moziki* know each other very well, frequently sharing the same profession.

The *moziki* also offers financial support to members in cases of special need. These needs are covered by an additional insurance system of loans and social assistance (Mayoukou, 1994). Each member is able to borrow money to finance a productive activity. The borrowed money must be refunded at a specified rate of interest within a fixed term. Non-members can also borrow money according to conditions defined by the association.

A *moziki* is characterized by mutually agreed rules that are respected by all members for the smooth functioning of the association. These rules stipulate the conditions of membership, the objectives of the association, the amount of each member's contributions and the group's organizational structure. Responsibility for keeping various accounts of the association and organizing meetings lies with the person called the *mama* or *papa moziki*.

With the exception of a *likelemba*'s more social function, *likelemba* and *moziki* are very similar, with almost identical economic goals that are realized through shared moral and cultural values of mutual assistance (Omasombo, 1992). They both bolster the economic needs of particular events experienced by the family of a member, such as birth, baptism or death through special fund raising.

A wide variety of social categories of people are involved in *moziki* or *likelemba*. At school, children use their pocket money to make *likelemba* contributions and are rewarded every weekend when one of them receives the money collected. Civil servants, teachers and craftsmen do likewise in their place of work. However, women urban market traders' *moziki* or *likelemba* are the most impressive. Many are members of more than one *moziki* or *likelemba* group. While there are large-scale traders among these women, the majority can be described as petty traders who are largely illiterate and depend on verbal rather than written transactions. Since the formal banking system in the country collapsed, many traders rely primarily on the informal financial system to finance their trading activities of local foods and manufactured consumer goods. Several depend on suppliers' credit facilities. Their financial activities involve frequent and significant transactions in cash. They often advance inputs to rural farmers and some even supply the market with foreign currencies.

The popularity and effectiveness of the *likelemba* or *moziki* as an informal financial system in Congo-Kinshasa relate to several factors. They are easy to join, the rules and procedures are easy to understand and accord with people's socio-cultural values. They are physically accessible. There is no expenditure on transaction fees and personnel, and no costs for evaluating the solvency of the borrower. Finally the costs of collecting loans are almost non-existent (Mojmir, 1989).

Moneylenders: The 'Bank Lambert'

In Congo-Kinshasa, as in other parts of the world, the formal sector views small-scale borrowers as riskier than large ones because of the difficulty of obtaining accurate information about them related to their geographical remoteness, illiteracy and unreliable incomes. The high minimum deposit collateral requirements that banks impose on borrowers effectively screen out the vast majority of small clients. Moneylenders have filled the gap, since they are willing to make small loans for various borrower purposes including emergency consumption. Moneylenders' procedures are simple and convenient, hence transaction costs are assumed to be zero or very low. On the other hand, borrowers face high interest rates.

Schumpeter (1939) theorizes that interest rates are controlled, like all other prices, by the supply and demand of capital. The supply of capital is a function of the profit that the entrepreneur expects and the reserve of money that the lender wishes to hold against an unexpected event. Real interest rates result from the tension between one and the other such that interest is a dynamic that would not exist in a static economy. If, as many people assume, developing countries like Congo-Kinshasa constitute a static economy, Schumpeter's thesis is paradoxical. Moneylenders and the clandestine bankers of Congo-Kinshasa charge exceptionally high interest rates taking advantage of people's immediate pressing need for loans. Moneylenders' collective powers are renowned. They are believed to collude in the provisioning of *Bank Lambert*[3] loans that are often allocated to a person who wants to start a commercial activity or alternatively needs money to cover expenses arising from a birth, medical treatment or school fees (*Revue Agriprimo*, 1979).

Bank Lambert loans work in the following way: a person borrows an agreed amount of money at an interest of 20, 30, 40, 50 or even 100 per cent per week or month. If at the end of the fixed period the borrower is unable to refund the totality of the money (the capital borrowed with interest) then he proceeds to the refunding of the interest and the capital which remains will produce further interest for a set period. If at the end of the fixed period, the borrower refunds only the capital, then the outstanding interest and unpaid capital continue to generate interest at the same rate.

In most cases, the borrower is unable to refund not only the capital but also the interest. The capital and interest are then tallied and constitute the principal on which new interest must be calculated. This operation can be repeated over many months for as long as the borrower is unable to pay back the capital and the interest at the agreed rate and within the time limit (Tambwe, 1983b). The borrower is condemned to seemingly never-ending cycles of debt and financial despair. The borrowers who fall victim to this situation are called *Martyrs du Puits 5* which refers to *Puits 5*, an underground mine owned by the Gécamine companies which exploit copper at Kipushi in Katanga (Nsaman, 1983).

The moneylenders do not pay much attention to how the loans are used but they are acutely aware of the whereabouts of their borrowers, who usually live proximate to their neighbourhood. They draw heavily on information obtained through personal, social and business relationships in order to pre-select clients. Most of the time, traders and landlords lend only to their customers and tenants. Savings collectors normally lend exclusively to their most regular depositors. While other moneylenders do not necessarily pre-select their clients, they rely heavily on recommendations of previous clients and the personal knowledge of applicants. But, if a loan for electrical equipment like a refrigerator is requested, moneylenders can expand to non-local borrowers. The terms and conditions of their loans are very flexible and timely. In general, no collateral is needed as the equipment itself serves as collateral. The threat of collection is regarded more seriously by moneylenders than by the formal sector because informal enforcement is easier than going through the legal system. For example, it is much easier for a landlord-lender to seize pledged equipment indefinitely than for a formal bank to do so.

Personal relationships, either within membership groups or through family members, are often instrumental in ensuring repayment. Informal lenders are more likely to use the threat of harm to property or person than to turn to the legal system, as usury is prohibited by Congolese criminal law.

Moneylenders follow currency fluctuations daily. If there is a currency devaluation, they quickly insist on the revaluing of the capital plus interest with the new value of the currency. Like other market agents in the Congo-Kinshasa informal economy, moneylenders must guard against price inflation. They adjust their debt calculations as soon as the prices for strategic products like fuel or the price of the dollar on the parallel market rise. The dollar exchange rate constitutes a reference for any person working in the informal sector. Its centrality to economic activity is examined in the following section.

Parallel market for foreign exchange: the *cambisme*

To understand the operation of the *cambisme*, some background information is required regarding income sources. Incomes of Congolese elites with a few exceptions are not principally derived from productive activity or subject to market competition. Rather they are of a rent-seeking character related to advantages associated with particular positions within the state apparatus. Therefore most commercial activities undertaken by and for the profit of Congolese elites depend, ultimately, on access to resources released by the state apparatus or the public sector (Leclercq, 1993). The importance of the parallel foreign exchange market in Congo-Kinshasa is linked to this phenomenon.

This parallel foreign exchange market always existed but it surged in importance in 1993 when the New Zaire (NZ) was created. The NZ was introduced by the former Prime Minister Faustin Birindwa, who was trying to suppress rampant inflation and depreciation of the currency.[4] In fact, the move was badly researched and ill-judged. The deadline for exchanging old banknotes for new ones was too tight. Further, the new banknotes were manufactured by a Congolese enterprise Egimex that was widely suspected of fraud. Several tons of paper was entrusted to the company's director who was contracted to deliver the equivalent in bank notes to the Central Bank. But, there was no supervision. The company failed to deliver all the printed banknotes to the Central Bank, diverting notes to the open market. Meanwhile, the lack of foreign currency in the Central Bank led to another form of fraud, as described by Boissonnade (1998: 185):

> ...the Central Bank manager presented to Mwamba Nozy[5] the difficulties that it had paying its debt of 40 million Deutsche marks claimed by the German printing company Giesceke and Devrient. Mwamba Nozy assured the bank manager that he could regulate the problem in the short term. Acting as an intermediary between the Central Bank and the German printing firm, Mwamba Nozy arranged for an alternative supply of currency notes from Argentina. In less than two months he flooded Kinshasa with counterfeit banknotes, which were virtually impossible to distinguish from the genuine ones. The Minister of Finance who had promised to suppress inflation was furious.

What is not specified is the way in which these unauthorized bank notes were injected into the market. The most expedient was the *cambiste* networks since they were in a position to disperse large amounts of money within a few days. They used procedures that have yet to be adequately investigated and are extremely difficult to penetrate given the tight networks in which *cambistes* operate.

In all the areas of the informal sector of the Congolese economy, relations linking members of a family, a clan or a religious group play a central role in inter-personal relations involving reciprocal favours, mutual confidence and trust. These trusting relationships create earning opportunities and provide access to certain scarce goods or services.

Managers of enterprises prefer to recruit among their 'brothers'. Family ties remain much stronger that those with the enterprise or with the state. The strategy consists of integrating mainly people of their own ethnic group into a network of clients, solidifying the power through the accumulation of dependants on the basis of common ethnicity, bonds of kinship, family friendship and neighbourhood or village of origin. For example, members of the Tetela ethnic group are dominant in the ownership of pharmacies because they are privileged in getting their supplies from a particular Tetela official in the Ministry of Health (MacGaffey, 1998).

Cambiste networks are similarly grounded in tight family clan or religious ties of trust expediting the injection of counterfeit banknotes into the market. *Cambistes*, located at the apex of pyramidal clientage networks, initiated the money market's distribution that quickly filtered down through the networks. This operation has to be made in a short period of time in view of the daily devaluations of Zaire's national currency. So, the *cambiste* on the top of the pyramid has the duty to maintain the trust of his *fournisseur*.

The operations of *cambisme* are carried out in many places, such as the central market, at the beach, in the streets and even in the stores maintained by West Africans and organized in the association called *Cedeao*. This name originally came from a West African organization called CEDEAO, the Economic Community of the States of West Africa. The informal association *Cedeao* of Kinshasa plays a significant role in the marketing of imported articles from Nigeria (*Groupe l'Avenir*, 2000).

Despite repressive measurements taken by the authorities in Congo-Kinshasa to prohibit the illegal exchange of foreign currencies, informal exchange transactions (*cambisme*) have continued. Organized into *moziki* associations, they are rapidly informed of any crackdown measurement as many female *cambistes* are thought to be *deuxieme* or *troisieme bureau*,[6] mistresses of powerful men in the state apparatus. It is precisely these ties that provide protection from the authorities who, theoretically, forbade *cambisme* (De Herdt and Marijsse, 1999).

Origin and role of female cambistes in Kinshasa

The origin of *cambisme* in Congo-Kinshasa can be traced back to the 1960s. At that time people spoke about the *changeurs*[7] of the Ngobila Beach down on the banks of the Congo River as well as across the river in Brazzaville.[8] The proximity between the two countries, Congo-Kinshasa and Congo-Brazzaville, combined with the existence of many ethnic links between people on both sides of the river largely supported the development of trade on the basis of informal business ties (Gondola, 1997).

Changeurs offered lower exchange rates than the banks for the CFA franc of Congo-Brazzaville and the franc of Congo-Kinshasa. At that time there were practically no women *changeurs*. Men dominated until the beginning of the economic crisis in the 1970s as the economic survival of families on fixed wages or salaries became an issue. Until then, men had not wanted their wives to earn an income, fearing that it would increase opportunities for infidelity (Bernard, 1972). Men were obliged to accept their wives' commercial activities because of the high cost of living.

Male behaviour and attitudes were being altered in other respects as well. Successful men had been in the habit of having mistresses, an open secret with their wives. A man's mistress was locally referred to as his *bureaugamie*, a play on the word polygamy and the French word for 'office', *bureau*. Most mistresses were educated and often met their lovers in the course of work. In any case, husbands used excuses about office work to cover for the time they spent with their mistresses. As the economic crisis deepened, men were increasingly forced to give up their second or third *bureau* to devote themselves more to their families' welfare. Their wives started to recover their individuality by taking initiatives to earn money for their families. They gravitated towards the informal sector, especially trade, and by the 1990s women controlled approximately 80 per cent of the businesses connected to regional trade and the parallel money markets (Kalombo Katumbanyi, 1997). Their activities were later extended to the border regions with Angola and the Central African Republic.

Between Congo-Kinshasa and Congo-Brazzaville, their trading activities were based mainly on food and small manufactured goods. They bought food products in Kinshasa to resell in Brazzaville and then bought printed wax clothes (*impreco*) to resell in Kinshasa. The majority had kiosks at the central market in Kinshasa where they sold various kinds of articles for women. Through their business connections, they started trading with Cameroon, Nigeria and Togo. In Togo, they discovered women traders *Nana Benz*[9] with whom they established business partnerships in the clothing trade, notably in Dutch wax printed cloth. Finally, thanks to the Congolese diaspora in Europe, they made business trips to Europe to buy Dutch wax printed cloth, to Antwerp for jewels and to France for shoes. Organized in *moziki* associations, they depute one of their members to travel abroad to buy these products.

As these activities became increasingly profitable, the possession of foreign currency for the purchase of products was ever more critical. Women had an *antenne*[10] frequenting different places where currencies were exchanged. The *antenne* was often a close female relative or friend. Later, attracted by the benefits of these exchange activities, most of them decided to take an active part in these activities joining alongside male colleagues in the informal foreign currency market.

Cambisme is to be found everywhere – at the Beach Ngobila or Beach Telecom, at the main railway station, in the central market and finally in Kinshasa's most important informal financial centre, the Wall Street of Kinshasa. Under the regime of former President Mobutu, Wall Street was the meeting place of *cambistes* where vast sums of Congolese currency (Zaire) were exchanged. The place became so integral to the economy that even ministers and former President Mobutu were seen buying dollars there for their official trips abroad (*Jeune Afrique*, 1999).

Organization of the informal currency exchange market

While Kinshasa's informal foreign currency market is subject to the forces of supply and demand, the fact that all *cambistes* in different parts of Kinshasa achieve arbitrage with roughly the same daily exchange rates demonstrates the power of the informal system of communication. In the absence of reliably functioning telephones and Internet facilities, Congolese *cambistes* fix their exchange rates on the basis of information received through personal networks. All the market agents are well informed about the availability and prices of goods and services through the *radio-trottoir*, the word-of-mouth radio of the streets. This diffusion of information is made more fluid by the ceaseless social contacts and individual visits made in search of lucrative activities (Leclercq, 1993).

The majority of *cambistes* are members of *moziki* associations. Apart from its role in mobilizing savings and mutual help, the *moziki* provides a forum for members to discuss their activities and business problems. The most active association is the *Moziki Sentiment Ngobila*, consisting of *cambistes* who operate at Beach Ngobila. Membership in this *moziki* is governed by a strict code of conduct involving adherence to minimum and maximum exchange rates. In cases of large amounts of money being exchanged, *cambistes* are under pressure to offer their customers a better rate. Members of the *Moziki Sentiment Ngobila* are not at liberty to go beyond the specified limits, whereas *cambistes* elsewhere are not so constrained. Whether or not the *cambiste* is a member of a margin-fixing *moziki*, she treats each customer differently. If the customer is unaccustomed to the currency market, the rate of exchange offered is less advantageous than for those who are regular customers.

The Congolese *cambiste* is often engaged in other activities as well. Most are traders of specific imported products who became *cambistes* in search of foreign currency to obtain their trading goods. In most cases they rely on friends or family members who help them to obtain starting capital and market know-how. They must know how to optimize business opportunities and save if they intend to become an independent *cambiste* one day.

Beside this network of friends, the Congolese *cambiste* works also with an *atalaku*, who assists the *cambiste* by attracting customers. The *atalaku* intercepts cars or people by shouting out exchange rates to potential customers. As the exchange rate is negotiable most of the time, the *atalaku* raises the rate a little to avoid undercutting his employer. At the end of the day *atalakus* are paid according to the number of customers they have acquired. Perseverance may allow the *atalaku* to become an apprentice *cambiste* and eventually to enter the circle of *cambistes*. This last stage requires extensive knowledge of the informal foreign-exchange markets.

More importantly, the *cambiste* needs to find a *preneur* who can supply her with foreign currency. Without him/her, the *cambiste* cannot operate. The *preneur* takes the local currencies of the *cambiste* and provides foreign currency. This raises two questions: how does the *preneur* obtain foreign currency, and why is s/he willing to convert it into a local currency known to be so unstable?

The *preneurs* are usually traders, who smuggle imported goods from foreign countries into Congo. The smugglers are generally educated people often professionals and salaried employees whose inadequate remuneration forces them to engage in the second economy (MacGaffey, 1991, 1998). They solve the problem of the unavailability of foreign exchange and therefore their inability to import the goods they need for their businesses through illegal trade (Vwakyanakazi, 1991). There is an enormous amount of primary export commodities that are smuggled out of the country and goods imported in exchange. This indicates the importance of illicit commerce in the Congolese economy. Most of the foreign currency comes from the illegal export of mineral resources to foreign countries, for example, the smuggling of diamonds. In 1979, the quantity of diamonds exported illegally from Zaire was estimated to be 68 per cent of official exports (MacGaffey, 1991).

Since the 1970s, the smuggling of gold and coffee to East Africa has become a means of accumulating wealth. In return for smuggled exports, manufactured goods, foodstuffs, vehicles and spare parts, fuel, construction materials and pharmaceuticals are imported. For those who do not smuggle or have no access to smugglers, personal connections to suppliers, such as the managers of the big import houses, are vital.

Smuggling remains the main source of foreign currency for *preneurs*. But they also have to organize their lives and businesses in Congo-Kinshasa and need local currency. The *cambiste* can assist in these matters. In turn, the *cambiste* leans on the apprentice *cambiste* who gains network contacts while working for the *cambiste*. The informal currency market vitally depends on social networking.

Conclusion

This chapter has documented the upsurge of informal financial markets in Zaire. As a consequence of this financial vacuum, the volume of informal financial activities has increased to fill the gap between credit requirements and supply of credit by formal financial institutions. Informal financial institutions have become an important vehicle for mobilizing household savings and financing small businesses. They serve market niches that banks cannot readily reach. The *cambisme* has become a reference market for all activities in the informal financial sector since so many informal activities in Zaire are based on the importation of foreign goods.

Social networking is the lynchpin of Kinshasa's informal financial markets. Networking is an activity in which the Congolese excel. When they perceive an occasion to obtain income, they deploy their business-directed networks of inter-personal relations to achieve that goal. However, the cardinal rule of the informal economy in Congo-Kinshasa is redistribution. Any participant in the informal economy must carry out redistribution of income not only from his/her own commercial activities but also from the system of network transfers to which s/he is a part.

The non-commercial redistribution of incomes, deeply embedded in values of social solidarity, is pivotal to the informal financial sector. These values link individuals by relations of affection or assignment. These relations are not restricted to members of a family, a clan or a tribe, although these ties play an important role. Networking is also prevalent amongst inhabitants of the same district, the alumni of a school, members of a religious sect or sports association. Mutual links form a framework that regulates informal activities in Congo-Kinshasa, where each one has the right to receive and the duty to give and where above all everyone shares (Leclercq, 1993). In other words, the redistribution motive follows the profit motive.

However, besides the stimulation of these activities, there is a negative effect on the economy. In the absence of any government social welfare provision, the system tends to privilege those who can provide services for themselves and worsens the situation for the less well-off and those with fewer opportunities. Informal distribution operates on the basis of trickle-down, but it is nonetheless rife with material inequality between and even within social networks.

Attempts to regulate the informal market have failed and the informal market has continued to grow regardless. In the absence of economic stability in the country, it is impossible to establish a less volatile and more equitable economy.

About the author

Mindanda Mohogu is a Congolese development consultant who has Bachelor's and Master's degrees from Antwerp University. His field of research is economic development, with special reference to the role of informal financial networks in developing countries. He has been a research associate at the African Studies Centre at the University of Leiden as well as at Amsterdam University in the Netherlands. He has conducted research surveys on diaspora and African remittance patterns in the Netherlands.

Notes

1. This fall of employment in the formal sector is not a new phenomenon. At independence more than 60 percent of the working population of Kinshasa had employment plummeting to 30 per cent in 1961, 34 per cent in 1967 rising slightly to 37 per cent in 1975 during the period of economic boom then falling again to 25 per cent in 1989.

2. This rate is represented by the ratio of foreign currency deposits to national currency deposits and represents the ratio between the money supply in foreign as opposed to national currency.
3. No bank in Congo-Kinshasa bears the name Lambert. It is borrowed from a Belgian bank, the Bank Brussels Lambert (BBL). In Congo, *Bank Lambert* means a loan with usurious interest.
4. The dollar was then worth 6 million Zaires (currency) and the New Zaire currency value was fixed at 3 million old Zaires.
5. Mwamba Nozy became known as *Pablo Escobar*.
6. Translated 'second or third office', jokingly referring to a man's mistress who occupies his 'working time'.
7. *Changeur* in French means someone who is involved in the act of exchange.
8. Kinshasa and Brazzaville are physically the most proximate capital cities in the world. They are separated by the Congo River. The crossing of this river by an ordinary high-speed motorboat takes no more than ten minutes.
9. They are very rich and famous and often drive around in Mercedes Benz, from which they derive the name *Nana Benz*.
10. *Antenne* is someone who acts on behalf of someone else to buy foreign currency.

References

Adams, D.W. (1992) 'Taking a fresh look at informal finance', in D.W. Adams and D.A. Fitchett (eds), *Informal Finance in Low-Income Countries,* pp. 5–73, Westview Press, Boulder, CO.

Aneza (1991) *Évolution de la Situation Socio-économique du Zaire de 1960 à 1990. Contribution de l'Aneza à la Conférence Nationale Souvéraine*, Aneza, Kinshasa.

Aryeetey E. and Hyuha, M. (1991) 'The informal financial sector and market in Africa: an empirical study', in A. Chibber and S. Fisher (eds), *Economic Reform in Sub-Saharan Africa,* pp. 125–36, International Bank for Reconstruction and Development/World Bank, Washington, DC.

Bernard, G. (1972) 'Conjugalité et rôle de la femme à Kinshasa', *Canadian Journal of African Studies* 2(6): 261–74.

Boissonnade, E. (1998) *Kabila Clone de Mobutu*, Editions Moreux, Paris.

Bouman, F.J.A. (1977) 'Indigenous Savings and Credit Societies in the Third World – Any Message?' paper delivered at the Conference on Rural Finance Research, San Diego, California.

De Herdt, T. and Marijsse, S. (1999) 'The reinvention of the market from below: the end of the women's money changing monopoly in Kinshasa', *Review of African Political Economy*, (80): 239–53.

Gondola, D. (1997) 'Jeux d'argent, jeux de vilains: rien ne va plus au Zaire', *Politique Africaines* 65: 96–111.

Groupe l'Avenir (La Bourse) (2000), 'Autopsie du Système Bancaire Congolais', 14 June 2000.

Jeune Afrique (1999) 'La chasse aux dollars est ouverte', no. 2023–2024.

Kalombo Katumbanyi, M. (1997) 'Crise economiques et l'emergence du pouvoir des femmes as sein des couples à Kinshasa', in Beauchamp, C. (ed.), *Démocratie Culture et Développement en Afrique Noire*, pp. 201–7, Harmattan, Paris.

Leclercq, H. (1993) 'L'economie populaire informelle au Zaïre: approche macro-économique', *Zaire-Afrique* 271: 17–36.

Lensink, R. (1993) 'Financial Liberalisation, Informal Credit Market and Imperfection Information', Research memorandum 555, Institute of Economics, University of Groningen, Gronigen.

Le Phare (1992) 'Pillages Cause de l'Ampleur de la Crise Economique à Kinshasa', no.180, 20 October, 1992.

MacGaffey, J. (1991) *The Real Economy of Zaire*, James Currey, London.

MacGaffey, J. (1994) 'State deterioration and capitalist development: the case of Zaire', in Berman, B.J. and Leys, C. (eds), *African Capitalists in African Development*, pp. 189–204, Lynne Rienner, Boulder, CO.

MacGaffey, J. (1998) 'Creatively coping with crisis: entrepreneurs in the second economy of Zaire (The Democratic Republic of the Congo)', in Spring, A. and McDade, B.E. (eds), *African Entrepreneurship, Theory and Reality*, pp. 37–50, University of Florida Press, Gainsville.

Marijsse, S. and De Herdt, T. (1996) *L'Economie Informelle au Zaire*, L'Harmattan, Paris.

Masangu, J.C. (1997) 'La Situation Bancaire au Congo', *Congo-Afrique* 319: 517–26.

Mayoukou, C. (1994) *Les Systèmes des Tontines en Afrique, Un Système Bancaire Informel: Le Cas du Congo-Brazzaville*, L'Harmattan, Paris.

Miracle, M.P., Miracle, D.S. and Cohen, L. (1980) 'Informal savings mobilisation in Africa', *Economic Development and Cultural Change*, 28(4): 701–24.

Mojmir, M. (1989) 'The role of the informal financial sector in the mobilisation and allocation of the household savings: the case of Zambia', *Savings and Development* XIII (1): 65–85.

Ngondo, A.P. (1996) 'Nucléarisation du ménage biologique et renforcement du ménage social à Kinshasa', *Zaire-Afrique* 308: 419–44.

Ngonga, N. *et al.* (1999) 'Persistance de la Dollarisation au Congo-Kinshasa: manifestation de la complémentarité ou de la substitution monétaire?', *Cahiers Économiques et Sociaux*, XXV (1), April (IRES): 25–55.

Nsaman, L. (1983) 'Le management face à la crise de l'administration publique zairoise. Quelques Témoignages Introspectifs', *Zaire-Afrique* 175: 271–80.

Omasombo, T. (1992) 'Economie populaire, état, capitalisme', in de Villers, G. (ed.) *Economie Populaire et Phénomènes Informels en Afrique*, Centre d'Étude et de Documentation Africaines (CEDAF), nos. 3–4.

Piettre, A. (1970) *Histoire de la Pensée Economique et Analyse des Théories Contemporaines*, Dalloz, Paris.

Revue Agriprimo (1979) 'INADES Formation', Abidjan 26(3).

Schumpeter, J. (1939) *Business Cycles*, McGraw-Hill, New York.

Tambwe, K. (1983a) 'Le likelemba et le muziki à Kinshasa: nature et problèmes socio-juridiques en droit privé zaïrois', *Zaire-Afrique* 177: 431–40.

Tambwe, K. (1983b) 'Le prêt usuraire: son histoire en général et sa pratique dans la société zairoise à propos de la pratique dite "Banque Lambert"', *Zaire-Afrique* 175: 281–93.

Vwakyanakazi, M. (1991) 'Import and export in the second economy in North Kivu', in MacGaffey, J. (ed.), *The Real Economy of Zaire*, pp. 43–70, James Currey, London.

World Bank (1997) 'Case Studies of Enterprise Finance in Ghana', Final Report, Washington, DC.

CHAPTER 5

Linking irregular economies: remaking transurban commercial networks through new forms of social collaboration

AbdouMaliq Simone

In light of intensified overcrowding of small-scale artisan production, retailing, hawking, and services provision in many cities, there is substantial competition for access to inexpensive consumables, machinery, electronics, building materials, markets and customers. While many of these transactions remain within a cash economy, there also exist complex barter and credit arrangements, bundling of disparate goods and services, low level 'futures trade' on basic commodity inputs, and a range of other speculative activities. The result has been the substantiation of economic links at all scales between almost all the major cities in Africa. The chapter discusses some examples of how these efforts to configure transurban exchange operate, particularly at medium scales of transaction. It also explores how particular styles and forms of affiliation and particular kinds of entrepreneurship and circuits of movement reciprocally shape each other.

Introduction

Actors in fluid African urban environments try to make collaborative action work, collective responsibility enforceable, and instruments of power effective and legitimate. These efforts give rise to an uneasy tension between the adoption of normative discourses concerning urban management and governance, the ways in which urban residents attempt to adapt to a vast range of new opportunities and crises, and the role of the city as a place of experimentation.

The capacity to generate stability – in livelihood, household organization and community ties – often now requires a continuously improvised pursuit of whatever ideas, practices, experiences, social cooperation and participation people can find. Notions of engagement permeate daily practices, where shifting the boundaries that divide work, religion, politics, geography and economics becomes an important aspect of managing everyday existence. Assumptions and domains are unsettled for the express purpose of continuously putting new identities, experiences, rules, and structures face to face, and thus diversifying the kinds of opportunities and resources that might be applied to everyday problems (Ranger, 1968; Boone, 1995; Bayart, 2000; Diouf, 1998).

These shifting engagements are not only compensatory. What Pardo (1996) described for the urban underclass of Naples largely holds true in urban Africa as well. People attempt to construct a proper and fulfilling life through an entrepreneurial orientation that depends upon diversifying the situations and persons with whom one transacts. A continuous interaction among these diversities is pursued. The workplace, the home, the neighbourhood and various processes of production, consumption, investment and favour-giving/receiving are used as sites for individual initiative and for diversifying one's socio-economic position. The all too frequent problem in the African context is the parasitic appropriation of this resourcefulness by the political elite that dominates much of the external engagement with the larger world where these actions, otherwise infused with deeply moral valuation, are steered into the instruments of crass accumulation for the few.

Accumulated years of popular disillusionment with the state, labour-intensive demands of securing basic needs, the entrenched negotiability of justice, and the effects of internationally mandated and supervised economic reform processes have largely overwhelmed the effectiveness of urban practices prioritizing social reciprocity and the continuous interaction of complementary diversity (see Bangura, 1994; Beall *et al.*, 1999; Bryden, 1999; Farvacque-Vitkovic and Godin, 1999; Mwanasali, 1999; Braathen *et al.*, 2000; McCulloch *et al.*, 2000). As a result, the mechanisms through which local economies expand in scale and coalesce into new political formations are often unclear, murky and problematic. They can entail highly tenuous and frequently clandestine articulations among, for example, religious and fraternal networks, public officials operating in private capacities, clientelist networks mobilizing cheap labour, foreign political parties, and transnational corporations operating outside conventional procedures (Hibou, 1999). With these economic scenarios come more flexible configurations of associational life, more deterritorialized frameworks of social reproduction and political identity, and autochthonous preoccupations with belonging (Geschiere and Nyamnjoh, 2000). As a consequence, the efforts of juggling contradictory scenarios of well-being become more volatile and uncertain.

The overwhelming visibility of urban poverty and collapsing physical and social infrastructures occlude the elaboration of circuits through which Africans are extending themselves into the world. In part, much of this extension tends to be Africans taking any chance of reaching better economic climates. Others go back and forth, increasingly to cities such as Dubai, Mumbai and Karachi, substantiating a more South-South chain of commodity transactions that has been building up over the years. On a larger scale, valuable primary commodities, such as minerals, are diverted from official national export structures into intricate networks where large volumes of under-priced electronics, weapons, counterfeit currencies, bonds, narcotics, laundered money and real estate circulate (Ben Hammouda, 1999; Constantin, 1996; Duffield, 1998;

MacGaffey and Bazenguissa-Ganga, 2000; Misser and Vallee, 1997; Roitman, 1998). The diversion can also include oil, agricultural products and timber.

What tactical positions are being adopted by entrepreneurs to understand what is taking place in diverse African urban economies, and to forge some kind of engagement with them? What new modalities of collaboration and competition are possible within shifting macroeconomic and political frameworks? Efforts to upscale cross-border, inter-urban trade are increasingly murky given heightened conflicts over the disposition of resources and the involvement of public actors in nefarious economic activities. Transaction costs are, as a result, often inflated even more than is customary in informal trade. Yet, the incessant hunt for opportunity on the part of small and medium-scale economic operators propels them into a wide range of provisional, ever-changing affiliations and practices aimed at identifying sources of low-priced inputs, small yet sustainable profit margins and available markets.

This chapter deals with operations at the micro level in an attempt to understand the social investments being made to continuously appropriate urban life as a resource for engaging livelihood opportunities beyond the constraints faced by local production and formal employment. It presents snapshots of two very different inner-city neighbourhoods, in Lagos and Johannesburg, to demonstrate the complexity of collaborative arrangements. These snapshots concern the interstices of a highly volatile reciprocal relationship between the attempt to access cross-border trade opportunities and the social arrangements residents must either configure or adopt to make such trade viable. In each instance, lowering transaction costs does not appear to be the overarching aim, but must be balanced with considerations about how to maximize opportunities and how to deal with immediate social relations and obligations.

Contextual factors

Emerging new forms of social collaboration applied to cross-urban economic transactions are being shaped by several key contextual factors. While not claiming direct causal connections, I want to outline the larger terrain on which these collaborations are taking place. First, the macroeconomic framework of these transactions has changed significantly along trajectories that amplify discordant national trade policies yet, at the same time, are beginning to entrench mechanisms and institutions that facilitate more fluid trade flows. For example, the Cross-Border Initiative in Eastern and Southern Africa and the emerging COMESA accords have significantly liberalized foreign-exchange systems by eliminating restrictions on current account transactions, dismantled non-tariff barriers (e.g. import quotas and licensing requirements), integrated inter-bank foreign-exchange markets, reduced maximum tariff rates and liberalized investment procedures (Fejgenbaum et al., 1999). Such steps create the possibility of opening up a broader exchange of commodities across cities within such regional frameworks and of diversifying the commercial structures that can potentially participate in such exchange. These moves are also intended to increase total output and take advantage of under-utilized capacity through increasing prices depressed by informal trade. Simulation models used by COMESA, for example, point to 82 per cent increases in intra-COMESA trade when informal trade is set at zero (Chirwa, 1997).

At the same time, there are changes in the intricate networks of diverse sectoral and national actors mobilized to circumvent cumbersome restrictions placed on cross-border trade. Whereas they once accorded albeit limited roles to various small-scale entrepreneurs, they are now losing ground to what often appear to be more formal corporate structures capable of rationalizing operations on a larger scale without the need for substantial mediation (Club du Sahel, 2000). In response, new entrepreneurial groups are also being formed as the costs of both travel and distributive trade increase. Individual traders may set up small, short-term consortiums to make bulk purchases, share transportation and importation costs. As these arrangements become more common, the traditional marketing networks become more fluid as well. Where once the disposition of goods was largely tied to a steady network of retailers and hawkers, the growth of distributive and cross-border trade, in response to market liberalization, means that traders are not assured of buyers for their goods (Benneh, Tims and Asenso-Okyere, 1997).

Efficiency gains in information management and the harmonization of trade policy and transportation are taking place at various speeds, reasserting national discrepancies and intersecting with political change and conflict. Shifts in the structure of trading networks are neither comprehensive nor unilateral. Even within regional regimes, tariff exemptions remain widespread, particularly as they apply to imports by the public and civil sectors, as well as to goods related to foreign-financed projects. Given the protracted struggles over resource claims in many countries, trade diversion still predominates in most instances and networks established to conduct informal trade are still relied upon to compensate for the highly fluctuating availability of many basic goods (Ackello-Ogutu and Echessah, 1997; Morris and Dadson, 2000). Unconventional trade is at its highest in states where chronic political crisis has undermined regulatory systems or where formal institutions function and retain some level of authority primarily through their participation in such unconventional trade (Ellis and MacGaffey, 1996; Flynn, 1997).

Despite new trade accords and the anticipation of substantial economic and customs integration in the coming decade, what rationalization that has taken place has tended to renovate and, at times, agglomerate the syndicates that conducted informal trade in the past. An intermingling of diverse entrepreneurial groupings, actors, turf and capacities takes place behind the veneer of what appear to be formal 'corporate' structures that, in reality, do not function like modern corporations (Azam, 2001).

Access to financing remains tight. For example, Nigeria has rarely been able to meet more than 35 per cent of the needs of its economic operators (Soulé and Obi, 2000). Additionally, policy reforms that are unable to appropriately sequence customs harmonization (through rate adjustment or recategorizing goods) with other free trade mechanisms will continue to encourage informal trade. For example, the Common External Tariff (CET) adopted by the West African Monetary Union in January 2000 will inevitably have a serious impact on Benin's economy, as it largely depends on the re-exportation of goods to Nigeria. Likewise, CET has increased the price of formal food imports by Niger from Nigeria by approximately 300 per cent (ibid.).

Historically, the formal enterprises of scale that do exist have tended to keep their supply chains heavily internalized, limiting opportunities for diversification and integration among distinct firms, as well as the scope of their operations. When entrepreneurs diversify, they tend to do so in different sectors within a given city rather than expanding into non-local markets. This method of diversifying acts as a means of spreading risk, maintaining personalized business connections, and dealing with the fear that growth will result in the owner relinquishing direct control over the enterprise (Billetoft, 1996). Regional exports have been an extension of import substitution, and thus do not experience the same competitive pressures of product development and quality as firms exposed to global markets (Salinger, 2001). Faltering opportunities for formal employment, large-scale population growth without concomitant gains in urban productive capacity, and the resulting increases in urban poverty give shape to an economic domain that brings together opportunities for individual initiative and for the substantial exploitation of labour. When workers are unable to bring anything to the table except their willingness to work, larger areas of the overall economy take advantage of this opportunity. As purchasing power declines, the need for affordable inputs increases. Inputs remain affordable by decreasing labour costs and/or the quality of the product.

While trade liberalization must confront developments ensuing from new environmental policies, food and supply standards etc., most African producers still tend to limit upgrades to the 'next lowest' value added product (Schupen *et al.*, 2001). As standards shift from product definition to process definition, formalized chains of artisan producers, which accessed opportunities in non-traditional niche export markets largely through the imposition of regulations limiting extractions of natural resources, are being squeezed out. Such a process re-emphasizes circumvention and trade diversion but with the need to substantially renovate existing entrepreneurial networks, both in the face of new trade and standards regimes, and the capacity of increased complicity between state actors and multinationals (Bayart, 2000; Hibou, 1999).

Of course these developments are embedded in what remain largely bifurcated urban economies. 'Real' urban economies remain oriented to market adaptation through labour mobility, low overheads, labour intensity and the minimal application of physical and financial capital. These 'real economies' constitute a potential key factor in accounting for why urbanization has continued even in periods of negative growth (Fay and Opal, 2000). A social logic that accords priority to the maintenance of extended family and community patronage systems, as well as mitigating disparities in accumulation possibilities, constrains independent economic action. These interdependencies have largely described how cross-urban trade and entrepreneurship have been organized. Elaboration of a so-called modern sector has been historically hampered by the absence of social groups possessing enough income to constitute an autonomous consumer base. The pace of population growth in Africa (2.5 per cent per annum) is expected to double the size of the population every 25–30 years. The modern sector can never absorb more than a small fraction of the urban population even at high growth rates (Lachance, 2000).

On the other hand, urban economies may not be actually as bifurcated as they appear. While many informal-sector entrants value the relative independence and flexibility incumbent in this sector, increasing numbers of informal-sector workers are engaged in highly dependent relationships with more formally organized economic operators.

Some of these relationships can be consistently lucrative. This is the case primarily for entrepreneurs who have plied earnings from other activities, often agricultural production, into investments in land, facilities and machinery used to attain subcontracting orders from the formal sector (Gore, 1994). Either through subcontracting or equipment-leasing relationships, informal-sector workers are often caught in highly exploitative relationships. Services are delivered or products produced at prices set by others as a means to access materials and markets that would otherwise be unavailable. The expansion of the informal sector in many African cities has largely been in the area of such subcontracting relationships. For example, having women doing piecework at home saves larger firms the costs of maintaining a formal labour force (MacHaria, 1997).

For the most part, 'real' urban economies require shared but essentially separate interests that are more amenable to continuously renegotiated social relationships of trust and collaboration (Hart, 1988). In yet other situations, kinship ties are used at particular stages in the operation of informal sectors, such as the task of locating apprenticeships. The use of these ties then gives way to an emphasis on personal relationships and loyalties when entrepreneurs launch their own businesses (Berry, 1985).

Macroeconomic facilities applied to encourage growth in urban economies have largely focused on supply-side factors, especially in terms of subregional trading regimes. Given the structure of existing trade networks, more emphasis could be placed on demand-side approaches that deal with networks of local authorities, contractors, civil society groups, chambers of commerce and so forth (Lachance, 2000). Indeed, even community-based and multi-associational operations are functioning with increasing scope. Urban quarters that not only serve as platforms for popular initiatives (e.g. waste management, micro-enterprise development and shelter provision) are readapting local modalities of cohesion and sociality to more regional and global frameworks.[1]

Thus, the intersection of new macroeconomic frameworks, structural adjustment, trade liberalization, the ongoing predominance of small and medium-scale 'real economies' with their own persistent social logic, the constraints on agglomeration, and changes in urban governance policies compel the elaboration of new forms of inter-mediation across urban economies. The intricate manoeuvres and debates among residents attempting to forge different ways of working together to expedite identifying and acting on livelihood opportunities centred on transactions between discrete cities, both in Africa and beyond, are aspects of this ongoing remaking of urban economies. The following snapshots attempt to point to some of the processes underway in the effort to forge such collaborations.

Obalende (Lagos)

Obalende is a neighbourhood located just east of the centre of Lagos Island. Ceded by colonial authorities to Hausa occupation and use, the area remains a key centre of Hausa life and entrepreneurship in Greater Lagos. The quarter is also popularly known as the 'city that never sleeps'. Indeed, a large number of local shops are open around the clock, but often trading in obscure items of seemingly little practical use. For many shops, what is sold inside is not important. Rather, there is a seemingly constant stream of visitors in and out of shops, and a constant flow of information exchange and consultations.

Obalende is the nerve centre of transnational trade operating with great reach and scale. Historically, large-scale trading and smuggling syndicates got their start in Obalende. While exceedingly wealthy businessmen and women may be involved at various stages in the conduct of trade, the quarter is largely the domain of small and medium-scale entrepreneurs. Each entrepreneur may have his or her own small shop, but they are continuously jockeying to participate in deals whose 'partners' and content are pieced together on a deal-by-deal basis. The continuous circulation of visits is part and parcel of a process of assessing what is going on and who is doing what, or is capable of doing or available to do something.

The assumption among participants is that each entrepreneur has established his or her own niche, expertise and networks that can be potentially rallied and fit into an unfolding scheme. The autonomy of the individual entrepreneur is necessary in fostering innovation. It is also important for emerging and provisional 'corporate' bodies not to have to devote resources to institutionalizing or reproducing themselves. However, a common Hausa identity and more structured and formalized participation in a variety of religious, community, guild and ethnic associations are important points of reference in this process.

What is particularly interesting in the elaboration of such entrepreneurial practices and floating syndicates is a series of tactics that have developed regarding ways of thinking about business and interacting with fellow entrepreneurs. They centre on which 'shopkeepers' should be visited and how. The process of assembling a business venture and the actors to be involved entail a highly visible process of 'shopkeepers' visiting each other and conveying a particular set of attitudes and stances in relationship to these visits. Yusuf may visit Al Haji Yahya, who then visits Ali, who in turn may visit Yusuf, who, together, may now make another visit to Yahya and so on. It is a process usually involving scores of actors and from it a specific constellation or 'team' will emerge to carry out a certain deal.

The deal is usually not anchored in a fixed or prescribed set of roles and investments that have been definitely negotiated and assigned. Rather, specific actors attain a sense of what they must do, where they must go and what they must commit over a specific time period from this complex process of interchange. This implicit sense of coordination does not obviate the need or practice of contractual relations and responsibilities. Certainly if a deal is to be successful, specific funds have to be deployed, goods have to be shipped, forms have to be signed, and so forth. But the sense of coordination and the understandings that actors attain as to what it is that they can contribute, as well as their experience of being part of some larger collaboration, are things that appear to emerge from this process of incessant visiting. At some unspecified point in the process, 'shopkeepers' simply know what to do and what others have to do.

These tactics of visiting are not written down, or even formally acknowledged as specific rules or practices. Rather, I have inferred them from discussions with various combinations of local entrepreneurs. Visits, and thus deals, should involve a constantly shifting combination of actors so that they continuously appear to each other in new and surprising ways. All participants are kept on their toes as a means of exploring each actor's potential. An important objective of this process is to repeatedly create new settings, that is, new compositions of actors otherwise well known to each other, where they can display certain opinions and behaviour.

This constant circulation of visits also ensures that there is a certain measure of ambiguity as to where a deal begins and ends. In this way, shopkeepers, even if not directly profiting monetarily from a given deal, are made to feel involved whether they are or not. In other words, it is possible for them to conclude that the deal might bring positive material rewards at some point in the future or lead to other deals in which they may become more directly involved. At the same time, this ambiguity is a way to distance actors who are deeply involved in especially unconventional or unsavoury deals. As such, this process enables actors to get away with acting as if they know more (or less) than they do about any given deal.

In this circulation of visits, participants must always talk to people they do not really need to talk to. Even if a prospective participant in a deal clearly knows the actors involved, they always go and see people who, as far as they know, have nothing to do with it. After all, this is a highly competitive environment of deal making, and inordinate levels and practices of competition could break up these shifting constellations of collaboration. Cooperation could be frozen and divided into strict sets of alliances that, in turn, could limit the resources brought to any particular deal or business opportunity. Even when it is seemingly superficial to the deal itself, this practice of talking to a wide range of people conveys that the participant in a particular deal is not necessarily after the markets, finance, etc., that they are after. Even though these others may not be part of the specific deal, they are offered an opportunity to say something about it, contribute to it, or learn from it. As this opportunity is availed now, the expectation is that it will be reciprocated at some point in the future.

At the same time, potential participants are usually very visible in what they are doing; they do not act as though they are sneaking around. They act as if they are seemingly indifferent to what people may think they are up to. At the same time, these visits also point to their efforts to be able to be noticed without being noticed, i.e. to be able to appear anywhere without their presence necessarily being relevant or having any implications to anything that is going on. This circulation of visits helps create a sense of neutrality for participants, enabling them to be present in a wide range of settings, and thus observe and participate in many conversations and transactions.

This is not to say that in all of these commercial interactions there is an absence of competition, rivalry, or secrecy. Indeed, this network of entrepreneurs works in various ways to assemble flexibility, resources, commitment, and knowledge that rest within a wide range of past experiences and potential collaborations to access and carry out specific economic activities. These assemblages must be reconstructed time and again to take advantage of what shopkeepers have learnt from past deals, of how their individual networks have changed, and of how the overall business climate is shifting. These practices of visiting and the assumptions behind them act as a means of keeping open the possibilities for assemblages to come and go, to be refashioned and redeployed.

Inner-city Johannesburg

The inner city of Johannesburg is one of Africa's most important sites for the intersection of informal trade networks operating across the continent and beyond. This position has developed in conjunction with the particular trajectories of demographic change in the inner city, as well as the increasing importance South Africa is assuming in many African domestic economies.

The race-based zoning of urban residential communities kept blacks out of the inner city for several decades. Accelerating white movement to suburban areas, coupled with economic recession, pushed up vacancy rates in the neighbourhoods of Hillbrow, Bertrams, Joubert Park, Berea and Yeoville and although it was officially illegal until 1991, blacks had begun moving to what was known as 'grey areas' in the mid-1980s.

The accelerated turnover of populations has itself provided a feasible cover, if not necessarily a major motivation, for the sizeable immigration of foreign Africans to Johannesburg (Bouillon, 1999). This migration, in turn, has substantially shaped the nature of inner-city life and commerce, further contributing to a process of internationalization. Because the inner city is one of the most circumscribed and densely populated urban spaces on the continent, with neighbourhoods such as Hillbrow made up of row after row of high-rise apartment blocks, this socio-cultural reconfiguration has, to a large extent, taken place invisibly.

Because the overwhelming majority of South African black inhabitants of the inner city are recent arrivals to Greater Johannesburg, conditions are wide open for the intersection of many groupings. Long displaced to the periphery of the city, the absence of stable black institutions within the inner city also contributes to the perception that it is becoming an increasingly desperate place, living on an edge without a strong core of cohesiveness.

What is perhaps most significant about the transformation of the inner city is not so much its character but the speed at which it has occurred. The sheer rapidity of demographic and economic change has created uncertainty as to what is possible to plan for and undertake (Reitzes, 1999). The uncertainty has caused sudden and substantial divestitures of all types that further impede adequate monitoring by adding a large volume of transactions to the quick pace of change. Insecurity has been intensified and, with it, the practice of getting rid of property cheaply.

In response to these changes, a measure of xenophobia prevails, whereby foreign Africans are blamed for an overcrowded informal trading sector, the growth of the narcotics trade and the general deterioration of the inner city (Reitzes, 1998). Many South African residents believe that it is because of such a foreign presence that government authorities and the private sector are unwilling to make investments in upgrading and service provision (Mattes *et al.*, 2000).

In an urban area with such demographic change, there are few grounds for anyone to cite and enforce a superseding claim to belonging. But this relative vacuum of belonging, i.e. a situation where almost no one presently living in the inner city can claim an overarching sense of origin or a protracted history of settlement, points out how, in the absence of effective governance, the feeling of belonging holds sway.

The narcotics enterprises that constitute an important component of the inner-city economy are commonly seen as the purview of Igbo-dominated Nigerian networks. While such composition may be generally true, these enterprises are by no means ethnically homogeneous or formed on the basis of national identity. Rather, in a business that has little recourse to appealing to the law or official commercial standards, the appearance of ethnic or national homogeneity conveys a certain impenetrability from external scrutiny, infiltration and competition. This pretence allows the enterprise to incorporate the diversity of actors it often requires in order to constantly change supply routes, markets and so forth.

In the commercial culture of the inner-city narcotics economy, the discrete tasks of importation, circumvention of customs regulations, repackaging, local distribution, money laundering, relations with legal authorities, territorial control, market expansion and plotting traffic routes are all complementary yet highly territorialized domains. Discrete 'units' usually administer each activity so that disruptions in one domain do not jeopardize the entire trade. Nigerian syndicates, which use the hotels in Hillbrow to accommodate a large transient population that in turn serves as a mask behind which to consolidate a steady clientele of drug users including sex workers, have instituted a particular governance structure (Kirk, 2000). The hotels, now largely managed by Nigerian syndicates, become discrete localities, housing not only workers in the drug trade but also Nigerians working in a wide range of activities. The syndicates dominate the governing committees that are established for each hotel, with their concomitant sets of rules. For example, no-go areas are often established for Nigerians and fines imposed for various infractions are then used for legal fees. Nigerians who are not involved in the drug economy are also called upon to provide a semblance of internal diversity, even if they are often used and manipulated (Osita, 2000).

The domains must be well integrated such that complicity and cooperation become the prevailing practices. Within one domain, each operator has a specific place and is expected to demonstrate unquestioning loyalty. This is the case even if the illicit nature and the practical realities of the trade create an incessantly open space for participants to take their chances and seek greater profits and authority outside the hierarchies that each syndicate attempts to rigidly enforce.

Thus, most inner-city residents know which hotels, residential buildings and commercial enterprises belong to which syndicates and to which nationalities these syndicates in turn belong (Reitzes *et al.*, 1997). Since any particular narcotics enterprise handles only certain facets of the overall trade, and leaves itself increasingly vulnerable if it expands in efforts to dominate more functions and more territory, spaces must also be maintained that clearly belong to nobody. However it is precisely within these spaces, which are often subject to the most vociferous claims of belonging, that the unpredictable may occur.

The drug economy, with its hyperactive sensibilities and codes of belonging, was able to largely entrench itself in Hillbrow and Berea because a dense, highly urbanized area with massive infrastructure was being vacated both of its former population and of financial and governmental resources. The modalities of operation of the drug business tend to provincialize certain parts of the inner city, to localize it in terms of clearly marked territories and 'fiefdoms'. But the definitiveness of organizations and territories is more a necessary performance than descriptive of actual operational practices. The more entrenched and expansive the drug economy becomes, the more it produces ambiguous interfaces. Ten years ago the identities of actors and territories were usually quite clear. It is now increasingly difficult to differentiate between supposedly discrete groupings, between illicit activity and legitimate investment, between consumption patterns and product availability, and between inner-city Johannesburg as an increasingly well-known site of the drug economy and other more invisible, and thus often advantageous, sites of operation.

In part, the ill-defined intersections between legal and illegal trade and the cross-fertilization of self-contained informal trade networks occur because of the social instability of the inner city. In an area where jobs are scarce, everyday life precarious, and the need to mobilize available social capital acute, the very act of counting upon those close to one becomes a practice that leaves an individual vulnerable to further difficulties.

As has been repeatedly pointed out by Graeme Reid, director of the Johannesburg Development Agency, a critical problem for local governance has been the instability of household composition within the inner city, particularly among South Africans. Families who reside in an apartment unit for several months frequently disperse, with new household arrangements being established in other parts of the inner city or elsewhere. In part, this instability is related to the intensifying uncertainty permeating everyday kinship relations. Individuals cannot interweave the details of their daily lives too closely to those of family members. If something goes wrong, if a member is HIV positive, or if a growing divide in economic capacity becomes apparent, one then becomes vulnerable to witchcraft accusations and thus vulnerable to being ostracized or killed. As a result, the very process of mobilizing social capital that is needed to elaborate a viable sense of belonging becomes extremely difficult. In its absence, the apparent capacity of foreign Africans to elaborate a sense of supportive social connectedness becomes particularly threatening, as it is perceived to provide immigrants with an undue advantage on which to thrive in this urban environment.

While immigrant networks depend on always activating a sense of mutual cooperation and interdependency, such ties are also often more apparent than real, especially as a complex mixture of dependence and autonomy is at work in relations among fellow compatriots. For many foreign Africans in the inner city, Johannesburg is neither the preferred nor final destination, especially at present (Sinclair, 1998). Its continental location and the degree to which the South African economy is increasingly intertwined with other African national and regional economies make the city more accessible than other European or North American destinations, despite the South African government's attempts at controlling immigration. The city's geographic location facilitates the petty to medium-scale conventional and unconventional trade activities that characterize a significant percentage of immigrant economies. From official commercial markets to informal ones in both Congos, Zambia, Angola and Mozambique, to name but a few of the predominant national settings, a substantial amount of their inputs either originate or pass through South Africa in a trade frequently controlled or at least mediated by South African-based immigrants (Perbedy, 1997).

The collapse of secondary and tertiary education across much of the continent, as well as appropriately compensated professional employment, has meant that South Africa both educates and provides professional positions for an increasing number of foreign Africans. A middle-class lifestyle progressively undermined at home can, in part, be recreated in urban South Africa.

But the bulk of foreign Africans increasingly represent a poorer, more desperate and less capacitated group, usually without the connections, resources or skills to secure opportunities in Europe or North America. I have conducted several follow-up informal surveys during the last two years in the buildings, churches, mosques, restaurants and nightclubs where I did initial field investigations in 1993–5. Immigrants now tend to be less educated, more engaged in lower scales of trade, and more dependent upon finding menial labour.

These largely anecdotal conclusions may mean that more skilled and well-paid foreign Africans have relocated to other parts of Johannesburg. But within the networks I have observed over the years, these residents have increasingly left South Africa after having implanted networks of associates to carry out various tasks incumbent in managing the deals their 'superiors' had previously negotiated. These deals have been centred upon incorporating the capacities that Johannesburg has to offer such as communications, transportation, and financial systems into pre-existing informal trade circuits. As many different entrepreneurial groupings converged upon Johannesburg to make use of these facilities over the past 15 years, the city also provided a platform where diverse groups could learn more about each other's operations and markets, and slowly begin to test the waters of collaboration. These efforts are oriented less toward immigrants establishing cohesive communities and niche activities along national or ethnic lines, but more towards building potentially synergistic relationships among the discrete specializations and skills of diverse entrepreneurial groups. For this purpose, there is decreasing investment in attempts to consolidate specific African national communities within the city.

Nevertheless, a sense of obligation persists in terms of the support immigrants provide to each other. This obligation can be functional only if it works in ways that are somewhat distinct from the norms that prevail in the contexts immigrants have left. One of the primary motivations for emigration is to attain the space necessary to accumulate some savings outside of the tightly knit family networks that can quickly eat up any earnings made at home. Accordingly, individuals insist upon some flexibility in how they manage their livelihoods, social lives and movements. The prevailing common sense is that groups can only provide and support each other as long as they have some flexibility to pursue various alliances, contacts and activities. They can follow up these new alliances only as long as they do not endanger their associates.

Such flexibility adds an additional comparative advantage: seemingly nonconvergent activities can be articulated in new and unconventional ways. In other words, opportunities are expanded by finding ways of putting together disparate activities within the overall framework of trust and solidarity prevailing among immigrant groups.

For example, the Soninke entrepreneurs, whose origins are in Mali and Senegal and who were some of the first pioneers in inner-city Johannesburg, have linked distinct areas of specialization built up over the years. By virtue of their long presence in Brazzaville, and the varying networks connected to different

Angolan political factions, the Soninke were able to dominate a highly lucrative trade in supplying different regions of Angola with consumer goods originating from South Africa.

Soninke traders, originally based in Dakar and Conakry, have also cultivated a wide range of activities in South-east Asia, particularly in the importation of textiles, clothing and electronics. They have built up substantial contacts at ports in Cape Town and Durban allowing the circumvention of custom controls under simulated re-packaging deals whereby containers are supposedly destined for elsewhere, often Luanda. By bringing together these formerly distinct networks, Soninke entrepreneurs can manipulate the loading and off-loading of varying goods depending on relative prices and market opportunities.

Continuous adaptations have to be made in this process given the fluid situations that prevail elsewhere on the continent. Service at Brazzaville's airport had been sporadic due to internecine conflicts over the past years. Closer direct relations between the Congolese and Angolan governments, with the progressive marginalization of UNITA in these bilateral relations, also had rearranged the trading picture. The presence of larger numbers of Angolan nationals within South Africa introduces additional competitive strains. In part, this fluidity deters entrepreneurs at any level from long-term and fixed commitment to specific trading strategies.

Flexibility is maintained only through keeping options open. One must be willing to take risks in forging new groupings and deals, many of which will not pan out. Middle-level informal traders sometimes incur heavy losses. To compensate for these, entrepreneurs stay close to a wide range of contacts and activities, often maintaining petty trade that is managed by compatriots, before venturing into other more risky, but highly profitable, activities. If successful, associates are brought in on a deal-by-deal basis.

Small-scale entrepreneurs also have to be cautious about larger syndicates muscling in and absorbing the trade routes and practices which they have opened-up. These syndicates can be formidable in scope and size. They use their links to governments and to powerful religious organizations to secure dominance over particular sectors and domains of trade.

Competition among syndicates does exist. However those operating within an overarching religious or ethnic framework, for example, relations between Hausa Muslims in Nigeria, Benin and Ghana and Senegalese and Guinean-based Tidiane Muslims, tend to agree on a division of commodities and territories. Such inter-ethnic cooperation is not specific to South Africa. It has emerged in other major African cities, most clearly in cities like Douala, Lomé, Lagos and Brazzaville. But in these cities, cooperation tends to emerge among a younger generation of entrepreneurs whose skills, reach and often ruthlessness are seen as a threat to established commercial interests. In contexts where ethnic identification can still mobilize great passion, ethnicity is used as a means of trying to curtail and break these efforts of a younger generation. As South Africa is a relatively new and lucrative territory of operation, there has also been substantial conflict in past years even here over who gets to do what. Nevertheless, working agreements have generally been rationalized in order not to compound the uncertainties that the agents of these syndicates face in South Africa.

Conclusion

Across Africa, there is a persistent tension as to what is possible to do within the city and the appropriate forms of social connections through which such possibilities can be pursued. Increasingly, more ephemeral forms of social collaboration are coming to the fore as a means of circumventing the intensifying contestation as to the kinds of social modalities and identities that can legitimately mobilize resources and people's energies.

Throughout these efforts the question remains as to how urban residents reach a larger world of operations, particularly in the pursuit of more normalized cross-border, inter-urban trade. Urban actors are seeking spaces for manoeuvre in which their ties to established territories of collective recognition are neither compromised by a multiplication of the arenas of action and identification, nor limit the room for manoeuvre across multiple sites of opportunity. This chapter has attempted to provide a limited yet provocative sense of what happens within the domain of the city itself that allows urban actors, often rooted in specific places, to operate outside these confines. It has attempted to open up more sustained and systematic investigation about how diverse communities attempt to maintain social coherence and cohesion while pursuing opportunities that would seemingly require behaviour and attitudes antithetical to the sustainability of such cohesion.

There are multiple geographies pieced together and navigated through the particular ways in which urban residents constitute connections among themselves and the ways in which these are folded along a series of other daily interactions. Within cities such as Johannesburg, and Lagos, there are numerous activities in which residents become involved across disjoined times and spaces. These activities do not necessarily obviate the need for local social mobilization in a conventional sense. But it is a task that does not seem to be directly addressed by such methodologies as grassroots activism, local democracy and social partnerships.

Across these cities there are inklings of the nascent emergence of different, almost inexplicable ways of people working in groups to put together spaces of operation that have no clear or fixed objectives or coordinates. After all, throughout urban Africa, the burden of change is often forced on those with the most to lose by change or the fewest resources to affect change. Change must be approached, then, as much through strategic stealth as through overt determination. This is used as evidence of a need for specific intervention, remedial action or constraints, where the focus is too often on what should be done, rather than what is actually being done (Flyvberg and Richardson, 1998).

About the author

AbdouMaliq Simone is a professor of sociology and urbanism at Goldsmiths College, University of London. He works on the reshaping of contemporary urban politics in large cities of Africa and South-east Asia. He is the author of *In Whose Image: Political Islam and Urban Practices in the Sudan* (Chicago, 1994) and *For the City Yet to Come: Urban Change in Four African Cities* (Duke, 2004).

Note

1. This is the conclusion of a broad range of initial field study reports under the auspices of the MacArthur Foundation/Council for the Development of Social Science Research in Africa Programme on Africa's Real Economies.

References

Ackello-Ogutu, C. and Echessah, P. (1997) 'Unrecorded Trade Between Kenya and Uganda', Proceedings of a Workshop held in Nairobi, Kenya, Technical Paper 58, Office of Sustainable Development, Bureau for Africa, USAID.

Azam, J-P. (2001) 'The Redistributive State and Conflicts in Africa', Oxford University, Centre for the Study of African Economics Working Papers WPS 2001.3.

Bangura, Y. (1994) 'Economic restructuring, coping strategies and social change: implications for institutional development in Africa', *Development and Change* 25: 785–827.

Bayart, J-F. (2000) 'Africa in the world: a history of extraversion', *African Affairs* 99: 217–67.

Beall, J., Crankshaw, O. and Parnell, S. (1999) *Urban Governance and Poverty in Johannesburg*, Report prepared for the Department for International Development, UK.

Ben Hammouda, H. (1999) 'Guerriers et marchands: elements pour une economie politique des conflits en Afrique', *Africa Development* XXIV(3/4): 1–18.

Benneh, G., Tims, W. and Asenso-Okyere, W. (1997) *Sustainable Food Security in West Africa*, Kluwer Academic Publishers, Dordrecht.

Berry, S. (1985) *Fathers Work for their Sons: Accumulation, Mobility and Class Formation in an Extended Yoruba Community*, University of California Press, Berkeley.

Billetoft, J. (1996) *Between Industrialisation and Poverty Alleviation: The Dilemma of Support to Micro-enterprises*, Centre for Development Research, Copenhagen.

Boone, C. (1995) 'States and ruling classes in post-colonial Africa: the enduring contradictions of power', in J. Migdal, A. Kohli and V. Shue (eds), *State Power and Social Forces*, pp. 37–61, Cambridge University Press, Cambridge.

Bouillon, A. (ed.) (1999) *Immigration Africaine en Afrique du Sud: Les Migrants Francophones des Années 90*, Karthala, Paris.

Braathen, E., Bøas, M. and Sæther, G. (eds) (2000) *Ethnicity Kills: The Politics of War, Peace and Ethnicity in Sub-Saharan Africa*, Macmillan, New York.

Bryden, L. (1999) 'Tightening belts in Accra 1975–1990', *Africa* 69 (3): 366–85.

Chirwa, J. (1997) 'The Impact of Informal Cross Border Trade on Price, Production, and Intra-COMESA Trade in East and Southern Africa', Regional
Integration Research Project, Canadian Institute of Development Research
and COMESA, Ottawa.

Club du Sahel (2000) 'Project Integration in West Africa: Options and Risks',
Document prepared for meeting of the Ministerial Lobby Group, 2–3
October, Paris.

Constantin, F. (1996) 'L'Informal Intenational ou la Subversion de la Territori-
alité', *Cultures and Conflicts* 21/22: 311–46.

Diouf, M. (1998) 'The French colonial policy of assimilation and civility of the
orginaires of the four communes (Senegal): a nineteenth century globalization project', *Development and Change* 29: 671–96.

Duffield, M. (1998) 'Post-modern conflict: warlords, post-adjustment states
and private protection', *Civil Wars* 1(1): 66–102.

Ellis, S. and MacGaffey, J. (1996) 'Research on Sub-Saharan Africa's unrecorded international trade: some methodological and conceptual problems',
African Studies Review 39(2): 19–41.

Farvacque-Vitkovic C. and Godin, L. (1999) *The Future of African Cities: Challenges and Priorities for Urban Development*, World Bank, Washington DC.

Fay, M. and Opal, C. (2000) *Urbanisation without Growth: A Not so Uncommon
Phenomenon*, World Bank, Washington, DC.

Fejgenbaum, J., Sharer, R., Thugge, K. and DeZoysa, H. (1999) *The Cross-
Border Initiative in Eastern and Southern Africa*, International Monetary Fund,
Washington, DC.

Flynn, D. (1997) '"We are the border": identity, exchange and the state along
the Benin-Nigeria Border', *American Ethnologist* 24(2): 311–30.

Flyvberg, B. and Richardson, T. (1998) 'In Search of the Dark Side of Planning Theory', Paper presented at the Planning Theory Conference, Oxford
Brookes University, 2–4 April, Oxford.

Geschiere, P. and Nyamnjoh, F. (2000) 'Capitalism and autochthony: the see-
saw of mobility and belonging', *Public Culture* 12(2): 423–52.

Gore, C. (1994) *Social Exclusion and Africa South of the Sahara: A Review of the
Literature*, International Institute for Labour Studies, Geneva.

Hart, K. (1988) 'Kinship, contract and trust: the economic organisation of migrants in an African city slum', in D. Gambetta (ed.) *Trust: The Making and
Breaking of Cooperative Relations*, Basil Blackwell, London.

Hibou, B. (1999) 'The social capital of the state as an agent of deception', in J-F.
Bayart, S. Ellis and B. Hibou (eds), *The Criminalization of the State in Africa*, pp.
69–113, James Currey/Indiana University Press, London and Bloomington.

Kirk, P. (2000) 'Suffering sleazy hotel syndrome: the illness is closely linked
to the explosion of the Nigerian drug trade in South Africa', *Daily Mail and
Guardian*, July 4.

Lachance, P. (2000) 'Africa's Real Economy and its Development Projects: Re-
thinking African Development Issues, the Case for Local Development',
OECD, Paris.

MacGaffey, J. and Bazenguissa-Ganga, R. (2000) *Congo-Paris: Transnational Traders on the Margins of the Law*, International African Institute in association
with Indiana University Press/James Currey, Bloomington and London.

MacHaria, K. (1997) *Social and Political Dynamics of the Informal Economy in African Cities: Nairobi and Harare*, University Press of America, Washington, DC.

Mattes, R., Taylor, D., McDonald, D., Poore, A. and Richmond, W. (2000) 'Still waiting for the Barbarians: South Africa's attitudes to immigrants and immigration', in D. McDonald (ed.), *On Borders: Perspectives on Cross-Border Migration in Southern Africa*, pp. 196–219, St. Martins Press, Cape Town and New York.

McCulloch, N., Cherel-Robson, M. and Baules B. (2000) 'Growth, Inequality and Poverty in Mauritania 1987–1996', Working Paper of the Poverty Dynamics in Africa Program, World Bank, Washington, DC.

Misser, F. and Vallee, O. (1997) 'Les Gemmocraties: L'Economie Politique du Diamant Africain', in Desclee de Brouwer, *Africa Report*, Organisation Geopolitique des Drogues, Paris.

Morris, G.A. and Dadson, J.A. (2000) 'Ghana: Cross-Border Trade Issues', African Economic Policy Paper 22, Office of Sustainable Development, Bureau for Africa, USAID.

Mwanasali, M. (1999) 'The view from below', in M. Berdal and D. Malone (eds), *Greed and Grievance: Economic Agendas in Civil Wars*, pp. 137–53, Lynne Rienner, Boulder and London.

Osita, N. (2000) 'The ability to squeeze water from a stone', *Daily Mail and Guardian*, November 8.

Pardo, I. (1996) *Managing Existence in Naples: Morality, Action and Structure*, Cambridge University Press, Cambridge and New York.

Perbedy, S. (1997) 'The participation of non-South Africans in street trading in South Africa and in regional cross-border trade', in J. Crush and F. Veriava (eds), *Transforming South African Migration and Immigration Policy*, South Africa Migration Project, Cape Town and Kingston.

Ranger, T. (1968) 'Connections between primary resistance movements and modern mass nationalism in East and Central Africa', *Journal of African History* 9: 37–53.

Reitzes, M. (1998) 'The Stranger within the Gates: Xenophobia and Public Leadership', Johannesburg, Centre for Policy Studies.

Reitzes, M. (1999) 'Patching the Fence: The White Paper on International Migration', Centre for Policy Studies, Johannesburg.

Reitzes, M., Tamela, Z. and Thulare, P. (1997) 'Strangers Truer than Fiction: The Social and Economic Impact of Migrants on the Johannesburg Inner City', *Social Policy Series* 60, Centre for Policy Studies, Johannesburg.

Roitman, J. (1998) 'Garrison-Entrepôt', *Cahiers d'Études Africaines* 150–152 (xxxvii-2-4): 297–329.

Salinger, B.L. (2001) 'Productivity, Comparative Advantage and Competitiveness in Africa', African Economic Policy Discussion Paper 35, Equity and Growth through Economic Research Program, USAID, Washington, DC.

Schupen, L. and Gibbon, P. with the assistance of Pedersen, P.O. (2001) *Private Sector Development: Policies, Practices and Problems*, Centre for Development Research, Copenhagen.

Sinclair, M.R. (1998) 'Solidarity and survival: migrant communities in South Africa', *Indicator South Africa* 15 (1): 66–73.

Soulé, B.G. and Obi, C. (2000) 'Prospects for Trade Between Nigeria and its Neighbors', Club du Sahel, OECD, Paris.

CHAPTER 6

Social capital or social exclusion? Social networks and informal manufacturing in Nigeria

Kate Meagher

This chapter explores the role of social networks in African informal enterprise development. It challenges negative perspectives regarding the capacity of African societies to form dynamic enterprise clusters through an examination of the development of two particularly innovative informal manufacturing clusters in the Igbo area of Nigeria. Tracing the institutional history, and networks of apprenticeship, labour, subcontracting, marketing and credit, it is shown that indigenous economic institutions have provided a basis for accumulation and economic efficiency, despite pervasive informality and state neglect. However, the economic strengths of Igbo social networks are shown to unravel in the context of drastic economic reforms and the increasingly predatory behaviour of the state, leading to the degeneration of these enterprise clusters into violence and economic decline. It is argued that radical liberalization and state withdrawal, rather than any intrinsic weaknesses of African culture, account for the failure of African social networks to foster dynamic enterprise development.

Introduction

Across Africa, extended programmes of political and economic liberalization have been accompanied by a dramatic proliferation of economic networks at all levels of society. Despite current enthusiasm about the critical role of networks in economic performance and global integration, African economic networks have done little to promote development. In studies of the contemporary role of networks in the global economy, African cases are conspicuous for their omission or their inclusion as special cases of failure (Castells, 1998; Schmitz and Nadvi, 1999; Wellman, 1999). This weakness is particularly notable in the case of small-firm networks, which have been celebrated as sources of economic dynamism in various parts of Europe, East Asia and North as well as South America, but have failed to display any similar potential in Africa.

While numerous examples of networked small-firm clusters have been identified in various parts of Africa (McCormick, 1999; Rasmussen *et al.*, 1992), examples of dynamic small-firm clusters breaking into export markets are rare. Amid celebratory research on the developmental potential of clusters in the Third World, Dorothy McCormick (1999) has pointedly asked why there are no successful small-firm clusters in Africa. In the face of prevailing tendencies to promote networks as the solution to market failure and state failure, African small-firm clusters provide an opportunity to understand more about the conditions that lead to network failure.

There is a growing tendency to locate the problem in African cultural deficiencies. Where commentators of the 1980s and early 1990s focused on the developmental potential of indigenous forms of social and economic organization, we are now told that African networks generate social liabilities rather than social capital. Some argue that in African societies, the development of effective networks has been blocked by redistributive institutions of kinship and community, or broken down by colonialism and rapid urbanization (van Donge, 1995). A more extreme, but currently fashionable position, is that African informal organization is perverted by its embeddedness in 'cultural repertoires' of clientelism, corruption, trickery, witchcraft, amoral attitudes to 'getting ahead', and the absence of an indigenous concept of public morality (Bayart, 1999). The central problem with these explanations is the core assumption that if networks fail to enhance economic efficiency and competitiveness, the problem lies in cultural inadequacies, not in the negative impact of economic restructuring on social and political cohesion. There is nothing in these analyses that tells us about the institutional limitations of networks *per se*, or about how the political and economic pressures of liberalization, as opposed to the inadequacies of African social and political culture, can cause networks to fail.

The question of why networks have failed to promote growth in Africa will be investigated here in the context of two informal manufacturing clusters in the town of Aba, in the Igbo heartland of southeastern Nigeria. The Igbo are an ethnic group famous for the density and dynamism of their associational life and informal economic organization, structured around such institutions as hometown associations, a variety of title societies, social clubs, credit societies, a well organized system of apprenticeship, and informal commercial networks spreading throughout West, Central and even Southern Africa (Forrest, 1994; Isichei, 1976). More importantly, the Igbo areas of Nigeria have recently attracted attention owing to the rapid expansion of informal manufacturing since the imposition of Nigeria's structural adjustment programme in 1986, especially in the towns of Aba and Nnewi (Brautigam, 1997). Although more has been written about Nnewi, Aba is more famous in the Nigerian context for its involvement in a range of local manufacturing activities. 'Aba-made' is a colloquial Nigerian expression for cheap, low quality goods, although some Aba manufacturers have successfully moved into higher quality niches.

In this chapter I will analyse the role of networks in informal shoe and garment manufacturing in Aba with a view to exploring why networks have failed to promote development in this very culturally and economically promising context. I will begin with an outline of the ways in which cultural and informal business networks have provided an organizational framework for the remarkable expansion of these two clusters. This will be followed by an account of how economic restructuring policies have eroded rather than liberated the organizational capacities of these networks. In the next section, I will show how contemporary forms of networking exacerbate tendencies toward differentiation, and undermine the economic potential of the clusters through a cost-cutting, low quality dynamic based on the deployment of affective ties in the context of severe economic stress. Finally, I will examine the vulnerability of popular organizational initiatives to the political designs of regional power holders.

The empirical material used in this paper derives from field research I conducted between October 1999 and September 2000, involving a sample of 132 firms across the informal shoe and garment sectors (Meagher, 2010). Throughout the paper social networks will be defined institutionally, as informal forms of organization, operating both within and outside the law. This represents a shift away from conventional 'nodes and flows' definitions, which define networks as conduits and bypasses, rather than as institutionalized informal structures of governance and power relations.

Social capital: Igbo economic networks and informal manufacturing

Informality and economic dynamism

The informal shoe and garment sectors are among the largest and most widely known informal manufacturing activities in Aba. They are organized in large clusters around the major input markets for their respective activities. Few formal sector firms operate within these clusters; indeed, the prevailing character of economic organization is decisively marked by informality. The indications of informality involve a range of factors, including the lack of official registration, the contravention of the most basic official labour and factory regulations, and, in many cases, operation in residential areas not zoned for industrial activity. Table 6.1 indicates the prevalence of these indicators of informality among the sampled firms. However, informality is not just a failure to operate according to legal norms; it also necessitates the development

Table 6.1 Indicators of informality in Aba's shoe and garment clusters

Sector	% Registered	% meeting basic provisions of Factory Act	% meeting minimum wage requirements	% operating within zoning regulations
Shoes	0.0	0.0	40.0	74.7
Garments	20.3	0.0	50.0	0.0
Total	9.9	0.0	44.4	38.1

Source: Author's fieldwork.

of alternative structures of entry, productive organization, and access to labour and productive infrastructure (Weiss, 1987). These alternative forms of organization constitute what are referred to here as 'informal economic networks'.

Particularly since the onset of economic liberalization, Aba's informal shoe and garment clusters have come to represent exceptional examples of informal organizational dynamism. In a town of approximately 750,000 inhabitants,[1] these two clusters generate a remarkable level of employment and economic turnover despite their informality, as indicated in Table 6.2. Between the two of them, these informal manufacturing activities account for 14,000 firms (slightly more if one were to count the dispersed firms outside the clusters), which generate employment for 36,600 enterprise heads, employees and apprentices, and an additional 21,000 temporary workers during seasonal periods of high demand.[2] More impressive still is their annual turnover, which amounted to US$162 million in the case of shoes, and $12 million for garments – figures that would amaze even Hernando de Soto. What is particularly unusual in the context of African informality is that the vast majority of these informal manufacturers specialize in their activity rather than practicing the kind of pluri-activity strategies common in contemporary Africa (Chazan, 1988).

History of informal shoe and garment production

This remarkable growth has taken place largely since the imposition of economic liberalization, but owes its realization to local cultural and economic institutions which have adapted to the needs and opportunities of the contemporary Nigerian economy. Although indigenous shoe and garment production were pioneered in Aba in the 1950s, their organization and cohesion is based on much older Igbo institutions of hometown-based occupational specialization. The characterization of the Igbo as an acephalous society tends to ignore the existence even in pre-colonial times of a range of pan-Igbo social, political and economic institutions that have contributed importantly to the legendary informal commercial success of the Igbo. These institutions include the Igbo institution of apprenticeship, which involves not only training but the provision of start-up capital, and institutions of suppliers' credit and

Table 6.2 Employment and turnover in Aba's informal shoe and garment clusters (1999–2000 season)

Sector	No. of firms	Long-term employment	Temporary employment	Annual turnover (US$ mil.)
Shoes	11,497	26,443	19,610	162.4
Garments	2,423	10,177	1,938	12.5
Total	13,920	36,620	21,548	174.9

Source: Author's fieldwork

customer advances accessed through links with organized networks of input and output traders.

Informal shoe manufacturing developed in Aba as the specialization of migrants from the former colonial district of Mbaise, a poor, particularly land-scarce area approximately 80 km north-west of Aba. Mbaise migrants turned to informal shoe production owing to its extremely low capital and skill threshold. The activity initially involved the use of simple hand tools for the production of crude sandals, often made from scrap materials. Over time, however, skills, equipment and materials became more sophisticated, and the production of contemporary 'fashion shoes' widened the market for informal producers. As informal shoe production grew it became embedded in input and output trading networks dominated by other, more prosperous, Igbo communities through whom Mbaise shoe producers gained access to much of the financing that fuelled the growth of the activity during periods of expansion in the 1970s and 1990s.

By contrast, informal garment production is the specialization of migrants from the more prosperous communities of the former colonial district of Bende, some 80 km to the northeast of Aba. Garment production is an activity with comparatively high capital costs, owing to the need for various types of domestic and even industrial sewing machines. Given the more prosperous character of the communities involved, indigenes of the area are also heavily represented in the networks of input and output trade for garment production. The greater wealth of the founding communities, combined with the greater continuity between the production and trading sides of the activity facilitated more rapid growth in the local garment industry, especially following Nigeria's ban on imported textiles in 1976.

Over time these communal networks have given rise to a complex division of labour and well-developed inter-firm subcontracting within the two clusters. However, a lack of subcontracting links with the formal sector highlights the limits of informal inter-firm networks. They are sufficient to organize activities among informal firms, but are rarely strong enough to bridge the formal–informal divide. The main problem, according to the formal sector firms interviewed, is not skill, as often supposed, but quality and reliability as a result of poverty and the unreliable infrastructural conditions of informal production.[3] This calls into question the adequacy of the financing available through trading networks, which appears inadequate for the development of a sufficiently high level of productive capacity to generate reliable links with the formal sector. It is worth noting in this regard that access to bank loans, rather than informal credit, proved to be a key factor in the extremely rare movement of Aba shoe firms from the informal into the formal sector.

Despite the absence of consistent subcontracting relationships with the formal sector, the integration of Aba's informal shoe and garment clusters into the far-flung trading networks of the Igbo commercial diaspora have sustained rapid growth in both clusters. In contrast to the prevailing assumption that African informal activities are largely dependent on local demand, Aba's

Table 6.3 Participation in informal distribution networks

Sector	% of enterprises with main market outside Aba	% of enterprises with distribution outside Nigeria
Shoes	98	83
Garments	39	27
Average	71	58

Source: Author's fieldwork

informal shoe and garment clusters supply markets not only across Nigeria, but across West, Central and Southern Africa, as indicated in Table 6.3. This integration into wide informal distributive networks is particularly pronounced in the shoe cluster, where 98 per cent of shoe producers claim their main market is outside Aba, and 83 per cent have at least some distribution outside Nigeria. This wide market reach is less pronounced among informal garment producers, owing to the stronger market for 'tailor-made' production in garments, as well as the higher participation of women who are less well integrated into the wider distributive networks. That said, 39 per cent of garment producers depended largely on distribution to areas outside Aba, and 27 per cent had some distribution outside Nigeria.

All in all, it is evident that Igbo society generated sufficient social capital to underpin the remarkable expansion of both the informal shoe and garment clusters. Despite the greater poverty of shoe producers, embeddedness in the wider economic networks of Igbo society provided channels of supply, distribution and financing that the shoe-producing community was unable to generate themselves. Within each cluster, patterns of inter-firm and intra-firm division of labour created new bases for the development of subcontracting and labour networks, which helped to mitigate the poverty of individual firms. Impressive as the organization and performance of these informal manufacturers appears, however, the limitations of their organizational networks are evident in their inability to establish reliable subcontracting links with the formal sector, much less penetrate into formal export markets.

Impact of economic liberalization on informal manufacturing networks

The belief that economic reforms would liberate the organizational capacities of informal economic networks proved sadly wrong in the case of Aba's shoe and garment clusters. On the contrary, reform policies triggered intense competition within informal manufacturing, owing to extreme pressures on livelihoods and rapid entry into the informal economy. These pressures served to undermine relations of cooperation and trust within the cultural and occupational networks that organized these activities. In the struggle for advantage, or mere survival, informal manufacturers as well as traders used all manner of personal networks to circumvent or contravene the informal institutional norms that previously regulated economic behaviour in these

clusters. The result was organizational fragmentation, increased differentiation, and the creation of a productive environment of increasing opportunism and uncertainty. The weakening of the structures of informal regulation
showed up most starkly in three areas: loss of control over entry, the erosion
of credit relationships in supply and distribution networks, and increased
differentiation among firms within the cluster.

Erosion of entry regulation

Rapid entry into informal manufacturing since economic liberalization has
diluted the original hometown networks that once regulated entry into informal shoe and garment production. Ninety per cent of informal shoe producers, and nearly 80 per cent of informal garment producers, have entered the
activity since the beginning of the Structural Adjustment Programme (SAP) in
1986. The expansion of markets for cheaper shoes and garments, combined
with a contraction of employment options in the formal economy, has resulted in increased entry of other Igbo as well as non-Igbo groups. Rather than
depending largely on kinship and hometown networks, entrants and producers alike have resorted to the mobilization of a wider range of ties in the search
for training and for labour. These include associative ties of neighbourhood,
friendship and church membership, as well as purely commercial ties, involving links through customers, or the selection of a master 'off the street' on the
basis of the samples hung outside the shop. Further penetration of the original occupational networks has occurred through links with input and output
traders, who use their connections with producers to find training for relatives
lacking the capital to enter into trading activities. A final category of new
entrants involved owners or workers in formal sector shoe or garment firms,
forced by retrenchment or declining salaries to set up as informal producers.

The result of these various pressures has been a dramatic decline in the
presence of the original occupational identities, particularly in the case of informal shoe production. At the time of the research, only 14 per cent of shoe
producers came from the founding Mbaise community, while 44 per cent of
garment producers came from the Bende area (Table 6.4). The greater success
of the original garment producing community in maintaining their control
of the activity is linked in part to the comparatively high capital costs of garment production, and in part to the strong representation of Bende indigenes
among traders and formal sector producers in the garment sector. However, a
further factor was the more limited growth of markets in garment production,
owing to increasing competition from imported Asian textiles, particularly
since the removal of the ban on textile imports in 1997, and the devaluation
of several Asian currencies during the same period. In the informal shoe cluster, by contrast, markets for cheap shoes have faced comparatively less competition, though illicit imports of second-hand shoes are considered a problem
and the penetration of cheap Asian shoes, called 'Dubai', have threatened the
lower end of the market since the end of 2000.

Table 6.4 Occupationally advantaged and non-advantaged identity groups (per cent)

Sector	Occupationally advantaged identities				Non-advantaged identities			
	Original producers	Related sub-groups	Trading groups	Total	Aba indigenes (Ngwa)	Other Igbo	Non-Igbo	Total
Shoes	14.1	8.5	15.5	38.1	23.9	32.4	5.6	61.9
Garments	44.3	16.4	16.4	77.1	8.2	14.8	0.0	23.0
Average	28.0	12.1	15.9	56.0	16.7	24.2	3.0	43.9

Source: Author's fieldwork

Although entry from a wider range of Igbo and non-Igbo communities is not in itself negative, it has tended to undermine the regulatory capacity of hometown-based occupational networks. Critical changes include the weakening of the key institution of apprenticeship and the erosion of the moral and reputation-based mechanisms underpinning trust and cooperation among firms. Ascriptive relationships play a key role in the ability of apprenticeship to maintain effective labour control, as well as labour protection and effective training. The negotiation of apprenticeships through associative and market-based relationships has seriously weakened these controls, leaving apprentices more prone to misbehaviour and leaving early, and masters more prone to exploitation of apprentices and inadequate attention to their training obligations. The practice of providing start-up capital to apprentices has declined markedly, and is almost exclusively restricted to relatives. Conversely, there is an increasing tendency toward written contracts and the payment of training fees, especially in cases where apprentices are linked to the master only by associative or market-based ties. However, the limited enforceability of these contracts, the changing economic incentives created by training fees, and the growing economic pressures on apprentices to finish their training as quickly as possible so as to start bringing in an income, have led to declining periods of apprenticeship. The result of these various forces is that apprentices tend to enter the business more poorly trained and poorly capitalized than was previously the case, and masters face a much more unstable, unskilled and unruly labour force.

Moreover, the lack of a defined basis of affinity among producers means that networks of reputation, trust and cooperation have become more fragmented. Organizational networks are now built up from an array of relationships including identity, friendship, church, and even membership in the same football club. Inter-firm relationships based purely on skills and reliability are also common, particularly at the upper end of the informal market. Unfortunately, far from broadening the basis of economic cooperation, the diversity of inter-firm networks has tended to create openings for the intrusion of opportunism into economic relationships between firms as producers attempt to circumvent business norms by manipulating affective ties. This is exacerbated by the intense livelihood pressure and competition for buyers that characterizes the productive environment in both clusters.

Erosion of informal credit systems

The combination of increased competition and squeezed profits among informal producers and traders alike has tended to undermine access to credit through input and output trading networks. Owing to the high cost of machinery, suppliers' credit has played a critical role in the expansion of informal garment production, while the advance system, which involves a 30–50 per cent advance payment from buyers, has played an important role in informal shoe production, and has also been important among poorer garment producers. Identity-based ties, in the case of garment production, as well as historically sedimented relationships between producer and trading groups, underpinned the reliability of these credit relationships, along with a strong reputation mechanism within producer and trader groups. However, the growing diversity of participation in both production and trade has tended to weaken trust and enforcement mechanisms between producers and traders.

From the perspective of trade, squeezed profit margins combined with liberalized economic conditions and expanding regional networks have produced high levels of non-Igbo participation in the output trade, as traders attempt to maximize their gains by bypassing their erstwhile Igbo correspondents. Not only Yoruba and Hausa traders from other parts of Nigeria, but indigenes of a wide range of West and Central African countries now come directly to producers in Aba to buy their goods. At the same time, producers are also caught between rising costs and intensifying competition for buyers, which tends to undermine profits and reliability. This has led to a shift toward 'cash and carry' relationships with both input and output traders. At the supply end of the market, there is a growing reluctance to offer, as well as to use, suppliers' credit because of the instability of markets. For instance, the Chairman of the elastic traders' union in the informal garment cluster says that hard economic times have destroyed credit relationships and trust with producers, even if they come from the same community. As he put it, 'By the time he can't repay me, that trust is no more there.... Formerly, on trust, you could release 100 dozen [units of elastic], but now if you give that out on credit, you could stay for one month without repayment'.

At the distribution end, competition and instability have also taken their toll. Weakened reputation mechanisms and increased competition have weakened credit relationships between producers and traders. Older producers in both activities noted that advances were less common now. A well-established shoemaker who had been 25 years in the business lamented that in order to keep a customer who offered advances, one had to be willing to accept almost any price, or risk the transfer of valuable custom to a producer willing to accept the terms. He observed that, 'competition wipes out long-term business relationships'. While producers continue to give credit if they can, in order to keep customers, customers are less prone to giving advances. Although some producers extend credit on the basis of trust built up through previous interaction or recommendation, the line between trust and desperation has become increasingly blurred.

Even where ascriptive ties between traders and producers have sustained credit relations, these relationships are increasingly governed by norms of social assistance rather than norms of economic reliability. Suppliers of shoe parts claimed that townsmen were the most problematic customers, because they exercised moral pressure to get credit, and then expected the trader to understand their problems when the time came for repayment. Associative ties, especially through church membership, were considered more reliable, but the preferred customer under contemporary economic conditions was the cash and carry customer. Among suppliers in the garment market, it was also felt that personal ties were not good for business. One supplier attributed the problem, not to the character of personal ties, but to instability of the economy. 'It is not you as a person that makes you to disappoint, but the economy of the country makes you to disappoint.'

Social liabilities and differentiation

While informal socio-cultural networks are often regarded as structures of occupational solidarity, recourse to personal networks in the organization of informal activities has tended to promote differentiation among informal producers. Differentiation has been fuelled by the entry of producers from a wider range of class as well as sub-ethnic backgrounds since the onset of economic liberalization. As shown in Table 6.5, 26 per cent of informal garment producers and 18 per cent of informal shoe producers came from formal sector and business backgrounds rather than from rural or informal artisanal and petty commercial backgrounds that have traditionally made up the informal sector. Eighty per cent of entrants from formal and business classes had entered the activity since the imposition of economic reforms. This new class of informal entrants, although often forced into informal manufacturing by adverse circumstances, brought with them an advantaged range of skills and social ties less available to those from rural or informal sector backgrounds. These included higher levels of education and stronger ties to better resourced and

Table 6.5 Class backgrounds of informal shoe and garment producers (per cent)

	Traditional informal classes			Formal and business classes		
	Rural	Urban informal	Total	Formal sector employee	Middle-level self-employed	Total
Shoes	40.0	41.4	81.4	11.4	7.1	18.5
Garments	31.1	42.6	73.7	14.8	11.5	26.3
Average	35.9	42.0	77.9	13.0	9.2	22.2

Source: Author's fieldwork

connected social groups. Thus, rather than being united by socialization into a common set of skills and productive relationships, informal manufacturers are now differentiated by the portfolio of ties to which they have access.

Differential socio-cultural backgrounds further contributed to these processes of differentiation. Entrants from areas well represented in the input or output trade of their activity often enjoyed advantageous access to credit or custom, while entrants from the original occupational group often had advantageous links to skilled training. Gender constituted an additional differentiating factor, since Igbo social and economic norms, while encouraging women to work or run businesses, structurally exclude them from the circles where significant loans and business contacts are accessed. Religious ties also played a role, as better-off producers used conversion to evangelical Christianity to distance themselves from less advantaged members of their sub-ethnic communities. Thus, networks of identity, class, religion and gender did not interact to form interlocking webs of ties uniting all members of the activity. Nor did they function simply as bridging ties that drew resources and business contacts from the wider economy into the cluster. Instead, they operated as both bridging and new bonding mechanisms through which structurally advantaged entrants were able to gain privileged access to resources, while simultaneously disembedding themselves from the redistributive pressures of their less fortunate fellow producers.

Networks of accumulation

In the garment cluster, the interaction of identity, religion and gender proved to be the central differentiating factors, while in the all-male shoe cluster the most successful production networks were marked off by the interaction of identity and class (Meagher, 2009). Among garment producers, successful performance was significantly associated with membership in one of the original occupational or trading groups. Despite increasing penetration by entrants from more advantaged class backgrounds, the original occupational group – Bende producers from traditional informal sector backgrounds – maintained a degree of closure by creating group boundaries through participation in evangelical churches. Lovejoy (1980) has described similar processes with regard to the role of Islam in the development of trading networks. The following cases illustrate some of these relationships:

> Mr. Kalu is a 36-year-old tailor specializing in Igbo men's wear. He is an indigene of Abiriba, one of the communities of old Bende area, and his father was a tailor. After completing secondary school, Mr. Kalu entered tailoring by serving a five-year apprenticeship with his father. To raise capital for his business, Mr. Kalu worked as a textile trader, an activity for which his town is famous, and combined the proceeds with start-up capital from his family. He now operates a well-equipped firm in the shop previously occupied by his father, with assets of nearly twice the average value of informal

garment firms in the cluster, though the business is not registered. Rather than using apprentices, he has five employees, all of whom are relatives and townsmen. He gets business from private customers as well as traders, particularly through friends and church members. Traders from Bende area are his most important source of distribution contacts outside Aba. He is a member of the Church of God, an evangelical sect, and his church association is the only association he participates in, in violation of the traditional Igbo norm of participation in one's village association.

However, membership in the original occupational group and evangelical conversion were not necessarily a path to success. While women were over-represented in the original occupational group, in evangelical conversion, and in completion of secondary education, female ownership had a strong negative association with firm performance. Youth, women and those from poor backgrounds found themselves trapped in structural factors that prevented their joining the inner networks of enterprise success. By contrast, well-educated male garment producers from other identity groups used participation in evangelical churches as a means of bonding with successful Bende producers. For example, a well established producer of men's suits from a non-Bende group claimed that his lack of identity-based ties with Bende producers was not a problem, since there were many of them in his church (Jehovah's Witness). While reasons for conversion are as much spiritual as economic, religious affiliation and conversion play a critical role in the structuring of economic networks.

In the shoe cluster, class rather than religion was a major determinant of successful business networks. People from the original occupational group tended to belong to established rather than evangelical churches, and evangelical conversions were less common in this sector. This reflects the greater economic insecurity of most shoe producers, which made them more reluctant to distance themselves from their ascriptive communities through religious conversion. However, those with advantageous class ties were able to build more outward looking networks, as the following case indicates:

Mr. Nwagbara, a man in his 40s, is a successful shoe and bag producer of Ngwa origins. A graduate of a polytechnic in Lagos, he started his working life as a salesman in a bag, shoe and chemical company in Western Nigeria. In the early 1980s, he left his job to set up his own small formal shoe firm in the commercial district of Aba. He is proud to reveal that he entered the production side of the business as an employer, not as an apprentice. Unfortunately, the market for shoes was poor in the early 1980s. Duties were high on imported goods, and inputs were scarce and costly. This led him to set up shop inside the informal shoe cluster, in order to benefit from the cheap labour and proximity to inputs. For markets, he is not dependent on the traders who frequent the shoe cluster, but pursues contracts from the formal sector. His first contract was to produce conference bags for a Nigerian university, which he got through an old school friend who introduced him to the person giving the contract. He maintains that for getting large contracts with the formal sector, personal background and image are important, as well as a reputation for delivering on previous jobs. He also emphasizes the importance of obtaining references from someone known to the contractor. Mr. Nwagbara puts a lot of store in dressing well, and has gained significantly from his wide business contacts obtained through his education and his time as a salesman in a formal sector enterprise.

Advantageous identity-based connections in the activity also created privileged access to resources and contacts, but only among those from more advantaged class backgrounds, who are more likely to be connected with large-scale traders and successful producers, rather than with small struggling operators. A producer of ladies' shoes from Ukpo in Anambra State, a town that specializes in the leather trade, built up his business from generous suppliers' credit and contacts from his townsmen. Although economic adversity had driven him into the shoe trade, the producer in question had completed secondary school, and had sufficient credibility and contacts with successful traders from his town to be able to establish a relatively successful informal shoe firm in one of the most skilled zones of the shoe cluster.

Networks of survival

Those excluded from these networks of advantage were confined to narrower, more poorly resourced personal networks made up largely of kinship, hometown, friendship and church ties with other equally disadvantaged producers and traders. They suffered from a lack of school, business, or ascriptive ties to people in more advantaged social positions. As a result, those from disadvantaged backgrounds were generally dependent on the moral sting of affective loyalties to get credit, discounts and customers, rather than using networks to build up wider business relationships. Dependence on the 'economy of affection' involved less advantaged producers in reciprocal obligations of assistance, requiring them to grant discounts and accept indefinite delays in payment from townspeople and friends. These obligations tended to undermine rather than enhance profits, as the following example shows:

> Sunday is a young shoe producer from Owerri in Imo State – a community with connections to the original occupational group. Although his father was a building contractor, the family had fallen on hard times, and Sunday was unable to complete secondary school or go into the trade. He entered shoe production 'because it is a poor people's business' and is therefore cheap to start. He served an apprenticeship with a townsman, but his master went out of business soon after Sunday gained independence. He worked as a journeyman for a couple of years to get some capital. Just after starting his own business, Sunday was forced to move to a new location by the Local Government. He lost all his contacts, and went out of business in six months. He borrowed money from an in-law to start up again.

He now runs a barely surviving business in a tiny market stall, which he shares with two other shoemakers. He has no suppliers' credit, because he buys from whoever is cheapest, which prevents him from building up regular business relationships with input traders. He also finds it difficult to get customers since he has little money for producing samples to attract them. Instead, he takes his goods once a week to Port Harcourt, a major city nearby, but has to sell cheaper there in order to attract business away from the established traders. He participates minimally in hometown and family networks because he feels they will bring little business to him, and will sap his resources. The one regular customer he has who is a townsman is his smallest and least reliable customer. On the whole, he says that friends are better than townsmen or church members. They share jobs with each other, but are more limited in the kind of social welfare demands they can make on each other.

In both the shoe and garment cluster, producers from less advantaged backgrounds routinely claimed that business from townspeople was not an advantage, since they tended to buy in small quantities, and they 'tended to owe'. However, networks of survival did not only affect the opportunities of individuals. They also influenced collective opportunities through their effect on the organization of production within small-firm clusters. At the inter-firm level, affective ties of kinship, community, church and friendship created a basis for widespread sharing of materials and equipment, as well as orders, information and designs. On average, 70–80 per cent of shoe and garment producers in the clusters shared these resources with fellow producers, though there was some reluctance expressed in the case of the two most sensitive resources, designs and orders. However, far from constituting a mutually supportive framework for resource-sharing and efficiency maximization among the poor – known in the literature as collective efficiency (Rasmussen, Schmitz and van Dijk, 1992) – these networks of survival have created a downward-levelling framework that prevents accumulation in any firm unable to detach itself from the constant pressures for assistance.

As McCormick (1999) and others have demonstrated, in fact, the embedding of affective networks in an economic environment of intense competition and livelihood pressure has generated 'collective inefficiencies' rather than the collective efficiencies promised by cluster theorists. Focusing on the disadvantageous dynamics of aggregation in weak institutional environments goes a long way to explaining the realities of informal manufacturing in Aba. Instead of attracting supplies of skilled labour and specialized suppliers, or generating technical innovations and increased quality, the Aba clusters suffer from the constant fissioning of firms as apprentices and employees leave to start their own businesses, intensifying competition.

At the level of suppliers, both clusters have been reducing rather than improving the quality of inputs supplied, because devaluation and declining access to credit leaves producers increasingly unable to afford quality inputs.

Among producers, mutual learning tends to take the form of passing on negative practices, such as copying designs of fellow producers, counterfeiting international brand names, and substituting inferior materials. Rather than stimulating technical progress, the combination of poor infrastructure, overcrowding of production areas, rising costs and declining prices has promoted the use of obsolete, second-hand machinery in the garment cluster, and the widespread abandonment of mechanized production in the shoe cluster. The clusters' reputation for poor quality production and opportunistic practices attracts traders of the same orientation, precluding entry into a higher market niche.

The end result in Aba is a productive environment characterized by a downward spiral of copying, undercutting, low quality production and technical regression – a parody of the prevailing image of successful small firm clusters. The contemporary literature on small-firm clusters has endlessly discussed the various advantages of clustering and cooperation, but has paid little attention to their disadvantages in contexts of weak formal instititional provision. This oversight belies an underlying ideological belief that small-firm clusters and the networks that regulate them will offer a viable substitute for state regulation. However, Aba's informal manufacturers saw things differently. As Table 6.6 indicates, nearly half of all firms in both clusters expressed doubts about the advantages of clustering, largely because of the negative production environment generated by copying, undercutting and poor infrastructure. Within an informal framework in which indigenous institutions of regulation have been eroded, and formal sector institutions do not apply, cooperation and affective norms, far from tempering competitive pressures with trust, generated a dynamic of opportunism, mistrust and cut-throat competition.

As previously indicated, the governance structure created by networks of survival has led to a situation in which accumulation is increasingly dependent on extrication from, rather than engagement with, the social and productive networks of the cluster. Producers who could afford to do so limited their involvement in sharing relationships, operating as sole occupiers of their shops where possible, in order to minimize the extent to which fellow producers could prevail upon them and copy their techniques and designs. More successful producers withdrew into larger closed premises within the cluster, which provided enough space for the centralization of production processes, and greater isolation from cooperative social networks within the cluster.

Table 6.6 Firms' attitudes toward clustering (per cent)

Activity	Advantage	Disadvantage	Mixed
Shoes	56.3	21.1	22.5
Garments	57.4	6.6	36.1
Average	56.8	14.4	28.8

Source: Author's fieldwork

Political capital: social networks and identity politics

The case of the Aba clusters has shown that neither the institutionalized networks of the informal economy, nor the personal networks deployed by individual operators, were able to create a coherent productive framework for small-scale manufacturing. Informal cultural and occupational networks, despite their embeddedness in local social institutions, were unable to cope with the competitive pressures and severe economic instability brought on by liberalization. The resulting recourse to personal networks, far from 'filling the gaps' in informal organizational capacity, only succeeded in fragmenting organizational strategies and further intensifying competitive and livelihood pressures.

The only form of informal organization with a potential for rising to the regulatory challenges posed by liberalization are informal occupational associations. With a basis of regulatory authority that is distinctly occupational rather than communal, informal occupational associations can provide a framework of cohesion independent of identity-based loyalties. Unfortunately, the role of informal occupational associations has been generally disappointing in African small-firm clusters (Haan, 1999; McCormick, 1999). The weakness of these associations is clearly exemplified in the case of Aba's shoe and garment clusters. Despite the timely emergence of occupational associations in both clusters, the combination of intense competition, inadequate access to resources, and weak institutional links with the state and formal sector has undermined their regulatory effectiveness as well as their autonomy from more powerful political interests.

In the garment cluster, there was one occupational association, formed in 1984, while in the shoe cluster, six independent associations had emerged at various times between the late 1970s and the late 1990s. The informal garment producers' association, known affectionately as 'Aba Garment', was dominated by the original occupational community, and had difficulty mobilizing new entrants from other communities, especially poorly capitalized entrants. Despite regular complaints about the need for regulation of prices and copying, less than 10 per cent of informal garment producers were members. The informal shoemakers' associations were more broadly-based in their membership and communal participation. The communal representation within association executives was roughly reflective of the origins of producers, and more than 80 per cent of producers were members of the association governing the area where they operated. Despite high levels of participation and legitimacy across community lines, occupational organization among informal shoemakers was critically weakened by its fragmentation into six separate associations, divided by jealously-guarded market administrative jurisdictions and local government boundaries that cut through the production area.

As a result of their organizational weaknesses and the informal status of their membership, the associations in both clusters suffered from the same basic inadequacies: an inability to provide basic business services (loans, technical training, joint procurement or marketing schemes) and effective economic regulation, particularly relating to entry and quality. Instead, their main roles involved lobbying the government for assistance, the mainte-nance of order within the production areas, and provision of social welfare services to members, largely funeral support. The garment association also assisted members with formal registration, and briefly ran a rotating loan facility, although it was wiped out within a short time by financial problems. In the shoe cluster, the huge number of firms, and the greater poverty of operators, precluded any attempt at organizing a loan facility.

Attempts at economic regulation were equally unsuccessful. Nominal price regulation existed in the garment cluster, but was not enforceable on non-members, who were in the majority. In the shoe cluster, attempts to regulate copying existed within subsections of the shoe associations, but were too iso-lated to limit the practice significantly. Quality control was enforced by one of the shoe associations, which seized the goods of anyone found using inferior materials, but this had little effect on declining quality and reputation within the cluster as a whole. The core of the problem was the lack of an institutional basis of authority. Given high levels of entry by various sub-ethnic groups, the associations lacked the moral authority of identity-based forms of organiza-tion. As associations of informal firms, however, they also lacked the official clout of formal institutional backing to enforce regulations on all members. In short, having moved beyond socio-cultural exclusiveness as an organizational strategy, the organizational effectiveness of informal occupational associa-tions required, not independence from the state, but access to resources and institutional authority through the state.

This dependence on the state was clearly reflected in the behaviour of oc-cupational associations in both clusters. Far from asserting their autonomy from the state, they turned toward the state as plants to the sun. All of the oc-cupational associations in both clusters had attempted to register at the state or even federal levels between 1984 and 2001. The garment association was at-tempting to use registration at the federal level to extend its mandate over all small-scale garment producers in Nigeria, in an effort to create an organized lobby for greater restriction of finished textile imports. The shoe associations turned to registration as a means of getting resources from the state, as well as competing for authority over each other. However, the fact that these associa-tions represented firms that were largely unregistered limited their ability to link up with the state through formal economic channels. Lack of registration of member firms, as well as social and class differences, excluded these associa-tions from the ranks of the organized private sector, including the Nigerian Association of Small and Medium Scale Industrialists (NASSI) and the Aba Chamber of Commerce (ACCIMA). The result was a tendency to form links with the state through incorporation into cliental networks with officials and politicians, who tended to make use of these links to serve their own personal and political agendas, rather than to address the occupational interests of in-formal manufacturers.

The tendency of links with the state to take the form of patron–client relations rather than accountable institutional linkages is evident at both the local and regional government levels. At the local government level, kickback relations between association executives and local government officials characterized the organization of services such as electricity or the construction and rental of workshop space. At the level of the regional government, obligations to provide basic infrastructural maintenance and development assistance never materialized, but the shoe associations were 'dashed' money and a transformer in return for mobilizing the votes of their constituencies in the 1999 gubernatorial elections. Rather than laying a developmental framework, these institutional networks created forms of organization lacking in transparency and accountability, often mobilizing the resources and support of informal producers against their own long-term economic interests. In other words, cliental forms of incorporation have tended to transform the social capital created by informal manufacturers' associations into political capital to serve the interests of more powerful political actors.

The most glaring example of this transformation of social capital to political capital is the case of the Bakassi Boys vigilante group, which has been the subject of a Human Rights Watch Report (2002). The Bakassi Boys arose from the informal shoemakers of Aba in November 1998 as a means of combating rampant armed robbery and organized crime, which were frightening away the non-local customers on which the activity depended. In the face of state indifference, and police corruption and inefficiency, the Bakassi Boys provided a second-best solution to the problem of law and order, which was critical to the survival of local economic activity. Although their methods of punishment were brutal, usually involving public dismembering and burning, the Bakassi Boys acquired a reputation for fairness and resistance to corruption that gained them overwhelming popular support in Aba, and in neighbouring Igbo states to which they later spread.

However, the Bakassi Boys' popularity proved their undoing, as politicians saw in the vigilante group a useful route to popularity and extra-legal control of state security. The need of shoemakers' associations for avenues of state recognition and assistance encouraged their cooperation with state-level initiatives to expand the operations of the vigilante group. Unfortunately, the rise of the Bakassi Boys was embedded in a wider political context characterized by struggles over the creation of state-level (as opposed to federal) police, tensions over the introduction of Sharia law in the north of the country, and growing pressures among Igbo governors to increase their clout at the federal level. These political objectives tended to overwhelm the original commitment of the vigilante group to local security and accountability, and, over time, turned them into yet another source of violence and insecurity until they were definitively quashed by the federal government in early 2006.

This process of political capture began with the involvement of the Bakassi Boys in ethnic riots in February 2001 in which hundreds of northern Nigerian migrants were killed. Not only did these riots undermine security in Aba, but they represented the first act of sectional violence ever associated with the Bakassi Boys, who had, until then, had a primary objective of making Aba safe for traders and sojourners from other parts of Nigeria and beyond. The negative economic effect on informal shoe and garment producers was felt immediately, since the riots frightened away northern customers for several weeks during a key business period linked to a major Muslim festival. In some parts of the shoe production zones business from northern Nigerian customers did not return to normal for up to one year. From the middle of 2000, increasing quasi-legal incorporation of the Bakassi Boys into the security arrangements of Abia State and the two neighbouring Igbo States of Anambra and Imo, transformed the vigilante group from a popular bid for law and order into a force for political repression in the run up to the 2003 and the 2007 elections (Ukiwo, 2002; Meagher, 2007). Ultimately, powerful political forces removed control of the vigilante group from the shoemakers that founded them, perverting the initial grassroots objectives of security and accountability that underpinned both the economic role and the widespread popularity of the Bakassi Boys.

Conclusion

At the beginning of this chapter it was argued that more systematic analysis of the performance of economic networks in Africa can yield valuable lessons about why networks sometimes fail to enhance economic efficiency. Such analysis requires us to transcend simplistic cultural explanations in order to examine the historical, institutional and political context in which networks develop and operate. The case of informal shoe and garment clusters in Aba was used to show both the extensive social capital generated by these clusters, as well as the ways in which their economic potential has been eroded by the pressures of liberalization, differentiation, survival strategies and political opportunism. As the Aba case study makes clear, the weakness of African small-firm networks does not arise from perverse cultural blue-prints, but from the weakness and instability of the institutional and political context in which such networks are embedded.

The cases presented here suggest three useful lessons regarding why networks have failed to produce sustainable economic growth in the Aba shoe and garment clusters, and in Africa more generally. The first is that the organizational capacity of identity-based and other informal networks is undermined rather than enhanced by rapid economic expansion and a lack of developmental support from relevant state institutions. As informal activities expand beyond the limits of informal regulatory institutions, the emergence of new structures of effective regulatory control depends heavily on the supportive role of the state, a point that has been recognized in critical analyses of small-firm organization in other parts of the world (Deyo *et al.* 2001; Portes *et al.* 1989), but continues to be ignored in much of the network literature on Africa.

The second lesson is that, where the state fails to take a hand in the development of new forms of organization and regulation, strains on informal organizational networks lead to differentiation and a shift to personal networks of advantage and survival which impede growth and exacerbate differentiation, uncertainty and opportunism. In short, networks generate social liabilities rather than social capital. These conditions tend to impede the development of 'collective efficiencies' in small-firm organization, and limit the formation of subcontracting links with the formal sector.

The final lesson is that weak formal institutions and the lack of incorporation into the formal economic framework encourage informal firms and occupational associations to turn to cliental forms of economic and political incorporation. In the process, informal networks are easily transformed from social into political capital, which leads to the fragmentation and demobilization of informal occupational interests in favour of the machinations of more powerful political forces. Far from strengthening the economic and political autonomy of informal economic actors, liberalization only weakens their organizational capacity. In an era in which networks are increasingly expected to bypass institutional and political weaknesses, the vulnerability of networks to disintegration and political hijack in the context of liberalization constitute lessons we cannot afford to ignore.

About the author

Kate Meagher is a lecturer in development studies at the London School of Economics. Her research focuses on the informal economy and non-state governance in Africa. She has carried out extensive empirical and theoretical research on cross-border trading systems and regional integration, the urban informal sector, rural non-farm activities, small-enterprise clusters, and informal enterprise associations, and has engaged in fieldwork in Nigeria, Uganda, and the Democratic Republic of the Congo. Degrees from the University of Toronto; the Institute of Development Studies (University of Sussex), and a D.Phil in Sociology from Oxford have been interspersed with lecturing and research positions at IAR/Ahmadu Bello University in Zaria, Nigeria (1991–7) and at the African Studies Centre, University of Oxford (2005–8). Current research interests centre on comparative approaches to non-state governance, the politics of economic informality and the impact of China on African informal economies.

Notes

1. Although the population was enumerated as 500,183 in the 1991 census, it was estimated by local government officials that approximately one-third of the regular population left town during the census in order to be counted in their villages of origin (Interview with official from the Population Department, Aba South Local Government, April 2000).

2. Some of these temporary workers include enterprise heads with no work of their own.
3. Interview with FAMAD shoe company (formerly BATA-Nigeria), April 2000 and July 2000; interviews with Leventis, Aba, United Equitable, Aba, and Presidential Tailors, Aba, April and July 2000.

References

Bayart, J-F. (1999) 'The "social capital" of the felonious State' in J-F. Bayart, S. Ellis and B. Hibou (eds), *The Criminalization of the State in Africa*, pp. 32–41, International African Institute, in association with James Currey/Indiana University Press, Oxford and Bloomington.

Brautigam, D. (1997) 'Substituting for the State: institutions and industrial development in eastern Nigeria', *World Development* 25: 1063–80.

Castells, M. (1996) *The Rise of the Network Society*, Blackwell, Oxford.

Castells, M. (1998), *End of Millennium*, Blackwell, Malden, MA.

Chazan, N. (1988) 'Patterns of state-society incorporation and disengagement in Africa' in D. Rothchild and N. Chazan (eds), *The Precarious Balance*, pp. 121–48, Westview Press, Boulder, CO.

Deyo, F.C., Doner, R.F. and Hershberg, E. (eds) (2001) *Economic Governance and the Challenge of Flexibility in East Asia*, Rowman and Littlefield Publishers, Lanham, MD.

Forrest, T. (1994) *The Advance of African Capital: The Growth of Nigerian Private Enterprise*, Edinburgh University Press for the International African Institute, Edinburgh.

Haan, H.C. (1999) 'MSE association and enterprise promotion in Africa' in K. King and S. McGrath (eds), *Enterprise in Africa: Between Poverty and Growth*, pp. 156–68, Intermediate Technology Publications, London.

Human Rights Watch/CLEEN (2002) 'The Bakassi Boys: the legitimation of murder and torture', *Human Rights Watch Reports* 14(5)A: 1–45.

Isichei, E.A. (1976) *A History of the Igbo People*, Macmillan, London.

Lovejoy, P.E. (1980) *Caravans of Kola: The Hausa Kola Trade, 1700–1900*, Ahmadu Bello University Press, Zaria, Nigeria.

McCormick, D. (1999) 'African enterprise clusters and industrialization: theory and reality', *World Development* 27: 1531–51.

Meagher, K. (2007) 'Hijacking civil society: the inside story of the Bakassi Boys vigilante group of south-eastern Nigeria', *Journal of Modern African Studies* 45:.89–115.

Meagher, K. (2009) 'Trading on faith: religious movements and informal economic governance in Nigeria', *The Journal of Modern African Studies* 45(1), 89–115.

Meagher, K. (2010) *Identity Economics: Social Networks and the Informal Economy in Nigeria*, James Currey, Suffolk, UK.

Portes, A., Castells, M. and Benton, L.A. (eds) (1989) *The Informal Economy: Studies in Advanced and Less Developed Countries*, Johns Hopkins University Press, Baltimore and London.

Rasmussen, J., Schmitz, H. and van Dijk, M.P. (eds) (1992) 'Flexible specialisation: a new view on small industry?', *IDS Bulletin* 23(3), July.

Schmitz, H. and Nadvi, K. (1999) 'Clustering and industrialization: introduction', *World Development* 27: 1503–14.

Ukiwo, U. (2002) 'Deus ex Machina or Frankenstein Monster? The changing roles of Bakassi Boys in eastern Nigeria', *Democracy and Development* 3: 39–51.

van Donge, J.K. (1995) 'The social nature of entrepreneurial success: three cases of entrepreneurial careers of Waluguru traders in Dar es Salaam', in S. Ellis and Y. A. Fauré (eds), pp. 188–202, *Entreprises et Entrepreneurs Africains*, Karthala-ORSTOM, Paris.

Weiss, L. (1987) 'Explaining the underground economy – State and social-structure', *British Journal of Sociology* 38: 216–34.

Wellman, B. (ed.) (1999) *Networks in the Global Village: Life in Contemporary Communities*, Westview Press, Boulder, CO.

Changing Work Patterns and Social Dynamics in Households, Communities and Nation-States

Body and soul: economic space, public morality and social integration of youth in Cameroon

Nantang Jua

As Cameroon's economic meltdown engendered a disappearance of conventional transition pathways, youths, determined to reclaim agency, began mapping out new paths with a view to reaching a final port of call. This required creating new social spaces as well as forms of capital. Connected youths sought to valorize this capital to access the state as purveyor of its accursed resources. The unconnected resorted to the extra-state realm, which provides a field of unlimited possibilities. A murky realm, it leads to a proliferation of magicians. Even the corporeal is valorized as underlined by the new visibility of football heroes and queens of the night in public spaces as well as their celebration. Transition of youths into these spaces while guaranteeing the youths newfound wealth and therefore social promotion and prestige does not insulate them from the economy of recommencement. But for this unlimited generation with fluid identities, this is not an insurmountable bar.

Introduction

Evidence of the disarticulation of African economies and their subsequent meltdown, attributable to Africa's fragmentary incorporation into neo-liberal capitalism, is proliferating, not least in Cameroon. Whether one attributes blame to the African response, as Afro-pessimists do, or to international financial institutions, the human suffering it causes remains the same. Its impact on youth, 'our silent other' and the 'lost generation', is readily observable in terms of society's dwindling capacity to integrate them socially (De Boeck and Honwana, 2000). Paradoxically, Cameroonian youth exude optimism and call themselves the 'unlimited generation'.[1] They constitute a counterculture that transgresses social limits and valorizes new forms of capital and space. Consciously reclaiming agency necessary for shaping their destinies, they refuse to be only acted upon and spoken for.

Youth is a socially, culturally and politically constructed category (ibid.; Comaroff and Comaroff, 2001). Thus quantifying the number of youths in any population is problematic. However numerous they may be, their presence is felt as the 'terrors of the present, the errors of the past, the prospects of a future, old hopes and new challenges' (Veloso cited in Comaroff and Comaroff, 2001: 92).

Youth's role in society comes to the fore in an environment of uncertainty in which social patterns and economic resources that were previously valued are unsettled, devalued or unattainable. Uncertainty here 'applies to both economic resources such as income opportunities, land, capital and political "goods" such as power, connections and influence' (Berner and Trulsson, 2000). This is observable in the realm of education where inequality as well as privilege are generated (Cruise O'Brien, 1996). However, education in Cameroon no longer produces the same privilege as in times of economic vibrancy, thereby denying many youth access to opportunities (Mbembe, 2001). Despite the disappearance of occupational pathways amidst national economic decline, the resilience of youth is striking.

Arguably, this optimism is attributable to the creation of new social spaces and forms of capital that enable youth to overcome the structural obstacles that would otherwise preclude many of them from attaining adult social goals (Wyn and White, 2000). On the whole, multi-positioning is the norm and many spaces that are manoeuvred into are transitional. Furthermore, the spatial movement belies the fungibility of capital. Youth and families adopt both deliberate planned and *ad hoc* strategies of action. In this way, the economy of street displaces the market economy in Cameroon (Berner, 2000). A youth counterculture is emerging as a means of managing that not only contradicts but also expresses Cameroon's economic quagmire. Various sub-cultures are accommodated within the counterculture, and it is the competition as well as cooperation between them that explains its chaotic nature (Werbner, 1996; Mbembe, 2001).

From economic growth to structural adjustment

Prior to 1986, social integration of youths in Cameroon was facilitated by a 7 per cent annual growth rate of GDP. Cameroon's economy was touted as 'a shining example for Africa' (Jua, 1991: 162). Ahmadou Ahidjo, Cameroon's president from independence until 1982, ensured judicious investment of revenue by 'tortoise walking' whereby 'if you keep your feet on the ground, you can feel the holes and go around them; but if you jump, you might land on one and get hurt' (Schiavo-Campo *et al.*, 1983). Structurally, the economy was dependent on the cash-crop production of coffee and cocoa. Industry remained underdeveloped and the public sector, as in most other African states, was swelling. The determination to stretch the state's outreach ensured its labour absorptive capacity.

In the five years following Paul Biya's appointment to the Presidency in 1982, the number of civil servants doubled to 160,000 causing the public-sector wage bill to balloon (Jua, 1991). Meanwhile, the country's oil production that came on stream in 1976 was a major contributor to Cameroon's 'Dutch disease', a condition in which the non-productive sector progressively outstrips the productive sector over time. The oil boom carried the seeds of its own destruction because the accumulated reserves of the oil economy were rapidly being dissipated.

Youth's preference for employment in the public sector was revealed in a 1985 survey (Lamlenn, 1985) (Table 7.1). About half of the sample population opted for state employment given that, in addition to the public sector *per se*, Cameroonian industry was overwhelmingly comprised of parastatal industries.

Even though salaries were good, rent-seeking was starting to surface. The public-service culture of employees was being edged out by aspirations of ostentatious consumption to the detriment of productive investments. Housing investments on the part of the civil service led to the mushrooming of exclusive neighbourhoods with names inspired by American television sitcoms, for example, Santa Barbara and Denver, as well as the tongue-in-cheek naming of one affluent neighbourhood *Quartier de la Douane* (Customs Neighbourhood). Reminiscent of the spatial residential divides engendered by colonialism, they constituted the symbolic architecture of power, empowering those living within these areas and prompting feelings of deprivation and insecurity on the part of the excluded.

Only 13 per cent of the youths stated a career preference for agriculture, which did not portend well for a country whose economic engine was agriculture. Decreasing government investment in this sector may have played some part in their disinterest.

Meanwhile, Cameroonian industry which was largely import-substituting in nature had a small domestic market and lacked foreign outlets given the similar nature of industries in neighbouring countries. The cumulative effect of various adverse economic factors marked the end of the Cameroonian economic miracle and the start of a steady decline in GDP between 1986 and 1989.

It is against this backdrop that Cameroon, prompted by the International Monetary Fund, embarked on a Structural Adjustment Programme (SAP) in

Table 7.1 Survey of youth's preferred sector of future economic involvement

Sector	Number	Percentage
Traditional agriculture	29	2.6
Modern agriculture	121	10.7
Public service	343	30.3
Industry	193	17.1
Commerce	112	9.9
Transportation	22	1.9
Other private business	152	13.4
Not stated/Do not know	159	14.1

Source: Lamlenn, 1985: 43

1988. SAP focused on reducing the public deficit and restoring the balance of payments. But despite deflationary measures and more than 20,000 ghost workers being laid off in 'Operation Antelope', the state still had a debt of more than 20 billion FCFA in payroll arrears in 1989. Salaries were reduced by 65 per cent between January and November 1993. While civil servants were still reeling from this shock, the FCFA was devalued by 50 per cent in January 1994 (Kouamé et al., 2001). Since consumption by civil servants largely drove the circulation of money in the economy, the effects of the foregoing measures were paralysing. Cameroon's per capita GNP dropped by 39 per cent between 1987 and 1997. As upward social mobility went into reverse, people devised coping mechanisms with a view to making ends meet.[2] Multiple livelihoods became the norm, as has been described for other parts of sub-Saharan Africa (Bank and Bryceson, 2001; Bryceson, 2002).

Salary reductions unsettled the positive correlation between cultural capital and income and engendered a status reversal. The older generation could no longer satisfy their household obligations to pay for family healthcare and school expenses, causing them to lose hope in the future as indexed by the decision of some to take early retirement.[3] No longer believing in the future, they invoked memories of the past. Contrary to Ahidjo's exhortation to Cameroonians in 1967 that they should '*enrichissez vous*' (enrich yourselves), policy declarations of the 1990s revealed that not only was Cameroon on a downward economic path but that social mobility was imploding as well (Mbembe and Roitman, 1995).[4]

Estimates of the national unemployment rate have varied from about half of the working-age population to the recent estimate of only 7 per cent as reported by the Minister of Employment, Labour and Social Insurance (*Cameroon Tribune*, 19 July 2001). World Bank (1994) figures confirm that a meteoric rise in Yaoundé's unemployment rate took place from 7 per cent in 1983 to 67 per cent in 1993. Despite this controversy over figures, there is an emerging consensus that unemployment is becoming a structural condition. Job opportunities in the formal sector have not increased despite a much-touted economic growth in the economy since 1999. Though SAP may have helped Cameroon to correct its macroeconomic policies through measures such as the reduction of the budget deficit, present trends have borne out Joseph Stiglitz's (2002) thesis that SAPs were a macroeconomic catastrophe resulting in high unemployment and limited growth.

Youth's formal job prospects have largely collapsed (Antoine et al., 2001) whereas formerly their parents enjoyed entry into a national labour market that could absorb everyone in the under-25 age category with at least a high-school diploma. Not surprisingly, these trends have had a dissonant effect on youth. Most youths no longer aim for good salaried jobs in the public sector to achieve 'their dreams about the future' (Lamlenn, 1985: 68). Mapping new biographic trajectories becomes imperative (Chuprov and Zubok, 2000).

The prevailing high unemployment rate affects some youths more than others. One's family and social connections help or hinder youth's employment search. President Biya has a habit of recruiting only children or protégées of the old party barons to the state's political commanding heights.[5] Meanwhile, the haemorrhage in public finances has pushed jobs beyond the reach of unconnected youths. To Biya's rhetorical question, 'what Cameroon would we want to leave for our children?', one youth retorted that Cameroon's leaders are 'eating as if there will be no tomorrow'.[6]

Youth discontent began crystallizing during their school years. Senfo Tonkam, the President of the National Coordination of Cameroon Students, sent a letter to Biya contending that higher education in Cameroon was 'sick and without repair' as evidenced in 'inadequate infrastructures, anachronism and arbitrariness' (*Cameroon Post*, 19 November 1990). Tonkam argued that university students in Cameroon were among the most wretched in Africa, facing poor housing conditions and nutritional levels, bad transport facilities, small scholarships, language barriers, and exploitation by their professors. Further, he requested that Biya look into the matter of growing unemployment rates among university graduates (Konings, 2002).

Tonkam's appeal failed to get a response. His group was identified with the opposition parties' clamouring for the introduction of liberal democracy in Cameroon. Instead of responding to the students' petition, the regime put an end to bursaries in 1990 with immediate and far-reaching effects. The amounts of these bursaries had been substantial. Thus, suddenly students from families that could not pay for their upkeep were excluded from university. Exclusion from tertiary education froze the movement between classes that was in gestation by denying the children of the poor the requisite cultural capital needed to access the subsumed class.

Lacking a future, these youths belonged to the 'lost generation'. Official discourse referring to them as the 'leaders of tomorrow' only served to highlight their plight. A popular comedian deformed Biya's call on youths to *retrousser les manches* ('roll back your sleeves') made in the 1987 at the onset of the crisis to *couper les manches* (translated in this context as 'cut off your hands').

Countering demoralization with political incentives: President Biya's youths

Smooth transitions from youth to adulthood afforded by job availability, security and income had guaranteed the political quiescence of the preceding generation of youths. In a survey of young people's attitudes, 84 per cent of a sample of 100 expressed disaffection for the state (Forkwang, 2002). With the disappearance of the certainty of a school-to-work pattern, the Cameroonian state recognized youth's potential for societal and political disruption, cognizant that job creation and political inclusion of youth were imperative for state stability. President Biya chose to dramatize his efforts by announcing the intake of groups of youths, no matter how small, into public-service employment. Thus, in his 2002 Youth Day speech, and with a view to conjuring up an image of a providential state, he reminded youths that 1,700 part-time primary-school teachers had been employed and 170 were in the process of being recruited.

Ostensibly to promote the ideals of 'rigour and moralization' while also gaining public visibility, some political entrepreneurs established a youth group called 'President Biya's Youths' (PRESBY) in 1996. Originally initiated in Yaoundé, the association now has national coverage with a reported membership of 120,000 and 7,900 officials (Forkwang, 2002). Reminiscent of Daniel Kanu's *Youths Earnestly Ask for Abacha* (YEAA) that orchestrated support for the Abacha regime in Nigeria, the organization has promoted political quiescence amongst the rank and file while conferring political leverage on its youthful leadership.

As Bourdieu (1984) argues, collective crisis triggers social shifts not least amongst youth whose differential reactions range from conformism to innovation. Conformists accept extant values and norms of society as well as the conventional modes of achievement while innovators map out new biographic trajectories. Youthful conformists in Cameroon gravitated to PRESBY.

In the context in which metaphors such as *njangi* ('you scratch my back and I'll scratch yours') are generally used to define the politics, PRESBY's growth in membership is largely driven by personal interest. Emphasizing reciprocal exchange, a national *Chargé de Mission* of PRESBY promised youths in Bui Division that joining the organization would deliver 'government favours' in the form of 30 scholarships to Bangladesh for those with Advanced Level certificates (Forkwang, 2002). Membership in PRESBY is commonly seen as a prerequisite for access to resources from the country's public and semi-public institutions. However, the payout is by no means guaranteed. Youths in PRESBY's rank and file face material disappointment, especially as everyone is obliged to pay membership fees. One young man explained that he had thought membership would help to recapitalize his failing business. With a view to proving his allegiance, he bought his uniform (a T-shirt), paid all the requisite contributions and devoted most of his time to PRESBY's activities. The net result was that his business folded and he was thoroughly disillusioned.[7] It is not uncommon for former members to view PRESBY as a scam designed by its leadership to appropriate money. The fact that PRESBY's national coordinator has yet to enunciate the organization's strategic vision and operational mechanics strengthens their view (*The Post*, 13 August 2001).

PRESBY's leaders are perceived as power brokers and feared even by provincial governors. Leadership positions are now coveted and fought over as demonstrated in the case of the South West Province. One of PRESBY's regional coordinators, Kendi, was removed from office when it was discovered that he was extorting money from people on the pretext that he would use the organization's connections to get them visas for European countries. His principal accuser was Provincial Secretary Enow Charles Eseme who replaced him at the helm of the organization then proceeded to embark on the same practices accompanied by boastful threats to anyone who challenged his power and authority.[8]

The frustrations of ambitious youth who have not been able to get leadership positions in PRESBY have prompted some to create their own movements. Among these are *L'Association des Camerounais Biyaristes* (ACB), *Jeunesse Actives pour Chantal Biya* (JACHABI),[9] *Movement of Youths for the Presidential Majority* (MYMP) and *Youths for the Support of those in Power* (YOSUPO). Similarly, they have tended to use their positions to extort money from public officials.[10] YOSUPO was formed by a group of young people who had worked closely with PRESBY's national coordinator but came to resent the fact that the national coordinator was 'eating alone' (*The Post*, 1 June 2001). Some officials have decried these venal practices. One of those who resigned from PRESBY argued: 'So long as one remains at the level of shouting the slogan "rigour and moralization", there would be no conflict with colleagues. The trouble only starts when you try to caution against or moralize them on issues like embezzlement and other corrupt practices' (*The Post*, 13 August 2001). Against this backdrop, it is clear that the overlapping professed goals of these groups do not provide a basis for cooperation. On the contrary, cooperation endangers their individual political space and leverage.

Creating new economic spaces: *Bricolage, débrouillardisme and zouazoua*

Though rewards of one sort or another may derive from belonging to youth organizations, most members do not depend on them financially. Like other youths, they actively participate in the informal economy or what has been referred to as the 'sidewalk economy', a space encompassing a full range of occupations from mechanics, barbers and dentists to food vendors (Decoudras and Lenoble-Bart, 1996). The adage 'need is the mother of invention' is continually played out here. The vibrancy of the informal economy rests on material scarcity. The term *bricolage* refers to the fact that commerce is based on inventive use of ready-at-hand materials of often questionable quality and durability. Cars that have supposedly lived out their life-span in Europe are given a new lease of life. It is not uncommon for the bodywork of a refrigerator to be used to patch up the body of a car. Mechanics may use scrap material of any description to make a new top cylinder gasket or deploy an old tyre to reinforce a bolt joint (Elder, 2000).

Along similar lines, *débrouillardise* (management) refers to the practice of seeing everything as repairable. Cellular phones, for example, can be fixed by anyone with the determination to do so. Mme Wam-ba Fotso's Siemens phone stopped working two weeks after she received it from Europe. She took it to her brother who is an electrical engineer. When he failed to diagnose the problem, the phone was taken to a computer expert. Ultimately, it was taken to a second-hand clothes trader who recently switched to repairing telephones at the Commercial Center in Market A in Bafoussam. All three of them gave a different diagnosis, ranging from starting problems to a defective battery and motherboard. Among the three *débrouilleurs*, the telephone repairer is intriguing because he was formerly a trader in second-hand clothing. As Ono-hiolo (2002) notes: 'Repair and maintenance shops are mushrooming where magicians without any expertise are making good business. For a majority of them, their only expertise is their aesthetical advertising boards. Those who are more daring even become itinerant repairers and in some cases ground-nut traders have transformed their stalls into repair workshops for cellular phones.'

The number of 'magicians' has ballooned. Fees for deposit and diagnosis of the problems in the case of cellular phones range from 2,500 to 5,000 FCFA. These add up to substantial earnings as it is common to find hundreds of phones in a workshop. Most are in fact second-hand phones imported from Europe that are defective from the outset. Furthermore, their maintenance problems are aggravated by their use as public phones. In Douala one frequently sees people seated at tables by the roadsides with cell phones that the public can use for a fee. These 'booths' now compete with the normal public phone booths. Adaptability of any article increases the owner's chances of a livelihood.

It would be mistaken to think that this informal economy, considered as more or less legal, is restricted only to poor neighbourhoods like Bépanda, Cameroon's 'far urban west' (Kouamouo, 2002: 34). Conquest and accretion of central spaces, even on a piecemeal basis, is important as presence here enhances the probability of victories in the 'war against uncertainty' (Mbembe, 2000: 271). This calculus explains the reticence of hawkers or street vendors to occupy the spaces provided for them in the market. In Douala, for example, they prefer to site themselves at the Deido roundabout where the town's main streets intersect. Admittedly, the need to escape the regulatory powers of the state plays a key role in choosing this location. It is easy for informal trades at this busy intersection to evade paying taxes on their goods, giving them a competitive edge over registered traders. They, in turn, have tried to retaliate by hiring people who can hawk their goods informally in this area, thereby blurring the distinction between formal and informal economies. The municipality has therefore tried to regain control of this central space by deploying a private militia, the Cobras, to attack the hawkers and seize their trading goods, as reported by one of the hawkers: '[t]hey weakened us with tear gas and started seizing our goods, even from the cigarette vendors. As for me personally, they seized watches valued at more than 200,000 CFA francs. I have lost all of [my] watches and I don't know how I can get them back' (Jua, 2000: 23).

Tax evasion is also the basis of the *zouazoua* trade. Illegally smuggled Nigerian petrol is popularly known as *zouazoua* in Cameroon. The trade has flourished because of the high level of taxation on local petroleum products[11] compared with *zouazoua* and the minimal start-up capital requirements for *zouazoua* trading.

Youths are mainly engaged in the *zouazoua* trade. Gender is not a barrier as evidenced by the Ikom Line Women. Aged between 18 and 25, they resorted to petrol smuggling because of their disdain for farm work or their lack of access to farmland (Niger-Thomas, 2000). In Mamfe, the Batcha Boys, who ranged between 16 and 35 years of age, controlled the trade in smuggled goods on the John Holt Beach at the Cross River, setting prices for offloading *zouazoua* from riverboats. Any attempt at government interference was deeply resented and one customs officer on night patrol on the beach in 1988 was killed. The trade spawned a number of other income-earning opportunities. For example, the Batcha Boys had female members who served in an auxiliary status, involved only in the sale of cooked foods, cigarettes and drinks to their male counterparts (ibid.).

The *zouazoua* trade was extensive because of the porous borders between the two countries. In Buea, capital of the South West Province, roughly 200 kilometres from Mamfe, gas points selling *zouazoua* sprouted up every few hundred metres. Business was so brisk that several petrol stations were unable to compete and others managed to stay in business only by switching their source of supply from the Cameroonian refining company SONARA to smuggled *zouazoua*.

The proliferation of informal gas points across the country represented an enormous fiscal loss to the state estimated at 30 billion FCFA per year (Ohayon, 1993). Emphasis on expanding the government's tax base under SAP made stopping this leakage imperative. To this end, strong pressure was exerted on local administrators to counter the trade. Their obligation to increase tax revenues by halting the trade in *zouazoua* was complemented by promotion as a reward for those who succeeded. Confronted with two choices – service to the state or supplementing their earnings – frontline officials opted for a win–win situation. Paying lip-service to the maintenance of law and order, they raided gas points but the petrol seized in most instances was never destroyed. It is generally believed that most was used for the benefit of the officials. It is this ambivalence that caused a Batcha Boy to note: 'How could we have stopped selling *funge* (*zouazoua*) when we have no other means of livelihood? They, who earn government salaries, seize *funge*. Instead of destroying it or putting the money (accrued from the sales) in government banks since they say they are keeping the law, they themselves make use of it and drive their cars. So they are criminals like we are' (cited in Niger-Thomas, 2000: 53). This, in the view of most people, made the state unfit to enforce the law of the land.

Against this backdrop, Biya created Opération Dorade, a military operation which, insofar as it involved the seizure and destruction of all *zouazoua*, adopted a tactic similar to a scorched-earth policy. Day and night raids were common. Soldiers stopped car owners on the road and asked them to siphon petrol from their tanks for control purposes. The soldiers succeeded in stockpiling large quantities of fuel that were used to initiate parallel distribution and trading networks. Senior officers acting under the pretext of re-establishing law and order were the biggest beneficiaries whose returns were only dented when *zouazoua* retailers succeeded in setting up rackets in collusion with junior officers, leaving their trade largely unscathed except for the higher transaction costs they paid.

Proceeds from the sale of *zouazoua* enabled some youths to embark on successful entrepreneurial careers. Though acknowledging the *zouazoua* trade as illegal, one of them ascribed its importance to the fact that it had enabled him to buy his fleet of cabs and sponsor his kin through university. He went further in justifying it by arguing that there is no public morality in the country as the leaders themselves have converted the state into a resource.[12] Others informed by world-class models of success and consumerism have used the proceeds to finance ostentatious lifestyles (Comaroff and Comaroff, 2001). Materialism, however, is not restricted to individual selfish gain. Alhadji Petel named his gas point 'Hollywood' for civic-minded developmental purposes: 'to start with, Hollywood is one of the great cities of the United States and I hope you're aware of the ambience that reigns there. A lively city at all hours, twenty-four hours a day; rich, pretty to live in. To me, Hollywood is money, cleanliness, wealth in general. Thanks to the resources I have from selling gas, I would like, if God permits, to make my entourage, my neighbourhood, a Hollywood. ...It's my dream, it's a point of reference' (cited in Roitman, 1998: 319).

Roitman (1998) has located the trade in *zouazoua* and other contraband in the context of political liberalization, emphasizing its symbolism for those engaged in it. People interpreted the meaning of 'democracy' as 'the freedom to engage in commerce regardless of means', with a view to escaping poverty.

Rent-seeking is not peculiar to the *zouazoua* trade. Its institutionalization and the impunity with which it permeates Cameroonian commerce are generally marked by the defiant attitude of those involved in it. Most rent-seeking goes unchecked because of the vertical nature of its operational networks and the heavy involvement of state officialdom at all levels. However, certain categories of people are periodically targeted as scapegoats or persistently harassed. Youth involved in contraband trade in urban areas are more vulnerable than youth operating in border areas. Two factors account for this. First, though SAP emphasized efficiency and maximization of revenue recovery, it also paradoxically reduced the capacity of the state to fulfil this goal. Downsizing government establishments and divesting state officials of their government vehicles deprived them of the personnel and logistical support to carry out tax collection. In many cases, the state was forced to enlist the assistance of on-site volunteers whose dedication to state revenue collection was questionable (Jua, 1991).[13] Second, and exacerbating the problems of border control, is the existence of youth as a floating population with commercial networks straddling national borders. Carrying multiple passports, youth can reinvent themselves in time and space so as to avoid any fiscal relationship with the state (Roitman, 1998).

Valorizing corporeality: Football heroes and queens of the night

Extenuating circumstances render permissible practices that would otherwise be considered only in the realm of the imagination in normal times. Everything becomes negotiable as new spheres of economic activity open up.

Increasingly youthful individuals realize that their bodies are a store of value that can be valorized and commoditized within various entertainment industries, notably spectator sports and prostitution (Berner, 2000). With the requisite knowledge, both indigenous and Western, the individual can capitalize on his/her body. Corporeality or body capital is the outcome of one's endowment from birth including one's capabilities, health history and entitlements to the labour of others. Stress is on innate qualities and their creative use.

Contrary to Kennedy's (1990) argument, education is now de-emphasized as it no longer guarantees access to privileges. However, families continue to be influential in decisions about their children's life choices[14] and parents have been actively involved in the choice of new corporeal trajectories for their children. This is illustrated in a programme broadcast by Cameroon Radio and Television entitled *Just for Fun*.[15] In one of the programme's short sketches, a woman is depicted returning home from work with a football for her son. In the ensuing dialogue, she urges her son, who was doing his mathematics homework, to play football so as to earn a lot of money like a neighbour's son: 'Don't you see that Kameni has even built a house for his mother? Where do you think that he got the money from?' The answer is football, which is generally seen as offering potentially huge returns on investment. The performance of the Indomitable Lions in the World Cup has led to a profound revalorization of football.

The national team members' earnings have received extensive press coverage. Furthermore, their demands for the prompt payment of their bonuses and their militant stand when they refused to leave France en route to the World Cup in South Korea/Japan until the government rectified defaults in their payments, are public knowledge. These footballers are recognized as people with tremendous economic power in terms of the magnitude and certainty of their earnings – so unlike most Cameroonians who are struggling for a livelihood in the informal sector.

Appreciation of football as a lucrative alternative pathway explains the mushrooming of sports academies in the country. In South West Province, three academies have been heavily over-subscribed. Kadji Defosso of the Kadji Sports Academy, arguably the most reputable in the country and one that has sold several footballers to European teams, calls this his *écurie* (stable). The academy owners' interests are in selling their players for large profits. Scouts now roam neighbourhoods in search of potential players eager to sign contracts with the dream of marching upward to the national and international football leagues. The boundaries between the accessible and inaccessible in the furtherance of their goals are overlooked and the fact that occasionally single outstanding individuals enjoy a meteoric rise from nowhere fuels the expectations of the youthful masses. Locational remoteness is not seen as an impediment. Afterall, Effa was recruited by a Belgian club during the finals of the holiday football championship in Oman, a small village in the heart of Cameroon's equatorial forest.[16]

Young Anglophones in the English-speaking part of Cameroon view football as a means to social but also political promotion in the face of their marginalization in the political arena.[17] Roger Milla, Cameroon's star football player, illustrates this point. His football prowess has made his name synonymous with the country. He received the *Chevalier de l'Ordre de la Valeur Camerounaise* (Cameroonian Knight of the Order of Valour) and was invited to be one of Cameroon's roving ambassadors with all the rights and privileges that go with such a title. Recently, his name appeared in the Larousse dictionary, significantly only the third Cameroonian (after Ahmadou Ahidjo and Paul Biya) to feature in this publication, and in spite of the fact that he does not have a university education. Since in popular Anglophone consciousness, the regime's policy is to devalorize all Anglophones or see them as deficient, the belief that they can gain national recognition or visibility by excelling in the international sports arena where aptitude and capability are privileged is now commonplace.

While young men's hopes and aspirations are pinned on the fame and fortune of a foreign football pitch, the actual success rate is extremely limited. By contrast, young women seeking glamour and fun in their working lives find a cash-yielding corporeal profession readily at hand. Prostitution attracts tens of thousands of young women, quickly robbing them of their youthfulness. In Douala, for instance, prostitution thrives at *Carrefour j'ai raté ma vie* ('my life has failed' roundabout). Explaining the sedimented history behind the name, Basile, a photographer whose studio is located there, attributed it not to the bar with nude dancers but to the presence of many *filles de joie* or *les reines de la nuit* ('queens of the night'). *Carrefour j'ai raté ma vie* seems to be an oxymoron but the meaning becomes clear when juxtaposed with the prostitutes' lexicon. Getting a potential client requires an 'attack' on their 'prey', generally men venturing alone into 'their territory' (Manu, 2002). The inference is that life is harsh, brutish and short in this Hobbesian space. Indeed, it is common for prostitutes to have difficulties feeding themselves, despite their extreme cost-cutting accommodation where five or more may share a one-bedroom apartment.[18]

Life is difficult but not desolate, and though desperate, the prostitutes are not despondent. They have the power to dynamize other sectors of the economy and, in recognition of this vibrancy, it is claimed: '*il y a mouvement* (there is movement) wherever there are *filles de joie*'. People are ferried by taxi or 'bendskin' (motor-bike taxi). Their clients fill the bars, nightclubs and inns as well as the casinos and game rooms. In effect, prostitution reduces the ranks of the army of the unemployed. Male youths earn fees for finding prostitutes for clients. Outside, women and children sell snacks and fruit. In the crowd, there are thieves who benefit from the cover of darkness to drag their victims to abandoned, half-finished buildings in the vicinity.[19]

Revalorization of commercial sex has led to an increased visibility for prostitutes who are no longer self-quarantined in specific neighbourhoods such as Nkané in Douala or Briquetterie in Yaoundé. Even student neighbourhoods have taken on the semblance of red-light districts. Producing a revised cartography, prostitution has new temporal dimensions as well, now being a 24-hour occupation rather than only nocturnal.

Historically, prostitutes in Cameroon were seen as underachievers, belonging to an uneducated, profligate underclass. However, with the arrival of economic uncertainty and the shifts that it has triggered in symbolic boundaries, even those endowed with middle-class values of diligence and social achievement have been known to invade this space. Their appropriation of this space is accompanied by optimism that it will bring about their upward mobility in stark contrast to the uneducated *filles de joie* who cannot combine cultural capital with their body capital to achieve a superior market position.

A case in point is Marie-Agnès B., who holds a Bachelor of Arts degree from the University of Yaoundé. In her own words: 'I know what I want: money. I have a lot of dreams and ambitions and I want my life to be a fairy tale. And to realize this, I have to look for money where it is found, that is to say, in men's pockets.' She stands in as the wife of foreign businessmen and facilitates their connections in the Cameroonian business milieu and works as an escort to closet homosexuals. For playing the latter role, an Italian businessman paid her a million CFA francs a week, which is the equivalent to five months' salary for a top Cameroonian civil servant (*Cameroon Tribune*, 1 December 2000). Unlike the women of *Carrefour j'ai raté ma vie*, she rents an apartment in Bastos, an exclusive neighbourhood occupied mostly by ministers and Yaoundé's diplomatic community.

Marie-Agnès B. is empowered by her language proficiency and level of education. Imitating prostitutes that she has seen in Western films, she has business cards to distribute to barmen and in hotels frequented by Europeans and the rich, and relies heavily on her cellular phone for contact with clients (*Cameroon Tribune*, 1 December 2000). By contrast, her counterparts at *Carrefour j'ai raté ma vie* lack the start-up capital to buy a phone and, in any case, most of their clientele are not in possession of mobile phones.

Pentecostal churches have tapped into the economic insecurities and guilt embedded in the expansion of prostitution. One Pentecostal congregation in Bamenda consists primarily of prostitutes. The attraction of this church and others is the millennium message to its 'brothers and sisters' that cites biblical evidence interpreted to mean that they can all become millionaires.[20] Of course, one cannot exclude the fact that the AIDS pandemic is causing them to think that belonging to the church may also help insulate them from this scourge (Gruenais, 1999).

Whole families benefit from the earnings from prostitution. Remittances are vital in a context where traditional safety networks are disappearing. Many families depend on remittances for their upkeep, and accepting money earned through prostitution is in itself proof that the cultural taboos against the practice no longer have the powers of sanction. Some parents even actively encourage this, attesting to a shift in valuation from the girl-child as an asset to the girl as proto-adult. The distinction is no longer made between dirty and clean money.

The spread of prostitution or what has been referred to as 'unbridled corporeal free enterprise' (van Dijk, 2001: 574) puts into broad relief some of the contradictions that haunt the state's role in defining public morality, even if this is only with a view to promoting governance. Cameroonian law identifies prostitution as a crime and prescribes a six-month prison term and heavy fines for prostitutes and their clients respectively. The tendency is to focus on the letter of the law while relegating the contradictions involved in its implementation to the background. The fact that men in high political office are some of the prostitutes' main clientele and see a symbiosis between sex and power helps to explain the slippage in adherence and enforcement of the law.

Wheel of fortune: Fungible capital and transitional space

Youth who manage to acquire quick and substantial amounts of money have become celebrities. Their social ascendancy has enabled them to rival the political class, as demonstrated by their consumer tastes and their tendency to move to the same neighbourhoods. However, while their newly found wealth is a means to social promotion and prestige, they still lack political power that would bring them into the national mainstream and give them immunity. To a large extent, only involvement in politics can insulate them from 'the economy of recommencement' (De Latour, 2001b: 170) while also enhancing their chances for more accumulation. This power is obtained either through invitation or opportunistically seeking political patronage and influence.

Youths who now enter political space are usually seeking to benefit from the generalized criminalization of the state. Honourable Lawrence Mongkuo, one of the youngest members of Cameroon's National Assembly, was caught in Paris with 30 kg of cannabis. When interrogated by the police, he claimed that the money earned from its sale was supposed to be used to finance his campaign. Following his return to Cameroon, he retracted this statement, saying that he accepted responsibility for the drugs in the hotel room simply to cover up for a friend.[21] Mongkuo had a diplomatic passport that shielded him from French jurisdiction but his behaviour has to be understood as part of the amorality of a disintegrating state whose representatives are no longer accountable to an electorate or civil-service code. Instead, the exchange relationships of patron-client relations serve as a popular ethical code for leaders that is readily transparent to all. Thus a member of the Assembly must invest personally in projects in his area of jurisdiction. Youth and others who hold elected office but lack economic power to serve as patrons in this way must engage in illicit activities to obtain the requisite finance. The moral rewards and hazards are clear.

Conclusion

Cameroon's structural adjustment programme marked the beginning of its economic decline and a breakdown in social integration. Youth, as the social category that was most vulnerable to these changes, reacted collectively by calling for macro-structural change and individually by mapping out new biographic trajectories needed to negotiate their transition to adulthood and to find an anchor in a context of uncertainty. State contraction and the disintegration of its regulatory role provided them with an opportunity to create alternative political and economic spaces. Some deliberately sought involvement with the state through PRESBY, while others concentrated on creating new economic spaces embracing *bricolage, débrouillardise* and tax evasion.

Innovation led to the mapping out of new occupational pathways and the normalization of hitherto ethically unacceptable practices like prostitution. New biographic trajectories such as prostitution and football have required the valorization of different kinds of capital, notably body capital. Ultimately success has depended on the composition of one's stock of capital.

Despite deteriorating job prospects in the national economy, youth were active agents, claiming control over their work lives and resource acquisition (Heinz, 2000). They have reacted creatively to uncertainty and devised a counterculture, pre-occupied with individual survival-cum-jackpot winnings rather than respecting the social contract that had hitherto bound them to society. The emphasis is on devising strategies for multiple livelihoods. Movement between spaces as well as multi-positionality characterizes the dynamics of youthful endeavour. Since adult status is seen as being entirely contingent on gainful employment, Cameroonian youths are in this sense different from their counterparts in the West who attribute value not only to work careers but also to leisure (Wyn and White, 2000).

Opting for trajectories that depart from those of their parents, and that are therefore seen as unconventional, may suggest that the latter are not involved in the making of their choices. Though largely individual strategies, those undertaking them in most cases are not necessarily the sole financial beneficiaries. The families of youths are often involved in decisions regarding the youth's working life, especially if they are destined to directly benefit from the earnings. Lack of parental involvement, as in the case of prostitution for instance, does not necessarily translate into moral disapproval insofar as they may readily accept remittances.

The state evidences a moral dilemma in which the laws on controlling prostitution are in place, but state officials do not implement them and are often personally supportive of a flourishing market for prostitution. Similarly, when law and order considerations have been pronounced by the state, the situation simply provides state functionaries with opportunities for rent-seeking either with a view to fostering economic livelihoods or accumulation. Individual and collective actions by state officials reveal the lack of a law-abiding morality in a period of chaos.

It is against this background that *sans souci* considerations become a defining principle in the everyday life of youths. Life becomes an adventure, a field of unlimited possibilities with no holds barred. In the words of Mbembe, they 'mobilize[s] not just a single "identity", but several fluid identities which, by their very nature, must be constantly "revised" in order to achieve maximum instrumentality and efficacy as and when required' (Mbembe, 1992: 5). Indeterminacy becomes an asset and helps explain their identification as the unlimited generation.

About the author

Nantang Jua is an associate professor and interim chair in the department of social sciences at South Carolina State University. His research interests are in international economic relations and the politics of the post-colonial state in Africa. He has published articles in several international journals such as *Africa, African Affairs, African Studies Review* and *Cahiers d'etudes africaines*. He has been a Senior Fulbright Fellow at the School of International Advanced studies in Johns Hopkins University in Washington, DC, a Rockefeller Humanities Fellow at the University of Michigan in Ann Arbor and Visiting Research Fellow at the African Studies Center in Leiden. He has also served as an international consultant for the United Nations Development Programme and the World Bank.

Notes

1. Though introduced into public space by the Cigarette Company, the phrase 'unlimited generation' has been colonized by the youth and its meaning subverted. Rather than referring to the cigarette, it is now used to describe youths who see their life chances as unlimited (Jua, 2001).
2. It became commonplace for university professors to use their cars at night as taxis or to earn cash on the side through the sale of home videos, cooked food or extra tutoring.
3. These decisions were predicated on a utilitarian calculus. By retiring, they earned benefits that were, paradoxically, more than their salaries. At the same time, they could begin to earn more income by contracting their expertise/services to the government at this juncture where the Washington Consensus was encouraging the promotion of local businesses (Jua, 2001).
4. See World Bank/IFC/MIGA, *Official Memorandum*, Annex 1, 15 November 1994, p.12.
5. See *Le Messager*, 7 July 2000. A.N., a son of Biya's friend who was a cadre in a bank in Douala, was appointed as Minister of Finance. T.M., who graduated from the University of Yaoundé with a law degree was named the Director General of the National Corporation for Oil Distribution. Commenting on malfeasance as a culture of this group, the Bishops of Cameroon noted in a pastoral letter: they 'can buy almost anything that

they want and offer the bribes necessary to obtain certificates' (Bishops of Cameroon, n.d., para. 26).

6. Author's conversation with a youth at the launching of the Social Democratic Front (SDF) in Bamenda, 26 May 1990.

7. Interview with a former PRESBY member in Likoko-Mimbea, 27 August 2001.

8. He extorted money from provincial parastatals including PAMOL, the South-West Development Authority (SOWEDA) and the CDC and collected money from state employees by threatening them with punitive transfers or cajoling them with promises of promotions. 'The situation was exacerbated in Meme Division and Kumba in particular (where) he even boasted that he will take over from Akpo Mukete as the (National) President of the YCPDM' (*The Post*, 17 November 2000).

9. JACHABI was launched at Yaoundé's Hilton Hotel under the patronage of Madame Chantal Biya, Cameroon's First Lady. This organization sought to promote her ideals, which were not well articulated to the public.

10. Illustrative of this is the case of Benakouma, an official of the ACB who was imprisoned for trafficking his influence (*Le Messager*, 1 September 1999).

11. The differentials between Nigerian and Cameroonian petrol prices accounted for the spiral in this trade. In 1993 Cameroonian petrol was 300 times more expensive than in Nigeria (*Africa International,* no. 266, November 1993, 49).

12. Conversation with a petrol seller during Opération Dorade, Buea, 1993.

13. The Egbekaw Beach Boys, an informal group not registered with the state, had full powers on the beach in Mamfe and helped the government in determining and collecting customs revenue (Niger-Thomas, 2000).

14. Forkwang (2002) found that 49 per cent of his survey of youthful respondents indicated that their families had some influence on their decisions about their life choices, while 46 percent said their families were *very* influential.

15. Monthly Cameroon Radio and Television programme aired in 2000.

16. As in most trading negotiations, falsehoods are used to increase the value of players. In this particular case, Effa, who had been suspended as a player in the second-division team of Fenerbache in Center Province for a two-year period, was presented as a Cameroonian national player (*Le Messager*, 15 October 2001).

17. For details on the Anglophone problem, see Konings and Nyamnjoh 1997.

18. Writing about this same phenomenon in Côte d'Ívoire, De Latour (2001a) notes that prostitutes' revenues are supplemented in some cases by petty theft, rackets and rip-offs. She also shows that the playing field is not level as the prettier prostitutes, who have a higher probability of attracting clientele, are referred to as *democrats* and the less attractive ones as *déchireuses*.

19. Such private and public structures left half-built as a result of the economic crisis abound and are the sovereign territory of thieves. The most notorious is the uncompleted high-rise ministerial building in Yaoundé,

dubbed *L'Immeuble de la Mort* (the House of Death), a space impervious to the forces of law and order.
20. This is common practice all over Africa. Traders have invested in religious temples and miracles are performed on demand. In one case in Nigeria, a minister of a Pentecostal church claimed that God had made him custodian of all the wealth in the Bermuda Triangle, empowering him to distribute it to his congregation. However, potential beneficiaries had to contribute an advance fee of ten per cent of the amount they hoped to receive (*Africa Confidential* 43(14), 12 July 2002: 2).
21. Sibatcheu, M. 2002, 'Me Mongkuo nie ses crimes' in *Le Messager*, http://www.lemessager.net/1356.

References

Antoine, P., Razafindrakoto, M. and Roubaud, F. (2001) 'Contraints de rester jeunes? Evolution de l'insertion des trois capitals Africaines: Dakar, Yaoundé, Antananarivo', *Autrepart* 18: 17–36.

Bank, L. and D.F. Bryceson (eds) (2001) *Livelihoods, Linkages and Policy Paradoxes*, Special Issue of *Journal of Contemporary African Studies* 19(1): 1–23.

Berner, B. (2000) 'Manoeuvring in uncertainty: on agency, strategies and negotiations' in B. Berner and P. Trulsson (eds), *Manoeuvring in an Environment of Uncertainty*, Ashgate, Aldershot UK.

Berner, B. and Trulsson, P. (2000) 'Structural change and social action in Sub-Sahara Africa: an introduction' in B. Berner and P. Trulsson (eds), *Manoeuvring in an Environment of Uncertainty*, Ashgate, Aldershot UK.

Bishops of Cameroon (no date) *Of Goodwill on Corruption*, Yaoundé.

Bourdieu, P. (1984) *Distinction*, Harvard University Press, Cambridge MA.

Bryceson, D.F. (2002) 'Multiplex livelihoods in rural Africa: recasting the terms and conditions of gainful employment', *Journal of Modern African Studies* 40(1): 1–28.

Chuprov, V. and J. Zubok (2000) 'Integration versus exclusion: youth and the labor market in Russia', *International Social Science Journal* 164: 171–82.

Comaroff, J. and Comaroff, J. (2001) 'Refléxions sur la jeunesse', *Autrepart* 80: 90–110.

Cruise O'Brien, D.B. (1996) 'A lost generation: youth identity and state decay in Africa' in R. Werbner and T. Ranger (eds), *Postcolonial Identities in Africa*, Zed Books, London.

De Boeck, F. and Honwana, A. (2000) 'Faire et défaire la société: enfants, jeunes et politique en Afrique', *Politique Africaine* 80: 5–11.

Decoudras, P. and Lenoble-Bart, A. (1996) 'La rue: le décor et l'envers', *Politique Africaine* 63: 3–12.

De Latour, E. (2001a) 'Métaphores socials dans les ghettos de Côte-d'Ivoire', *Autrepart* 18: 151–67.

De Latour, E. (2001b) 'Du ghetto au voyage clandestin: la métaphore héroïque', *Autrepart* 19: 155–76.

Elder, T. (2000) 'The way of the bricoleur', in B. Berner and P. Trulsson (eds), *Manoeuvring in an Environment of Uncertainty*, Ashgate, Aldershot UK.

Forkwang, J. (2002) 'An "Unlimited Generation"? Youth, Intersubjectivity and the State in Cameroon', Paper presented at a conference on 'Understanding Exclusion, Creating Value: African Youth in a Global Age', 7–10 June, Dakar, Senegal.

Gruenais, M-E. (1999) 'La religion préserve-t-elle du Sida? Des congregations religieuses Congolaise face à la pandemie de l'infection par HIV', *Cahiers d'Etudes Africaines*, XXXIX (2)154: 252–70.

Heinz, W.R. (2000) 'Youths' transition and employment in Germany', *International Social Science Journal* 164: 161–70.

Jua, N. (1991) 'Cameroon: jumpstarting an economic crisis', *Africa Insight* 21(3): 162–70.

Jua, N. (2000) 'Spatial politics and political stability in Cameroon', *Dialogue and Reconciliation* 1: 35–60.

Kennedy, P. (1990) *African Capitalism: The Struggle for Ascendancy,* Cambridge University Press, Cambridge.

Konings, P. (2002) 'University students' revolt, ethnic militia and violence during political liberalization in Cameroon', *African Studies Review* 45(2): 179–204.

Konings, P. and Nyamnjoh, F.B. (1997) 'The Anglophone problem in Cameroon', *Journal of Modern African Studies* 35(2): 207–29.

Kouamé, A., Kishimba, N., Kuépié, M. and Tameko, D. (2001) *Crise, Réformes des Politiques Economiques et Emploi à Yaoundé,* Les Dossiers du CEPED, no. 64, Paris.

Kouamouo, T. (2002) 'Bépanda-Cameroun: un Far West urbain', *L'Autre Afrique* 22: 34–5.

Lamlenn, B.S. (1985) 'Cameroonian Youths in Transition', Institute of Human Sciences, March (unpublished manuscript), Yaoundé.

Manu, P. (2002) 'Carrefour J'ai Raté Ma Vie', *Le Messager*, http://www.lemessager.net/

Mbembe, A. (1992) 'Provisional notes on the postcolony', *Africa* 62(1): 3–37.

Mbembe, A. (2000) 'Everything can be negotiated: ambiguities and challenges in a time of uncertainty', in B. Berner and P. Trulsson (eds), *Manoeuvring in an Environment of Uncertainty,* Ashgate, Aldershot UK.

Mbembe, A. (2001) *On the Postcolony,* University of California Press, Berkeley.

Mbembe A. and Roitman, J. (1995) 'Figures of the subject in times of crisis', *Public Culture* VII(2): 323–52.

Niger-Thomas, M. (2000) 'Women and the art of smuggling in western Cameroon', *CODESRIA Bulletin* 2–4: 45–61.

Ohayon, P-Y. (1993) 'Que faire face à la baisse des recettes?', *Africa International* 266: 48–9.

Onohiolo, S. (2002) 'Les Sorciers du Cellulaire', *Le Messager*, http://www.lemessager.net/1361.

Roitman, J. (1998) 'The garrison – entrepôt', *Cahiers d'Études Africaines* XXXVIII: 297–329.

Schiavo-Campo, S., Roush, J.L *et al.* (1983) 'Private Sector: The Tortoise Walk: Public Policy and Private Activity in the Economic Development of Cameroon', USAID Evaluation Special Study, No. 10, March, PN-AAL-004.

Stiglitz, J. (2002) *Globalization and Its Discontents,* Allen Lane, London.

van Dijk, R. 2001, '"Voodoo" on the doorstep: young Nigerian prostitutes and magic policing in the Netherlands', *Africa* 71(4): 558–86.

Werbner, R. (1996) 'Multiple identities, plural arenas', in R. Werbner and T. Ranger (eds), *Postcolonial Identities in Africa*, pp. 1–25, Zed Books, London.

World Bank (1994) *Cameroon: Diversity, Growth and Poverty Reduction*, World Bank, Report no.13167 CM, Washington DC.

Wyn, J. and White, R. (2000) 'Negotiating social change: the paradox of youth', *Youth and Society* 32(2): 165–83.

CHAPTER 8

Between family and market: urban informal workers' networks and identities in Bissau, Guinea-Bissau*

Ilda Lindell

People making a living in the informal economy of Bissau, Guinea-Bissau, make use of a variety of social networks and of multiple identities. This chapter discusses both those networks that facilitate accumulation and those that sustain survival. It explores the relation between social networks and identity formation in a changing urban work environment. Social networks constitute arenas for the formation of identities, including both the reaffirmation of deeply rooted kinds of affinities and the construction of alternative senses of belonging. At the same time, networks are constructed through the instrumental deployment of identities. However, while identities may be multiple and flexible and networks continuously constructed, the individual's choices of identities and networks are not unconstrained. They are limited by the power that is exercised within and through networks and by practices of exclusion. Material constraints may also discourage many from enacting other identities to which they may aspire, because of the trade-offs involved.

Introduction

The conditions under which African urban dwellers make a living have changed significantly in the context of policies of structural adjustment and a marginal position in the global economy. In the face of poor availability of wage jobs and declining real wages, urbanites increasingly rely on informal ways of income earning. Thus, while most African cities have long been characterised by the presence of an 'informal sector', they are now experiencing new waves of 'informalization' (Bryceson, 2006; Hansen and Vaa, 2004). Large segments of urban informal workers have however experienced a decline in incomes, as urban purchasing power has fallen, operation costs have risen and exploitation has intensified under conditions of adjustment (Lindell, 2002; Meagher and Yunusa, 1996; Lugalla, 1997; Brand *et al.*, 1995). In this informal economy characterized by uncertainty, earning a living rests on networks of

personal relationships that provide a degree of material security, access to resources and predictability in exchanges.

This chapter is about the social networks that urban informal workers engage in for income earning in the deeply informalized economy of Bissau,
Guinea-Bissau.[1] It uncovers the diversity of forms of social collaboration, both
those that are based on age-old roles and identities and those that are giving
breath to new, alternative kinds of affinities, and how the two kinds may relate
to each other. Individuals' choices of networks and identities in the changing
work context are assessed in the light of existing structural constraints, including processes of exclusion from networks, the persistence of patriarchal
structures and an environment of economic hardship.

'Social capital', social identities and social context

Social networks of assistance in the market are increasingly being interpreted
as a form of 'social capital'. This concept is not new but the version of 'social
capital' that has attained hegemonic status in development discourse is of
neo-liberal inspiration, drawing extensively on the work of Robert Putnam.
In this discourse, 'social capital' is presented as a solution to a wide range of
problems.[2] Among other things, the presence of 'social capital' is considered
to necessarily lead to higher incomes and improved market performance. 'Social capital' is attributed an all-explanatory power and a universal role. In
these analyses 'social capital' is usually detached from its social context and
from specific cultural repertoires. By focusing solely on the positive features
of 'social capital', the power structures that 'social capital' may both contain
and be inserted into become invisible, and so does the role of agency. A truly
dynamic view of 'social capital' is thus missing in this discourse.[3]

As some have noted, the dominant neo-liberal 'social capital' discourse
has been oblivious of more productive conceptualizations, such as Pierre
Bourdieu's (1993). In his work, 'social capital' is conceived of as socially constructed and as implicated in the reproduction of social stratification, and
thus not separable from its social context. In his view, social capital is closely
connected to cultural and symbolic capital, which necessitates an analysis of
the cultural and ideological content of social networks. I look upon social
networks as constructed and as sites of negotiation of norms and roles. They
are social fields where both cooperation and struggle among participants may
occur. Social networks also relate to wider structures in society, in the sense
that they may reproduce those structures but may also hold the potential to
undermine them (Lindell, 2002).

The new wave of studies of 'social capital' in the market has been more
interested in its economic functions rather than in its role in identity creation
or in its social, cultural and political dimensions. Identity formation and social networks seem however to be closely related. As identities are relational
and constructed through daily practices, social networks may be conceived of
as one potential means for identity formation. In turn, social networks may

be constructed through the instrumental deployment of identities, including repeated practices of exclusion from and inclusion in those networks. Individuals may bear fluid and multiple identities that may be kept in a functional balance, as often stressed in the literature (Werbner, 1996; Ferguson, 1999; Simone, 1999). But the power that is exercised within and through networks, I will argue, may stand in the way of individuals' choices. It will be shown that material constraints also play a role, as the enactment of alternative aspired identities may sometimes jeopardize material assistance premised on other affinities, something that urban impoverished people may not be in a position to do.

Available analyses of social networks sustaining income activities and related identities in the new economic environment tend to take divergent directions. Some emphasize the revival or adaptation of age-old affinities in market-based networks, sometimes reportedly entailing elements of domination (Macharia, 1997; Diouf, 2000). Others contend that new kinds of social networks in the market are fostering alternative identities away from 'traditional' ones – often referring to the transformation of female identities and with little consideration for structural constraints (Tripp, 1989, 1997). This chapter attempts to give a more nuanced picture of the relation between social networks and identity formation and displays the great diversity of identities at work in networks. It shows how the above two kinds of networks may coexist and interact. It will be argued that networks may be simultaneously the means for the development of new alternative identities as well as for the reaffirmation of older affinities. They may both reproduce social divisions in society and cut across (or even subvert) these divisions, possibly creating opportunities for new identities to be forged. What these networks based on new kinds of affinities are able to achieve will be assessed in the light of wider structural constraints.

The discussion will be based on data collected between 1992 and 2002 for a study on livelihoods and social networks among disadvantaged groups in Bissau. The main target respondents were food traders and households. In-depth interviews were conducted with members of about 45 households and about 60 food traders – most of these were small-scale women traders but a handful of wholesale and import–export firms were also included. Most of the interviewed traders were selected on the basis of a household survey. The survey encompassed about 10 percent of the population of two neighbourhoods, in a total 453 households, and focused on the food and income strategies of households, including trade activities. Qualitative interviews were also conducted with local elders, a variety of key informants and government officials with responsibilities in the management of urban food trade.

Informalization of work in Bissau

Bissau is a small but rapidly growing capital city of less than half a million inhabitants. The industrial sector has always been small and has further declined in the last couple of decades, along with a shrinking public sector. In the face of this narrow range of options for income generating activities, the majority of Bissauans rely on informal activities for survival.[4] Among these activities, the one that emerged as by far the most common activity pursued by members of the households surveyed was trade, particularly retail trade of food items (including drinks and charcoal). There has been a visible explosion in the number of food traders, reflected in the appearance of numerous unplanned market places in the city.

In spite of its extremely peripheral position in the global economy, Bissau has been the stage of a large flow of international commodities since the mid-1980s, particularly the export of unprocessed cashew nuts and the import of rice and other basic foods. Following the liberalization of the economy, a small number of merchants accumulated considerable profits through these import–export activities, by taking advantage of the difference in the international prices for the two commodities. Large numbers of urban dwellers also earn a living by engaging in activities related to this international trade. This is the case for production and sale of cashew wine, one of the most important income activities for (non-Muslim) women, as well as the case of retailers of imported rice (van der Drift, 2002; Lindell, 2002). In addition to these, growing numbers of men in the city have become dependent on casual work such as shipping and loading of import and export goods. Other urban dwellers make a living by trading in other commodities, such as vegetables, fruits and fish, some of which are locally produced.

The majority of the food trade enterprises registered during the household survey were small-scale, consisting mainly of one-person enterprises. The majority of the traders were unable to keep any savings and a large share spent most of their incomes on food. These were thus largely survivalist enterprises, many of which were constantly on the verge of collapse, under the pressures of heightened competition, slack demand, high costs of operation and household needs. Beyond these general trends, there were patterns of differentiation in the informal food economy. It is very difficult to generalize about these patterns as they varied for each sub-sector and cut across ethnic groups and genders. But women seemed to be over-represented at the lower end of the informal economy, in small-scale and low-income activities. The larger-scale and profitable segments of the economy seemed to be dominated by men, particularly men of ethnic groups originating from the Eastern part of the country – often referred to as Muslim groups. These patterns of differentiation followed a certain division of labour along gender and ethnic lines that were visible in food trade activities in the city. Women from coastal ethnic groups (Pepel, Mancanha, Manjaco) accounted for the greater share of women food traders in Bissau and were most numerous in the trade of fresh foods, though they also engaged in the retailing of imported foods such as rice. Male traders from the Eastern ethnic groups (Mandinga, Fula) increased greatly in numbers in the city since the mid-1980s. They came to dominate the supply of imported foods and meat. Within this general division of labour, small traders diversified their trade activities by switching commodities seasonally or by trading different commodities simultaneously in order to minimize risks.

Since formal sources of assistance were not available to small traders, they relied extensively on social networks to sustain their income activities. The remainder of the chapter presents examples of the varied nature of such networks and discusses implications for identity formation in the work context. The discussion will focus on the networks of groups involved in the food economy, particularly traders but also day workers linked to international commodity flows.

Networks and the affirmation of historical identities

Hierarchical networks of accumulation

The cashew–rice economy in Guinea-Bissau has been structured into hierarchical networks, within which cashew nuts and imported rice circulate. Such hierarchical networks consist of import–export firms at the top, wholesalers or middlemen at the intermediate level, and cashew producers and rice retailers at the bottom.[5] Wholesalers and middlemen participating in these networks often get informal credit from their suppliers, which usually requires a good deal of subordination to these patrons. These informal contracts are often based on kinship, ethnic and religious affinities, particularly Islam. Merchants and traders originating from the neighbouring countries and members of the Islamized ethnic groups from the Eastern parts of the country are particularly well represented in these networks. These groups have strong historical trade traditions. They have had groups of professional traders since centuries back and have long valued trade as a profession. Since the 1980s a share of them has been in a position to take advantage from trade liberalization.

The successful trading careers of some members of these groups seem to generate aspirations and a re-evaluation of identities among individuals from other ethnic groups in the city with different worldviews and work traditions. These individuals have begun to value trade as prestigious work, sometimes to the annoyance of their seniors.[6] Some individuals even abandoned their ethnic origin to identify themselves as a Fula or a Mandinga instead. Carrying these identities seemed to be perceived as opening the possibility for penetrating prolific vertical networks and for entering the few channels of social mobility available to Bissauans in the existing political economic context. This suggests a conscious and instrumental use of identities, which has been reported as an important strategy by urbanites to adapt to changed conditions in African cities (Ferguson, 1999; Simone, 1999). Clearly, these identities are also contingent, reflecting changes in public morality and in the balance of social and economic forces in society. A trader-related identity was hardly one would have aspired to in earlier times when the Guinean state regarded private traders as immoral elements in society.

However, these vertical networks dominating the Guinean economy seemed to be quite exclusionist and the switching to a more suitable identity was not an option commonly available to the majority. Some 'outsiders' to these networks were eager to participate in them and often expressed frustration about the great difficulties in penetrating them. This exclusionism may lead to a certain hardening of ethnic identities currently occurring elsewhere in Africa, where the distribution of economic opportunities evolves along ethnic lines (Bangura, 1994; Simone, 1998, 1999). While there are many exceptions, the above trends in Bissau's food commodity market suggest reinforcement rather than a blurring of age-old ethnic–gender specializations in trade, and of related identities.

Family embeddedness of women's businesses

The second example of forms of support for market activities involving historical hierarchical relations pertains to the social networks of women traders. Guinean women, particularly women of coastal ethnic groups, have been involved in trade activities since pre-colonial times. The lifting of restrictions on trade was followed by a great increase in the number of women traders in the city. While interviewed women traders engaged in a variety of networks for support, relatives emerged as a particularly important source of support. Access to a selling site and marketing skills were in several cases gained through a senior female relative. Male relatives often assisted with preparatory work for commercial gardening, with building a market table or a shade. Close relatives were by far the most common source of credit, particularly husbands and male relatives. In addition, a share of the women traders sold goods they produced on land controlled by male relatives or governed by customary norms privileging male seniors.

In the large literature about the position of women in connection to urbanization and income opportunities, perspectives have changed through time but seem to oscillate between two general positions. One long standing position has stressed the opportunities that towns and the market may open for the autonomy of women from the control of husbands and male kin, the positive effect of women's access to income on established male and female roles, the market place as a crucial liberating space for women, and the variety of sources that towns offer for the construction of women's identities (Cutrufelli, 1983; Liljeström *et al.*, 1998; Young, 1992). Some writers have also made celebratory descriptions of women's empowerment in connection with women's increased participation in income activities and market-based networks, in the context of economic liberalization (Tripp, 1989; Sow, 1993). On the other hand, a range of studies illuminates women's subordinate positions in the urban labour market and the 'informal sector', the persistence of patriarchal dominance both in the wider society and in the home and the limitations of women's groups as spaces for expanding women's power and re-inventing female identities (Rosander, 1997).

The considerable dependence of interviewed female traders in Bissau on the family, and particularly on male relatives, suggests the need for caution in interpreting women's intensified involvement in the market as being automatically liberating from domestic structures and as enabling women to construct alternative identities. The importance of the family embeddedness of women's businesses is not exclusive to women traders in Bissau, rather it has been noted in other contexts (Dennis, 1991; Ndiaye, 1998; Sow, 1993). But one may look upon this kin assistance as both an asset and a constraint for small traders. A supportive kin and husband and a husband that was able and willing to contribute to household expenses emerged as key factors for the stability of the businesses of the interviewed women traders. At the same time, this dependence may limit their individual options.

The family embeddedness of women's businesses varies considerably, even within the same study setting. This reflects the variety of family and domestic situations in which women are inserted, the range of available kin in town, its responsiveness and material assets and how gender roles are defined in different ethnic groups. Among a wide range of situations, some interviewed women traders lived in corporate groups that were able to provide them with a degree of material security, others had exited the control of the extended family and a share of them headed their own households.[7] A deeper study of the role of women's networks for their empowerment would need to consider these variations, as well as women's varying embeddedness in networks in the market. These differences may have implications for the extent to which women are free to pursue alternative identities.

The above described patterns – tightly drawn networks of accumulation along ethnic/religious lines and women traders' dependence on kin support – reflect wider trends in Africa towards an intensified 'familiarization' of businesses and affiliations in the market (Macharia, 1997; Ndiaye, 1998; Meagher and Yunusa, 1996). This has raised concerns that such a trend may reinforce traditional axes of subordination and the position of dominant figures in the family while eventually constraining independent action or open confrontation. But the dependence of businesses on family and ethnic structures is only one side of the picture. There are networks that draw on different kinds of affinities and gather people with different senses of belonging. It is to these networks that I turn now. Whether they offer an alternative for small-scale traders to disengage from the above kinds of support will be discussed later in the chapter.

Networks and the invention of alternative identities

Market women invest in alternative networks of support through which they may potentially carve out a space of autonomy from networks of assistance within the patriarchal family and create a platform for bargaining for a better position. As women were spending a growing number of hours at the market, their market activities were often perceived as a threat by men and male

seniors in the domestic field.[8] In the words of a senior male, the biggest problem in his neighbourhood, as he saw it, was 'women's disobedience to their
husbands; now they make their own decisions, influenced by their colleagues
at the market place'. Some respondents seemed to rely solely on market-based
networks for their security. In this section I will present the most common
types of market-based networks that women traders and male day workers
use, which potentially nurture alternative identities that cut across traditional
divisions.

Naturally, market-based networks are themselves not necessarily free from
oppression. The credit agreements that many traders had with suppliers may
guarantee secure access to commodities but in many cases entailed exploitation or sexual concessions (Lindell, 2002). These relations cannot be generalized as they vary for each commodity. Here I will focus on more general
kinds of social arrangements in the market that were commonly used by respondents and on collaborations among people sharing the same condition or
position in the market, and thus potentially more egalitarian in nature.

Traders handle practical problems by engaging in a variety of collaborations based on friendship and affinities developed in the market. They share
crucial information for daily business decisions, concerning for example supply and demand conditions and prices at different supply sources. Within
the same market place, traders selling the same type of product tend to agree
on a single price, in order to avoid disputes. Retailers often assist each other
in the sales, in the payment of the market fee and some may even get a loan
from a colleague when business is going badly. I often encountered pairs of
women traders that cooperated closely. These kinds of partnerships have been
noticed among women informal traders in other African cities (Tripp, 1989;
Brand *et al.*, 1995). As they usually trade in the same commodity, they ac-
company and help each other throughout the workday, pool their resources
when needed, and help sustain each other's businesses through the frequent
setbacks. These were usually women in a similar (often poor) material situation and their collaboration seemed to be particularly vulnerable to the effects
of market shocks.

Rotating savings groups

There are more institutionalized forms of cooperation in the market which
cut across traditional divisions, and which I will exemplify with rotating
savings groups and redistribution groups of casual workers. The occurrence
of rotating savings groups among women informal traders in Africa in the
absence of formal sources of credit is well known in the literature (Ardener
and Burman, 1996; Niger-Thomas, 2000). This is a widespread form of saving
in Bissau, found in all layers of society but divided along income levels. It consists of a group of people who regularly contribute an agreed amount of money into a common pool. Members then take turns in collecting the gathered
sum. According to respondents, these savings groups help them save for more

occasional expenses such as clothes, medicines and burial ceremonies. But the groups also help to keep members in business and provide a safety valve for the trader and his or her dependants. When one member's business is on the verge of collapse or is threatened by unexpected expenses in the household, turns may be altered to assist that person. Occasionally, participation in a savings group helped traders to increase the scale of operations – although one should consider the limitations imposed by the general conditions of heightened competition and shrinking demand.

Savings groups take a great variety of configurations. Some emerge around old lines of affiliation, for example among people from the same compound or lineage, where chances of holding people accountable are perceived as higher. But perhaps more commonly, savings groups often join people sharing the same type of business and working location. Among traders, these groups are typically based on acquaintances created at the market place and gather people of different ethnic backgrounds. In spite of their apparently inclusive nature, these groups are inherently selective, as they are structured along income lines, i.e. the ability to pay an agreed amount of money, and thus gather traders with similar scales of business.

Redistribution groups of casual day workers

Large numbers of men in the city are dependent on day work activities. Casual work has certainly increased in the city, as it has elsewhere in Africa and beyond (Bangura, 1994; Gibbon, 1995). This may be interpreted as a result of both retrenchment and the extensive use that merchant capital is making of casual work in the context of economic liberalization. In Bissau, day work comprises a great variety of activities, including loading and shipping work for import–export firms. The latter activities take the form of short-term work tasks that are performed by collective work groups, on the basis of unwritten collective contracts. Among these groups of casual workers, some had developed practices of redistribution of incomes and assistance. For example, should only some members of the group get day work, the other members who did not, could count on receiving a share of the incomes. Members also assist each other in need. 'If I get day work', one participant explained, 'I separate a share and give to the first two members that I encounter'. When he himself did not find day work, he 'circulated' in certain places until he met one of the others. When he and his family were out of food, he sought help from other members in the group and if the latter had something to give or lend, they could not refuse. Willingness to work and honesty were requisites for being part of the group. Ties among participants are sometimes premised on kinship but friendship seems to be a widespread basis for the formation of such groups. Frequent interaction within the group for both work and leisure purposes probably facilitates accountability between members and compliance with the rules.

These groups of day workers are usually composed of men from a wide variety of ethnic groups and neighbourhoods in the city. In this sense, they differ considerably from the exclusive vertical networks mentioned above and from ethnic or family based networks, and thus possibly counteract the social fragmentation and the 'localisms' that are visible in Bissau as well as in other African cities (Bangura, 1994; Simone, 1998). These networks of casual workers connecting neighbourhoods and bridging diverse ethnic affiliations require of participants that they bear flexible and diverse identities. In addition, a share of these workers continue to be subsistence farmers on lineage land around the city and to be part of extended kin groups with own systems of rules and own identity references. They have mixed these two types of work historically in Bissau and apparently been able to balance these distinct roles and experiences (Lindell, 2002). In the past, being members of corporate kin groups did not prevent them from developing a class consciousness related to their work conditions at the port. These 'dual workers' would later be at the forefront of the struggle against colonialism. Only the future will tell whether today's casual workers will mobilize again on the basis of this shared identity, across ethnic divisions, and give political content to their assistance networks, in order to contest their exclusion from the vertical networks of accumulation and to demand a larger share of the profits that the latter command.

Caught between family and market

The networks described above cut across traditional social divisions and potentially create space for the construction of work identities that are not bound to family and ethnic group. The potential of these networks to fully bloom and provide alternatives to tradition-based support seems however to be constrained by the internal structure of the networks as well as wider processes and the position of participants in the wider society. The reformulation of identities that these networks eventually encourage cannot be separated from material considerations. Many descriptions of market-based networks, such as savings groups, tend to be overoptimistic by portraying them as emancipating from oppressive domestic structures (Sow, 1993; Tripp, 1989, 1997). Issues of differential access and sustainability are often glossed over, with little consideration for the wider social and economic context in which these networks exist. These are the issues considered in this section, in relation to the networks described above.

The issue of differential access to market-based networks can be illustrated by savings groups in the study setting. These groups are inherently selective, as mentioned above. The poorest traders were usually excluded. An important share of the traders interviewed had in fact stopped participating, due to very low and irregular incomes, to the necessity of spending the entire earnings on food, due to ill health in the household and to the frequent collapse of their businesses. The general decline in real incomes and the increasing precariousness of income activities for many under conditions of structural adjustment seems to be eroding this as well as other kinds of collaborative efforts among traders at the lowest income levels.[9] This seemed also to be the case of support groups among day workers. As the pool of urban men dependent on this kind of work for an income grew, day work opportunities became increasingly sporadic according to respondents, and exploitation by employers has probably increased. Not surprisingly, the size of incomes earned and then redistributed among workers was very low. In this context, such redistribution practices seemed to be under serious threat.

Returning to small-scale women traders and their significant dependence on kin support, one needs to consider then whether market-based networks are a viable alternative to disengage from kin-based assistance, where the latter is perceived as oppressive. For many women traders, the insecurity of their market incomes, their eventual exclusion from supportive networks in the market and the erosion of the material bases of these networks may perpetuate their dependence on the assistance of relatives and force them to comply with patriarchal authority in the home and the kin group (at least in those instances where the latter guarantee a minimum of security). 'Rebellious women', I was told by a senior man, 'are usually women who have money, who have the economic strength to stand on their own'.

Particularly women living in extended family groups in the study setting had reasons to avoid challenging patriarchal authority in those groups. Male seniors control the assets of the compound, such as houses, agricultural fields around the city and the largest stores of staple food, which they may use to assist compound members in a day of need. A 'rebellious' behaviour may jeopardize these material benefits. In addition, the head of the extended domestic group holds substantial spiritual authority over members of compounds derived from his privileged relation to the ancestors. Most Guinean women are generally dependent on men for access to important resources such as land for subsistence or commercial production. Men are ascribed extensive rights over the children born by their wives. A separation from a husband often implies the loss of important rights for women in these respects. These and other areas of male privilege make up a complex set of constraints on women's lives which act to restrict their exit options and hold back their bargaining strength. The consequences of women's increased participation in the market for their own empowerment are not straightforward, as sometimes is implied. Market women in Bissau, as in other societies in West Africa, have long trade traditions and have long enjoyed a degree of autonomy in their income activities. Most of the respondents keep their own money separately from their husbands' and decide upon the use of their own incomes. Many did not show their incomes to their husbands, although at least as many did. The significance of women's control over their own earnings becomes more relative however when considering that almost half of the (527) traders in the household survey spent all or virtually all of their trade income on food for the household. The fact that women usually do not know the size of their husbands' incomes is also instructive in this context.

In sum, while policies of liberalization have opened income opportunities for women, male authority over their lives is not necessarily waning, given the precariousness of those income activities under conditions of adjustment, the continued importance of patriarchal structures of security provision and the persistence of a variety of male privileges to the detriment of women. In addition, while new forms of solidarity are visible in the market, they are not necessarily replacing old ones. These persistent domestic patriarchal structures may interact with the subordinate conditions that many women experience in the market – for example in relation to the practices of both suppliers and local government – to hamper a true empowerment of these women (Lindell, 2002). In some instances, gender, ethnic and class differences overlap and eventually reinforce each other, to the disadvantage of many market women in Bissau.

Conclusion

This chapter explores the relation between social network construction and identity formation in a changing urban work environment. The focus has been on how the construction of networks and identities relates to wider structures and processes in society. One aim was to illustrate two apparently contradictory trends taking place in the study setting: some social networks seem to be reinforcing established roles and social divisions along ethnic and gender lines and facilitating the revival or maintenance of traditional roles and identities; other networks bridge over social divisions and provide platforms for the invention of identities away from historical senses of belonging.

Participants in hierarchical networks of accumulation in Bissau make use of skills and identity references with deep historical roots as they attempt to meet the challenges of economic liberalization. Their perceived success has generated aspirations of participation and a re-evaluation of 'valued work' and identities among elements of other groups. However, these networks seem to have remained highly exclusivist, narrowly drawn around ties of kinship, ethnicity and religion, blocking access to this possible channel of social mobility. Women, among the excluded from this male world, engage in other types of networks. A significant share of them was dependent on the assistance of male relatives to keep their businesses afloat. This casts doubt on simplistic interpretations that see a direct connection between women's increased participation in the market and in market networks and their emancipation from patriarchal structures. As family support is anchored in patriarchal domination within the household and the extended family, women traders' continued dependence on this support may weaken their bargaining strength and hamper the independent construction of female identities. The above network configurations suggest a reaffirmation or persistence of deeply rooted affinities, long established social divisions in society and historical relations of domination. This may restrain the individual freedom of subordinated individuals in these networks and discourage them from enacting other identities to which they may aspire.

But informal workers also invest in social networks that cut across deeply rooted social divisions and 'traditional' identities. These networks counteract social fragmentation and create opportunities for constructing alternative senses of belonging. In some cases, these alternative affinities are compatible with traditional norms in family-based networks. But for women traders, a tension exists between their involvement in networks in the market and gender relations in the domestic field. Women's networks in the market potentially provide an alternative to family support, but are limited in a number of ways. First, their social networks are vulnerable to the effects of adjustment policies. As resources for redistribution and assistance become scarce, poor informal workers' collaborative efforts are undermined. The often bleak prospects of these efforts call into question the sustainability of the alternative identities they nurture. Second, many of these networks are selective and exclude the poorest groups. If participation in trading networks away from the family is a means to construct alternative identities, this raises the issue of whether this is a luxury that only a share of informal workers can afford.

In sum, urban informal workers invest in a variety of social networks and make use of multiple identities in order to survive in the contemporary urban work environment. However, the examples discussed here suggest that this is not an unconstrained juggling of identities. Individuals' choices are constrained by power being exercised within and through networks, by practices of exclusion from networks and by real material limitations. For some people options seem limited, as they find themselves caught 'between family and market' and are compelled to stay in relations of assistance that are oppressive in order to keep their businesses going. Their continued participation in kin and ethnic-based networks of assistance should not be interpreted as necessarily meaning a lack of consciousness or as a propensity to stay attached to tradition. Rather, continuing to fulfil traditional roles and to display historically rooted identities while other identities seem to be at hand, may hide subversive values and aspirations, which may eventually surface when respondents perceive conditions to be ripe.

About the author

Ilda Lindell is an associate professor at the Department of Human Geography, Stockholm University and a researcher at the Nordic Africa Institute, Uppsala, Sweden. She is the author of *Walking the Tight Rope: Informal Livelihoods and Social Networks in a West African City* (2002, Almqvist and Wiksell, Stockhom), which deals with processes of informalization and how vulnerable groups are dealing with the changes. Her current research focuses on informality and urban governance and on collective organizing in the informal economy in African cities, including the links of such organizations to international movements. Her publications on these latter topics include articles in *Urban Studies*

(2008, 45:10), in *Geografiska Annaler* (2009, 91:2), and in *Habitat International* (2009, 33:4), forthcoming articles in *Global Networks*, *Third World Quarterly* and *Journal of Southern African Studies*, and book chapters. She is the editor of *Africa's Informal Workers: Collective Agency, Alliances and Transnational Organizing in Urban Africa* (2010, Zed Books/The Nordic Africa Institute, London/Uppsala), and of a special issue in *African Studies Quarterly* (2010).

Notes

* This article builds on my published doctoral thesis (Lindell, 2002).
1. 'Informal workers' are workers that do not enjoy the protection of state law, including the self-employed.
2. See World Bank, (2000, 2002), Narayan and Prittchet (1997), Narayan (2000). See also empirical studies by Barr (2000), Fafchamps (1996), and Bigsten *et al.* (2000).
3. For a critique of 'social capital' see Fine (1999), Portes (1998), Harriss and Renzio (1997), Harriss (2002), Putzel (1997) and Levi (1996).
4. According to the household survey, only a minority of the households depended exclusively on regular wage work whereas more than half relied on activities that lacked written contracts, paid sick leave and a regular income – common attributes of 'informal work'.
5. This is based on interviews with heads of two import–export firms, six rice wholesalers and key informants, as well as on a couple of studies of the Guinean trade sector (Crowley, 1993 and La Mettrie, 1992).
6. This was the case amongst the Pepel of Bissau, whose seniors defined 'the Pepel identity' as hard working farmers, during interviews. This group had cultivated the fields around Bissau for centuries.
7. About one third of the households were headed by women in the two surveyed neighbourhoods.
8. This has also been documented for women traders in Tanzania (Pietilä, 2002).
9. See Meagher and Yunusa (1996) for similar changes in credit groups in urban Nigeria.

References

Ardener, S. and Burman, S. (1996) *Money-Go-Rounds: The Importance of Rotating Savings and Credit Associations for Women*, Berg Publishers, Oxford.

Bangura, Y. (1994) 'Economic restructuring, coping strategies and social change: implications for institutional development in Africa', *Development and Change* 25(4): 785–827.

Barr, A. (2000) *Collective Action and Bilateral Interaction in Ghanaian Entrepreneurial Networks*, Working Paper 182, World Institute for Development Economics Research, Helsinki.

Bigsten, A., Collier, P., Dercon, S., Fafchamps, M., Gauthier, B., Gunning, J., Oduro, A., Oostendorp, R., Patillo, C., Soderbom, M., Teal, F. and Zeufack, A. (2000) 'Contract flexibility and dispute resolution in African manufacturing', *Journal of Development Studies* 36(4): 1–37.

Bourdieu, P. (1993) *Sociology in Question*, Sage Publications, London.

Brand, V., Mupedziswa, R. and Perpetua, G. (1995) 'Structural adjustment, women and informal trade in Harare' in P. Gibbon (ed.), *Structural Adjustment and the Working Poor in Zimbabwe*, pp. 132–214, Nordiska Afrikainstitutet, Uppsala.

Bryceson, D. (2006) 'African urban economies: searching for sources of sustainability', in D. Bryceson and D. Potts (eds), *African Urban Economies: Viability, Vitality or Vitiation?*, pp. 39–66, Palgrave Macmillan, New York.

Crowley, E. (1993) *Guinea-Bissau's Informal Economy and its Contributions to Economic Growth*, USAID (unpublished), The Hague.

Cutrufelli, M. (1983) *Women of Africa: Roots of Oppression*, Zed Press, London.

Dennis, C. (1991) 'Constructing a "career" under conditions of economic crisis and structural adjustment: the survival strategies of Nigerian women' in H. Afshar (ed.), *Women, Development and Survival in the Third World*, pp. 88–106, Longman, London.

Diouf, M. (2000) 'The Senegalese Murid trade diaspora and the making of a vernacular cosmopolitanism', *Codesria Bulletin* 1, 19–30.

Fafchamps, M. (1996) 'The enforcement of commercial contracts in Ghana', *World Development* 24(3): 427–48.

Ferguson, J. (1999) *Expectations of Modernity: Myths and Meanings of Urban Life on the Zambian Copperbelt*, University of California Press, Berkeley.

Fine, B. (1999) 'The developmental state is dead – long live social capital?', *Development and Change* 30: 1–19.

Gibbon, P. (1995) 'Introduction', in P. Gibbon (ed.), *Structural Adjustment and the Working Poor in Zimbabwe*, Nordiska Afrikainstitutet, Uppsala.

Hansen, K. and Vaa, M. (2004) 'Introduction', in K. Hansen and M. Vaa (eds), *Reconsidering Informality: Perspectives from Urban Africa*, pp. 7–24, Nordiska Afrikainstitutet, Uppsala.

Harriss, J. (2002) *Depoliticizing Development: The World Bank and Social Capital*, Anthem Press, London.

Harriss, J. and Renzio P. (1997) 'Missing link or analytically missing? The concept of social capital', *Journal of International Development* 9(7): 919–37.

La Mettrie, D. (1992) 'Rapport Technique Diagnostic sur le Commerce de Cereales en Guinee Bissau', FAO, (unpublished), Rome.

Levi, M. (1996) 'Social and unsocial capital: a review essay of Robert Putnam's Making Democracy Work', *Politics and Society* 24(1): 45–55.

Liljeström, R., Magdalena, M., Masanja, P. and Urassa, E. (1998) 'Cultural conflicts and ambiguities' in M. Rwebangira and R. Liljeström (eds), *'Haraka, Haraka, Look before you Leap': Youth at the Crossroad of Custom and Modernity*, Nordiska Afrikainstitutet, Uppsala.

Lindell, I. (2002) *Walking the Tight Rope: Informal Livelihoods and Social Networks in a West African City*, Stockholm Studies in Human Geography 9, Almqvist & Wiksell, Stockholm.

Lugalla, J. (1997) 'Development, change and poverty in the informal sector during the era of structural adjustment in Tanzania', *Canadian Journal of African Studies* 31(3): 424–516.

Macharia, K. (1997) *Social and Political Dynamics of the Informal Economy in African Cities: Nairobi and Harare*, University Press of America, Lanham, New York and Oxford.

Meagher, K. and Yunusa, M-B. (1996) *Passing the Buck: Structural Adjustment and the Nigerian Urban Informal Sector*, UNRISD Discussion Paper 75.

Narayan, D. (2000) *Voices of the Poor: Can Anyone Hear Us?* World Bank, Washington DC.

Narayan, D. and Pritchett, L. (1997) *Cents and Sociability: Household Income and Social Capital in Rural Tanzania*, World Bank, Policy Research Working Paper 1796, Washington DC.

Ndiaye, F. (1998) 'L'impact de la vie familiale sur l'activité entrepreneuriale des femmes au Sénégal', *Africa Development* 23(3/4): 149–161.

Niger-Thomas, M. (2000) *Buying Futures: Cameroonian Women in the Formal and Informal Sectors*, PhD thesis, Leiden University.

Pietilä, T. (2002) 'Drinking mothers feeding children: market women and gender politics in Kilimanjaro, Tanzania' in D.F. Bryceson (ed.), *Alcohol in Africa: Mixing Business, Pleasure and Politics*, pp. 197–212, Heinemann, Portsmouth, NH.

Portes, A. (1998) 'Social capital: its origins and application in modern sociology', *Annual Review of Sociology* 24: 1–24.

Putzel, J. (1997) 'Accounting for the "dark side" of social capital: reading Robert Putnam on Democracy', *Journal of International Development* 9(7): 939–49.

Rosander, E. (1997) *Transforming Female Identities: Women's Organizational Forms in West Africa*, Nordiska Afrikainstitutet, Uppsala.

Simone, A. (1998) 'Urban social fields in Africa', *Social Text* 56: 71–89.

Simone, A. (1999) 'Thinking about African urban management in an era of globalization', *African Sociological Review* 3(2): 69–98.

Sow, F. (1993) 'Les initiatives féminines au Sénégal: une réponse à la crise?' *Africa Development* 18(3): 89–115.

Tripp, A. (1989) 'Women and the changing urban household economy in Tanzania', *Journal of Modern African Studies* 27(4): 601–623.

Tripp, A. M. (1997) *Changing the Rules: The Politics of Liberalisation and the Urban Informal Economy in Tanzania*, University of California Press, Berkeley/Los Angeles.

van der Drift, R. (2002) 'Democracy's heady brew: cashew wine and the authority of the elders among the Balanta in Guinea Bissau', in D.F. Bryceson (ed.), *Alcohol in Africa: Mixing Business, Pleasure and Politics*, pp. 179–96, Heinemann, Portsmouth, NH.

Werbner, R. (1996) 'Multiple identities, plural arenas' in R. Werbner and T. Ranger (eds), *Postcolonial Identities in Africa*, pp. 1–26, Zed Books, London and New Jersey.

World Bank (2000) *Entering the 21st Century*, World Bank, Washington DC.

World Bank (2002) *Building Institutions for Markets*, World Bank, Washington DC.

Young, K. (1992) 'Household resource management', in L. Ostergaard (ed.), *Gender and Development: A Practical Guide*, Routledge, London.

CHAPTER 9

Sweet and sour: women working for wages on Tanzania's sugar estates[*]

Marjorie Mbilinyi

Structural adjustment policies engendered profound changes in Tanzania's rural society and economy, many unintended and unanticipated. Smallholder peasant farming is in crisis, while large-scale commercial farming has regained its footing as a prime force in export-driven agriculture. Gender relations within smallholder households have been strained by the crisis and, at the same time, help to sustain the reproduction of both farm sectors. The smallholder sector's increased need for unpaid family labour, mainly of wives and dependent youth, has led to major gender conflicts, as many family labourers escape the family farm into alternative employment as wage labourers on sugar estates and smallholder farms or in non-farm activities. Women have gained more economic power resulting from their increased labour-force participation and new income-earning capabilities. This has been accompanied by the tragedy of falling male employment and a decline in male incomes. Both women and men peasants struggle to survive, however, in the context of growing landlessness and proletarianization in areas dominated by the sugar estates and other plantations.

Introduction

This chapter highlights the differential impact of sugar-estate expansion and the crisis of peasant agriculture on women and men within smallholder house-holds in Morogoro district, Tanzania, during the late 1990s, in the midst of Structural Adjustment policies and other dramatic reforms in macroeconomic policy. Of central interest is the smallholder sector's increased need for unpaid family labour, mainly of wives and dependent youth, and dialectically, the escape of the same family labourers into alternative employment away from the family farm as wage labourers on sugar estates and smallholder farms or in non-farm activities. Analysis of the position and conditions of male and fe-male workers in the rural sector centres on who has access to and control over resources in the household, community and workplace. Power relations, heav-ily influenced by the interaction between capitalist and smallholder farming, determine not only the kind of employment women obtain compared to men but also differences among women in their control over land, labour and cash incomes.

The first section of this chapter briefly discusses the experience of structural adjustment in Tanzania, before turning to the circumstances that prevail in smallholder farming in Morogoro and the growing significance of unpaid family labour in smallholder production as well as competing labour demands exerted by the sugar industry at Mtibwa. The third section examines the significance of wages for women labourers in the sugar industry and the effect that their increased control over cash has on household gender relations. The final section considers the pressures women face as their standard of living declines and patriarchal relations weaken in the household.

Destiny of large and smallholder farming under structural adjustment

Agriculture in Tanzania consists of smallholding peasant farmers, medium-scale commercial farmers and large-scale capitalist enterprises owned mainly by private and transnational corporations. These farming systems differ radically in terms of their access to land, credit and labour. Outgrower schemes combine smallholding peasant farmers' production with large-scale capitalist management, and sometimes give rise to successful medium-scale commercial farmers who may, in turn, rely on hiring peasant labourers.

Certain cash crops such as sisal, sugar cane, tea, coffee and ornamental flowers are grown wholly or partially by large-scale capital-intensive growers.[1] Other crops are primarily peasant crops, notably cotton and cashew nuts, and still other crops are produced in both sectors (tea, coffee and cashew nuts). Sugar-cane outgrower farmers produce an increasing share of sugar-cane output, locked into a symbiotic relationship with sugar-cane estates.

Agricultural performance

The ostensible goal of structural adjustment policies (SAP) implemented in Tanzania in the mid-1980s was to increase productive output by economic investment, increasing efficiency in the allocation of resources by reorienting the economy towards export rather than domestic markets, reducing inflation and improving the balance of payments (Msambichaka *et al.*, 1995). Tanzania's economy was expected to become more competitive on the world market if production costs were reduced by devaluation, more stringent controls over labour were imposed, and wage cutbacks were introduced.

However, Tanzanian agricultural performance has been disappointing in contrast to the original optimistic forecasts that were used to rationalize the reform process. With the exception of tea, the marketed output levels of most of Tanzania's major export crops throughout the 1980s and up until 1991 failed to surpass those achieved during the 1970s.[2] Contrary to representations by mainstream discourse, structural adjustment and neo-liberal reforms did not stimulate peasant agriculture production. However, major capital investment was pumped into the large-scale agricultural sector that began to register increases in output during the 1990s.[3] Horticultural exports, especially roses and other flowers, have risen. Nevertheless, peasant agriculture has continued to erode in the 2000s.[4] Traditional exports, including coffee, tobacco and cotton, have declined to 21 per cent of total export value while non-traditional exports have ballooned to 79 per cent, which includes minerals, horticulture products and tourism (Tanzania Gender Networking Programme, 2006).

One of the key explanations for the stagnation of peasant agriculture has been the decline in distribution and consumption of farm inputs (Msambichaka and Naho, 1995). The removal of input subsidies for smallholders and the failure of private traders to supply fertilizer and improved seeds in liberalized input markets seriously constrained production.

Peasant farmers' rates of return for tobacco, coffee, tea, sugar and rice declined in many areas of the country during the 1990s,[5] creating growing regional differentiation as a result of the rolling back of support services and infrastructure for smallholder farmers. Under economic liberalization, farmers located near major market centres or good transport lines were able to benefit most from reforms, whereas farmers in distant or more remote locations experienced producer prices offering minimal or no increase in real terms largely due to the faster increase in the price of farm inputs and consumer goods (ibid.).

The poor incentive structure of agriculture was a major cause of agriculture's dismal performance during the 1990s (Tanzania, Ministry of Agriculture 2001; Tanzania, Minister for Finance and Economic Affairs, 2008). Real producer prices of export crops have declined over time thus enhancing the deterioration in terms of trade, and the sector was overtaxed. Moreover, the farmers' share in export prices remained low at the end of the decade, ranging from a low of 22 per cent for pyrethrum and 35 per cent for tea (largely a plantation crop) to a high of 75 per cent for fire-cured tobacco and 65 per cent for cashews. The producers' share remained below 60 per cent for all other major exports, as in the pre-liberalization era.

Plight of peasant agriculture

Male and female smallholder farmers reported increasing difficulty in sustaining farm production and in caring for their families during the 1990s, as documented by micro-level research (Kashuliza and Mbiha, 1995; Koda, 1994; Mbilinyi, 1995, 1997; Mbilinyi *et al.*, 1999; Turuka, 1995).

Our study's focus group discussions with villagers in Mbogo and Lusanga, Morogoro region in 1997 revealed farmers' views. When asked to compare the situation in 1997 with five years earlier, the following comments were recorded:

Commodities are available, but life is hard, there is no money. What you sell does not match with what you buy. Crop prices are too low and the prices of what we buy too high. (man)

Yes, yes times are hard, we farmers are being hung by the neck! We sell at low prices compared to farm input prices, which are high, *pesa ngumu sana* [money is hard to come by]. (woman)

Fertilizer prices, especially that of urea, are higher for us villagers than for the sugar estate. Urea bought on credit is more expensive because it's a business venture. Mtibwa Sugar Estates sell fertilizer at a lower price because they are the major buyers of the sugar cane from outgrowers. The private trader who sells fertilizer ups the price on the excuse that it is a free market after liberalization. (man)

There's no income in farming. (woman)

In the past our incomes were better. Now things are available but we are not satisfied because of our low incomes. Life is especially difficult for the women who depend on us men. (man)

Income levels have not been keeping up with farmers' increasing workloads. Men's incomes from agricultural export crops have plummeted. Women, dependent on the good will of male household heads to ensure that they benefit from their labour input in family export crop production, have been feeling the pinch. They have become increasingly engaged in separate market-oriented activities whereas previously they relied on their husbands' earnings for family purchases. Men's contracting access to cash has engendered a push–pull reallocation of intra-household labour and welfare, and tensions have risen in domestic relations against a background of uncontrollable external forces.

Sugar and spite: Morogoro peasant farmers and the Mtibwa sugar estates

Under colonialism, Morogoro was renowned for its large-scale sisal plantations. In the post-colonial period, it became the country's major supplier of peasant-produced horticultural products. Of growing importance now, is the area's production of sugar that combines large-scale estates and medium-sized commercial farms with peasant household efforts in outgrower schemes. At Mtibwa and Kilombero, sugar cane has become a significant smallholder and commercial farm crop, grown by peasant outgrowers and medium-scale commercial farmers on a semi-contractual basis to the large sugar companies there. Unlike most peasant export crops, sugar cane experienced increasing output from the mid-1980s to the mid-1990s (Toke, 1995). Most of Tanzania's sugar cane is produced on these estates but the share coming from sugar outgrowers tripled during this period and was largely responsible for the growth in overall output.

Peasant outgrower production

Relations between the estates and the outgrowers have altered over time, as have ownership patterns in the industry. The sugar estates were originally owned by private companies and became parastatal companies after nationalization in the late 1960s and early 1970s (Sterkenburg and van der Wiel, 1993). The government sought to increase outgrower production to boost income redistribution and rural self-employment in the 1970s. However, the area under outgrower cane declined during the 1980s in response to low producer prices and a lack of adequate farm support services from both government extension services and the estates. Historically, the estates were expected to provide outgrowers' credit support for machinery to clear, prepare and plant the land and even provided hired labour to weed, harvest and transport cane during peak seasons. Under pressure of rising costs in the 1980s, the estate management scaled down its outgrower support.

Since 1990, outgrower production has increased because of improved producer prices, better communications between company management and outgrowers, the involvement of management themselves in outgrower farming, and the creation of outgrower associations in Kilombero and Mtibwa. Reorganization led to the loosening of restrictions on management participation in outgrower production during the early 1990s, giving management an added incentive to be supportive of outgrowers, although with the possibility of a conflict of interest in the long run (Mbilinyi, 1995). The result has been an increase in the area under outgrower cultivation, increased yields and increased output (Sterkenburg and van der Wiel, 1993: 11). At Mtibwa Sugar Estates, the share of total cane provided by outgrowers grew from 17 per cent in 1988/89 to 57 per cent in 1995/96 (Mtibwa records,1997, personal observation).

Outgrowers, however, were not sheltered from the rising costs of production that Tanzanian peasants were experiencing generally. Normally it took 14–16 months to harvest the first crop after planting but thereafter the annual crop yields measured up to 30 tons per hectare. Outgrowers experienced a loss during the first harvest followed by positive returns thereafter, although weeding and fertilizer costs and charges for cane cutting, loading and transport were additionally incurred and they paid 30 per cent interest on the loans they received from the estate (Toke, 1995).

Peasant outgrowers tried to defray their costs by using unpaid family labour instead of hired labour for furrowing, planting, weeding and fertilizer application (Toke, 1995). Around the Mtibwa Estates, a growing number of women and youth in farm households were co-opted into outgrower sugar production on highly exploitative terms. They came to perceive this as coerced unpaid family labour (Mbilinyi, 1997).

Peasant landlessness and proletarianization

There was another downside to the blossoming of sugar output: peasant farmers were losing land to the estate. Nationally, landlessness was becoming an issue as the government pushed a land reform bill through parliament, bowing to international pressure to liberalize land markets and to expand foreign investment in large-scale agriculture, mining and tourism.[6] The majority of Tanzanian farmers and other citizens lacked information about the contents of the land bills in question and were not invited to share their views.[7]

Morogoro regional and district authorities reported several sites of rural land conflict: a large farmer sought 20,000 acres of land in one case and local villagers protested against land alienation and demanded redistribution of large farms. Peasant farmers in Lusanga and Mbogo villages spoke bitterly about the purchase of village land by medium-scale outgrower sugar-cane farmers. They and their children and grandchildren were already experiencing real landlessness (Mbilinyi, 1997).[8] In the past, one acre in Lusanga sold for Tsh 50,000 (US$1 = Tsh 700) whereas in 1997 the price had more than doubled and villagers could no longer afford to buy land. Farmers with the means to do so had to rent land in neighbouring villages for as much as Tsh 10,000.

Major inroads were made into village land by the sugar company and later by medium-scale sugar outgrowers, many being from the estate's top-level management who farmed commercially on their own account. This affected household land access, as revealed by interviews in 1997:

> I was born in 1925 and arrived here when I was 16 years old. We used to get big yields of maize. When they came and opened up the factory, conditions both worsened and got better. We got money for our land but ended up hungry. Now company bosses rule us and benefit from our land. We have nowhere left to farm. (elderly man)

> I have got forest land but I lack the means to farm it, and then the rains fail. That's why some of us sell the land, at least we can eat thanks to the money. (woman)

A steady proletarianization process was underway in the villages surrounding Mtibwa Sugar Estates in the 1990s. The opening up of land to market forces was taking place alongside labour-market expansion. The reaction of one medium-scale outgrower was as follows:

> I buy a plot along with the people who used to live on it. After the purchase, I find the farmer on my doorstep. "What is it?" I ask. He replies: "You bought my farm, didn't you? How am I going to eat? You bought me as well."

It is in this context of increasing land pressure that waged work at the sugar estate has become very attractive. Formerly, the estate had to recruit labour from faraway districts like Njombe and Iringa. However by the early 1990s the estate could find plentiful supplies of labour locally. Estate managers attributed the ready availability of casual workers to economic hardship and drought (Mbilinyi, 1995).

However, as the estate labour force has grown, workers' militancy has emerged, especially among the young male cane-cutters. The cutters, numbering more than a thousand strong, young men, have developed the organizational and negotiating skills necessary to defend their interests. The labour situation at Mtibwa Sugar Estates became volatile in 1996 when cutters went on strike and later rioted in protest over the management's failure to backdate an agreed wage increase to the beginning of the season. The estate management eventually conceded to their demands to preclude further work stoppages.

Women working at Mtibwa sugar estates

From the 1980s onwards, substantial numbers of women peasant farmers residing in neighbouring villages around the Mtibwa Estates began seeking work on a daily casual basis to earn cash with which to purchase basic foodstuffs.[9] This has to be viewed in the light of a general expansion of female participation in micro and small-scale enterprises in both rural and urban areas of Tanzania during the SAP era (Katapa, 2000; Mbilinyi, 1997, 2000; Shundi, 2000). A growing number of rural women began earning cash incomes as casual farm workers on neighbouring plantations and large farms or through off-farm activities such as petty trade, food preparation and sales, homebrew beer sales and artisanry, a pattern that has been discerned elsewhere in Africa during this period (Bryceson, 1995).

Women's employment and working conditions

In 1997, full-time workers on the estate numbered approximately two thousand, 17 per cent being women, mostly drawn from the poorest stratum of the rural population.[10] The majority of female workers were casual labourers employed as weeders. Their conditions of employment contrasted markedly with the permanent workers who had a variety of rights according to national labour legislation, which included protection of employment, annual paid leave, family health services, sick pay, three-months paid maternity leave and minimum wage scales. Many permanent workers had access to housing on the plantations.

Seasonal temporary 'regular' workers, a large proportion of whom were male cane-cutters, had some of the same rights as permanent workers: minimum wage scales, health services, housing in many cases and work bonuses. Pay scales were determined on a piece-rate basis, however, whereas most non-field permanent workers received monthly wages. Most seasonal workers, by definition, were migrant workers, some of whom were directly recruited by the company. The conceptual lines between the two were vague and subject to the whim of management and the power of collective action among workers, as shown in their strike action. Management was especially concerned about the explosive outcome of housing hundreds of young men in single-sex compounds, often six to a room. The residential and work environment provided ample opportunity for men to share grievances, raise awareness and plan action. That militancy among sugar-cane workers might be a logical response to low wages and poor working conditions was never mentioned.

The Mtibwa Sugar Estates encouraged women to become casual labourers, providing incentives such as sugar and sometimes maize for those who attended regularly and fulfilled their work tasks. So many village women sought work that some had to be turned away.[11] In 1992, only 14 per cent of the permanent labour force was female (Mbilinyi, 1995). In the next five years, permanent staffing levels were cut by 26 per cent. Women were less adversely affected by the retrenchments than men, suggesting that management valued the use of female labour in the wake of the estate's labour unrest. Women were perceived as less militant and could be hired on casual terms for lower wages year after year without workers' benefits such as maternity leave having to be paid (ibid., 1995, 1997, 2000). Nonetheless, women workers at Mtibwa Sugar Estates were a minority in a male-dominated industry and plantation society, and were subjected to a macho work environment.

In contrast to both the permanent and the seasonal temporary workers, women casual workers were paid on a daily piece-rate basis in the field without any workers' benefits, with the exception of basic health services for the individual worker. They were not satisfied with their working conditions, complaining that their tasks were too heavy, they lacked transport from the camp to the field, their health was endangered due to over-work, no workload adjustments were paid during pregnancy, and safety precautions and protective clothing to guard against fertilizers and other agro-chemical usage were unavailable (ibid., 1995). Not surprisingly, women guards and hospital workers were relatively more satisfied with their working conditions than the field workers.

Despite their reservations about the work, women continued to seek employment on the plantation because they lacked alternatives. Smallholder farming no longer provided sufficient income and their weeding work was a vital means of tiding their families over during the rainy 'hunger' season before the harvest when people's food stores were depleted. They worked to earn enough money to buy maize. There was similar casual work available on the larger outgrowers' farms at somewhat higher wages but this was less secure employment and did not afford women workers and their children access to the Mtibwa company hospital, a highly valued perk.

Wage levels did not keep up with the rising cost of living and were considered far too low by all categories of workers. Many claimed that they barely covered a quarter of their needs and women felt compelled to pursue additional income-generating activities in addition to their subsistence agricultural work. Several farmed paddy as a food and cash crop, often by opening up new forest land. Full-time workers in the security and hospital departments complained

that they lacked free time to carry out trade or farm, and relied at least partially on hired labour. Only the top-level management and professionals could
afford to hire large numbers of labourers and, with their advantaged access
to estate land, they became successful medium-scale sugar outgrowers. Field
workers had far less access to land and lacked the cash needed to hire others.
Whatever farming they did was on marginal company land and directed towards meeting household food consumption needs. Male workers who were
married relied on their wives to take the lead in farming.

Women's workloads were intensifying with gender dynamics within the
household shaping the nature of the work women performed and the degree
of control over the products and income they earned.

Not-so-happy families: intra-household struggles over unpaid domestic labour and women's wages

Smallholder farming in Morogoro has traditionally been characterized by a
patriarchal internal structure whereby elderly men dominate power relations
with the household. Historically, the patriarchal farming system was based
on the exploitation of the unpaid labour of women, youth and other household dependants in the production of crops and other produce for household
consumption and sale. With the introduction of large-scale plantations and
associated male wage labour, this patriarchal system and the unpaid labour
of women and youth subsidized the cost of reproduction of the waged labour
force employed in large-scale capitalist farming.

The growing scale of female wage labour in the large-scale agricultural sector is not only reflective of a new relationship developing between the smallholder farm sector and the large-scale capitalist sector but also introduces
tensions within smallholder peasant farming. The decision by women and
youth to seek waged employment is not simply a response to an emerging
labour market but reflects a qualitative change in status from unpaid to paid
labour, a social as well as economic transition with profound implications for
household relations (Mbilinyi, 1997).

Intra-household division of labour

Amidst the decline in men's cash earnings and the compensatory increase in
women's wage labour and income-generating activities, there was no evidence
that the division of labour within the household altered to facilitate these
changes. In a recent survey of Morogoro village labour patterns, women farmers spent an average of 6.7 hours per day in agricultural production, 4.7 hours
per day in reproduction activities and 3.5 hours in food preparation, cooking
and water collection (Rwambali, 1990). Hardly any farm activities were carried
out solely by men, not even in the case of cash crops. Most operations were
done jointly or by hired labour, children and relatives (the other category),

and some by women alone. The concept 'joint' was nebulous: what portion of joint was actually that of women?

Lazaro (1996) found that women working or living on plantations in Morogoro devoted an average of 4 hours per day to food-crop production compared to 1.6 hours by men. There was no major difference between married and single women (4.4 and 4.8 hours respectively) whereas married men put in less time than single men (1.7 and 2.8 hours). Her explanation was that married men relied on their wives' input into the farm. Women also devoted more time to domestic reproduction activities: 5 hours compared to 1.3 hours for men.

Similar gender patterns were revealed in my interviews with Mbogo and Lusanga villagers in 1997. Men did hardly any cooking, laundry, water collection or childcare. This was carried out by wives and mothers with the assistance of their male and female children, except for cooking which rarely involved boys. Mbogo villagers reported that some men cooked if their wives were ill and no one else was available. Those with bicycles also helped to carry water, especially if the water source was far from home.

Most farm operations in both villages were carried out by all household members regardless of sex or age, especially hoe cultivation, planting, weeding, harvesting and transport. In Mbogo, everyone took part in clearing the land but Lusanga villagers insisted that this was largely the male head's responsibility. Food storage was carried out by men in Mbogo and by women in Lusanga but marketing of the crop was solely carried out by men in both locations. Men were responsible for protecting crops from pigs, a common problem in Lusanga, while women and children scared away birds. In Mbogo, everyone reportedly shared this task.

Decision-making in farmer and worker households

Men continued to dominate most key decisions related to agricultural production. In Lusanga and Mbogo villages, the only decision that was unambiguously reported to be joint was that of what kind of crops to grow. Households farmed paddy and maize, with cash returns mainly controlled by the men. Men were in charge of the sale of these crops, with joint consultation in some households. Women in Lusanga were the major decision-makers as to where to plant but in Mbogo this was a joint decision. Men controlled sales of cattle and goats, while women were responsible for the chickens, although people in Mbogo said there was some consultation involved. Decisions over the allocation of cash proceeds from crops were dominated by men, with the possibility of consultation in some cases: 'In 3 out of 100 households!' according to one woman in Lusanga.[12]

However, in the light of changing circumstances, women increasingly participated in household economic decision-making processes. Women earned extra cash incomes from beer brewing and the sale of homemade doughnuts (*maandazi*) and other foodstuffs that were sold at kiosks, but it appears that the evolving pattern of household members' participation in wage work at the Mtibwa Sugar Estates was most critical to the changing status.

Lazaro (1996) carried out a detailed analysis of income and expenditure patterns in workers' households on Morogoro plantations. As women earned more cash income, they were becoming more assertive. Single women, like single men, had more or less complete control over how they spent their income, and over other resources. When asked who had the final decision on how a household's income was spent, 89 per cent of conjugal households with a non-income-earning wife answered that it was the husband, with the remainder reporting that both men and women had a say. However, women earning some form of income were deciding how to use their own earnings or they also gained decision-making powers over joint income. Radical changes were taking place in some households and co-habiting relationships where wives/girlfriends were employed on a regular basis and their husbands/partners were either unemployed or lacked regular cash incomes. Some women reportedly used their income to dominate and exert power over the men, just 'as men normally do'.

Conversely, married men in full-time plantation work were faced with a new situation. They were responsible for providing for household consumption needs on the basis of cash earnings, while their wives produced most of the household's direct food requirements. In the past, most male plantation labour was of a migrant nature whereby men were non-resident in their home areas. Women produced subsistence food and managed the household in their husbands' absence, whereas they were now doing so in their presence.

This proximity afforded women better awareness of their husbands' finances and led them to be vocal about what they saw. Many village women accused men of squandering their money on alcohol and other women. Mtibwa workers raised the same issue of financial irresponsibility. Male workers hastened to point out that wives did not trust their husbands when they reported that their incomes had decreased, or that they had no more savings. The decline in male incomes led to increased marital conflict. Several of the village women and field workers interviewed conceptualized their present marital relationship as one where 'women marry men', as opposed to the normal Kiswahili expressions *ameolewa* (feminine: she was married to him) and *ameoa* (masculine: he married her) inferring that men are the active and women are the passive partners in the act of marriage. Criticizing this reversal of accepted gender roles, one female field worker at the sugar estate noted: 'Men used to heed the marriage law and provide for their wives. Nowadays they shirk their responsibilities.'

Marital conflict increased amidst growing economic hardship and poverty, and the female perception that men were not carrying their share of family responsibilities (Mbilinyi, 1995). Many widowed and divorced women stated that they had chosen not to remarry: 'Why add another child to the household?', 'I don't want another burden (*mzigo*)' or as one Mtibwa field worker put it: 'Who in their right mind would accept problems?' (*Nani atakubali matatizo?*).[13] Women resented the fact that men no longer earned sufficient cash for their families' needs nor did they provide obligatory labour inputs into farming and other non-farm activities.

Young men and women were choosing not to marry (ibid.). The young men explained that they lacked the resources necessary, such as land, a house and enough cash income. Rural unemployment and the general economic slowdown were considered to be major obstacles. In Lusanga village, people said that young men were in a rush to earn money and often forgot other priorities such as marriage and farming. Mbogo villagers attributed the delayed marriage patterns to the land crisis: 'Without land, how can our young men marry?' Young women had regular sexual partners and bore children but increasingly chose not to marry because they feared the 'costs of having a husband'. According to some Mtibwa workers, parents even encouraged their daughters not to marry because of the problems facing married women.

These views reflect the impact of falling male incomes and growing under- and unemployment on gender relations at household level at a time when cash requirements were steadily increasing. The decline in male incomes was due to an amalgam of factors already cited in this chapter: falling returns for export and other cash crops, cutbacks in formal employment, and the growing scarcity of fertile land and water supplies in the region. The solution to the cash shortfall brought other tensions in its wake. Women and men were divided over many gender issues but confronting the same basic livelihood crisis and growing poverty arising from the fundamental restructuring of Tanzanian agricultural production.

Ousting patriarchy or obliterating the peasant family?

The legitimacy of economic reform depends on the degree to which it delivers its promises of improved well-being, higher incomes, reduced poverty and greater access to basic social services for the majority of rural and urban people. The income gap between rural and urban areas was estimated to have doubled during the 1970s and 1980s (Msambichaka and Naho, 1995). Poverty was more widespread and deeper in the rural areas as compared to urban centres. The incidence of poverty rose during the mid 1990s after an earlier decline. Surveys indicated that nutritional intake was inadequate for between a quarter and a half of all Tanzanian households.[14] Farmers were poorer than non-farmers in rural areas and farmers without cash crops were poorer than those who produced them, holding farm size, education and other factors constant (Tanzania Poverty Reduction Strategy Paper, 2000). In 2001, 38 per cent of the rural population was still living in poverty, another indicator that neo-liberal policies have not led to significant rural development nor increased incomes for the rural majority (Tanzania, Bureau of Statistics 2002; Tanzania, Research and Analysis Working Group, 2005).

Poverty has a qualitative, subjective dimension that cannot be captured in economic measures (Mbughuni, 1994). When asked to assess their welfare during the 1990s compared with the previous five years, Mtibwa workers stressed 'hard times' (*maisha magumu sana*). The rising costs of living in terms of basic foodstuffs, like cooking oil, and school fees were cited. It was generally acknowledged that there were more goods in the shops as a result of economic liberalization but they asked: 'What's the good of them when we cannot afford to buy them?' '*Leo pesa hamna. Motisha hamna.*' (Today there's no money, there's no incentive.)

The majority of plantation workers at Mtibwa Sugar Estates (MSE), Kilombero Sugar Company (KSC) and TPC said that conditions had worsened. Field workers, guards and the more privileged workers in the office and hospital shared similar views as expressed in the following verbatim quotes emanating from focus-group discussions:[15]

> *Sawa kabisa* (absolutely) – you try to do some business. The money you get is so little, it's not enough for your consumption needs. (woman, MSE)

> Right now women carry a heavy load. First of all, there's divorce. Men run away when they see how costly a family is. (village chairperson)

> Prices are increasing but the salaries are still too low. They are really killing us. I can't afford cooking oil. We just boil the food. We have fish twice a month, on payday. That's when we buy soap and maize for *ugali*. There's no money left over to pay the development tax or to buy myself clothing. I pay people to produce charcoal, which I sell as a supplementary income, but I can't afford to use it myself – it's too expensive. We use firewood instead. I get free medical services but have to pay for my children. It's Tsh 150 for the medical card, a bed is Tsh 1,000 if they are really sick and the daily outpatient charge is Tsh 300. People try to leave without paying – we can't afford it. (woman weeder, aged 26, KSC)

> Look at the price of things! One piece of *khanga* costs Tsh 750. A length of cloth to sew a dress costs Tsh 5,000, and we get maybe Tsh 2,000 at the end of the month, or less after deductions. (woman weeder, aged 31, KSC)

> Tsh 4,000 is not enough pay. You pay Tsh 700 for the rent of one room for you and your children. You have to pay for school fees and uniforms. Even when you and your wife are working and each contributes something, there is not enough. (male weeder, aged 30, KSC)

> Prices of food like maize have risen. Meat is beyond our reach – our incomes are too low. In 1986/87, prices were low. Even Tsh 3,000 was enough to live on. Nowdays a *khanga* from Kenya costs Tsh 2,800 – your pay is gone! I don't know where we are heading. (woman irrigation worker, aged 40, TPC)

> Low wages – but you need many things. You cannot afford anything important, all the money goes on food. (woman weeder, aged 27, TPC)

Your child passes his exams to enter secondary school but you can't afford to pay the school fees so he misses his opportunity for further education. (male irrigation worker, aged 48, TPC)

Malnutrition is increasing. Among every 10 children, only one is fully fed. (village health worker)

There are no textbooks in school because the prices are so high. Life is difficult for everybody – parents, students and teachers – different from the past. (school teacher in Lusanga)

Life is getting harder every year. The cost of living goes up, the value of money drops. (woman clerk, aged 23, TPC)

In spite of all these hardships, many women workers at Mtibwa Sugar Estates felt that they were better off than in the 1980s because of their employed status. Wage employment, even on a casual basis, was preferable to full-time farming because at least 'they were sure of *some* income whereas farmers had nothing'. In Lusanga, a man pointed out that: 'Women's involvement in trade has resulted from hard times. In the past there were no women at the market but now there are many'. He was referring to restrictions on women entering the market in accordance with local Islamic norms that had prevailed in the area but were now being flouted.

While women were gaining some degree of control, men felt a loss of control, a sense of hopelessness and foreboding about their future in peasant agriculture, as the following quotes from men indicate:

Conditions look good but we don't have the resources. Our hands cannot support us and provide all our needs.

We farmers use the hand hoe and cannot produce much. There is no future in hand-hoe farming, it's mere subsistence.

We are mixing life with politics. A Lusanga resident doesn't know morning or evening what he'll eat. Conditions are very difficult. People live by faith alone. Things are there but who has the means to buy them? Life is not good. We just try our luck.

Conclusion

The results of economic reform policies have been mixed in terms of overall agricultural performance, with positive and negative consequences for women farmers and workers, and other self-employed persons. Clearly a minority of the population has benefited from the changes that have occurred in Tanzanian rural society. Moreover, gender relations have been transformed with more economic power for women, resulting from their increased labour-force participation and income-earning capabilities. This has accompanied the tragedy of falling male employment and a decline in male incomes.

Smallholder peasant farming, at least as it exists today, is at risk. The increasing monetary costs of farm production and dependence on tradable goods and services such as farm inputs and equipment have marginalized smallholder farmers and fuelled the increasing concentration and control over land and labour by large-scale capitalist enterprises. This tendency has been bolstered by a shift in orientation of state services in support of large-scale capitalist ventures rather than smallholder farming. Increasing marginalization in land ownership to the point of landlessness, especially among youth and women, is contributing to the increasingly part-time nature of farming on the part of the poor. The growing dependence on non-farm incomes for household subsistence is closely linked to the steady withdrawal of family labour from smallholder farming and women's and youth's aversion to unpaid family-labour demands.

A transformation of class and gender relations in agricultural production is underway. The gender relations that underlie the patriarchal farming system are no longer tenable. Women and youth are voting with their feet and with their hands to reject unpaid family labour amidst the growing immiseration of the majority of rural people, the collapse of viable commercial smallholder farming and the entrenchment of large-scale capitalistic agricultural enterprises. Women and youth have resisted pressures to increase unpaid family labour in crop production and have sought alternative off-farm self-employment or waged work in large-scale agriculture. In effect, they are replacing unpaid family labour in the fields with the extremely low wages and poor working conditions of sugar estates, and growing vulnerability to HIV/AIDS.

Organizations that seek people-centered sustainable development strategies have to confront the enormity of the oppression and exploitation that maintains the so-called 'community' in rural Tanzanian society. The capacity of the household and the community to reproduce themselves has been seriously undermined. The decline of public social services has become a politically explosive issue. Rural areas are being increasingly neglected, as indicated by falling levels of education and the rampant AIDS epidemic.

Village farmers and plantation workers who participated in our 1997 Mtibwa study shared a common vision of an activist state, which would protect their interests *vis-à-vis* company management and the vagaries of the market. Parents accused the government for its failure to develop an employment strategy that would ensure that their children had something meaningful to do and the means to maintain themselves. Women were angry at official neglect in ensuring that men carried out their parental responsibilities. Plantation workers were especially alarmed by the increase in child abuse and believed that the government had an active role to play in supporting efforts to stop male violence against women and children.

At the same time, farmers talked about the need to organize themselves so as to protect their control over village land and the commons around it. Joint action was also recognized as necessary for the creation of a bottom floor to producer prices, below which farmers would not sell, thereby protecting their farm incomes from the inroads of private traders. Activities of the Women Worker Committees of the Tanzania Plantation Agriculture Workers Association (TPAWU)[16] are a good example of initiatives that were being taken then by women workers to organize themselves. Feminist activists can contribute their analytical skills to this popular education process, along with advocacy and lobbying for desirable policies at all levels of society. As Mtibwa workers concluded at the research feedback workshop: 'We don't have to agree with the World Bank about everything!'

About the author

Marjorie Mbilinyi, formerly professor of education at the University of Dar es Salaam where she taught from 1968 through 2003, is a scholar activist and founding member of several feminist/gender-oriented organizations and networks in Tanzania and Africa, including the Tanzania Gender Networking Programme, the Feminist Activist Coalition which TGNP hosts, Women's Research and Documentation Project, the Tanzanian and African Participatory Research Networks and Gender and Economic Reforms in Africa, GERA, as well as recently joining the African Feminist Forum, AFF. She has extensive experience in participatory organizing, pedagogy and research at national and community level, linked to feminist advocacy and activism. Her recent publications include several co-edited books, *Activist Voices* (2003, Tanzania Gender Networking Programme [TNGP], Dar es Salaam), *Against-Neoliberalism* (2003, TGNP, Dar es Salaam), *Nyerere on Education* (2004, HakiElimu, Dar es Salaam) and *Food is Politics* (2002, Rural Food Security Research Group, Institute of Development Studies, University of Dar es Salaam) and the journal article 'Rooting transformative feminist struggles in Tanzania at grassroots', *Review of African Political Economy* 2009, No. 121: 435–442 (with Demere Kitunga).

Notes

* I gratefully acknowledge the assistance of Ave Marie Semakafu and Julius Mwabuki in carrying out research on the sugar estates in 1995 and 1997, respectively, and workers at the Mtibwa, Kilombero and TPC sugar estates and villagers and leaders of Lusanga and Mbogo villages, Morogoro Rural District, for their participation in extensive discussions connected with this study (Mbilinyi, 1997).
1. Relatively few studies have examined the large-scale capitalist sector in spite of its long and continued significance in Tanzanian agriculture (Maganya, 1994; Mbilinyi 1991, 1994, 1995, 1997).
2. Peak years for marketed output were: cotton: 1973, coffee: 1973, tea: 1979 which was only surpassed in 1990 and 1991, tobacco: 1977, cash crops: 1974, sugar: 1978, sisal: 1964 and pyrethrum: 1967 (Tanzania, Bureau of Statistics, 1994). World Bank (2000: 71–2) figures indicate the following peak years for production output of three of these crops during the period between 1982 and 1998: cotton: 1993, coffee: 1993, cashew: 1998.

Production of cotton and coffee has since declined with sharp fluctuations, whereas cashew output fell from 1986 to 1990, after which there has been a steady rise.

3. Most mainstream commentators argue that agricultural production declined after independence, and even more so after the Arusha Declaration Policies of 1967, only to be rescued by the liberalization policies of the late 1980s and 1990s. Analysis of both sides of the debate is found in Mbilinyi (1994).

4. The only sector that did not register increased growth was agriculture, declining from 5.8 per cent in 2004 to 5.2 per cent of GDP in 2005 (Tanzania, Bureau of Statistics, 2006).

5. See Kimambo, 1994; Majengo, 1994; Mdadila,1996; Mwaikambo, 1995; Toke, 1995; Turuka, 1995; Kashuliza and Mbiha, 1995.

6. See HakiArdhi, 1996, 1997; Kamata, 2003; Mhina, 1996; Mvungi 1995.

7. A coalition of non-governmental and community-based organizations worked for more than a year to oppose the land reform process and to publicize information about it as widely as possible, under the leadership of HakiArdhi. In the end, the campaign succeeded to get women's rights to land incorporated into the Village Land Act. However ultimate control over land remained in the hands of the Executive Branch of government, and struggles over land have intensified in response to mass land appropriations by private investors in mining, tourism and agriculture (Kamata, 2003).

8. I am grateful to Richard Mabala who drew my attention to the land issue in Mbogo village and shared his preliminary research findings.

9. Lazaro (1996) also noted that before the 1980s, local women did not go to work on the sugar and sisal plantations.

10. The women estate workers were relatively uneducated compared with women in the nearby villages. Roughly one third of the estate's labour force was employed on a casual or seasonal basis, for whom written records were not available.

11. Similar age and marriage patterns had been observed in 1992, suggesting a different labour pattern in the sugar industry at Mtibwa than in the tea industry. Women farm workers on private tea plantations in Rungwe District, Mbeya were largely young, unmarried daughters living at home who were looking for a cash income before getting married and setting up their own households in the late 1980s and early 1990s. Mtibwa's female workforce was older and more settled (Mbilinyi 1989, 1991,1995).

12. Kaihula (1995) also found a similar pattern of contradiction as women entrepreneurs accessed and controlled more income. Their husbands expressed anxiety about the perceived threat to their former position as heads of household but they also appreciated the contribution that women made to the household income.

13. See Mbilinyi, 1991; Mbilinyi, 1995; Chale and Mukangara, 1997; Lazaro, 1996 and confirmed by several women villagers in the Mtibwa 1997 fieldwork.

14. Twenty-seven per cent of the people were unable to afford enough food to meet nutritional requirements (Tanzania, Bureau of Statistics, 1993)

and 48 per cent could not meet all their basic food and non-food needs (Tanzania, Poverty Reduction Strategy Paper, 2000).
15. Author's translation (Mbilinyi, 1995: 133–5).
16. These committees in association with the MWEMA project, which was then supported by the ILO and Danida, carried out gender awareness and training activities, supported worker negotiations with management to seek more gender balanced work conditions and terms, and increased women's participations in the unions.

References

Bryceson, D.F. (1995) *Women Wielding the Hoe,* Berg Publishers, Oxford.
Chale, F.S. and Mukangara, F. (1997) *'Taarifa ya Utafiti, Wilaya ya Mbeya Viji-jini'*, Tanzania Gender Network Programme (TGNP), Dar es Salaam.
HakiArdhi (1996) Workshop on Debating Land, 3 April, Dar es Salaam.
HakiArdhi (1997) Consultative Conference of NGOs and Interested Persons on Land Tenure Reform, 15–16 May, Dar es Salaam.
Kaihula, N.A.M (1995) 'The Effects of Wives' Economic Power on Gender Relationships in Tanzania Households', MA thesis, University of Dar es Salaam.
Kamata, N. (2003) 'People, state and resources' in M. Mbilinyi M. Rusimbi, C.S.L. Chachage and D. Kitunga (eds), *Activist Voices*, pp. 91–105, Tanzania Gender Network Programme/E&D Ltd, Dar es Salaam.
Kashuliza, A.K. and Mbiha, E.R. (1995) 'Structural adjustment and the performance of the agricultural sector in Tanzania, 1980–1990', in P.G. Forster and S. Maghimbi (eds), *The Tanzanian Peasantry*, Avebury, Aldershot, UK.
Katapa, R. (2000) 'Gender Patterns in Employment in the Informal Sector', Women's Research and Documentation Project (WRDP), Report on Institutional Strengthening of the Ministry of Community Development, Women's Affairs and Children, Prepared for the Italian Association for Women in Development (AIDOS), Dar es Salaam.
Kimambo, E.C. (1994) *1993/94 Industry Review of Tea*, Ministry of Agriculture, Marketing Development Bureau, Dar es Salaam.
Koda, B. (1994) 'Gender, Agriculture and Rural Development in Tanzania', Paper presented to Institute of Development Studies Women's Study Group Seminar on Achievements and Constraints of Women in the Past Twenty Years, Dar es Salaam.
Lazaro, E.A. (1996) 'Women in the Household Economy: The Case of Agricultural Plantations in Morogoro Region, Tanzania', PhD thesis, Sokoine University.
Maganya, E.N. (1994) 'Of large-scale and small farms', in U. Himmelstrand, K. Kinyanjui and E. Mburugu (eds), *African Perspectives on Development*, James Currey, London.
Majengo, O.J. (1994) *Tobacco Marketing Review 1993/94*, Ministry of Agriculture, Marketing Development Bureau, Dar es Salaam.
Mbilinyi, M. (1989) 'Plight of women plantation workers', *Sauti ya Siti*, September.

Mbilinyi, M. (1991), *Big Slavery: Agribusiness and the Crisis in Women's Employment in Tanzania*, Dar es Salaam University Press, Dar es Salaam.

Mbilinyi, M. (1994) 'Restructuring gender and agriculture in Tanzania' in U. Himmelstrand, K. Kinyanjui and E. Mburugu (eds), *African Perspectives on Development*, James Currey, London.

Mbilinyi, M. with Semakafu, A.M. (1995) 'Gender and Employment on Sugarcane Plantations in Tanzania', ILO, Working Paper 85, Geneva.

Mbilinyi, M.J. (1997) 'Women Workers and Self-Employed in the Rural Sector', Report prepared for ILO and presented at ILO/Tanzania, Ministry of Labour and Youth Development National Workshop, 30 July-1 August, Dar es Salaam.

Mbilinyi, M. (ed.) (2000) 'Gender Patterns in Micro and Small Enterprises of Tanzania', Ministry of Community Development, Women's Affairs and Children (MCDWAC), Women's Research and Documentation Project (WRDP), Italian Association for Women in Development (AIDOS), Dar es Salaam and Rome.

Mbilinyi, M., Koda, B., Mung'ong'o, C. and Nyoni, T. (1999) 'Rural Food Security in Tanzania: The Challenge for Human Rights, Democracy and Development', Institute of Development Studies, Rural Food Security Policy and Development Group, presented to Launching Workshop (July).

Mbughuni, P. (1994) 'Gender and poverty alleviation in Tanzania', in M.S.D. Bagachwa (ed.), *Poverty Alleviation in Tanzania*, Dar es Salaam University Press.

Mdadila, J.M. (1996) *1994/95 Market Review of Maize and Rice*, Ministry of Agriculture, Marketing Development Bureau, Dar es Salaam.

Mhina, E. (1996) 'Improving Information on Women's Contribution to Agricultural Production for Gender Sensitive Planning', FAO/URT, preliminary report, Dar es Salaam.

Msambichaka, L.A., Kilindo, A.A.L. and Mjema, G.D. (eds) (1995) *Beyond Structural Adjustment Programmes in Tanzania*, University of Dar es Salaam, Economic Research Bureau, Dar es Salaam.

Msambichaka, L.A. and Naho, A. (1995) 'Agricultural sector performance under SAP in Tanzania', in L.A. Msambichaka, A.A.L. Kilindo and G.D. Mjema (eds), *Beyond Structural Adjustment Programmes in Tanzania*, University of Dar es Salaam, Economic Research Bureau, Dar es Salaam.

Mvungi, A.A.K. (1995) 'Towards a people-based approach: a case study of Mwanga District', in P.G. Forster and S. Maghimbi (eds), *The Tanzanian Peasantry*, Avebury, Aldershot, UK.

Mwaikambo, W.S. (1995) *Coffee Marketing Review 1993/94*, Ministry of Agriculture, Marketing Development Bureau, Dar es Salaam.

Rwambali, E.G. (1990) 'Women and Co-operatives in Rural Development in Tanzania', MSc thesis, Sokoine University, Morogoro.

Shundi, F. (2000) 'Gender patterns in employment in micro and small enterprises in Arusha Municipality and Arumeru District', in M. Mbilinyi (ed.), *'Gender Patterns in Micro and Small Enterprises of Tanzania'*, Ministry of Community Development, MCDWAC, WRDP, AIDOS, Dar es Salaam and Rome.

Sterkenburg, J. and van der Wiel, A. (1993) 'Structural Adjustment, Sugar Sector Development, and Netherlands Aid to Tanzania', Paper at Global Change, Structural Adjustment and Access Conference, 29–31 March, Amsterdam.

Tanzania (2000) *Poverty Reduction Strategy Paper*, Prepared by the Tanzanian Authorities for the International Monetary Fund, http://www.imf.org/external/NP/prsp/2000/tza/02/index.htm. [last accessed 17 November 2009].

Tanzania, Bureau of Statistics (1993) *1991/92 Household Budget Survey*, Planning Commission, Dar es Salaam.

Tanzania, Bureau of Statistics (1994) *Selected Statistical Series 1951–1991*, Planning Commission, Dar es Salaam.

Tanzania, Bureau of Statistics (2002) *Household Budget Survey 2000/01*, President's Office, Dar es Salaam.

Tanzania, Bureau of Statistics (2006) *Economic Survey 2005*, President's Office, Dar es Salaam.

Tanzania, Minister for Finance and Economic Affairs Mustafa Haidi Mkulo 2008, 'Introducing to the National Assembly the Status of the Economy Report for 2007', 13 June, Dodoma.

Tanzania, Ministry of Agriculture (2001) 'Revised Draft Agricultural Sector Development Strategy', Consultation Draft (30 May), Dar es Salaam.

Tanzania, Research and Analysis Working Group (2005) *Poverty and Human Development Report 2005*, Dar es Salaam.

Tanzania Gender Networking Programme (2006) 'Is the 2006/2007 Budget Pro-Poor and Gender Sensitive? Need for a New Alternative Budget Framework', *Gender, Democracy and Development Digest 2*, Dar es Salaam.

Toke, S.B. (1995) *1993/94 Industry Review of Sugar*, Ministry of Agriculture, Marketing Development Bureau.

Turuka, F.M. (1995) *Price Reform and Fertiliser Use in Smallholder Agriculture in Tanzania*, LIT Verlag Munster, Hamburg.

World Bank (2000) *Agriculture in Tanzania since 1986*, Washington, DC.

SECTION IV

Occupational Change and Public Policy

CHAPTER 10

Shifting out of gear: households, livelihoods and public policy on the South African Wild Coast

Leslie Bank

Since the transition to democracy in South Africa, rural development policy has not been consistently and clearly defined. In the mid-1990s, the main focus of government policy was on meeting basic needs through service delivery projects in rural areas under the so-called Reconstruction and Development Programme (RDP) of the African National Congress. This changed in the late 1990s when basic service delivery was supplemented with the introduction of market friendly, neo-liberal policies, which aimed to attract more foreign investment and deepen market relations throughout the society. In rural areas, this shift was manifested in a renewed focus on small-scale commercial farming in the former Bantustans and in the formation of 'commodity groups' in rural villages, as a means of generating new livelihoods options and alleviating poverty. This chapter investigates the impact of the latter policy changes on the social dynamics within rural households, on gender and generational relations and on the livelihood and occupational profile of the members of a single rural community in the Eastern Cape, South Africa's poorest province.

Introduction

In 1996 the African National Congress (ANC) government in South Africa adopted the market-friendly neo-liberal Growth, Employment and Redistribution (GEAR) policy framework in order to speed up economic growth and development delivery in the country. The main aim of GEAR was to attract greater volumes of direct foreign investment to establish an annual six per cent national economic growth rate by 2000, which would boost exports and create 400,000 new jobs every year (Binns and Nel, 2001: 3). To ensure that economic growth and investment were not confined to the larger metropolitan areas, it was also announced that 11 Spatial Development Initiatives (SDIs) would be created to draw private-sector investment into new 'development nodes and corridors' in areas of 'under-utilized economic potential', especially in the former homelands. By 2000, it was clear that the GEAR programme was struggling to deliver on its promises. Instead of creating a million jobs nation-ally, the formal sector of the economy shed over 500,000 jobs between 1996 and 2000 (*Economist,* 2001). In fact, GEAR's inability to generate jobs emerged as the most important political issue, next to the HIV/AIDS crisis, in the 2004 South African general elections (*Mail* and *Guardian*, 15–22 April 2004).

Direct foreign investment had arrived in restricted quantities and was con-centrated in the major metropolitan centres. This created great difficulties for many of the SDIs, which were struggling to get off the ground (Kepe *et al.*, 2001, van Wyk, 2003). In the Eastern Cape, the country's poorest province and the location of two SDIs created in the mid-1990s, poverty has deepened and unemployment has grown over the past decade. De-industrialization at the national and regional levels has taken a heavy toll on the region as many migrant and commuter workers, especially in the former Transkei and Ciskei homelands, have lost their jobs. The withdrawal of industrial decentralization subsidies supplied by the apartheid state since the 1970s for firms operating in homeland towns has resulted in the loss of over 50,000 local industrial jobs in these areas (Bank, 2003). Districts on the Transkei coast were among the most severely affected by retrenchments in the mines in the 1990s (Ngonini, 2003).

Along the Transkei Wild Coast, which was zoned as an agro-tourism SDI in 1996, standards of living have dropped, even in areas directly targeted by SDI projects and initiatives. A longitudinal study conducted by CIETAfrica (2001) found that by 2000 over 30 per cent of households in this area had no land under cultivation and that the average cash value of food produced by house-holds had decreased by over 10 per cent since 1997. Employment rates, which hovered around 15 per cent for women and 25 per cent for men, were also seen to be declining steadily. But perhaps most strikingly, the survey revealed a dramatic increase in household debt. In 2000, 43 per cent of households had at least one member who had tried to obtain a cash loan or credit, which was twice as many as in 1997. By 2000, 41 per cent of households had active loans, mostly with local shopkeepers, compared with 17 per cent in 1997. The aver-age loan was over US$200. The report's main conclusion was that households on the Wild Coast were getting progressively poorer. They were growing less food, had less income for consumption and had lower levels of employment and higher levels of debt in 2000 than in 1997. Reports of similar trends have emerged from other parts of the province and are confirmed by the results of the 2001 census, which shows that unemployment in many rural areas of the province is now above 70 per cent (South African Census, 2001).

The failure of the SDI programme to deliver on its promises, together with a widespread recognition that rural poverty is worsening in the Eastern Cape, especially in the eastern part of the province, has generated consider-able scepticism within the province about the capacity of GEAR-style poli-cies to meaningfully tackle rural poverty. This realization has coincided with a more general disillusionment with the consequences of Structural Adjust-ment Polices in Southern Africa as a whole and has initiated calls for greater attention to be given to food security (Ellis, 2003; Scoones and Wolmer, 2003). In the Eastern Cape this concern was strongly reflected in the work of the Provincial Growth and Development Plan (PGDP) research team in 2003, which identified increased food production as a key development priority for the next decade (Provincial Growth and Development Plan, 2004; *Daily Dispatch* 12 September 2003). The approach advocated by the PGDP was for an agriculture-led growth strategy with a strong emphasis on food production and poverty-alleviation measures. The earlier GEAR obsession with foreign investment, agro-business, export crops and the formation of commodity groups has given way to a much stronger emphasis on local resources, markets and the reactivation of family farming, especially in and around the former homelands.

The Massive Food Programme (MFP), launched in the Eastern Cape in 2003, captures the spirit of this thinking. The programme, which is to be progressively expanded offering a range of opportunities for rural smallholder households to expand maize production in the former homelands with state subsidies, extension services and technical support. The main aim of the programme was to revive maize production, to reduce poverty and stimulate a new agricultural market in locally produced maize.[1] Only two years earlier, Local Government Minister Sydney Mafamdai told the South African cabinet that the rural development vision was 'a radical one in that it envisages transformed rural economies which move away from subsistence modes of economic activity to productive, sustainable and growth enhancing economies activities, and many of the current projects are not sustainable because they are biased towards poverty alleviation and are not explicitly developmental' (*Daily Dispatch,* 11 July 2001). He went on to lambaste 'resource poor' and 'subsistence-orientated' farmers as inhibiting development, as agents of environmental degradation, and as barriers to effective economic diversification and entrepreneurship in rural areas.

In the PGDP approach 'subsistence' and 'development' were not presented in such oppositional terms. In fact, resource-poor farmers were penned into new programmes, such as the MFP, at the bottom end of the rural development ladder, as rural producers who might, with time, develop into 'emerging farmers'. The changing perception of the resource-poor farmers owed much to the influence of donor-driven rural livelihood frameworks emphasizing poverty alleviation. Indeed, this framework highlights the capacity of rural households to use collective household strategies, such as intensification or diversification, to work their way out of poverty and to achieve sustainable livelihoods. This is envisaged as the path from struggling rural family farms to efficient commercial smallholder farms. As Scoones and Wolmer (2003: 2) note:

> In more recent times rural development policy has been constructed around a particular narrative centred on the assumed efficiency of the small family farm. Agriculture, as the mainstay of the rural economy can, it is argued, be transformed through technology transfer, supported by effective extension

and input supply and credit systems. Efficient and productive small farms would produce sufficient food to eliminate food insecurity, provide opportunities for labour, and form the basis for broader rural growth.

This emphasis on family farming as the key to both poverty alleviation and development is, of course, nothing new in South Africa or the Eastern Cape. In fact, the basic orientation of rural development policy during the homeland era was predicated on the promotion of family farming units of various kinds. The Tomlinson Commission of the 1950s, which laid the foundation for homeland economic policy, identified two types of rural farmers in the homelands – subsistence-oriented rural households that provided labour to the migrant economy and efficient small-scale commercial farming households – and argued that the apartheid government should find ways of supporting both categories. In 2004, a similar model was being advocated for the Eastern Cape but, unlike Tomlinson who saw the two categories of farmers (worker-peasants and small commercial family farms) as very different, the MFP policy framework seems to envisage that some 'resource-poor farmers' or what it now calls 'homestead producers' will, with the correct blend of support from the state, become efficient small family farmers.[2]

But how realistic are such schemes to revitalize family farming and food production in a context where many rural households have drifted away from agriculture and where gender and generational relations in rural areas have become increasing fraught? The aim of this chapter is to interrogate the influential rural livelihoods framework, which informed a new confidence policymakers perceived in the capacity of poor rural households to revitalize food production. In the discussion below, I begin by exploring some of the assumptions that inform the framework, especially in relation to questions of household coherence and occupational profiles and preferences, and to test these against changing rural realities in the Eastern Cape, paying special attention to developments in the Mooiplaas location of the former Ciskei. I argue that the livelihoods model takes inadequate account of the extent to which rural social relations have been transformed with the collapse of apartheid and the introduction of new rural development policies under the ANC government. The betterment-style patriarchal family farms built up by the apartheid government in rural areas as a means of servicing its wider economic and political objectives have unravelled in the face of far-reaching political and economic change since the 1980s. Under these conditions, male authority and power have been challenged, both within the household and beyond, as women have gradually consolidated control of post-apartheid village economies in many areas. For these women, a return to betterment-style family food farming would imply giving up the gains they made during the 1990s, notably their ability to control their own labour and economic choices. These changes and their implications for new policies, especially those that depend on high levels of household cooperation to achieve their objectives, are discussed in this chapter.

Framing livelihoods, conceptualizing households

Sustainable livelihoods approaches have their roots in Amartya Sen's (1981) path-breaking 'entitlement approach' to the understanding of famine and poverty. In the 1980s, Sen initiated a radical shift from the earlier supply-side understandings of famine by highlighting the role of demand-side factors, such as rights and entitlements, to the ability of households to access food. In a similar vein, the sustainable livelihoods framework starts by investigating how people use resources to construct a livelihood at the local level, rather than by beginning with the usual macro-level analysis of different economic sectors. The approach usually seeks to establish what sorts of assets and re-sources exist at the household and community level and explores what com-binations of these are required to protect households from poverty and to reduce their levels of vulnerability.

In recent reviews of the application of livelihood perspectives, Colin Mur-ray (2000, 2002) suggests that the 'sustainable livelihoods' framework (ad-opted by DFID) potentially offers a dynamic and historical perspective on changing livelihoods by focusing on complex 'cause and effect relationships' and 'iterative chains of events' from the local level. He sees the approach as holistic and capable of transcending discrete sectors – urban and rural, indus-trial and agricultural, formal and informal – through multiple analysis and cross-cutting strategies and approaches (2000: 116–17).

However, Murray also states that one of the weaknesses of the approach is that it under-estimates the impact of major shocks such as rampant inflation, civil conflict and mass redundancies in highlighting the 'vulnerability context' in which households operate. Swift and Hamilton (2001) concur when they note that the central focus on 'local dynamism' and on 'household welfare and agriculture', in particular, has created a danger that longer-term political and economic processes will be missed. Bryceson (1999) has taken this further, suggesting that those using this approach need to be careful to distinguish clearly between cyclical changes and more structural-level changes in African rural economies. She asserts, as I do here, that processes of de-agrarianization – namely a shift away from agrarian lifestyles and occupations – have not been adequately acknowledged since the 1980s.

Other critics have focused on the methodological weaknesses of the liveli-hood approach and the reliance on a neo-classical economic language of as-sets, capitals and 'multipliers' to explain complex social processes. Whitehead (2002) has recently suggested that, while economists might be comfortable conceptualizing market and non-market elements of householding within a single framework, this would not necessarily be the case for those working in anthropology, sociology or political economy. She notes:

> From the perspective of the latter disciplines, assets are of course relational: systems of access and distribution and systems of exclusionary access are intrinsic to the idea. They become torn out of their relational context in the shift to the language of neo-classical economics to explore livelihoods.

The analogy between sustainable livelihoods assets-capital and the attributes of financial capital, which are central to this paradigm cannot be pushed too far without losing the relational and processual elements that are so essential to considering livelihoods.

While some now call for a deeper understanding of the social dynamics of householding, few have questioned the centrality given to the household as basic units of analysis within the framework, although Bryceson (2002a, b) does allude to this in terms of declining household social and economic coherence. Indeed, irrespective of the disciplinary approach adopted, the spotlight invariably falls on the *household* – on its assets, its internal structures of power, its systems of resource allocation and its strategies for survival or accumulation. As Frank Ellis (2000: 31), one of DFID's leading advisors on livelihoods, explains:

> it is the rural household that is taken as the main social unit to which the framework is applied. This is applied by the use of the term 'livelihood strategy' in which the household as a social unit is observed to alter its mix of activities according to its evolving asset position, and the changing circumstances it confronts.

In the rural context, it has been noted that households may construct any one of a variety of 'household strategies'. In African rural contexts, many scholars, including Ellis, have recently emphasized the tendency towards 'livelihood diversification', which is defined as 'a process by which rural households construct an increasingly diverse portfolio of activities and assets in order to survive and improve their standard of living' (ibid.: 15). However, other household strategies might offset other economic processes, such as livelihood intensification, extensification or migration (Swift and Hamilton, 2001).

However, to propose, as Ellis (2000) and many others do, that households are central to the perspective begs the question of how those using the perspective should locate rural households within broader social, economic and political processes. Unfortunately, neither Ellis nor his colleagues provide a clear answer to this question. This leaves the issue of households hanging in the air. On the one hand, the concept seems to be used as a convenient shorthand for the measurement of resources, as a sort of vessel which contains rural people's most valued assets, while on the other, it is presented as a social agent – 'an individual by another name' to use Folbre's (1984) formulation – a thinking and acting unit which devises strategies, weighs up options and maximizes resources (Moore, 1994). In presenting his analysis of households, Ellis (2000) specifically warns that those who use this perspective should be careful of the 'cultural relativism of post-modern approaches' that see households as everywhere 'constituted in culturally specific ways'. To accommodate variation and diversity, he advocates that researchers apply a 'bargaining model', which assumes that households function as effective social units but within the context of internal conflicts and tensions over resources.

But what seems to be advocated here is a notion of households that is not only located outside of culture, but of capitalism and modernity as well. It is appended to the view that rural households are (or at least until recently have been) part of relatively autonomous peasant sectors. Ellis's argument thus draws on evolutionary models, especially those of a neo-Marxist articulation of modes of production kind, that present the relationship between peasants (or rural households) and capitalism as one of mutual exteriority (Kahn, 1992). As a result, the basic approach to the analysis of rural households tends to focus on exclusion, marginality and vulnerability. In reflecting on this structural situation, many studies have emphasized how rural households restructure themselves to survive on the margins or how they have strategies to overcome exclusionary tendencies. In these debates, rural households have generally been presented as 'black boxes' with their own internal dynamics, constantly adapting and responding to changes in the structural conditions within which they are made to survive. But far less has been said about the increasing fragility of rural households and their inability to hold themselves together under conditions of stress associated with social transition. In the discussion below, I highlight these latter concerns in relation to my field research in the villages of the Mooiplaas location during the late 1990s and again in 2001.[3]

Constituted migrant family farms

The Mooiplaas location consists of a wedge of former mission land located between the national road and the coast, to the east of the coastal city of East London in the Eastern Cape. Betterment planning was implemented in Mooiplaas in 1958. There was no overt resistance to the measures in this area, despite the fact that some families lost considerable amounts of land and livestock in the process. Part of the reason for this was that the area was only consolidated into a single location after the 1936 Land Act and did not have a history as a single united community. The betterment process in Mooiplaas constructed 14 villages, each of which was placed under the control of headmen and divided into arable, residential and fenced grazing zones. The consolidation of new villages occurred through the aggregation of formerly scattered households into single compressed settlements in which each family was given a certificate of occupation that entitled them to a residential site with a garden, an arable field of one or two acres, and access to grazing land. The administration of land was left in the hands of headmen who had the power to allocate land within the village. The headmen were, in turn, responsible to the Department of Native Affairs which held overall responsibility for implementing and managing betterment.

The betterment era saw rural stability being built on the platform of domestic patriarchy that was entrenched at the community level through the empowerment of chiefs and headmen through the tribal authority system. This vision was inscribed in the Bantu Authorities Act of 1951, which strengthened rural patriarchy by enhancing the power and influence of headmen. The idea of a direct chain of command running from the Natives Affairs Department through the tribal authority system was fundamental to the thinking behind this legislation. Given this structure of power, it is not surprising that the implementation of betterment and the tribal authority system involved systematic discrimination against unmarried women and widows. Women like Mrs Falase, a widow from Ngxingxolo village, found that while she had worked her husband's lands prior to betterment, she was denied access to her own field after betterment. She said that it was the policy of the Trust not to give women land, 'if you had no husbands, there was no chance that you would get anything more than a residential site with a garden, if you were lucky'. Mager (1999: 125) writes that in many parts of the Ciskei, betterment officials attempted to compensate women who lost land with temporary jobs on betterment projects, such as fence building, terracing and conservation work. She suggests that these offers of work were not well received by men, who wanted the employment for themselves.

In trying to assist smaller male-headed households to farm 'better', the state focused on providing inputs, advice and training to increase household agricultural output. They provided government tractors for ploughing as well as seed and fertilizer for fields and gardens. White agricultural extension officers stressed the need for new progressive farming techniques to be adopted and for households to establish their own economic independence in the village. The themes of self-realization, independence and self-sufficiency were constantly emphasized during their field visits, as well as at the agricultural shows and demonstrations held fairly regularly in Mooiplaas during the 1960s and 1970s. In an effort to raise levels of household production and to encourage greater household self-sufficiency, women were also targeted for special attention. As one woman explained:

> They were keen to encourage development and household self-sufficiency. This entailed training us in all aspects of self-sufficiency like baking, all types of crafts, home economics and farming. At the time [the 1960s] delegates would be chosen from the villages here to go for training at Debe's Nek [a small town in the Ciskei]. Delegates would stay at the centre for a week with each day dedicated to learning new skills. On the last day of training we would be taken on a tour of development projects in the area and would see what some farmers had achieved under the supervision of teams from the Fort Hare Agricultural School and Fort Cox College of Agriculture. This scheme was for all interested parties until it collapsed in the 1970s. (Interview 7 June 1999, Mrs Tofu, 75 years old)

In Mooiplaas, the efforts of state officials to encourage household autonomy and self-sufficiency received strong support from local headmen, some of whom became increasingly critical of the so-called uncooperative traditionalists, or *amaqaba*, in the villages who were reluctant to adopt 'progressive ways' (Bank, 2002). Residents of Ngxingxolo village, for instance, remember how headman Koyana unashamedly sided with Christianized families in the village during the 1970s. It was alleged that he would go from door to door in the village gathering up children who were working at home and force them to go to school. With the help of his council, he also outlawed stick fighting in the village, except during initiation, and did everything in his power to persuade 'red families' to abandon their traditions and rituals and to start attending church.[4] The betterment model anticipated the creation of rational and efficient migrant family farms in areas like Mooiplaas that could subsidize the bachelor wages paid to migrants in the cities, while at the same time keeping women and children gainfully occupied in the rural reserves and homelands (Wolpe, 1972). The ascendance of more educated headmen in the Ciskei, like Koyana, was a feature of the restructuring of the tribal authority system under apartheid in the 1950s. As it became clear that the position of headman now came with a regular state salary and required some level of literacy, many better-educated candidates with a claim to such positions stepped forward and were favoured by the state, which wished to see the wheels of the new rural bureaucracy and betterment plans running smoothly (Mager, 1999).

New opportunities, fractured households

Unlike many other rural districts, Mooiplaas was not targeted as a recruitment centre for the mines during apartheid. The 14 villages were too small to justify a dedicated Chamber of Mines recruiting centre. This meant that men from the villages went to the general government labour bureaus in the East London district which had been revamped in the 1960s, and tended to be allocated unskilled jobs in Cape Town, especially on the docks. They were usually housed in single-sex municipal hostels in Langa. Others found jobs in East London where they were also often forced to find accommodation in hostels. Many of these men only returned to the location once a year, leaving the job of maintaining their family farms to their wives and daughters. Throughout the 1960s, women stuck to their tasks in the countryside and only took up seasonal labour occasionally on white-owned farms around the location. But this changed in the 1970s with the expansion of the state's new homeland industrial decentralization programme that targeted areas on the fringes of East London as centres for new industrial investment. By the mid-1970s, dozens of new textile and furniture factories had been set up in places like Fort Jackson, Berlin and Zwelitsha – all within relatively easy commuting distance of Mooiplaas. This process gained momentum in 1981 when state-funded subsidies and incentives for companies seeking to move to the homelands were quite significantly increased. In the Ciskei alone, this programme was responsible for creating over 30,000 new industrial jobs between the mid-1970s and 1980s (Black and Davies, 1986).

By the 1980s, with increasing numbers of young women from the villages seeking wage employment, household levels of agricultural production dropped and were further affected by intermittent drought. From the point of view of the betterment planners of the 1950s, the pendulum had swung too far away from agriculture, and the very households they were hoping to create were now increasingly sites of gender and generational tension. Husbands felt that their wives were not paying enough attention to their gardens and were showing too much interest in urban jobs and opportunities. Wives argued that tilling the soil was no longer a viable basis for building the homestead and that the extra income they could earn outside the location was vital to the survival of their households.

Children were also affected by these divisions and began to argue that if their mothers were losing interest in farming, why should they be expected to work in their gardens? The changing political situation in the rural areas also affected the balance of generational power. By the mid-1980s, young men from the villages were moving around in packs, refusing to obey the headmen and threatening many older residents of the location, who were terrified that they might be identified by the comrades as 'collaborators'. One of the striking features of the struggle of the 'comrades' against the tribal authority structures in Mooiplaas and other similar areas in the 1980s was that they made no real effort to replace headmen with 'civic structures' that were dominated and controlled by the youth. In fact, with the collapse of apartheid, youth were generally more eager to leave the villages than to dominate them politically.

In the late 1980s, unemployed youth from Mooiplaas left the rural location in droves to find better opportunities in the cities. A considerable number ended up in the informal settlements of Duncan Village in East London but many others travelled further afield to Cape Town, Durban and Johannesburg in search of a better life (Bank, 1997). Their enthusiasm to leave was often fuelled by changes in the cities, especially East London, where comrades had seized the old Duncan Village location and opened it up for new immigrants, especially 'progressive youths', from the surrounding villages. Once young men started leaving, the young women followed. A crippling drought gripped the Eastern Cape in the late 1980s and young women became deeply disillusioned with their roles as homemakers and agricultural workers in a context where agriculture was showing no returns (Moodie, 1992).

By the early 1990s, figures on the composition of new informal settlements in East London showed that, in many of these areas, women outnumbered men and that the average age of household heads was less than 30 years. As the youth left, established migrants and commuters began to lose faith in the project of building their family farms in the villages. Many stopped remitting income as frequently as they had previously and some simply gave up on the idea of returning home, seeking instead to set up a base for themselves in the urban areas where new housing projects were being established for people with jobs.

In the post-1994 period, the saving grace for many rural households, which had been depleted of social and economic resources, was the increase of social welfare grants and pension payments to blacks. These payments, which had been racially determined in the past with blacks receiving pensions only once every two months, were suddenly equalized and increased, ensuring that households with older members suddenly found themselves better off than many of those who had previously had a number of migrant workers. The shift from remittances to welfare grants as the main source of household income in the villages also meant that there was a shift of power in these households away from men to women, who made up more than two-thirds of welfare recipients. In short, by the 1990s, the betterment images of economically stable rural households that made a living from the combination of migrant remittances and family farming had all but been shattered in Mooiplaas. Instead, these models of functional productive families had been replaced by increasing numbers of economically and socially weak female-headed households that neither farmed effectively nor received regular remittances from absent industrial workers. By the mid-1990s most households were heavily dependent on state welfare grants for survival.

In the DARE survey I conducted in Ngxingxolo village in Mooiplaas in 1998 it was found that there were very high levels of absenteeism among men and women in the 20 to 40 year age cohort. Over 40 per cent of all those who were absent from Ngxingxolo were under the age of 30 years, and over 80 per cent were under 40 years. Most of them were living in East London and were unemployed. Few sent anything home to help their parents and they were said to only visit their rural homes once or twice a year. As one old woman explained, 'I only seem to see my sons these days when they have no money in the city and want me to give them some of my pension'.

The tendency of men to stay away was more pronounced than that of women, who often sent children home to stay with their grandmothers. These women were likely to be more regular in their home visits and were the most reliable in terms of bringing cash and groceries home with them to help their parents out. But few young women showed any real interest in returning to the village on a full-time basis, preferring to stay in the city where they said that there were more opportunities to earn a living. It was only when women were in their forties and fifties and found it increasingly difficult to find work in the urban areas that they started returning home.

The DARE survey showed that welfare grants and pensions were the main source of household income. There were 69 welfare recipients in 56 of the 100 households sampled. Most of these income-earners were old women, often widows, who were also the heads of their households. Moreover, only 6 per cent of households claimed that they received regular remittances in 1998 and only 20 per cent of the economically active population in the village were in some form of full-time employment. The situation was deteriorating rather than improving because of ongoing job losses in the industrial and manufacturing sectors in East London and the surrounding towns. This further weakened the capacity of households to act as effective cooperative units.

The unravelling of the rural 'betterment households' had serious implications for the agricultural output of households in Ngxingxolo. Out of the 100 DARE survey households, a third produced no maize at all, while a further 28 per cent produced less than one bag of maize in their gardens. Of the remaining

42 per cent, 25 per cent of households produced between 2–5 bags, leaving only 17 per cent of households with an output of more than 5 bags of maize in that year. One of the reasons for the very low maize yields was that some households had divided up their gardens into smaller parcels of land on which they grew certain vegetables, like spinach, beans or pumpkins, thus abandoning older inter-cropping practices. One of the other factors that played a role was the lack of ploughing and planting equipment in the village. Only three households owned a plough and there was only one planter in the 100 households sampled. Moreover, due to stock theft and increasing suspicion between white farmers and black villagers in the area, some of the local white farmers who had helped villagers with ploughing in the past withdrew this service, leaving the villagers in the lurch.

Problems like these did not emerge overnight and it became clear from our life-history interviews that the pathetically low crop yields recorded in 1998 were by no means exceptional. The fact that 70 per cent of households owned no more than basic hand tools is indicative of a much longer-term disengagement with productive agriculture in the village. Without the necessary equipment it was said that it could cost as much as R1000 (US$1 = R7) to pay for inputs, machinery and labour to get one garden under full production. This was more than most households could afford (Bank and Qambata, 1999).

Shifting into GEAR with commodity groups

In the 1990s as men and women struggled to piece together livelihoods within a context where households lacked social cohesion and commitment to common goals, the public policy framework in rural areas changed with the arrival of post-apartheid administration. By the mid-1990s, a new set of policies were in place which aimed to transform agricultural production in rural areas away from its subsistence orientation to a more market-oriented approach. The formation of commodity groups that would bring producers together and pool resources was seen to be a major vehicle in achieving this objective. It was felt that, if properly organized, such groups could service export markets for commodities such as wool, mohair, butternut and beef. In practical terms, the Eastern Cape Department of Agriculture initially focused on creating pig farming, poultry and wool commodity groups, while the Department of Welfare encouraged groups of poor or single women to come together to create bakery projects or vegetable gardens.

The Welfare projects identified rural women and female-headed households in particular as being extremely vulnerable to poverty, and thus focused on getting such women to work together in small projects. The programmes of the Department of Agriculture and Land Affairs were less gender biased, and focused instead on viable commodities for export. However, in practice, beef and wool farming projects tended to be dominated by men, while pig and poultry projects were under the control of women.

The importance of women as market-oriented farmers was given additional recognition in various other ways, such as the creation of the 'female farmer competition', which was launched nationally in 1999. The categories under which awards were granted included 'top export producer', 'top producers for national markets' and 'top producer for informal markets'. The creation of awards such as these was not only indicative of the department's desire to encourage market-oriented production, but also of the state's desire to empower rural women. The decision to create new opportunities for rural women had also been central to the development agenda of NGOs in the Eastern Cape. Organizations such as the Border Rural Committee and others working in the field of land reform and rural development have invested an enormous amount of energy and resources in campaigning for women's rights. In fact, it might be argued that the extent to which the empowerment of women was a major component of the government's rural development policy strategy owes a great deal to the work of NGOs.

Thus, from a policy point of view, it needs to be noted that in addition to the advocacy of households as the critical agents of rural social change of the 1990s, there was a strong shift in policy away from the idea that the rural economy must necessarily be managed and controlled by men. Quite the opposite, rural social change policy efforts became focused primarily on women. However, it needs to be stressed that while the policy framework changed significantly over the preceding decade, the implementation of policy was extremely uneven.

During the 1990s, Mooiplaas was one of the areas in Eastern Cape Province where local people were exposed to new policy interventions and where NGOs were active. One of the reasons for this was that during the political revolts of the 1980s a number of progressive NGOs assisted Mooiplaas residents in their struggle against forced removal. After the removals were called off, many of these organizations continued to work in the area, shifting their role from one of political support to development assistance.

In promoting rural projects, NGOs in particular have paid special attention to the plight of women and offered a range of training courses and practical support in educational, farming and small-business projects. This involvement created local jobs, with some village residents finding part-time or even full-time employment as field-workers and community advisors. These contacts quickly triggered a sophisticated knowledge of how the development sector works and the intricacies of changes in land and agricultural policy. Although many of the formal job opportunities in the development sector went to men, local women proved to be the most adept at 'reading' new development initiatives and devising strategies to maximize the potential benefits. They had been quick to realize that they were a valued constituency for development agencies and learned the art of presenting themselves as 'targets' for development interventions by emphasizing certain identities and underplaying others.[5]

I was amazed at the rapidity of their learning curve as I observed women in Mooiplaas handle development agents and officials over the past five years.

They appreciated that outside development agents generally do not like to spend more time than they have to in the field and that it is important for them to be on time for meetings and take notes and even prepare minutes, so that the process of delivery is not unnecessarily delayed. Some women acquired cell phones to ensure that they were easy to contact. They organized themselves into highly responsive units and networks with a cross-cutting membership that could be quickly mobilized as and when new development projects were discussed. One of the points that women frequently stress during meetings with development agents is that it is better to speak to women because they are organized and effective, rather than wasting time on men who do not seem to understand the advantages of working together.

But not all the women in the villages had the ability to operate as brokers and thus there was a core group of women in each village who always acted as the go-betweens in negotiations. Most of these women had matriculation-level education, as well as the benefit of various NGO training courses, and some experience of working outside Mooiplaas. Women like Maureen Mbane and Zinzi Tofu, who were both in their late thirties, were self-confident and capable of interacting effectively in a range of different contexts. Maureen had been a supervisor in a city clothing and shoe manufacturer's firm before being retrenched in 1996 and returning to the village after a long period of unemployment in the city. Zinzi Tofu had worked for years in a tourist shop at the former Transkei border post on the Kei River before it closed down in the early 1990s and she too returned to the village to look after her elderly mother.

The ability of women to adopt and perform multiple identities and to communicate the necessity of these social skills to those located in their networks was crucial to their success. In one context they presented themselves as representatives of landless people, while in others as small-scale entrepreneurs, and in yet others they acted on behalf of malnourished mothers. These women, whom I refer to as 'development junkies', played out a range of social identities and managed to attract fairly substantial development resources into Mooiplaas in the 1990s. In line with current government policy, most of these resources were allocated to commodity groups but there were other development initiatives that women controlled as well, such as the pre-school movement.

In the process of responding to the development context, women in Mooiplaas tended to disconnect themselves from household-based identities, stressing a range of other social identities and associations. This was perhaps not surprising given the extent to which rural households have unravelled in this area since the 1980s. But it was also directly related to the fact that women generally felt that if development resources were channelled through households, they might inadvertently fall under the control of men. And this was something that many women seem determined to avoid. It was also one of the rationales that the women gave for not including men in their savings groups, credit clubs and commodity groups. They tended to use cultural arguments saying that men have no place getting involved in pig, poultry and beadwork or curio projects because these were 'women's activities'. But this did not stop women from becoming involved in 'men's commodity groups', like the beef project. When asked about their involvement in this project, the women proposed a different set of arguments, claiming that times had changed and that women should not be typecast.

During the 1990s, Ngxingxolo village became the most successful of all the location villages in establishing commodity groups. Part of the reason for this was that the village had a history of interaction with NGOs and managed to use these contacts to gather information about new links and opportunities. By 2001, the active commodity groups in this village included the Masikhanye Pig Farming Group, the Mashilakhe Sewing Group, the Nomzamo Poultry Group, the Masikuhuthale Beadwork Group, and the Khaya la Bantu cultural tourism group, which were all run, controlled and managed by women. There were also two other groups – the leatherwork group and the beef farmers' group – that were dominated by men. Yet it is interesting to note that neither of these groups had achieved much success in attracting development funding. The beef farming group, for instance, only started submitting proposals to the Department of Land Affairs and Agriculture in 2001 to give them the start-up capital and training for this project.

The relative power of men and women within this field was vividly displayed in June 2001 when I invited a group of visiting foreign journalists to come with me to Mooiplaas to view the 'small projects' being developed there. I gave the villagers two days' notice of the visit but when I arrived the women had arranged a reception party for the journalists that included a display of the work of various commodity groups as well as a cultural performance of songs and dances for the visitors. The events took place at a local pre-school and were attended mainly by women and children.

The two male-dominated commodity groups, the beef farming and leatherwear groups, were also present, but they sat away from the main group of women in the shadows near the school ablution blocks, chatting among themselves. They were barely visible and when the journalists eventually got round to talking to them, one of the women who had organized the event took it upon herself to speak on their behalf, only occasionally giving them a chance to interrupt her with points of clarification. The event, as the journalists themselves remarked, was a dramatization of the power and confidence of women as development agents in the village.

My study of the dynamics of the commodity groups revealed that despite the women's astute organizational efforts, the impact of the commodity groups on rural welfare was not pronounced. First, contrary to the way these groups were presented by policy-makers, they were generally fairly poorly resourced and generate only very small profits for the participants. In none of the cases recorded were the commodities produced and sold able to generate enough income to sustain all the initial members of these groups. In fact, between 1997 and 2001 most of the groups shrunk in size from around ten to five members, but they nevertheless survived and were still in business four years after they were initially encountered. To be sure, they constituted activities that generated bits and pieces of additional income that needed to be combined with other income sources, especially pensions and welfare grants, in order to allow these rural women to survive.

Second, many of the groups themselves were dependent on the state and the donor community for continuous support in order to keep their businesses going. In many cases women managed to acquire and aggregate 'development funds' from a number of sources. In the case of the piggery project, for instance, the women cleverly sourced development funds from both the Department of Land Affairs and Agriculture and the Department of Welfare by representing the project both as a 'poverty-relief project' and as an 'entrepreneurial venture'. Some of the projects also received additional help from NGOs and donor organizations. In most instances these funds proved to be critical to the ability of the projects to function with any level of success, showing again that state transfer and resources are primary sources of livelihood income in many rural areas.

Third, and most importantly for the argument developed in this chapter, the activation of commodity groups largely occurred in Mooiplaas not as a mechanism to expand and strengthen local household-based economies but as an alternative to these. In Mooiplaas, the growth and consolidation of female networks and opportunities both in the form of commodity groups but also in the explosion of female savings, grocery and credit associations further weakened rather than strengthened the socially incoherent and moribund household economy. The rural youth, many of whom lived in slums on the fringes of towns and cities, were mostly unemployed and very often both unwilling and unable to make much contribution to their households in the village. Older men, who had also lost their power and purpose in the village, felt emasculated and moved around the village shadows, like 'domestic nomads', scratching around for income and opportunity wherever they could find it. They complained bitterly about the power, influence and resources that women had taken for themselves, saying that when they used to work in the cities, they controlled the purse strings and the decision-making processes in their households. With these kinds of tensions playing themselves out, households were hardly in a position to operate as the rational decision-making units that the livelihood approach assumes.

Conclusion

During the 1990s, rural areas in South Africa became increasingly disconnected from the industrial core of the economy as a result of large-scale retrenchments and the decline of the migrant labour system. The plight of the rural poor had been further exacerbated by the collapse of homeland industrial decentralization areas, leaving tens of thousands of local and commuter workers in the former homelands without jobs. Exactly what these processes meant for rural communities, households and individuals is still poorly understood in South Africa. The current wave of donor-funded livelihood audits and household surveys has done very little to deepen our understanding of the changing rural social relations. Part of the reason for this is that many of these enquiries tend to employ a set of *a priori* assumptions about the significance of households as units of collective action and strategic decision-making in rural areas.

Rural research has been hindered by the continued currency of theoretical models and approaches that have situated rural households outside of capitalism and modernity. Such approaches, I argue, have ignored the extent to which rural households have themselves been shaped from within the larger political economy and how they have been internally restructured by the very policies against which they have reacted. It is only when we begin to make these connections that the full impact of the rising levels of structural unemployment, the collapse of patriarchal apartheid social and political institutions and the significance of new policies can be fully appreciated.

Using the DARE case-study material and survey results from the Mooiplaas location outside the city of East London, I have suggested that rather than standing as defensive bastions of hope and cohesion in a sea of political and economic change, rural households have themselves crumbled under the pressure of change. I have argued that the apartheid rural restructuring in this area during the 1950s and 1960s sought to reconstitute large extended families into smaller and more functional rural households that were expected to farm as families on small plots of land, while at the same time accessing wage remittances from the cities. During this period, the ability of households to hold themselves together socially depended critically on the enforcement of apartheid laws restricting mobility, on political stability in the countryside, and on the ability of the urban economy to deliver the jobs necessary to subsidize household agricultural production in the villages. In Mooiplaas, the first two conditions fell away in the mid-1980s with rural revolt and out-migration, while the third collapsed with increasing unemployment in the villages and declining levels of wage remittances. The result has been that households have become socially fragmented as members have dispersed, often retaining very tenuous links with their rural kin in the villages. I suggested that it is indeed ironic that the strongest links that now exist between the village and the city are those constructed between mothers and daughters, not fathers and sons as was anticipated in the patriarchal apartheid models of the 1950s and 1960s. In the absence of regular remittances from the cities, rural individuals and households have become more and more dependent on state transfers, especially pensions, for survival.

This context of domestic strife, fragmentation and incoherence in Mooiplaas has created the backdrop for the introduction of new rural development policies. In the 1990s, as argued in the above, the centrifugal tendencies within households encouraged women to move into commodity groups, stimulating the creation of new feminized social networks that seized the local economic initiative away from men, but without adding a great deal of value to the village economy. In this context, the proposed shift in development policy away from commodity groups and back to family farming and food security was potentially a positive move in the Eastern Cape because agricultural land in the former homelands was still under-utilized and there was increasing evidence of hunger and malnutrition in many rural communities. But the challenge for the state was to present a re-engagement in farming, especially family farming, as a potentially exciting and rewarding option. This was extremely difficult in situations like Mooiplaas where gender and generational relations were fraught with tension and mistrust and where exclusive forms of cooperation, such as those seen in gender-specific commodity groups and savings, seemed to be undermining the capacity for households to embark on new livelihoods strategies.

With the South African government shifting from GEAR's emphasis on attracting investment to a more local focus on new programmes to address poverty and reduce vulnerability in rural areas like Mooiplaas, it is crucial for both the state and donor agencies to recognize that they cannot assume that rural households operate as functional economic decision-making units that will be ready and able to take up new agricultural pursuits, or even that they will be capable of working together as social units for the achievement of common sets of objectives. These assumptions need to be carefully assessed in each individual case and may prove to be wishful thinking on the part of livelihood theorists and policy-makers alike.

About the author

Leslie Bank is an associate professor and director of the Institute of Social and Economic Research (FHISER) at the University of Fort Hare in South Africa. He is trained as an anthropologist, but works extensively on issues of public policy and socio-economic trends in South Africa. He has published widely in the field including a book entitled *Home Spaces, Street Styles: Contesting Power and Identity in a South African City*, Pluto: London, 2010.

Notes

1. My assessment of the MFP programme is based on presentations of the core elements to the PGDP process by senior Eastern Cape agricultural officials in 2003. In August 2003, a set of advertisements ran in the Eastern Cape print media and on radio inviting rural communities and households from the former homelands to apply for inclusion in the programme (see *Daily Dispatch* 19 August 2003).
2. In terms of small-scale production, the two tiers in the MFP system are practically and conceptually linked. At the upper level, the MFP seeks to establish groups of commercially oriented maize farmers in 'targeted' areas who will, with state support, farm aggregations of 'more than 50 ha of land within a radius of 15 km of other aggregations that add up to

at least 200 ha', while at the lower level, the MFP will strengthen household production through the new Siyazondla Homestead Production Programme, which was also launched in 2003. The latter programme sets out to make it 'easier for households with access to arable allotments to engage in lease arrangements (using a range of payment mechanisms, including share of the crop) with aspirant farmers who wish to participate in the MFP' (Provincial Growth and Development Plan, 2004: 8–9). Later in the document, it is pointed out that, lest we get the wrong impression, 'the aim [of the homestead programme] is not to turn every person in the former Bantustans into a farmer, rather to address food vulnerability at the household level and support the diversification and strengthening of household livelihood strategies, while also supporting surplus crop production where appropriate' (ibid., 2004: 15).
3. Under the auspices of the Deagrarianization and Rural Employment research programme (DARE), funded by the Netherlands Ministry of Foreign Affairs, I conducted extensive fieldwork and a survey of 100 households in Mooiplaas location in 1997–98 and thereafter again in 2001. I would like to acknowledge this support from the Dutch government and the African Studies Centre in Leiden, the Netherlands, and also express my thanks to Deborah Bryceson, the DARE research programme coordinator, for her useful comments on an earlier version of this chapter. The views expressed here are, however, those of the author alone. This survey work will hitherto be referred to as the DARE survey.
4. A distinction was made in many parts of the Eastern Cape at this time between so-called *abantu basesikolweni* or School people, who seemingly embraced Westernization, European values and Christianity, and the Reds, also known as the *abantu ababomvu* or *amaqaba*, who were distinctive and easily identified in rural areas because they still smeared their bodies with red clay and vehemently resisted and rejected European and Christian influences.
5. For an interesting comparison with similar development projects in the Lubombo SDI zone on the Kwazulu-Natal coast, see van Wyk (2003). Overall, van Wyk takes a much more negative perspective of these programmes than I do. She sees them as exploitative and as packaging women as ethnic stereotypes, while I emphasize the agency of women in using development resources to challenge male power and authority in the village economy.

References

Bank, L. (1997) 'Urbanization in the Eastern Cape', *South African Labour Bulletin* 4(2): 42–50.
Bank, L. (2002) 'Beyond red and school: rural livelihoods, gender and tradition in the Eastern Cape', *Journal of Southern African Studies* 28(3): 631–49.
Bank, L. (2003) 'Socio-Economic Indicators and Settlements in the Amatola District', Research Report for the Amatola District Council's Land Use Planning Team, April 2003.

Bank, L. and Qambata, L. (1999) 'No Visible Means of Subsistence: Rural Liveli-hoods, Gender and Social Change in Mooiplaas, Eastern Cape. 1950–1998', African Studies Centre Working Paper 34, Leiden.

Binns, T. and Nel, E. (2001) 'Supporting Local Economic Development in Post-Apartheid South Africa', Rhodes University, Institute of Social and Economic Research, Seminar paper.

Black, P. and Davies, W. (1986) 'Industrial Decentralisation in the Ciskei', Rhodes University, Institute of Social and Economic Research, Working Paper 22.

Bryceson, D. (1999) 'African rural labour, income diversification and liveli-hood approaches: a long-term development perspective', *Review of African Political Economy* 80: 171–89.

Bryceson, D. (2002a) 'The scramble in Africa: reorienting rural livelihoods', *World Development* 30(5): 725–37.

Bryceson, D. (2002b) 'Multiplex livelihoods in rural Africa: recasting the terms and conditions of gainful employment', *Journal of Modern African Studies* 40(1): 1–28.

CIETAfrica (2001) *Impact Assessment of the SDI of the Wild Coast*, 1997–2000, East London.

Economist (2001) 'South Africa Survey', 24 February 2001.

Ellis, F. (2000) *Rural Livelihoods and Diversity in Developing Countries*, Oxford University Press, Oxford.

Ellis, F. (2003) 'Human Vulnerability and Food Insecurity: Policy Implications', Forum for Food Security in Southern Africa, Theme Paper, no. 3, Overseas Development Institute, mimeo, London.

Folbre, N. (1984) 'The feminisation of poverty and the pauperisation of mother-hood' *Review of Radical Political Economics* 16(4): 78–88.

Kahn, J. (1992) *Constituting the Minangkabau: Peasants, Culture and Modernity in Colonial Indonesia*, Routledge, London.

Kepe, T., Nsebeza, L. and Pithers, L. (2001) 'Agri-tourism Spatial Development Initiatives in South Africa: Are They Enhancing Rural Livelihoods?', *ODI Natural Resource Perspectives* 65.

Mager, A.K. (1999) *Gender and the Making of a South African Bantustan*, James Currey, Oxford.

Moodie, D. (1992) 'Town women, country wives: migrant labour family poli-tics and housing preferences at Vaal Reef Mines', *Labour, Capital and Society* 25(1): 421–55.

Moore, H. (1994) *A Passion for Difference*, Cambridge, Polity.

Murray, C. (2000) 'Changing livelihoods: The Free State, 1990s', *African Studies* 59(1): 10–32.

Murray, C. (2002) 'Livelihoods research: transcending boundaries of time and space', *Journal of Southern African Studies* 28(3): 489–509.

Ngonini, X. (2003) 'Rural Livelihoods and Social Welfare in Pondoland', Uni-versity of the Witwatersrand, Unpublished research paper, Johannesburg.

Provincial Growth and Development Plan (PGDP) (2004) 'Summary of the PGDP Programmes for the MTEF, 2004–2007', Province of the Eastern Cape, South Africa.

Scoones, I. and Wolmer, W. (2003) 'Livelihoods in crisis', *IDS Bulletin* 34(2): 1–14.

Sen, A. (1981) *Poverty and Famines: An Essay on Entitlement and Deprivation*, Clarendon Press, Oxford.

South African Census (2001) 'Eastern Cape Report', South Africa Statistics, Pretoria.

Swift, J. and Hamilton, K. (2001) 'Household food and livelihood security', in S. Devereux and S. Maxwell (eds), *Food Security in Sub-Saharan Africa*, ITDG Press, London.

van Wyk, I. (2003) '"Elephants Are Eating Our Money": A Critical Ethnography of Development Practice in Maputaland, South Africa', University of Pretoria, Faculty of Human Sciences, MA thesis, Pretoria.

Whitehead, A. (2002) 'Tracking livelihood change: theoretical, methodological and empirical perspectives from North-East Ghana', *Journal of Southern African Studies* 28(3): 575–98.

Wolpe, H. (1972) 'Capitalism and cheap labour-power in South Africa: from segregation to apartheid', *Economy and Society* 1: 425–56.

CHAPTER 11

Fair or foul play: taxation of women entrepreneurs in Cameroon[*]

Margaret Niger-Thomas

In Cameroon, women entered labour and commodity markets to ensure basic subsistence of their households during the widespread economic recession of the 1990s. The Cameroon government instituted new taxes at the local level in an attempt to integrate all economic activities and to eliminate the informal sector where the vast majority of women entrepreneurs were found. For the first time, women entrepreneurs were required to pay tax on their own account. This chapter assesses the rationale of the country's 'global tax', its implementation and the response of female entrepreneurs. It is argued that an abrupt imposition of the global tax on women's informal sector activities made women exceptionally vulnerable and recommends a more conducive and enabling environment for women's income-earning activities which would assist their efforts while affording transparency of tax collection.

Introduction

One of the far-reaching effects of global economic restructuring is a decline in real incomes for households in many parts of the world. As a result, women increasingly are entering labour and commodity markets in an attempt to make ends meet. Once there, they are often vulnerable to the gendered dynamics of the market in which they are operating. In Cameroon, as in most other African countries, the law on taxation however is applied without discrimination to men and women. Most discussions on trade and the laws that underpin it have been gender-blind. According to Mejia and Riley (1997: 1):

> Trade is discussed in economic and political terms, but the differential social and economic impact of changing trade patterns on women and men has not been considered relevant.

On the insistence of the World Bank, the Cameroonian state instituted new taxes at the local level in an attempt to encompass all economic activities and to eliminate the informal sector. Since the mid-1990s, there has been a persistent effort on the part of the state to decentralize the taxation system, and thereby intensify its relationship with local communities. The Global Tax policy in Cameroon was adopted in 1995 as part of the government's on-going search for alternative measures to alleviate the effects of economic stagnation. Like other taxes, this tax is implemented throughout the country and is meant to integrate the informal sector of the economy as a sphere of activity operating within the state. It represents the state's consistent efforts to eliminate the dualism between the formal and informal sectors with a view to formalizing the entire economy.

This chapter explores state taxation reforms in the context of rural and urban case studies. Both study areas are found in South-west Province of Cameroon. Limbe is a primarily urban location with a town population of 44,561 out of a total district population of 64,878 and is situated on the coast at the foot of Mount Cameroon. Mamfe is in the interior, a sparsely populated forest area of 47,218 people with an urban population of only 13,844 (Cameroon 1987 census).

With the introduction of the Global Tax, petty trading became more liable to taxation. Furthermore, women entrepreneurs were targeted for the first time, producing a sudden economic jolt. Under the new law, trade activities were randomly and arbitrarily slotted into various tax categories.

Research elsewhere shows that the informal sector activities in developing countries often operate in contravention of existing legislation and by-laws. Several studies have argued that the fault lies in the country's legal system rather than informal sector workers (de Soto, 1989; Fombad, 1994). In Cameroon, the arbitrary way rules are applied generates what could be called an 'informal taxation system', which repeatedly surfaces attention on corrupt practices. One female entrepreneur in Limbe commented that turning a blind eye to those who do not pay taxes while individual tax collectors' pockets are being catered for, has been the order of the day for years.

Furthermore most entrepreneurs, especially women, keep no records of their income and expenditures. Hence taxes are levied arbitrarily. Kaldor (1970: 172) states that:

> The extension of tax to small traders, artisans, or professional persons meets with serious administrative difficulties, as there is no way of ascertaining income where no proper books are kept, and no regular accounts are prepared or audited.

This chapter considers how different categories of people, notably early entry and already established female entrepreneurs, as opposed to female formal sector employees who more recently initiated informal activities, reacted to the introduction of the new tax law. 'Early entry entrepreneurs', otherwise referred to as 'old timers', traditionally dominated the informal sector of the economy until the late 1980s. These women depend on the informal sector for their main source of livelihood. 'Recent entry', or 'newcomers', refer to female entrepreneurs who have primarily been employed in formal sector jobs but started penetrating the informal sector since the late 1980s and 1990s.

What has been the impact of the Global Tax? Can it be seen as a means of bringing women's economic activities into the limelight and ridding them of persistent invisibility? How has it affected female entrepreneurship? What are the moral underpinnings of the exchange relationship between women entrepreneurs, whether individuals or groups on the one hand, and the state on the other? The first section of this chapter describes conflict between the state and women entrepreneurs in relation to newly-introduced market controls, before examining the Global Tax's implementation, and its differential impact on early and recent entry women entrepreneurs in the informal sector.

Battleground between entrepreneurs and state officials

Antagonism between state officials and Cameroonian women traders is illustrated by a bush meat market incident that occurred in Mamfe in 1993. The scene described below gives a vivid picture of the chaos and confusion created by regulations imposed seemingly arbitrarily on certain sectors of society. The situation was instigated by the decision to implement a ban on bush meat.[1]

> The setting is the main Mamfe market at about 3 p.m. on a Friday afternoon in 1993. My attention was drawn to what was going on between female entrepreneurs and state officials in relation to the law on bush meat sales. The actors are bush meat sellers (all women) and forest guards (all men).
>
> As I stood at the entrance to the section of the market where general foodstuffs and meat sellers congregated, I suddenly heard a whistle. Bush meat sellers had been given the signal and they had to act fast. Women were disappearing with their basins of meat. They hid them on top of market shades and under tables on which other items were displayed, while others were hurriedly covered with dress lengths and various food items. In a few seconds, two fierce-looking forest guards dressed in green khaki shorts and shirts appeared, searching for bush meat. The guards had appeared without any warning, like soldiers in a sneak attack against their opponents, the women bush meat sellers. There was total confusion as the guards combed the market.
>
> A basin of meat belonging to one of the women who was still struggling to hide her wares was seized by a guard. Women shouted abuse at him: 'How can you come to attack women when the hunters are in the forest?' yelled one of the women. 'Has the market become the forest where animals are found?' The woman whose meat had been seized pursued the guard and pleaded for her basin of meat to be returned, but to no avail.
>
> 'For over 10 years now, I have been selling bush meat and taking care of my family. There was no such law. What is this new type of government that is doing nothing to help us but wants to kill us and our children?' asked the woman whose meat had been seized. 'You have been cheating the government all these years because you don't pay tax. The law now says animals should not be hunted because hunting affects the environment,'

replied the forest guard. 'Environment is what? You found me selling not hunting. The government should control the hunters who are men in the forest and not the sellers,' retorted the woman. 'If the hunters stop hunting, we will stop selling.' 'Yes, but if you also stop buying, the hunters will stop hunting,' the forest guard said, clinching the argument.

While this dialogue was going on, the other guard was struggling at the other end of the meat section with two women who were holding on tightly to another basin of meat. Other women joined in the struggle and began pulling the meat out of the basin piece by piece. They jeered and shouted.

I later discovered that the meat seized by the guards was auctioned off to workers in government offices. When I tried to talk to one of the forest guards, he was not willing to enter into any discussion and his only response was: 'It is not your business to question where the money goes. We are only doing our jobs.'

Beating around the bush meat

The forest guards were enforcing the law enacted to control wildlife whereas the women, with no formal source of income, were capitalizing on resources available within their environment. Many of the women perceived the state as a threat to their existence. A male trader who had witnessed the scene labelled the forest guards as thieves, 'reaping where they did not sow'.

In 1996, I went back to the market. On several occasions in both Limbe and Mamfe markets, I found a team of tax collectors going from one section of the market to another, harassing traders who would not pay their taxes. I asked my informants in Mamfe whether they were still being harassed by forest guards. One of them responded:

> Now we pay the new tax to the government and we can sell in peace. Forest guards can no longer seize our meat and feed their families. Sometimes they come on Saturdays for controls and we pay a small fee of between 500 FCFA and 1,000 FCFA [US$1 = FCFA600–700, 1996–99], depending on how much meat they find in our basins. They are ready to compromise because they also help themselves from the money we pay.

Clearly, the payment of taxes on bush meat has evolved with constantly changing rules. The forest guards not only enforce the rules, they also bend them. Bush meat sellers, and female entrepreneurs in the informal sector generally, had not been subject to tax until 1992 when the Department of the Environment and Forestry began collecting quarterly fees. Meat sellers became obliged to pay a daily market fee to Mamfe Rural Council of 50 FCFA to 100 FCFA, and also a veterinary fee. Since colonial times, a national law formally required individuals who dealt in wildlife produce to purchase a licence. However, the delegate of the Ministry of the Environment and Forestry in Mamfe at the time told me that these licences had never been purchased by the female bush meat sellers who complained of its high cost – a full 100,000 FCFA per year. Subsequent laws were passed in 1974, 1981, and 1994 to regulate forestry, wildlife and fisheries.[2] With the reinforcement of the law to control wildlife in the early 1990s, the general tendency was for the Department of the Environment and Forestry in Mamfe and elsewhere to force bush meat sellers to purchase licences. This led to scenes like the 'bush meat scene' in the Mamfe main market. As one of the forest guards reported:

> We would have loved to pursue only the hunters, most of whom have no licences, but it is absolutely impossible to find them since they hide in the forest. Our target has been to discourage these women from selling bush meat because they never buy licences, nor do they like to pay taxes to the government. You can find them in the Mamfe main market and especially at Ajayukndip which is the headquarters of bush meat sales. Buyam-sellams (traders who buy food supplies from rural dwellers to sell in urban centres) are there every Sunday. If they stop buying, the hunters will stop hunting.

However, the harassment and seizure of bush meat did not solve the problem. The women who sold bush meat had no other source of livelihood apart from subsistence farming. Most had relied on this trade for years to educate their children and provide for their families. Thus the sale of bush meat had become a way of life. Apart from the financial benefits, bush meat was the main source of protein in their families' meals. When meat was seized, it was either shared amongst the forest guards themselves or sold off cheaply to the public. Some of the meat might also be given to top-ranking government officials in Mamfe whereas the women whose meat was seized went back home empty-handed after a hard struggle. They lost the money used to purchase the meat and the profit they could have made, as well as the time and energy spent trekking through thick forest to buy from the hunters.

Amoral economy: fluctuating and blurring taxation levels

Due to the refusal of bush meat sellers to purchase licences they considered too expensive for their type of trade, the wildlife service had to look for other measures to make sellers pay a fee to the state. This led to the imposition of a quarterly fee of 6,000 FCFA in the early 1990s. A few years later, this local arrangement changed and sellers were asked to pay a weekly fee of 1,000 FCFA to the wildlife service, 500 FCFA to the veterinary office and 300 FCFA or sometimes 400 FCFA to the council. Forestry officials went to the market every Saturday to collect these fees. The amount for each week was 1,800 FCFA or 7,200 FCFA a month. In cases of default, basins of meat were confiscated. Before 1995, every bush meat seller was expected to pay a total of 86,400 FCFA a year in taxes to the state.

With the advent of the Global Tax in 1995, bush meat sellers were not excluded. They were obliged to pay the following amounts.

In total, these entrepreneurs paid 50,000 FCFA to 60,000 FCFA yearly. When compared to the taxes demanded before the advent of the Global Tax,

Table 11.1 Taxes paid by bush meat sellers

Registration fee at the Forestry Office	10,000 FCFA
Weekly tax (paid to the Game branch)	500-1,000 FCFA
Global Tax	5,000-6,000 FCFA
Weekly veterinary fee	200 FCFA
Daily council fee	100 FCFA

Source: Author's field data, 1999

this amount was smaller but nonetheless more significant because it was being enforced in the market place. Consequently, the 'old-timer' bush meat sellers were experiencing lowered profit margins. As one informant commented:

> Before 1993, there were only about 10 full-time bush meat sellers in this market. Today, there are about 50 of us and most of the newcomers dodge paying taxes. They prefer to move about the town to sell during the week. On Saturdays, they remain at the other end of the market where they will not be taxed. After the tax collectors leave the market, then they come and sit with us to sell their bush meat.

The irony is that since some income goes into state coffers through tax payments, and informally also into the pockets of those who collect wildlife fees, these women are no longer harassed. As the delegate in Mamfe told me in July 1999: 'The few workers who go out to collect the fees levied on bush meat put the money in their pockets and report that they are still educating the women on the need to buy licences for their businesses'. The state makes the laws and the officials in control bend them to reap maximum benefits for themselves, especially in times of crisis. If the state, and especially those in formal state control, can bend the rules they make, it is not surprising that entrepreneurs themselves use various strategies to evade the rules and regulations of taxation to their own advantage.

Before the introduction of quarterly fees in 1992, and their revision in 1995, a market fee for the municipality was paid daily. Even though considered quite small (50 FCFA or 100 FCFA), some traders still avoided paying it. The introduction of higher taxes during a period of economic recession, and greater competition in trade made things far more difficult for the entrepreneurs. The scene of chaos amongst the market sellers necessitates reflection on the moral economy of the Global Tax as well as on other forms of state taxes newly introduced.

Most women when asked why they worked or carried out trade activities said it was for their family and the need to augment family income. The ultimate goal of female entrepreneurs is to cater for the household and meet the demands of extended family relations. Women's growing entry into the informal sector throughout Africa has been seen in terms of a household livelihood crisis (Omari, 1989; Bryceson, 1999).[3] Women informal sector traders saw the tax reform as robbing them of their hard-earned monetary returns.

Having never been taxed before and being suddenly forced to pay amidst an economic depression, the traders' resentment against state tax enforcement welled up.

In his general study of peasant–state relations, Barrington Moore (1978: 5) remarks that one reason for resentment is that: 'One can be angry because one feels that the existing rule is itself wrong and that a different rule ought to apply'. This was the case with some informants who felt that, rather than imposing tax on them, laws should be passed to improve roads, living conditions, health facilities, etc. This feeling led to tax avoidance strategies, especially with the introduction of the new tax reform.

Government's tax reform strategy

Tax payments are, of course, a vital aspect of the economy of Cameroon. Davey (1974: 2) mentions three main goals for taxes: first, to transfer resources for socially and economically beneficial purposes; second, to stabilize the economy (or at least to avoid upsetting it); and third, to redistribute wealth between the rich and the poor. He sees these goals as universal, yet it is clear that they acquire particular implications in developing countries. In general, the tax systems comprise both direct and indirect taxes. As already seen, there have been frequent changes over the years in the tax system in Cameroon. However, my focus in this chapter is on the abolition of the Poll Tax, the implementation of the Global Tax and the response to this by female entrepreneurs in Limbe and Mamfe. Part of the women's moral outrage to the Global Tax relates to its striking difference with the previous Poll Tax as explained below.

Poll tax

The Poll Tax was instituted by the British colonial administration in parts of Cameroon in order to involve indigenes in the colonial economy. Adult males from the age of 18 whose income could not be assessed, and as such did not pay personal income tax, paid a yearly Poll Tax of 3,000 FCFA up to 1994/5. This applied mostly to males in rural areas or those who were not involved in any kind of formal public-sector employment or private enterprise. With the Poll Tax, no distinction between employed and unemployed males was made. Women were not directly involved in tax payments but in most villages in the Mamfe area they contributed indirectly through their husbands' tax payments. In polygamous households, each wife contributed according to her position in marriage, with the first wife often contributing more. Women regularly had to rescue not only their husbands but also their brothers during tax raids by paying on their behalf. This practice continued until the Poll Tax was abolished and replaced by the Global Tax. An important change is that the new tax policy has shifted the burden pointedly onto rural women by engaging them in direct tax payments.

Global tax

As part of the state's proclaimed process of liberalization and democratization, a number of laws and other subsidiary legislation were enacted as of 1990. As Fombad (1994: 511) noted:

> For the first time, informal activities such as clandestine transportation, itinerant trading, street vending, home-operated restaurant and beer-drinking places popularly known as 'chicken parlours' or 'circuits' were now recognized as legal and required to be registered and, thus, pay taxes under new and apparently more flexible terms.

The Global Tax was instituted at the World Bank's behest to integrate the informal sector into the formal economy and to revamp the country's ailing economy. It represented the first step taken by the government to establish the financial autonomy of the municipal councils directly responsible for its collection. Unlike the Poll Tax that was a head tax, the Global Tax is paid according to the commercial activity of the individual concerned. It is for this reason that it is sometimes called an 'Activity Tax'. While the Poll Tax was only paid by adult males, the Global Tax is supposed to be paid by everybody involved in any kind of trade activity. It is separate from the business licence (commonly called *patente* in French) that was only paid by certain categories of businesses. There were two types of *patente* class A1–A15 and class B distinguished by the type of business, the turnover, and the size of the business. *Patente* had to be paid for most activities operating from permanent stalls. However, the majority of female commercial activities were carried out in open spaces and were therefore excluded from payment.

With the tax reform, new categorizations were made for tax assessment, covering all kinds of commercial activities, whether operating from built-in stalls or in open spaces. All businesses, which prior to the new law fell under the business licence class A12–A15, now have to pay the Global Tax. People who pay the Global Tax do not have to pay income tax, turnover tax or a business licence. All those whose capital per year is less than 15 million FCFA fall under the Global Tax. Four main categories can be distinguished (Table 11.2).

Table 11.2 Global tax categorization (1999)

Categories	Amounts
Category A	0–20,000 FCFA
Category B	21,000–40,000 FCFA
Category C	41,000–50,000 FCFA
Category D	75,000–100,000 FCFA

Source: Article 50 New 1997/8 Finance Law[4]
N.B. The gap between Category C and D emanates from the government's own records. Category D applies to an echelon of more capitalized businesses mostly owned by men, whereas women's businesses are primarily restricted to Categories A–C.

These four categories of taxes cover about 122 economic activities. The average *patente* paid per taxpayer prior to 1995 was 43,000 FCFA in the country, while the average Global Tax is about 2,500 FCFA for Mamfe and 1,500 FCFA for Limbe.[5] While the Global Tax is less financially demanding than the *patente*, its implementation has raised real problems in different parts of the country. People question the rationale of paying taxes and in particular the Global Tax that embraces all categories of people in business. Typical female activities are mostly represented in Category A with the lowest tax payment. Included in this category are itinerant food vendors, itinerant vendors of drinks and water, tailors or seamstresses with fewer than five machines and working alone or with apprentices, food vendors without an establishment, hairdressers with one to two employees, school canteens, vendors of raffia or palm wine, vendors of foodstuffs (*buyam-sellam*), dealers in hides and skins, vendors of firewood, etc.

The categorization of the Global Tax and its implementation has had diverse impacts on male and female entrepreneurs. In the next section, a classification of female entrepreneurs in Mamfe according to various trade activities allows an analysis of female entrepreneurs' responses in this area and their reactions to the Global Tax. But, as one of the tax officials in Mamfe noted:

> For those who had hitherto been paying the patente, the Global Tax was well received after initial misgivings since those taxpayers had been taking it as an additional burden. However, for others who had never paid the patente or business tax, it was naturally not well received and this explains why the assessment started in October rather than July (the end of the financial year) as the government had intended. The majority of women had to be informed and then made to pay business taxes for the first time in their lives. (Mr E., April 1996)

Carrot and stick: implementation of the global tax

Strategies for implementing the Global Tax were left to the discretion of each municipal council. However, a general trend observed in both Limbe and Mamfe was for council employees to work in close collaboration with the Department of Taxation. This made it possible for municipal councils to be well informed about the new tax policy. Entrepreneurs, especially women, were informed in small groups according to their trade. Failure to respond to tax measures sometimes led to the incorporation of public security officers in the team that went out on tax drives.

Mamfe women entrepreneurs falling into line

Mamfe women discussed in this chapter are mostly old-timers and a few newcomers (formal-sector workers) operating at the level of micro and subsistence entrepreneurship.[6] Micro entrepreneurs have fixed workshops that are an extension of their place of residence, or a stall some distance from home. Their asset bases ranged from 150,000 FCFA to 1.3 million FCFA and they paid taxes that ranged from 12,000 to 20,000 FCFA. Among the 69 female entrepreneurs studied in Mamfe, only 5 had fixed premises. The majority of women interviewed (64 in number) were subsistence entrepreneurs with a capital base of 5,000 FCFA to 150,000 FCFA. They owned temporary market stalls or stands. Most were generating an income mainly by extending their household and formal activities to include sewing, the selling of food, second-hand goods and beauty products, and giving extra classes. These women had never been taxed but were now expected to fall into Category A as micro entrepreneurs paying 0–20,000 FCFA.

Taxes for most women in Category A of the Global Tax were assessed arbitrarily. Even though various categories were well defined by the state, those concerned with the tax's implementation opted for a further specification of the criteria for assessment. This depended on the place, trade activity, seasonality of the business and sometimes on the personal relationship between the tax assessor concerned and the taxpayer. Trade activities were grouped and taxed, though differences were still common. In practice, different amounts were imposed especially for petty trading and in the foodstuff business where most women were engaged.

Some entrepreneurs who had been used to paying the *patente* found a change in the amount they had to pay when they went to the tax office for assessment for the Global Tax. Even though some informants felt there was a general reduction in tax rates, there was still a feeling of mistrust of the state. Scepticism seemed to prevail in the minds of women who had lost confidence in the system due to structural adjustment and the hardship they were going through at a time of crisis. This was expressed in some of the comments made:

> At least this time, the government has thought of us and reduced the patente. Instead of 26,650 FCFA for my hairdressing salon, this time I paid 12,000 FCFA. But one can never trust this government, they may pretend to please us so that we vote for them in the council elections and after that they change. (C.O., aged 36, married, 1996)

Even though Global Tax rates were less than the *patente*, many women were still resentful. Tax assessment was easier for those who had been accustomed to paying the *patente*, but many entrepreneurs were suddenly being taxed for the first time with the implementation of the Global Tax. The majority of female entrepreneurs included in this study fell within Category A of the Global Tax, with incomes ranging from 0–20,000 FCFA. This group comprised mostly subsistence entrepreneurs and a few small-scale businesswomen who were paying taxes for the first time. One tax collector commented: 'Women complain a lot, they resist tax payment more than men. But the officials are only there to execute orders despite complaints from women.'

Table 11.3 Population of global tax payers in Mamfe, 1995/6–1998/9

Year	Male	Female	Total	% female
1995/6	325	126	451	28
1996/7	365	288	653	44
1997/8	724	346	1070	32
1998/9	379	324	703	46
Total	1793	1084	2877	38

Source: Statistics from Mamfe Department of Taxation (1996–1999)

In Mamfe, I collected statistics on female and male Global Tax payers over a period of four years (see Table 11.3). An attempt was also made to classify female Global Tax payers according to their trade activities to identify how different categories of female entrepreneurs were responding to the Global Tax.

Table 11.3 shows that the trend towards increasing numbers of taxpayers is erratic, with women constituting an increasing proportion of the total although not consistently. More male than female entrepreneurs were paying Global Tax in Mamfe with the highest number found in the financial year 1997/8. This could be explained by the fact that an attempt was made to implement the farmers' Global Tax of 3,000 FCFA for the first time in this year. But as the Chief of Taxation in Mamfe reported, female farmers resented paying and gave various excuses leading to a reduction in female tax contributions.

From Table 11.4, it is clear that most female taxpayers in Mamfe are taxed on their trade in general foodstuffs. In this field, start-up capital is usually small, ranging from 5,000 FCFA to 10,000 FCFA. Before the Global Tax was instituted, most women selling foodstuffs only paid a small market fee. With

Table 11.4 Types of female entrepreneurs paying the global tax in Mamfe 1995/6–1998/9

Activity	1995/6	1996/7	1997/8	1998/9
Petty trading	18	19	35	24
Foodstuff (including buyam-sellam)	36	165	177	160
Off-licence	23	18	26	36
Lodging facility	2	2	2	2
Tailoring	9	14	19	32
Hairdressing	13	15	18	23
Eating places	19	22	20	11
Transport	1	3	5	1
Drugs sales	2	2	1	1
Bush meat and smoked fish	–	28	31	27
Palm wine	1	–	–	–
Second-hand goods	2	–	12	7
Total	126	288	346	324

Source: Statistics from Mamfe Department of Taxation (1996–1999)

the new tax reform, and following harassment by tax officials, they were forced to pay taxes. From interviews with tax controllers in the market and other officials, it was clear that women selling foodstuffs were unusually aggressive towards tax collectors. As one tax official remarked: 'They defend themselves with their mouths.' To deal with this group of women, tax collectors in Mamfe tried to split them up into smaller groups according to the different types of commodities they sold, and thus make them aware of the importance of paying taxes. For example, in the case of women selling *garri* (cassava farina), once the tax workers succeeded in convincing five women to pay the taxes they owed, the others were exposed to even more harassment and were likely to follow suit. Since the number of people to be taxed was far lower in Mamfe, these entrepreneurs experienced more harassment by local officials since their local council was seriously under-resourced especially with the new system of direct taxation by the local government.

Limbe women eluding the global tax net

Most of the women interviewed in Limbe were higher income formal sector workers, often operating at home or in offices but not in open markets except for a few visible large-scale businesses. These women (155 in total) were found at all the five levels of entrepreneurship mentioned earlier, although the majority were micro and subsistence entrepreneurs just as the women in Mamfe. The situation in Limbe differed from that in Mamfe. 'One of the problems,' noted the Divisional Chief of Taxation in Limbe, 'is how to cover the informal sector completely using the Global Tax'. In 1996, when I carried out field research, foodstuff sellers and petty traders in the open market in Limbe were not yet taxed and up until April 1999, the situation had not changed. This category of entrepreneurs no doubt constituted a substantial number of women entrepreneurs. At the time of my interviews, Limbe urban women were less heavily taxed than Mamfe rural women. The informal sector in Limbe is larger than that in Mamfe due to its urban nature, but given that their business premises were often tucked away within the confines of their residential home rather than on full view in the open market, women's trade activities were more difficult to identify, let alone be taxed.

In Limbe, the Global Tax had not yet been extended to all the actors and trade activities concerned. In the course of an interview with the Chief of Taxation on 30 April 1999 in Limbe, the chief recounted the experience of a team of tax collectors in Limbe's main market:

> Attempts have been made to reach market women with the Global Tax but these were met with total rejection. A team of tax officials went out some time last year and concentrated on the area where women packed their foodstuffs for daily sales. These women were asked to pay 8,000 FCFA in tax. They complained that they had never paid taxes and that the amount was too high. The tax officials tried to force them to pay by locking up the

stall where the goods were packed every evening after daily sales in the open market. It became a battleground and as you know, women battle with their mouths. I was surprised to see a group of women, about 15 in number, talking aloud and entering our premises. They stormed into my office, everyone complaining at the same time. I managed to calm them down and asked one person to lodge their complaint. I saw this as an opportunity to inform the women about tax payments. I took about 15 minutes to educate them on the new tax system and why they should pay taxes. Despite all my explanations, some were still not convinced. They could not see why the government should start taxing them now when life seems so hard with the economic crisis. Well, as a government representative, all I did was to insist on the need for tax payments if the situation in the country was to change. In order to please them, I asked them to pay 4,000 FCFA instead of the 8,000 FCFA that they had been taxed. They went back happier.

An attempt to make market women in Limbe pay the Global Tax met with fierce protest. One day in March 1998 a group of women traders from Limbe market marched to the Department of Taxation in protest against tax payments. At about 9 a.m., women selling food items had just set up their stalls when a team of five tax collectors burst in on the scene. They concentrated on the section for food sales where most of the market women were to be found. These women had always paid a market fee of 50 FCFA or 100 FCFA, but no tax *per se*. Most were not even conversant with the new tax law. As the collectors moved from one table to the next, they demanded a tax payment of 8,000 FCFA for the sale of foodstuffs, but nobody was willing to pay. 'We saw this as too much for us at a time of crisis when we are experiencing very poor sales,' commented one of the women. The tax collectors tried to enforce payments by locking up some of the packing stores and seizing food items. The market woman recounted the event:

At this point, we started shouting abuse. Some women even threw cocoyams at them. When the tax collectors left the market, 15 women were immediately selected to march to the Department of Taxation with their complaints. The female entrepreneurs in this sector of the market had organized a *njangi* group to which they made daily rotating contributions. The president of the group led the protest. As they marched to the taxation office, the women shouted "NO TAX, NO TAX, NO TAX". The noise they made drew the public's attention, and women and children by the roadside joined the crowd. In order to appease the women, the delegate talked to them in a calm manner and asked them to pay 4,000 FCFA instead of 8,000 FCFA.

However, very few women had paid up by the time of my interview with them in April 1999. Women did not feel morally bound to pay taxes to the state which lacked legitimacy in their eyes. As one informant in Limbe market commented: 'The government always wants to take and yet it gives nothing.

Why should we suffer when it is said that oil brings money and yet we are in Limbe with the SONARA and there is still a crisis.'[7] Apparently having seen how difficult it was to deal with the market women who stormed his office in 1998, the Chief of Taxation felt it necessary to carry out more 'sensitiza-tion' before enforcing taxes. He told me that effective tax collection of this group of traders might only begin in the 1999/2000 financial year. Teams of tax controllers and council workers were being sent out into the field to try to educate potential taxpayers, especially women. Seminars were organized for taxpayers, but female entrepreneurs rarely attended such gatherings. Different strategies of implementation were required for different groups of actors and trade activities.

The not-so-global tax: a regressive taxation system

The Global Tax's premise was that everyone who earns should pay tax. How-ever, the implementation of the Global Tax in Limbe and Mamfe does not seem to have taken into consideration most of the activities carried out by recent entry cohort entrepreneurs. These women, who constitute most of the wealthier people straddling the formal and informal divide, manage to slip through the tax net more easily.

Differences between Limbe's and Mamfe's tax base highlight the contrasts between the early entry cohorts (old-timers) who have been actively engaged in informal sector work for many years usually in low-earning petty trade and the recent entry cohorts (newcomers) who surfaced during the 1990s. While the government experiments with various strategies to integrate the informal sector into the formal, tax officials focus on the early entry cohort entrepre-neurs and their activities. They tend to be poorer and more vulnerable than the recent entry cohort. Several reasons account for the vulnerability of the former. As one of the tax officials in Mamfe noted:

> The Global Tax did drive many people into the open. It also sent some back into the shadows like those who packed their wares and took them into their houses in residential districts where second-hand clothes for sale hang over the doors ready to be folded and packed away at the sight of a tax collector on duty. (Mr E.A. aged 44, married, 1997)

Those who were driven into the open were mostly early entry cohort entre-preneurs. Trade location is an important determinant as to who pays Global Tax and who does not. From Table 11.4 it can be seen that most of the activi-ties taxed are those carried out in the open market or in stores located along the roadside and open to customers. The bulk of such activities are carried out by female early entry cohort entrepreneurs. These women have no other source of income and operate from their houses hidden in residential areas, a fact that imposes limitations on their client network. To stabilize their activi-ties and to remain in business, they have to comply with rules and regulations in the Global Tax. Indeed these female entrepreneurs have to obey the premise of the new government policy as summarized by the Assistant Delegate of Taxation in his interview with me: 'Do whatever kind of business you think fit but be within the law'.

Most early entry entrepreneurs found it strange to be taxed and they continue to complain about the new tax reform. However, the recent entry cohorts are less bothered. From their homes and offices they conduct businesses, managing to operate largely outside the official gaze and rarely getting called upon to pay taxes.

In Mamfe, none of the recent entry cohort entrepreneurs I studied paid Global Tax or any other form of tax even though their trade activities could be taxed following the rates for Global Tax stipulated by the government. In Limbe, out of 155 female recent entry cohort entrepreneurs interviewed, only nine were paying some form of tax. Examples of such female entrepreneurs included women who owned sewing workshops, hairdressing salons, restaurants, off-licence bars, transport businesses and the exceptional case of a large-scale entrepreneur who owned a housing estate.

Considering the location and the type of businesses carried out by about 90 per cent of the recent entry cohort entrepreneurs in both areas of study, it was extremely difficult to monitor their activities and convince them to pay taxes.[8] The times and places of these activities were not clearly defined, hence tax collectors found it difficult to control such activities. The example of clerical workers and others whose formal work environment constituted their market space can be cited. Most of these women were also itinerant business people. Some women even sold from their bedrooms and through telephone contacts. The mechanisms put in place for the control of the Global Tax were either limited or inefficient in relation to this category of female entrepreneur.

Before the 1980s, civil servants were exempted from business activities, but now everybody is free to become involved in business. How many people actually stay within the law remains an open question especially since the introduction of new tax systems like the Global Tax and the recent Value Added Tax.[9] Generally in Cameroon, as in most African countries, taxes are paid with great reluctance. This may be a result of the poor exchange relationship between the state and society. The population does not seem to be deriving as much as it had expected from the state even when taxes are paid. It is felt that only a few people in certain privileged positions benefit from what is commonly described as the 'national cake'. This feeling is all pervasive among entrepreneurs, especially those in the Mamfe area who have to travel on poorly maintained roads to Nigeria, Bamenda or Kumba to buy goods.

Some entrepreneurs paid their taxes fearful that their stalls might otherwise be locked up. However, most female entrepreneurs have not yet accepted the rationale of paying state taxes. As a group of women selling lunch meals around the park in Limbe complained to me: 'The taxes we pay are not fixed. It all depends on the tax collectors. They are free to tax us as they like. After all they are the government and they have the right to steal from us.' Another food seller nearby added: 'It is always the men imposing on us. How many women have you seen going round with those tax collectors?' Because of its efforts to introduce new taxes and revise old ones to absorb the informal sector, the state is perceived as being exploitative and even described as a thief. The manner in which the individuals and community perceive the state determines their exchange relationship with it. This has led to tax rejection and all forms of evasive tendencies by businessmen and women.

The Global Tax was instituted after the collapse of the formal economic sector and following the expansion of the informal sector in the 1990s. Almost everyone, including state officials and employees, had to fall back on the informal sector. Thus, the government found it necessary to forge formal entry into this sector through the imposition of new taxes. After ten years in existence, to what extent are economic activities subject to the Global Tax? Is it possible for the informal sector in Cameroon to be wiped out after a long period of economic recession, and all categories of entrepreneurs struggling to come out of poverty? Is it a matter of theory or reality? Evidence suggests that the Global Tax is inflexible in theory (the law) but flexible in practice (implementation of the law).

Three years after my original study, I revisited Mamfe and Limbe to hold discussions with tax officials and assess the effects of the Global Tax. At the Department of Taxation in Limbe, one of the officials commented as follows:

> The more we endeavour to implement the new tax, the more those in the informal sector look for new strategies to evade tax collectors. More and more avenues are created everyday, especially by women, which cannot be controlled by official tax collectors.

The informal sector has always been perceived as clandestine, unregistered and illegal, resulting in taxes either not being paid at all or being paid incorrectly. De Soto (1989: 3) notes that the informal sector is a euphemism for the illegal sector. Tax evasion strategies are common hence informal sector agents who obey the law and pay taxes have to operate in especially narrow profit margins relative to those who evade taxes. It is the people's spontaneous and creative response to the state's incapacity to satisfy the basic needs of the impoverished masses. Economic liberalization presents more opportunities to all classes of people and especially women operators in the informal sector.

In Cameroon, it prompted policy-makers to focus on an area of the economy that was previously marginal to the state. Women informal sector entrepreneurs had generally operated outside both the country's tax and trade licensing structures. Not surprisingly, they attempted to evade the Global Tax. Tax avoidance strategies can be delineated by the type of trade activity carried out. While the act of avoiding taxes is sometimes pre-meditated and consciously undertaken, in some cases it is subconscious. The female entrepreneurs resorted to a range of tax evasion tactics including: early morning market sales, attending evening or night markets, absenteeism,[10] sales at periodic markets, mobile shops and itinerant sales of cooked food, collaborative sales, indoor markets, and bribery. Bribes paid by entrepreneurs at the numerous police and *gendarmerie* checkpoints along the road are seen as a substitute for official taxation. As one of the female entrepreneurs remarked:

> The bribes we give to government officials on the road or at the airport when our goods arrive are more than enough to make up for taxes. If we don't pay direct taxes, it is no problem, because we have already paid indirectly along the road.

In effect, government officials taking bribes discourage tax adherence.

Conclusion

This chapter has focused on the impact of the Global Tax on female entrepreneurship in Limbe and Mamfe. It has assessed the rationale of the new tax, its implementation, and the response of female entrepreneurs.

In the face of challenges posed by the economic crisis and SAP, women in all walks of life are becoming more involved in income generation. As a consequence, the state is trying to enlist women as taxpayers. The Global Tax represents a redistribution of the tax load. Poorer women, who normally would not be taxed, are now paying the Global Tax because of their commercial activities. State representatives and development economists tend to argue that women's contributions to development will remain invisible if their economic activities are not taxed. But it could also be argued that if women's informal sector activities are given a conducive environment in which to operate and be allowed to grow, they will automatically become visible, also for taxation.

The Cameroonian state abruptly imposed the Global Tax with the aim of formalizing all trading activities. While some women entrepreneurs were forced to pay taxes due to harassment by tax officials, others deployed tax avoidance strategies to retain their business's normal profit level. Women advanced a moral argument against tax payment arguing that the taxes were unjustly being enforced at a time of economic recession when the cost of educating their children had increased with the imposition of school fees, which had never previously been demanded, not unlike cases of moral outrage engendered by taxation documented by Thompson (1963) and Scott (1976). So too, public health facilities were being curtailed and the costs of daily life had increased. Women were, therefore, preoccupied with the idea of 'making up what has been lost'. They believed they were catering for the genuine needs of the family and that took precedence over state claims.

Women traders felt that they had the right to defend themselves from taxation. It was for this reason that a group of 15 Limbe market women marched on the Department of Taxation in protest. Meanwhile the state saw tax payment as a civic duty of the economically active population. These opposing views, based on sound moral arguments, resulted in a battleground as exemplified by the bush meat sellers and forest guards in Mamfe. Society and the state were diametrically opposed with little common ground between them.

The Global Tax had several limitations yet it was clear that the Cameroonian state had to collect taxes for the common good. Nonetheless the common good was proving to be far too common and less than good in the eyes of Cameroonian women entrepreneurs. While the World Bank insisted on regularizing the tax situation in Cameroon, the women traders felt that their living standards had been compressed too much and that they had justifiable reasons to subvert state actions. Not feeling indebted to the state nor trusting towards state officials, women entrepreneurs' imperative was to evade rather than pay taxes.

About the author

Margaret Niger-Thomas is an anthropologist and member of the department of women and gender studies at the University of Buea. She also works in the Cameroonian civil service holding the position of regional delegate for women's empowerment and the family. Her research interests span the formal/informal sector of the economy, female entrepreneurship, taxation policy, social capital, group initiatives and networking. Her publications include: *Buying Futures: The Upsurge of Female Entrepreneurship crossing the Formal/Informal Divide in South West Cameroon* (Leiden University, 2000), 'Women's Access to and Control of Credit in Cameroon', in *Money-Go Rounds*, (Ardener and Burman [eds], Berg, 1995) and 'Revisiting Smuggling in Mamfe, Cameroon', in *From Modern Myths to Global Encounters: Belonging and the Dynamics of Change in Postcolonial Africa* (van der Kwaak, Spronk and Willemse [eds], CNWS Publications, Leiden, 2005). She is the founding president of Manyu Women's Self-Reliance Foodstuff Co-operative, the chairperson of the Women's Information and Co-ordination Forum (WICOF) a regional NGO based in Buea, Cameroon and the technical adviser of the Forum for Christian Women's Empowerment and Development (FOCWED).

Notes

* I wish to acknowledge the editorial suggestions of Deborah Bryceson in this chapter.
1. 'Bush meat' is also called 'smoked meat' in urban centres. When hunters kill wild animals in the forests, they dry or smoke the meat before selling it. Buyers and sellers of bush meat have always been women, and this trade is a lucrative source of income for several women in the Mamfe area.
2. Decree No. 95/466/PM of 20/7/95 laid down new conditions for implementing wildlife regulations in the country.
3. In his study of the rural informal sector and household economy in Tanzania, Omari (1989) explained that: 'Rural women get involved in the informal sector as a means of improving the household economy and of reducing the effect of rising costs by budget supplementation'. It is

clear that in the current state of economic recession both rural and urban women are faced with the need to supplement their household income.

4. It should be noted that the Global Tax rates of the 1995/6 Finance Law have been revised following Finance Law No. 07/014 of 18/7/97.

5. Figures were obtained from the Department of Taxation in Limbe and Mamfe. Due to the urban nature of Limbe, there are more economic openings that bring in income to the council coffers, thus, accounting for the low average Global Tax paid in Limbe. In peri-urban Mamfe, the situation differs in that the sources of council revenue are limited, hence the higher average Global Tax paid compared to Limbe.

6. I have identified five levels of female entrepreneurship in south-west Cameroon: 'giant women' or large-scale, 'big women' or middle-scale, small-scale, micro and subsistence entrepreneurs (Niger-Thomas, 2000:74 and 1997).

7. SONARA (Société Nationale de Rafinerie) is the acronym used for the National Oil Refinery Corporation in Cameroon based in Limbe.

8. Statistics are from the author's field data.

9. The Value Added Tax (VAT) in Cameroon was introduced on 1 July 1998, but became operational only on 1 January 1999.

10. 'Absenteeism' refers to the practice of some female entrepreneurs dodging from their market places at the sight of a tax collector. They pretend to be absent for a while but stay close by and watch their items unnoticed. Once the tax collectors have left that particular sector of the market, the 'absentee entrepreneur' reappears on the scene.

Bibliography

Bryceson, D.F. (1999) 'African rural labour, income diversification, and livelihood approaches: a long-term development perspective', *Review of African Political Economy* 80: 171–89.

Cameroon, Ministry of Economic Affairs and Planning (1987) Demo 87 Second Census, Directorate of Population Census.

Davey, J.K. (1974) *Taxing a Peasant Society: The Example of Graduated Taxes in East Africa*, Charles Knight and Co., London.

de Soto, H. (1989) 'Structural adjustment and the informal sector', in J. Levitski (ed.), *Microenterprises in Developing Countries*, pp. 3–12, Intermediate Technology Development Publications, London.

Fombad, C.M. (1994) 'Legal aspects of the informal sector in Cameroon', *African Journal of International and Comparative Law* 6(3): 504–15.

Kaldor, N. (1970) 'Taxation for economic development', in M.C.Taylor (ed.), *Taxation for African Economic Development*, pp. 158–77, Hutchinson Educational, London.

Mejia and Riley (1997) 'Women workers and the global economy'. *Newsletter of the Association for Women in Development*, 2(1).

Moore, B. Jr. (1978) *Injustice: The Social Bases of Obedience and Revolt*, Macmillan, London.

Niger-Thomas, A.M. (1997) 'Combining the Formal and Informal: Cameroon Women and the Livelihood Crisis', Unpublished paper from the PAAA Annual Conference, Accra, University of Legon.

Niger-Thomas, A.M. (2000) *Buying Futures: The Upsurge of Female Entrepreneur-ship Crossing the Formal/Informal Divide in Southwest Cameroon*, Centre for Non-Western Studies Publications 95, Leiden.

Omari, C.K. (1989) 'Rural Women, Informal Sector and Household Economy in Tanzania', United Nations World Institute for Development Economics, Helsinki.

Scott. J.C. (1976) *The Moral Economy of the Peasant: Rebellion and Subsistence in South East Asia*, Yale University Press, New Haven and London.

Thompson, E.P. (1963) *The Making of the English Working Class*, Vintage, New York.

CHAPTER 12

Occupational change, structural adjustment and trade union identity in Africa: the case of Cameroonian plantation workers

Piet Konings

This study focuses on the profound changes in the position of workers and trade union identity on the Ndu Tea Estate established in the Bamenda Grassfields of Anglophone Cameroon by the end of the British Trusteeship era. Local male peasants, who were excluded from inheriting family property, used to have a high stake in plantation labour, perceiving it as an avenue to accumulate and gain status in the local community, and they tended to strongly identify with the local trade union, relying on it for the protection of their interests. The severe economic crisis and subsequent structural adjustment programme in the late 1980s brought about a dramatic deterioration in workers' conditions of service, and they rapidly lost whatever confidence they still had in the union leadership, accusing it of collaborating with the management in the planning and implementation of a series of anti-labour measures. As a result, they now are inclined to by-pass the union and to defend their interests by engaging in a variety of informal and collective modes of resistance.

Introduction

It is now widely recognized that wage workers were among the most seriously affected by the economic crises and Structural Adjustment Programmes (SAPs) of the 1990s in Africa. SAPs conventionally prescribed devaluation, major cuts in public expenditure, privatization, rehabilitation or elimination of most parastatals, as well as liberalization. As a result, wage workers were faced with managerial efforts to intensify supervision and increase labour productivity, retrenchments, curtailments in pay, suspension of benefits compounded by soaring consumer prices and user charges for public services.

The World Bank attempted to justify these anti-labour measures not only in economic but also in political terms (Bangura and Beckman, 1993; Adesina, 1994; Gibbon, 1995). They argued that the historical influence of African trade unions has led to excessive levels of wage employment, inflated wages and a pro-urban, pro-worker allocation of public funds. It is interesting to observe that this view approximates earlier populist positions regarding 'labour aristocracy', 'urban bias' and 'urban coalition', all of which portrayed workers as a privileged minority, pursuing narrow self-interests at the expense of the urban poor and peasantry in coalition with the urban elite (Waterman, 1975; Lipton, 1977; Bates, 1981). Although these views have been severely criticized by various authors (Jamal and Weeks, 1993; Adesina, 1994; Thomas, 1995), they were nevertheless used by African leaders, like Rawlings in Ghana, to legitimize the implementation of SAP measures and to suppress trade union opposition (Kraus, 1991).

Given the formidable challenge SAPs posed to trade unions in Africa, there was a surprising dearth of studies on the actual trade union response to SAPs. Existing studies focus mostly on the national level. They show that some trade union centres, notably in countries like Zambia, Ghana and Nigeria where trade unionism managed to preserve a certain degree of autonomy *vis-à-vis* the state in the post-colonial era, attempted to oppose SAPs (Akwetey, 1994; Panford, 1994; Hashim, 1994). This opposition, however, proved unsuccessful in the end. SAPs seriously weakened the position of trade unions in African states. Mass retrenchment of labour in the public and private sector led to substantial losses in trade union membership and trade union revenues, whilst government abolition of legislative provisions concerning job security, participatory rights or guaranteed collective bargaining rights, and outright government oppression of any trade union oppositional action, forced trade unions' backs against the wall.

In these circumstances, there was little the trade unions could do for their suffering members. Increasing job insecurity and falling real earnings forced the rank and file to search for alternative sources of income, 'straddling' between the 'formal' and 'informal' sectors and subsistence farming, as well as engaging in illicit income-generating activities such as theft, corruption, black-marketeering and prostitution. The 'fusion' of labour markets ensured the survival of workers, but, according to some authors (Jamal and Weeks, 1993), it also signified the virtual collapse of the wage-earning class as a distinct entity. Consequently, trade unions faced a deep crisis of identity. It would appear that they have not yet devised any new strategies to deal with their dramatic loss of membership and the fusion of labour markets.

Even less research was done on the impact of such changes in trade union bargaining strength and labour markets on workers' trade union identity. Studies of industrial workers in Nigeria contradicted each other. Some claimed that workers no longer had faith in their unions and were inclined to embark instead on individual survival strategies and income-generating activities (Oloyede, 1991). Others argued that workers often still relied on their unions to settle individual and collective grievances (Isamah, 1994). Still others pointed out that workers combined individual survival strategies with union activities. For example, Bangura and Beckman (1993) illustrate how workers attempted to pursue individual strategies via trade union actions: their actions were directed at obtaining levels of termination payment that would enable them to set up farms or petty transport and trading operations.

These studies caution against easy generalizations. There may indeed be a considerable variation in workers' trade union identity under SAPs, dependent on factors such as the differential impact of SAPs on economic sectors, the historical strength of trade unionism, the location (urban/rural) of affected enterprises, among other factors. In this study the focus is on changes in trade union identity during the economic crisis and SAP in rural Cameroon on the Ndu Tea Estate. The estate, established in the Bamenda Grassfields of Anglophone Cameroon in 1957, was owned by an English–Indian multinational, the Estates and Agency Company Ltd (EAC) until 1977, when it was transferred to the Cameroon Development Corporation (CDC), a huge agro-industrial parastatal whose main estates are located in the coastal areas of Anglophone Cameroon (Konings, 1993).

Estate production and occcupational change at Ndu

In 1957 the EAC began constructing a tea estate at Ndu, a small town situated in the Donga-Mantung division of the Bamenda Grassfields. It was at that time the only agro-industrial enterprise in the entire Bamenda Grassfields and one of the few enterprises in the region offering wage employment.

The local population belongs to the Wimbum, the most important ethnic group in the Donga-Mantung division. Wimbum society, like most other societies in the Bamenda Grassfields, is characterized by a highly complex socio-political form of organization headed by powerful, even sacred, chiefs. The chief of Ndu is the most influential of the Wimbum chiefs and for this reason is seen by some as the leader of all the Wimbum. The chief is assisted by quarter-heads, councillors and a number of other important (hereditary) title and office holders. Efforts to rise within existing institutions to a position of influence and prestige are common throughout the population and internal flexibility is thus introduced into an otherwise stiffly stratified social system (Probst and Bühler, 1990). In fact, traditional institutions have from time immemorial co-opted prominent members of the community within their ranks. The most common mechanism is to honour such persons with a non-hereditary title. Titles and membership of titled societies become important pieces of 'symbolic capital' and an object of accumulation (Goheen, 1993).

There used to be a clear sexual division of labour. Women were largely responsible for food farming while men hunted and traded in livestock, kola nuts and palm products (palm oil, palm wine and raffia). A considerable number of men were engaged in lucrative long-distance trade in kola nuts to Nigeria. Following the example of Fulani in the area, they also began raising cattle. After the Second World War, there were two significant changes in men's roles. Firstly, there was a steady increase in male labour migration to the coastal plantations, especially to CDC estates. Secondly, the introduction of arabica coffee growing provided a new, major source of revenue for men.

With the opening of the estate, the EAC management began to recruit local male labour. This was by no means accidental. It was the outcome of two potentially conflicting factors: the capitalist preference for female pluckers and the 'traditional' male control over women's vital productive and reproductive labour (Kaberry, 1952; Goheen, 1993). In prior negotiations between the chief of Ndu and the EAC on the local community's supply of land and labour for estate production, the company had proposed employing female pluckers for various reasons. There was a general belief in management circles that women were *naturally* more suited to picking tea (they had 'nimble fingers'), more docile (they were accustomed to subordination), and cheaper (their income was defined as supplementary to that of the so-called breadwinner, namely the husband). The company's long experience with tea plucking in India and Sri Lanka had strengthened this managerial belief (Kurian, 1982). The idea of enjoying similar benefits on a tea estate in Cameroon must have been particularly attractive to management. The chief, however, strongly opposed the company's proposal, saying that:

> women are responsible for farm work. That is why we call them 'mothers of the farm'. They are also responsible for feeding and caring for the household. Women are very important people, but they are expected to obey male orders. Employment on the estate would incite women to neglect food production and household work, to behave 'headstrongly' and independently, and even to become 'harlots'.

He insisted instead on employing local male labour as a prerequisite for allowing the estate to be set up in his area of jurisdiction. This condition would not only halt the migration of local male labour to coastal areas but would also avert the construction of labour camps, which were frequently found on the coastal estates. In this way he hoped to safeguard not only 'traditional' male control over women's productive and reproductive labour, but also the continuing integration of male workers into the local community and their loyalty to traditional code of ethics and authority patterns. He finally agreed that women could be employed on the estate for specific activities, notably weeding, on a casual or temporary basis, provided their employment would not affect their productive and reproductive responsibilities in the local community. It was not until 1983 that his newly elected successor – a university graduate – allowed the employment of women as pluckers on a permanent basis.

The newly created estate never experienced any shortage of labour. Wage-earning opportunities were few in the area, and manpower resources abundant. The local population increased from approximately 17,000 in the mid-1960s to approximately 35,000 in the mid-1980s. The labour force expanded from 300 in 1957 to 1,750 in 1987. It has remained predominantly male (94 per cent). Generally speaking, estate workers are men who have failed to be selected as the successor to the family head. In Ndu, as elsewhere in the Grassfields, there can only be one such successor, who is not necessarily the eldest son. After his installation as head of the family, he has control of all family property. Estate work is highly valued by the non-successors, as it enables them to escape from the successor's control and to build up an independent existence. It also serves as an important avenue to social mobility in the local community.

The majority of non-successors use part of their wages to achieve specific objectives which can 'compensate' them for the loss of the successorship and enhance their status within the local community. One can usually observe a certain pattern in the pursuit of these objectives: a man first attempts to build a house and marry one or more wives who can look after the cultivation of food; he then tries to set up a coffee farm and raise cattle, and eventually to invest in the acquisition of honorific titles which give the non-successors, like the hereditary office and title holders, access to power and wealth in the community. This is naturally a difficult project. It takes years of hard labour for low-waged estate workers to achieve even some of these objectives. As a result, male workers showed long-standing commitment to their jobs: 53 per cent of the male labour force in the mid-1990s were employed on the estate for more than 10 years. In a situation where supply was far greater than demand, labour was often recruited through informal channels. One consequence of this was that jobs tended to be 'monopolized' by certain families. Workers often approached their direct superiors to recommend their sons or other relatives for employment when vacancies occurred. The management was usually inclined to accept such recommendations if they came from workers who were known as being hard working and committed.

The Ndu male workers have continued to resist female employment on the estate (Konings, 1995a). Only 6 per cent of the mid-1990s labour force consisted of women. Most of them were pluckers who were recruited since 1983 following an agreement between the newly elected chief of Ndu and the CDC on permanent female employment. The women tended to be younger and better educated than the men and were usually those who wanted to escape from 'traditional' farm work and male dominance, but were not yet able to find any employment other than plantation work. Hence, they tended to be less committed to their jobs than male pluckers.

It would be difficult to describe plantation workers as 'labour aristocrats' (Loewenson, 1992) given the relatively low remuneration they receive for their hard labour. Ndu pluckers were placed in category 2 (semi-skilled workers, zone 2 of the primary sector) of the standard national classification of occupations, being entitled to a monthly basic wage of approximately FCFA 25,000 (US$1 = FCFA 441). Primary sector wages were the lowest in the country; industrial semi-skilled workers in the urban areas earned about FCFA 35,000. Primary sector wages also appeared lower than the average household income in the area, estimated by Goheen (1996) at about FCFA 447, 270 a year. Goheen, however, admits that her income figures were skewed somewhat by the fact that several households in her sample were headed by relatively wealthy men; households headed by men with wage/salaried jobs had substantially more income than those where male employment was confined to farming.

Moreover, quite a number of Ndu pluckers were unable to earn the basic wage, mainly due to the link between the remuneration of workers and the system of task work operating on the plantations.

Completion of the daily task set by the management entitled a worker to the daily basic wage; non-completion was punished by a *pro rata* payment. Because of their low remuneration, estate workers usually displayed a rather ambivalent attitude towards plantation labour. In some ways they valued it for providing them with a regular source of income. In other ways they had an acute feeling of exploitation and subordination in the labour process. Para-doxically, the close links workers continued to maintain with their local com-munity appeared not to be an obstacle to class action. In several ways, such ties increased workers' inclinations to resist control and exploitation in the labour process.

First, they seemed to stimulate workers' efforts to resist capitalist norms and authority and to preserve a certain degree of autonomy at the workplace. For instance, managerial staff frequently complained about the alarming rate of absenteeism on the estate. A few examples illustrate the close connection between absenteeism and the continuing adherence of workers to local norms and authority:

> During the annual harvesting period in August-September the men are cus-tomarily obliged to assist the women in transporting the harvest from the farm to the compound. As this period approaches, the rate of absenteeism on the estate tends to rise.

> Ndu has the largest market in the Donga-Mantung Division. Market days are not only of great economic importance, but are also social happenings. On market days workers are often either absent or leave the estate before closing time.

Second, they may have fuelled workers' demands for better conditions of service because workers tried to invest any capital derived from wage employ-ment in their social advancement within the local community.

Third, they could have provided workers with an 'exit option', protecting them against severe managerial disciplinary action, in the form of dismissal.

Trade unionism on the Ndu estate and structural adjustment

On 27 July 1958 a trade union, the Ndu Estate Workers Union,[1] was founded on the estate due to the determination and organizational skills of what Mil-len (1963) has called an 'outside' leader. This leader was Mr E.Y.K. Barthson who had been active as a journalist in Lagos. Living in Ndu, he had been in-vited by senior estate workers to organize a union.

The new union was immediately opposed by the estate management and the chief, who regarded it as a threat to their authority. Both continually in-timidated workers to discourage them from joining. Eventually, however, they realized they could not impede the growing popularity of the union because it persevered in defending workers' interests. The union's successful organization of a first strike in 1962 boosted worker confidence in its leadership and forced the chief and the management to recognize the union. Gradually, both came to accept the union as the 'normal' mediation channel between workers and management. The union's persistent struggle for improvement in the workers' living and working conditions triggered a rapid growth in union membership. By 1968, a year after the introduction of the check-off system on the estate, it was estimated that more than 90 per cent of estate workers were paid-up union members. Ndu workers at that time demonstrated a remarkable degree of participation in union affairs:

> Each time we convene an Annual Conference we get nearly every registered and potential member present and eager to attend so that it looks more like a general meeting than a conference as stipulated in sections 5 to 7 of our constitution. On the other hand, previously we had encouraged General Meetings of workers every month. At these meetings workers prefer to discuss not only the difficulties facing them on the estate but all the matters that should be handled by the Annual Delegates Conference.[2]

Obviously, the relatively small size of the union allowed for close contact between the leadership and the rank and file, as well as more ready participation in trade union affairs. Active participation in the union enabled Ndu workers to exercise a considerable measure of control over the union leadership's representation of their interests.

In 1972 trade unionism in Cameroon was put under state control, with the aim of transforming trade unionism from a vehicle of labour resistance into an instrument of labour control. Unions were henceforth expected to play a major role in national development, especially through the education of workers on the 'need' for increased production and constant 'dialogue' with employers. In a subsequent reorganization of trade unionism, the Ndu Estate Workers Union was dissolved and its members were requested to join a newly created Divisional Union of Agricultural Workers of Donga-Mantung (DUAW).

State control over the union together with a virtual statutory prohibition of strike action formed a serious obstacle to the new union's representation of workers' interests. The situation was aggravated by the union's lack of funds, as a result of the introduction of a new system for distributing the check-off contributions which prevented the union from paying staff members, holding regular meetings, and organizing trade union activities. Little wonder that the rank and file lost confidence in their leadership, a condition that was manifest in an increasing number of 'illegal' strike actions after 1972 which the union could not control (Konings, 1995a). The economic crisis that hit the CDC from 1986 onwards further weakened the union's bargaining position *vis-à-vis* the management.

There is no doubt that the sharp fall in commodity prices on the world market and the 40 per cent increase in the value of the CFA franc relative to the US dollar (which made CDC commodities even less competitive on the world market) were the principal causes of the virtual bankruptcy of the corporation. The CDC suffered a loss of about FCFA 19 billion between 1986 and 1991. Nevertheless, there were other factors that also contributed to the emergence and continuation of the crisis. First, there was the political elite's inability or unwillingness to stop the imports of cheap tea and palm oil, which impeded CDC sales on the domestic market. Second, there were frequent reports of the managerial elite's involvement in massive embezzlement, reckless expenditure, waste, and power struggles. It is therefore understandable that many workers did not believe that the management could effectively combat the crisis (Konings, 1995b).

The government had previously subsidized parastatal enterprises annually, irrespective of performance, but faced with a severe economic crisis in the second half of the 1980s, it was no longer able to render any assistance to the CDC. To save the corporation from total collapse, the management was forced to adopt a series of adjustment measures aimed at cost reduction and productivity increases, including intensified task work, drastic cuts in workers' salaries and fringe benefits, and retrenchments. This managerial strategy for economic recovery was reinforced in 1989 when the government adopted a World Bank and IMF-inspired SAP which demanded, among other things, a restructuring of the parastatal sector. The CDC was then obliged to sign a four-year performance contract with the government, under which the corporation was expected 'to meet certain standards of efficiency and to become self-supporting and profitable'.[3] Soon after the signing of this contract, the CDC General Manager announced a managerial crusade against 'undisciplined and unproductive' workers.

The various adjustment measures brought some relief to the company's liquidity problems but its survival remained precarious. It was not until January 1994, when a 50 per cent devaluation of the CFA franc made CDC products more competitive on the world market, that prospects for economic recovery appeared. Six months later the government surprisingly announced the privatization of the corporation, prompting feelings of job insecurity among the workers. After vehement protests by the workers and the regional population as a whole, the actual privatization was postponed (Konings, 1996).

In response to the corporation's unprecedented crisis, the union presidents on the CDC estates decided to assist the management in its struggle for economic recovery. There were a number of factors behind this decision. Since the reorganization of trade unionism in 1972, the unions had become accustomed to solving problems with the management and the state through peaceful negotiations rather than through confrontation. In this particular case, the union presidents agreed with the management that, given the corporation's inability to secure any loans or public subsidies during the crisis, cost reduction and productivity increase were absolute prerequisites for economic recovery. Furthermore, they were assured by the management that no one in the corporation would be exempted from making sacrifices for the sake of economic recovery. They also hoped that the implementation of an adjustment programme would safeguard the jobs of the sizeable CDC labour force estimated at about 15,000.

On 23 August 1987 the union presidents agreed with the management on a substantial increase in the productivity required of estate workers. For example, the daily quota required from tea pluckers was raised from 26 to 32 kg of green leaves. When the corporation's financial position continued to deteriorate, management proposed further austerity measures to the union presidents. Following negotiations, a new agreement was signed on 6 January 1990, which entailed drastic cuts in the salaries and fringe benefits of all workers and managerial staff, amounting to some 30 to 40 per cent of their previous incomes. The most draconian measure, however, was the introduction of a compulsory savings scheme, forcing workers to save at least 15 per cent of their basic salary to aid the corporation's recovery.

In the wake of the political liberalization process in the country, the unions regained a certain degree of autonomy in 1991. The union presidents then became more responsive to the sufferings of the workers and began to criticize the adjustment programme they had previously supported. At their urgent request, the CDC General Manager organized a meeting to review the January 1990 agreement. During this meeting on 1 March 1992, the union presidents insisted upon the termination or modification of the workers' financial contributions to the corporation's economic recovery. They justified this remarkable change in the union's position as follows.

First, the union had expected that the increased output and financial sacrifices of the workers would have forestalled, or at least minimized, any retrenchments. This had proved to be wishful thinking as the management had embarked upon mass layoffs of workers. Between 1986 and 1990, the labour force at the Ndu Tea Estate had been reduced from 1,750 to 1,333. Labour retrenchment has been facilitated by the new Labour Code of 1992 which allowed employers to lay off workers during 'an unfavourable economic situation and internal reorganization' without previous consultation with the Labour Office or unions.

Second, the unions had expected the government to take appropriate measures to stabilize the prices of essential commodities and to standardize the wages of the agro-industrial parastatals. This had not happened. Neither had the National Social Insurance Fund continued to pay family allowances to the workers. In fact, prices had skyrocketed after the political opposition's 1991 'ghost town' campaign,[4] wages had been frozen since July 1985, and taxes had increased by 100 per cent. As a result, CDC workers 'would now seem to be carrying out forced labour as the majority of the labour force has no take-home wage at the end of the month'.[5]

The management, however, refused to go beyond some minor concessions in relation to the January 1990 agreement. The union presidents then declared a collective trade dispute on 13 May 1992. When the management tried to employ delaying tactics, CDC workers went on strike from 21 to 26

May 1992. After this strike, the management agreed to various amendments of the January 1990 agreement including the reintroduction of certain fringe benefits.

Although there was a certain improvement in the relationship between the union leadership and the CDC management after these amendments, tensions and conflicts continued to simmer beneath the surface. The union presidents complained regularly about the management's lack of consultation with the unions and shop stewards, while the management, in turn, constantly insisted that, in a situation of crisis, the unions should have concentrated on an increase in labour productivity rather than on the representation of workers' interests.

Ndu workers and trade union identity under structural adjustment

The SAP and the union's extensive cooperation with the CDC management in the planning and implementation of adjustment measures had a disastrous effect on trade union membership and the rank and file's trade union identity.

A considerable number of workers ceased to be union members, because they were laid off by the management during the economic crisis and SAP. Although Ndu workers maintain close links with the local community, which serves as a kind of social protection against retrenchment, retrenchment nevertheless thwarted workers' social mobility projects in the local community. Best off were usually the older workers who had been able to invest part of their savings in coffee production, cattle rearing, trade or other entrepreneurial activities. Nonetheless, even for some of these men, survival became precarious during the economic crisis: by the early 1990s the government had not paid them for their coffee for over two years.

Worst off were usually the young men and women who lacked the financial resources to continue building up an autonomous existence. They were often looked upon as social failures. A man who had not been able to establish at least a coffee farm commanded no respect in society (Manga, 1984). An educated woman who refused to engage in 'traditional' farm work and to subordinate herself to male control through marriage was seen as 'lazy' or 'loose'. In their efforts to earn some income and preserve a certain degree of autonomy towards the family head, a growing number of young men and women were forced to engage in petty trade – often in smuggled or stolen goods – and to accept all kinds of casual, menial jobs. Some young men formed work groups offering their labour to local farmers (Courade, 1994). Others decided to migrate to urban centres to try their luck, some returning to their hometown after a while, having failed to secure gainful employment during the crisis (Gubry *et al.*, 1996). Still others started growing food, a domain previously reserved for women, to earn some cash. They often experienced difficulties in finding land for food cultivation in an area where land had become an increasingly scarce commodity due to estate production, coffee farming and cattle grazing. Being engaged in a traditionally female occupation, they also risked social ridicule and consequently had to farm in the forest where land was still available and where they could not be seen.

Educated women wishing to escape from 'traditional' farm work and male control had often no other choice than to prostitute themselves. Given the continuing male opposition to female employment on the estate, it was not surprising that male workers and shop stewards brought strong pressures to bear upon the management to fire women first whenever retrenchments were necessary.

An increasing number of union members were also inclined to retire 'voluntarily' from the estate. This was mainly due to the growing demotivation of workers with the intensified control and exploitation at the workplace and their dissatisfaction with the union's defence of their interests during the crisis. While some workers were still reluctant to resign and thereby lost their monthly wage income, however meagre it may have been, others were no longer interested in keeping their job at any cost, especially having lost confidence in the corporation's eventual recovery. The latter wanted to collect their long-service awards and gratuities and their voluntary and compulsory savings, and invest the capital in farming, trade and other potentially lucrative activities such as taxi-driving or setting up a bar or shop.

A tiny minority of the remaining labour force continued to identify itself with the union, relying on it to protect its interests. The vast majority of workers, however, lost whatever confidence they still had in the union and employed a variety of strategies to cope with the managerial adjustment measures. Some of them opted for a single strategy, others for several strategies, simultaneously or consecutively.

A number of tea pluckers became survival-oriented in the climate of insecurity and tended to acquiesce in any economic recovery measures the management introduced, however stringent, for the sake of keeping their jobs. They tried to impress the management with above-average output and avoided conflicts with their supervisors. This intensified the element of competition in the labour process, undermining the previously high degree of solidarity among workers who shared similar living and working conditions.

Unexpectedly, most workers still seemed to cling to the strategy they had always employed in times when the union had failed to protect their interests and 'deliver the goods': engaging in individual and collective modes of resistance. It should be noted, however, that collective actions became more sporadic than in the past. This is understandable, since collective actions were extremely risky in a situation where strikes were virtually outlawed and were likely to elicit severe managerial reprisals in the form of summary dismissals.

When the union president, Mr Johnson Tanto Massa, informed the Ndu workers of the union's agreement with the management on an increase of task work from 26 to 32 kg of green leaves, workers complained that the new norm was too high, as many of them already experienced difficulties in reaching the old quota. They protested against the agreement in various ways. They refused to re-elect Mr Johnson Tanto Massa in the DUAW executive elections shortly afterwards and instead voted a non-estate worker, Mr G.N. Majam, a brother of the chief of Ndu and a clerical worker in the local coffee cooperative, into office. In addition, they started a go-slow in November, which resulted in all of them being paid a *pro rata* rate. The pluckers agreed to raise output only after the estate manager promised to allow some of their representatives to visit the other CDC tea estates to investigate whether their colleagues on these estates were also carrying out the new norm.

Promptly after the signing of the January 1990 agreement between the management and the unions, the newly elected union president, Mr G.N. Majam, barely escaped being beaten up by angry workers when he informed them of the terms of the agreement. Because of Majam's total failure to obtain the workers' consent, the CDC General Manager himself had to come to the estate to seek their cooperation. At a mass meeting, he stressed that non-acceptance of the drastic cuts in their real incomes would inevitably lead to the closure of the estate. This left the workers with no other choice but to comply.

A year later, on 4 January 1991, workers went on strike. After the severe cuts in their income, they were angry because their family allowances had not been paid for 18 months and because they had not enjoyed Christmas advances as had their colleagues on other CDC estates. Attempts by the Labour Department, management and the union to settle the strike failed. After an appeal had been made to the chief of Ndu on 7 January to intervene, the latter promised the administration that he would order the workers to return the next day. The workers indeed came to the estate on that day, but they left by 9 a.m. Only after family allowances were paid on the following day did they finally resume work.

Notwithstanding the sporadic collective actions, workers had become more inclined to resort to individual informal actions which were more difficult for the management and state to control. The CDC Annual Reports document managerial concern with the increasing rate of uncompleted work, absenteeism and workers' insubordination at the workplace. Apparently the managerial crusade against 'undisciplined and unproductive' workers had not yet been successful. In addition, workers were engaged in a variety of informal actions such as sabotage and involvement in illicit income-generating activities, to protest against the reduction in their incomes. Some pluckers did not keep to the plucking standards: they mixed bad leaves with good ones, a practice which enabled them to complete their task faster and to achieve more weight and income. Others cut the tea bushes and prunings and used them for firewood, while others stole tea from the factory and sold it to middlemen. The management periodically complained that the theft of tea had reached unprecedented levels since the economic crisis and had caused serious losses to the company.

Conclusion

Economic crisis and SAP brought about a serious decline in trade union membership and in the rank and file's trade union identity. Workers no longer union members after retrenchment or 'voluntary' retirement from the company attempted to eke out an existence in the local community with varied success. While young men and women usually found it hard to survive, older workers were more likely to be successful. In the course of their working careers the latter had often been able to invest their savings in various forms of self-employment, including coffee farming, cattle raising, trade and business, and in the purchase of honorific 'traditional' titles which were potential sources of political and economic power in the local community.

Several authors (Lubeck, 1986; Peace, 1979; Oloyede, 1991; Warnier, 1993) have shown that West African workers aspire very intensely to self-employment since it commands far more social respect and prestige than wage labour. Workers place considerable weight on the entrepreneurial ethos prevailing in most West African societies, and they are therefore inclined to look upon wage labour as an unavoidably 'transitional phase in a moment of social ascent'. They greatly admired any of their colleagues who succeeded in setting up some kind of business, well aware of the 'many sacrifices such an achievement demands from an ordinary worker'.

This entrepreneurial ethos served to fuel workers' militancy when their efforts for self-employment were being threatened by declining incomes and deteriorating working conditions. Faced with a relatively large increase in task work and a dramatic cut in their real incomes during the economic crisis and structural adjustment, most union members rapidly lost whatever confidence they still had in the union leadership's bargaining power and became inclined to engage in various forms of individual and collective forms of resistance.

As a result of these developments, the union encountered a serious crisis of identity. Management and state constantly tried to impress upon the union leadership that workers should take their due share of the sacrifices necessary for national recovery and that it is the union's responsibility to solicit the workers' cooperation. The cooperative role the state-controlled unions were willing to play during the economic crisis and structural adjustment compromised their representation of workers' interests. Moreover, the union leaders were often not properly consulted by the management in the planning of austere adjustment measures, but they were nevertheless requested to assist in their implementation, thus risking accusations by the rank and file of 'betrayal of workers' interests'. Workers saw it as a situation whereby they made sacrifices for the economic recovery of the company while the political and managerial elite 'continued to loot the parastatals'.[6]

Although the union achieved a certain measure of autonomy *vis-a-vis* the state during the political liberalization process in the 1990s and became more concerned to defend workers' interests, the logic of structural adjustment continued to constrain its ability to defend members' rights effectively. In only a few cases were the unions able to challenge some of the management's more stringent anti-labour adjustment measures (Konings, 2006).

In October 2002, the CDC was finally privatized. The government sold the estates to a South African consortium, Brobon Finex PTY Limited and the estate was renamed the Cameroon Tea Estate. The unions were not consulted about the privatization of the CDC estates. The management ignored the unions, even refusing to enter into any negotiations with the union leaders about the introduction of drastic measures to alter the labour process, including growing casualization of the labour force, outsourcing of certain tasks to contractors, increases in task work, a 50 per cent slash of wages, and non-payment of various fringe benefits. Given this situation, the workers had no other choice in the defence of their interests but to resort to a variety of formal and informal protest actions, notably protracted strikes (Konings, 2003).

The usual management response to strike actions was summary dismissal of strikers. It was only after state intervention in a long and violent strike in 2006 that the management was prepared to pay dismissed workers their termination benefits. Little wonder that the rank and file lost confidence in the union leadership, and new recruits refused to join the unions, well aware of management's hostile attitude towards trade unionism.

Contrary to government expectations, the privatization of the tea sector has not given rise to an increase in the quality, output and sales of tea, due not only to severe mismanagement but also to frequent labour protests against the deteriorating conditions of service.

About the author

Piet Konings is a senior researcher at the Africa Studies Centre, Leiden, the Netherlands. He has carried out extensive research on labour, trade unionism and political developments in Ghana and Cameroon, and has published widely on these topics. His latest books include *Negotiating an Anglophone Identity: A Study of the Politics of Recognition and Representation in Cameroon* (Leiden: Brill, 2003) and *Crisis and Creativity: Exploring the Wealth of the African Neighbourhood* (Leiden: Brill, 2006).

Notes

1. In 1963, the union changed its name to Cameroon Union of Plantations, Industrial and Agricultural Workers (CUPIAW).
2. See letter of General Secretary of CUPIAW to Registrar of Trade Unions, dated 17 July 1968, in File MTPS/WCD/BU.99, CUPIAW.
3. See Report of the Consultation Meeting with the Ministry of Labour and Social Insurance at Provincial Level by Mr P.M. Kamga, dated 28 October 1989, in File MEPS/SWP/Bu.134, vol. 4, General Correspondence CDC.
4. This was a campaign of civil disobedience organized by the opposition parties to force the Biya regime to call a national conference. It involved

the stoppage of all work, all trade, and all traffic in the towns, except on Friday evenings and Saturdays, resulting in huge personal and public financial losses and an aggravation of the economic crisis.

5. See Minutes of the Second Appraisal Meeting of 6 January 1990 Agreement between the CDC Management and the Workers' Unions which was held in the General Manager's Office on 14 March 1992, in File MTPS/IDTPS/SWP/LB.2, Vol. 27, Complaints from CDC.

6. See Labour Day Speech by Mr C.P.N. Vewessee, President of FAWU, on 1 May 1991, in *Messager (e)*, 13 May 1991, p. 4.

References

Adesina, J. (1994) *Labour in the Explanation of an African Crisis*, Dakar, Codesria Book Series.

Akwetey, E.O. (1994) *Trade Unions and Democratization: A Comparative Study of Zambia and Ghana*, University of Stockholm, Stockholm.

Bangura, Y. and Beckman, B. (1993) 'African workers and structural adjustment: A Nigerian case-study', in A.O. Olukoshi (ed.), *The Politics of Structural Adjustment in Nigeria*, pp.75–91, James Currey, London.

Bates, R. (1981) *Markets and States in Tropical Africa: The Political Basis of Agricultural Policies*, University of California Press, Berkeley.

Courade, G. (ed.) (1994) *Le Village Camerounais à l'Heure de l'Ajustement*, Karthala, Paris.

Gibbon, P. (ed.) (1995) *Structural Adjustment and the Working Poor in Zimbabwe: Studies on Labour, Women Informal Sector Workers and Health*, Nordiska Afrikainstitutet, Uppsala.

Goheen, M. (1993) 'Les champs appartiennent aux hommes, les récoltes aux femmes: accumulation dans le région de Nso', in P. Geschiere and P. Konings (eds), *Itinéraires d'accumulation au Cameroun*, pp. 241–71, Karthala, Paris.

Goheen, M. (1996) *Men Own the Fields, Women Own the Crops: Gender and Power in the Cameroon Grassfields*, University of Wisconsin Press, Madison.

Gubry, P., Lamlenn, S.B., Ngwé, E., Tchégho, J.-M., Timnou, J.-P. and Véron, J. *et al.* (1996) *Le Retour au Village: Une Solution à la Crise Economique au Cameroun?*, L'Harmattan, Paris.

Hashim, Y. (1994) 'The State and Trade Unions in Africa: A Study of Macro-Corporatism', Institute of Social Studies, PhD thesis, The Hague.

Isamah, I. (1994) 'Unions and development: the role of labour under structural adjustment programmes', in E. Osaghae (ed.), *Between State and Civil Society in Africa*, pp. 123–52, Codesria Book Series, Dakar.

Jamal, V. and Weeks, J. (1993) *Africa Misunderstood*, Macmillan, London.

Kaberry, P.M. (1952) *Women of the Grassfields: A Study of the Economic Position of Women in Bamenda, British Cameroons*, HMSO, London.

Konings, P. (1993) *Labour Resistance in Cameroon*, James Currey, London.

Konings, P. (1995a) *Gender and Class in the Tea Estates of Cameroon*, Avebury, Aldershot, UK.

Konings, P. (1995b) 'Plantation labour and economic crisis in Cameroon', *Development and Change* 26(3): 525–49.

Konings, P. (1996) 'Privatisation of agro-industrial parastatals and Anglophone opposition in Cameroon', *Journal of Commonwealth and Comparative Politics* 34(3): 199–217.

Konings, P. (2003) 'Privatisation and ethno-regional protest in Cameroon', *Afrika Spectrum* 38(1): 5–26.

Konings, P. (2006) 'African trade unions and the challenge of globalisation: a comparative study of Ghana and Cameroon', in C. Phelan (ed.), *The Future of Organised Labour: Global Perspectives,* pp. 361–95, Peter Lang, Oxford and Bern.

Kraus, J. (1991) 'The political economy of stabilization and structural adjustment in Ghana', in D. Rothchild (ed.), *Ghana: The Political Economy of Recovery*, pp. 119–55, Lynne Riener Publishers, Boulder CO and London.

Kurian, R. (1982) *Women Workers in the Sri Lanka Plantation Sector*, International Labour Office, Geneva.

Lipton, M. (1977) *Why Poor People Stay Poor: Urban Bias in World Development,* Temple Smith, London.

Loewenson, R. (1992) *Modern Plantation Agriculture: Corporate Wealth and Labour Squalor,* Zed Books, London and New Jersey.

Lubeck, P. (1986) *Islam and Urban Labor in Northern Nigeria: The Making of a Muslim Working Class*, Cambridge University Press, Cambridge.

Manga, S. N. (1984) 'Deux Opérations de Développement Agricole dans la Province du Nord-Ouest du Cameroun', Institut des Sciences Humaines, Yaoundé.

Millen, B.H. (1963) *The Political Role of Labor in Developing Countries*, The Brookings Institute, Washington DC.

Oloyede, O. (1991) *Coping Under Recession: Workers in a Nigerian Factory,* University of Uppsala, Uppsala.

Panford, K. (1994) 'Structural adjustment, the state and workers in Ghana', *Africa Development* 19(2): 71–95.

Peace, A. (1979) *Choice, Class and Conflict: A Study of Nigerian Factory Workers,* Harvester Books, Brighton, UK.

Probst, P. and Bühler, B. (1990) 'Patterns of ontrol on medicine, politics, and social change among the Wimbum, Cameroon Grassfields', *Anthropos* 85(4–6): 447–54.

Thomas, H. (1995) *Globalization and Third World Trade Unions: The Challenge of Rapid Economic Change*, Zed Books, London and New Jersey.

Warnier, J.-P. (1993) *L'Esprit d'Entreprise au Cameroun*, Karthala, Paris.

Waterman, P. (1975) 'The "Labour Aristocracy" in Africa: introduction to a debate', *Development and Change* 6(3): 50–64.

CHAPTER 13
With or against the odds? Professionalization of the labour force in Tanzania

Pekka Seppälä

Tanzanian vocational education levels and formal sector employment opportunities have increased dramatically since national independence. However, the improvement has slowed down during the 1980s and 1990s due to the country's economic difficulties. Many formal sector employees were forced to engage in sideline activities to make ends meet. The chapter discusses whether this tendency towards sidelining should be perceived as a deterioration of work ethics, or whether it should be understood as a rational and culturally shaped solution to combining work, economic well-being and social life. The alternative interpretation of professionalism is based on the relevance – valid in the prevailing Tanzanian context – of income diversification and clientelistic social networking premised on congeniality, politeness and human respect aimed at attracting and maintaining clients.

Introduction

Classical sociology presents the advancement of the division of labour as a key variable in the integration of modern society. Theorists such as Emile Durkheim, Max Weber and Talcott Parsons associated the social division of labour with societal development in which face-to-face relationships were progressively replaced with contractual relations. They argued that clearly delineated occupations in a modern society create stability and predictability upon otherwise loose associational ties. Although economic development facilitates the social division of labour, development cannot take place smoothly without the state acting as a regulatory and supervisory agency. The state must operate a bureaucracy, stimulate growth of other professions, promote corresponding vocational education, and impose regulatory controls over entry into the more demanding professions. In this way professionalization is interwoven with the project of modern nation-building.

This chapter analyses the relationship between professionalization and the economy in Tanzania. During the 1980s and 1990s, Tanzania experienced a protracted economic crisis which seriously reduced salary levels, the commitment to work in the formal sector and professional ethics in a western sense. Rather than imposing value judgements it can be argued that a different form of professionalization prevailed, a more diffuse form which, although deviating from western norms, cannot be equated with failure or corruption.

This chapter begins by defining and reviewing trends in professionalization in sub-Saharan Africa (SSA) generally, and a section on the development of education, professional employment and the labour force in Tanzania follows. Occupational diversification and its impact on professionalization are discussed and compared in the light of three theoretical approaches.

Professionalization in the nation-building project

Professionalization means an occupational change where, due to division of labour, the workers are guided by more precise work competence requirements and job ethics. Historically, nation-building and professionalization were very much top of the agenda for newly independent sub-Saharan African countries in the 1960s and 1970s. In Tanzania, as in many other African countries, the instrument for achieving this goal was primarily a strong state with heavy reliance on state planning rather than market forces. It was believed that modernization would be attained through education and subsequent professional employment. Given the central role of the state as a provider of professional employment, the nexus between the state and professionalization was intrinsic and clear.

The change that took place during the 1980s and 1990s arose from the weakening of the state rather than from the weakening of the ideology of professionalization. SSA countries were still striving to extend their formal systems of education and create growing numbers of professional specialists. However, government resources to implement such policies were meagre. Educational standards decreased in several countries because of a decline in the quality and availability of education. Primary school enrolment for SSA dropped from 79 per cent in 1980 to 73 per cent in 1992–3 (World Bank, 1997). The number of positions in the public sector fell while salaries of professionally competent staff declined, even though the share of wages and salaries in government expenditure continued to increase. At the same time, the formal private sector revealed a limited capacity to increase professional working opportunities.

The weakening of professionalization can be viewed normatively from two perspectives. From the perspective of nation-building (with its planning orientation), the shift can be perceived as a symptom of a societal process which, if allowed to develop too far, could lead to the abandonment of modernization. From this perspective, deprofessionalization is a societal illness. However, a totally different conclusion is drawn by neoliberal ideologists. They argue that state-guided professionalization simply led to the swelling of state structures without any positive feedback to society. The state became a self-contained bureaucratic system exploiting its citizenry through clientalistic relations. Lack of competition within the bureaucratic cadres hindered the development of real professional capacities,[1] resulting in unproductive bureaucratization (World Bank, 1995).

It seems that it is not possible to bridge these two views without reference to functional aspects of professionalization. In order to advance the discussion, three approaches to professionalization are delineated which represent different instrumental objectives, namely:

- *'state-guided professionalization'* where professionalism is achieved and guaranteed by bureaucratic controls over the formal qualifications of workers;
- *'market-oriented professionalization'* which is associated with the development of market specialization through job experience and skills training and which leads to increasing exchange relations and higher productivity; and
- *'culturally-conditioned professionalization'* where modes of work and livelihood are seen within a specific cultural context. Professionalization arises from the individuals' search for livelihood giving rise to diversified skills, work flexibility and a blend of inter-personal relations of trust and accommodating service to customers.

State-guided professionalization emphasizes the importance of government and bureaucratic controls in an ordered society. In creating and enforcing professional standards, the state is seen not only as a gatekeeper but also custodian of the professional workforce. Conventionally, only the state and very large private enterprises have been able to provide working opportunities and the structure for professional standardization. The utility of producing a professional labour force is functional only to the extent that other essential factors of production (e.g. capital, markets) are available. When these are lacking, professionalization loses its significance.

In 'market-oriented' professionalization, the need for professionalization is seen in a more open way. Professionalization refers to the increase of a skilled workforce more than to the institutionalization of controls governing standards of professional competence. It entails the economy's capacity to *generate an employed labour force*. The crux of the model of market-oriented professionalization is how to increase basic and vocational education to facilitate productive formal employment or informal self-employment. In this vision, professionalization is more broadly attainable especially as basic and middle-level training can be part of on-the-job training schemes.

In actual fact, the conventional approach to professionalization which underlines the state-guided and market-oriented approaches could be viewed as the inappropriate projection of the western model in alien settings. In this sense, professionalization may generate opportunities and justifications for exploitation without any positive impact on the living standards of the majority of the population. At the very least, in Tanzania, the projection of either of the two approaches results in semantic confusion. Professionalism in the western sense is the privilege of very few. For most Tanzanians, the official work place is a part of a wider livelihood strategy. People need to create their own labour opportunity networks to supplement low salaries and compensate for the limited economic scope of formal employment. The economic networks and capacities are fundamentally shaped by existing moral, cultural and social conventions. In this chapter, the merits and demerits of a third model, that of culturally conditioned professionalization, is discussed and contrasted with the two other western normative models. But in order to do so, some historical background is required.

Trends in education and employment opportunities in Tanzania

The number of people with a university education was very small on the eve of independence in 1961. African professionals were estimated to total only about 30, while all other professionals were Asian or European by origin. British colonial authorities had invested very limited resources in the Tanganyikan educational system.

The independent Tanzanian government immediately began to address this situation after seizing the reins of power. The Tanzanian economy made good progress during the first decade after independence but then started to falter in the 1970s. Currently Tanzania continues to be amongst the poorest countries in the world. Although some positive economic improvement has been noted during the last few years, no indications of positive development can be seen in formal sector employment or in food production. Economic growth is largely limited to specific areas such as tourism and mining.

The Tanzanian population increased from approximately 10 million in 1964 to 34 million in 2002 (Tanzania, 2003a). The labour force increased roughly in similar proportion. In 2000 there were roughly 18 million people of working age[2] in Tanzania, most living in rural areas. Approximately 70 per cent were under 30 years of age and the overwhelming majority had little or no formal education.

Table 13.1 Economically active labour force in Tanzania (2000/01)

	Total	Men	Women
Geographic distribution (%)			
Urban	19.2	18.9	19.5
Rural	80.8	81.1	80.5
Formal education			
None		20.5	31.8
Some primary		29.2	22.1
Std 7		43.9	42.2
Secondary+		6.4	3.9
Total number	17.8	8.7	9.1

Source: Labour Force Survey 2000/01 (Tanzania, 2003b)

Formal sector employment accounts for less than 10 per cent of the employed population. For the individual worker, livelihood can comprise a combination of 'official wage employment', i.e. 'professional employment', and 'income generation'. Official waged employment in contemporary Tanzania rarely provides a guaranteed adequate income. For this reason, it is more often than not supplemented with other income-generating activities. When juxtaposing official employment with income generation it cannot be assumed that the latter is secondary to the former, nor that the application of professional skill is restricted to the former. In other words, professional work can be 'official' or income-generating in nature. The professional skill to conduct work is not restricted to a fixed address. In the literature on the Structural Adjustment Programme (SAP) and privatization, the private sector is often cited as the source of new employment. Even though the private sector is growing while the state sector is contracting, the private sector remains the smaller sector. During the mid-1990s, it employed an estimated 320,000 people compared with 490,000 employees in the formal public sector (World Bank, 1996). Within the public sector, employment in social services (education, health services etc.) far exceeds employment in industry. Parastatals provided two-thirds of Tanzania's formal industrial employment in 1992 (Bol, 1995). Thereafter, the government started a massive operation to downsize the parastatal sector, which caused the industrial sector to contract still further.

The future of formal employment is likely to depend heavily on state policies towards public sector employment. Throughout the 1990s there were calls from foreign donors for 'good governance'. This embraces, among other things, a reduction in public sector employment through the screening of all public organizations, the closure of unviable units, a reduction of commercial or quasi-commercial functions in viable units and cutbacks in employment in remaining organizational branches. Implementation of reform began in the parastatal sector in 1993 and has advanced well in some fields and slowly in others. By 1998, two-thirds of parastatals had been sold or liquidated. A similar type of reform was implemented in the sphere of public administration with 50,000 redundancies in the civil service by 1998 (Therkildsen, 1995). Donors nonetheless pressed for further cuts.

A more positive trend in labour force expansion has taken place in the informal sector. The significance of the informal sector depends on its highly debated conceptualization (Collier *et al.,* 1986; Maliyamkono and Bagachwa, 1990; Bagachwa, 1993; Sarris and van den Brink, 1993; Chachage, 1995; CIBR, 1995; Havnevik, 1993; Bryceson, 1997). According to a government labour survey, one in three households had an informal sector activity in 2000 as opposed to one in four the decade before. The rise was especially apparent in the urban areas where 61 percent of households in 2000 compared with 42 percent in 1990 had an informal sector activity. In rural areas, the percentage over the same timeframe rose from 21 to 26 per cent (Tanzania, 2003b).

Factors enhancing and constraining professionalization

From the perspective of bureaucratic professionalization there are broadly four factors that could increase the professionalism of the labour force. These are vocational training, professional associations, certified entry requirements to employment, and an incentive system based on a hierarchical salary pyramid.

At the time of independence in 1961, the rate of African children attending primary school was around 15 per cent (Lugalla, 1993). Since then considerable improvement has taken place. Roughly 70 per cent of the primary school age population attend school (Table 13.2). Almost 10 per cent of the labour force has received some vocational training while the literacy rate in the country has approached 70 per cent. The general trend appears positive but critics note the declining enrolment rates and the low quality of primary and secondary education and lack of interest in practical/technical training during the 1990s. Regardless of the limitations in public sector employment opportunities, education is still biased towards clerical and academic positions (ibid.; Samoff, 1994; Swantz, 1997).

During the 1960s and 1970s, the Tanzanian educational system was egalitarian with an emphasis on universal primary education. Elite high schools did not exist, in contrast to neighbouring Kenya where they were very important. During the implementation of structural adjustment, the egalitarian emphasis quietly disappeared. Cost-sharing policies led to increases in school fees. Real school costs considerably exceeded the nominal low fees charged (TADREG, 1997). The cost of a school uniform, school materials such as books and paper, and contributions for the maintenance and expansion of the school that parents were obliged to pay pushed costs beyond the capacity of many parents. Primary school attendance started to decline. Meanwhile the

Table 13.2 Primary education and adult literacy in Tanzania

Year	Literacy rate amongst adult population (%)	Primary school gross enrolment rate (%)	Secondary school enrolment rate (%)
1970	n.a.	33	2
1980	59.2	90	3
1985	60.7	83	3
1990	62.1	75	5
1995	67.8	78	5
2000	n.a.	66	n.a.
2005	n.a.	106*	n.a.

Source: Association for the Development of Education in Africa database and World Bank development indicators, 1970–2005
* The massive percentage increase in enrolment documents the reinstatement of universal primary education following a long period of declining enrolment in response to SAP cutbacks in education and the implementation of 'user costs' policies. The 106% figure reflects that some older non-primary aged students enrolled given that they had not had the means to do so earlier.

distribution of secondary schools became highly skewed. New private schools were constructed in wealthy urban and rural areas and run by parents. Moreover, given the lack of resources in the country's two universities, an academic elite appeared consisting of people with esteemed foreign, especially western, university degrees.

Professional associations represent a form of voluntary self-regulation. This supplements state control mechanisms for enhancing professionalism. Through associations, professionals strengthen their identity, while creating external boundaries and internal hierarchies (Abbott, 1988). Some associations have a history of functioning effectively as substitutes for labour organizations during times when the labour movement was politically controlled. However, Tanzanian professional associations have historically tended to be limited to circles of people with high levels of education. Some of the associations (e.g. political scientists and economists) conduct seminars displaying impressive academic standards.

During the 1990s, organizations of commercially minded people with far less education formed, for example the associations of cashew nut traders and traders dealing with precious stones. These groups, under the loose banner of a professional association, aim to serve as a pressure group or 'voice' of civil society *vis-à-vis* the state.

When it comes to creating a system of certified entry into public sector employment, the British civil service was historically the central reference point. British certification of professions was the blueprint for Tanzania's system and has continued to exert influence long after independence. From the perspective of state-guided professionalization, a major problem has been the lack of rigour in applying formal criteria in public sector recruitment. In the face of formal criteria, recruitment on the basis of politics and kinship has been widespread. Consequently, only two per cent of civil servants had diplomas or higher education certificates in 1988. Some two per cent had secondary education at A-level, 24 per cent had O-level qualifications and the remaining 72 per cent of civil servants were primary school leavers (NORAD, 1995). The formal British-based system of entry requirements had lost strength because heterogeneous aid projects emanating from various donor countries had created their own educational and professional categories during the postcolonial period. The Folk Development Colleges, which imitate a Scandinavian model, are interesting. For many students, the value of the colleges was limited because they did not provide certificates, which were considered comparable to those from other Tanzanian training institutions.

Recent moves to privatize the social services have led to a reduction in the number of professional cadres subject to professional entry requirements stipulated by the state. This was especially apparent with respect to private health clinics, which have mushroomed during the 1990s. Professional employment did not always follow the procedures nor meet the stipulated standards of public facilities. After a period of hesitation, the government intervened and began licensing private health clinics.

Progression up an official wage scale is believed to enhance professionalism. The wage structure of government employees is very hierarchical and reflects the educational pyramid (Hazlewood *et al.*, 1989). However, most employees cannot survive on current inflation-affected wage levels. During the 1980s, the official average salary decreased some 80 per cent in real terms (Bol, 1995). On the other hand, when fringe benefits are included, salaries increase in value for higher-level officers who often receive perks such as access to chauffeur-driven vehicles, housing allowances, etc. Recent donor-instigated salary reforms have tried to narrow the yawning gap between low and middle-level income groups. In actual fact, donor involvement tends to create an additional wedge in Tanzanian income differentiation. A Tanzanian professional elite employed in development aid projects has emerged which receives salaries comparable to those of foreign experts. Through their command over disproportionately large resources and conspicuous consumption, the aid elite (both local and foreign) has seriously undermined the morale of their co-workers receiving lower salaries.

The erosion of salary levels outside elite circles has been the prime reason for a decline in professional work ethics. The impact of declining salaries has provided the main impetus for employees to diversify their sources of income. Diversification, common among government employees, has become a widespread phenomenon throughout Tanzanian society, encompassing people from all walks of life.

Diversification and the division of labour

Diversification refers to the supplementation or displacement of a main source of income by an economic agent's operation of several different income-generating activities in parallel. In Tanzania, the existence of multiple sources of income at a household level is widespread. The World Bank (1996) estimates that 78 per cent of all households have more than one source of income. The figure is slightly lower among the poor compared with the better-off, but without noticeable differences between rural and urban areas. Diversification entails flexibility in the allocation of labour time and other resources to various activities. The term 'de-agrarianization' covers the rural pattern of diversification *from* agriculture (Bryceson, 1996). In urban settings, diversification often means a shift *from* wage labour so that labour time can be more freely allocated to various tasks.

Diversification has been studied using alternatively the individual, household or enterprise as the unit of analysis. Our discussion concentrates on the level of an individual or 'actor'. However, it is useful to discuss briefly the other units of analysis. The 'household' is a valid starting point because labour tasks and incomes tend to be shared by household members. Some academic commentators hold that the household is an amorphous entity and the communality or 'common cooking pot' of households varies a great deal. Although this observation is justified, it does not negate the validity of household analysis but rather necessitates a closer look at the economic integrity of the households under study.

Using 'enterprise' as the unit of analysis reveals other facets. Large- and medium-scale entrepreneurs tend to have a wide portfolio of entrepreneurial activities (Trulsson, 1997). Similarly, many informal sector entrepreneurs also divide their resources between trading, personal/communal services and agriculture (Seppälä, 1996). Diversification at the enterprise level can be partly explained by 'forward' and 'backward' linkages of products and partly as a diversification of the entrepreneur's portfolio to minimize risks. Among small-scale entrepreneurs, the analysis of diversification is often synonymous with diversification of the household unit of production.

At the individual level of analysis, the ways in which diversification has evolved can be traced through formal occupational categories. State employees are illustrative. Public sector wages drastically declined to a degree that it was remarkable that state employees did not resign *en masse*. The fact that they did not can in part be explained by the social status and minimal basic security provisions received through employment. It is practical to work at one's official job at least some days or hours during the week because of fringe benefits or illegal 'rents'. The working place provides important contacts and market information, which can be used in sideline activities. Furthermore, employment within the state apparatus gives one a better vantage point for assessing policy changes, which, in Tanzania's volatile economy, may provide a competitive edge to one's business.

Teachers exemplify a category of government employees who have low wages but who still prefer to keep their official positions. Usually they have no access to fringe benefits apart from accommodation. Payment of their salaries, however, is often delayed for as much as six months. In order to make a living, three-quarters of primary and secondary school teachers in a 1990 survey reported that they had sideline activities. The most popular was agriculture, a third of secondary school teachers were engaged in private tutoring and 18 per cent were petty traders (Lugalla, 1993; Tripp, 1997).

Many medical doctors are also engaged in farming and keeping chickens commercially. More controversially, state-employed doctors tended to supplement their official salaries with private medical practices during off-duty hours in the face of a government ban on private medical practice. Eventually, the government had to relent on its ban and the change of rules has helped to make activities more visible and accountable to public health regulations (Tripp, 1996).

Occupational diversification in Tanzania has a long history linked to and facilitated by kinship structures, intertribal relationships and clientage networks of the precolonial and colonial periods. During the precolonial period, the provisioning of all social services was organized through these channels and the providers were simultaneously part-time farmers or herders. During the colonial period, the rotating movement of labour between labour demand areas (plantations and towns) and the labour supply areas (labour reserves) meant a spread of skills and reduced the proportion of the population (especially men) solely engaged in cultivation (Bryceson, 1990). Rather than exposing diversification as a completely new phenomenon, it should be seen as an already existing tendency, which has taken on new forms during recent decades. In short, diversification is embedded in Tanzanian culture and politics.

In the first few decades of independence, diversification was a political issue that went under a different label. President Nyerere stated that Tanzania's socialist society needed to be guided by a public administration of high morale and occupational dedication. For this reason, he launched a party leadership code of conduct, which prohibited the civil service from engaging in private businesses and sideline activities. This policy aimed to prevent civil servants from using public resources to capitalize their private enterprises. The policy was partly successful in reducing corruption and mismanagement until the economy deteriorated and the purchasing power of salaries drastically declined. Many civil servants were forced to engage in sideline activities in fields of activity unrelated to their training or occupation to ensure an adequate livelihood for their families. When President Mwinyi came to power he relaxed the policies towards sideline activities and eventually the party abandoned the leadership code.

Culture of diversification

Given the clandestine nature of income diversification in the 1970s and early 1980s, and the lifting of sanctions against it only recently during the era of structural adjustment, occupational diversification is loaded with contradictory moral connotations. Nevertheless, the practice is so deeply embedded in the everyday experience of Tanzania's population that it is the starting point for any discussion on livelihood strategies.

Invariably diversification strategies involve some form of entrepreneurship. In Tanzania, entrepreneurship is characterized by open networking, to the extent that the borderline between entrepreneurship and social interaction is, often consciously, dimmed. In everyday life, the distinction is hard to discern. This is reflected in the term *shughuli* (Kiswahili for 'activities'), which can be translated as 'business' to refer to utilitarian economic projects or simply 'daily activities'. This hints at the fact that occupational diversification relies upon the utilization of social networks for utilitarian purposes but this utilitarian conduct has to be concealed to be effective. An ideological emphasis on egalitarianism and community welfare, and the need for a good reputation related to the maintenance of one's social networks require investments in 'cultural capital'. 'Cultural capital' diverts resources away from directly utilitarian and commercial purposes and directs 'business' to matters like kinship and friendship, funerals and feasts. Intricate webs of social relationships mesh the accumulation of cultural capital with economic capital. Investment in cultural capital pays off in times of economic difficulty. Thus a haphazard and difficult market situation does not usually cause a personal catastrophe for wealthier people because they are able to use their social networks as economic safety nets. The ultimate advantages of clientage networks and cultural capital investment lie in exceptional situations (Seppälä, 1998).

In the economic literature it is convincingly argued that the survival of small enterprises is based on their flexibility and self-exploitation, i.e. underpricing of work related to the use of uncosted family labour. When there is a market, it is flooded with entrepreneurs and prices are drastically lowered. When there is no purchasing power, entrepreneurs close their projects and pursue other activities. In this context, diversification is synonymous with self-exploitation and flexibility. However, it has, in the same way as social networking, the function of minimizing risks. People who have diversified their economic activities are able, in a situation of sudden setback in one activity, to substitute other income sources. The importance of risk avoidance is hard to exaggerate in a country like Tanzania where a natural catastrophe such as harvest failure or an abrupt political decision can alter one's work situation suddenly.

Normative analysis of professionalization

Professionalization, especially its formalist interpretation, has been criticized as a meritocratic way of legitimizing hierarchical power relationships and maintaining artificial boundaries, which hinder occupational development. The proponents of professionalization argue, on the other hand, that it protects professionals, increases their job security and strengthens their work ethic.

Given the limited period of time in which educational opportunities have been available to the Tanzanian population, the problem of excessive meritocracy has hardly surfaced. The critique emanating from the market-oriented perspective has many adherents in Tanzania. They argue that professionalization combined with rigid state administration may create positions and structures, which are dysfunctional to institutional capacity. By contrast, bureaucratic professionalization has been defended as a cost-efficient way of regulating education and public sector employment and, that this formalism is not a hindrance to the market supply of labour outside the public sector. The full extent of bureaucratic professionalism is applicable only to limited government functions and to a fraction of the labour market, even in western societies.

The concept of culturally-conditioned professionalization avoids the circularity of the debate because it challenges the notion of professions as ahistoric categories. Freidson (1986) argues that systems of occupations should be analysed in national and historical frameworks rather than as a fulfilment of abstract criteria. He gives examples of fundamental differences in national traditions within Europe. If various European traditions differ so markedly, there are strong grounds for acknowledging the possibility of a distinctive system of professions developing in Tanzania.

As has been argued here, occupational diversification has become the most pervasive feature of Tanzania's labour force. Western formalists have argued that diversification with its compromised time allocation and resource borrowing tends to become a *modus operandi*, 'infecting' working places, work ethics and the whole of society. Sideline activities are seen as undermining the functioning of formal organizations, diminishing their efficiency and creating informal organizational structures (Hyden, 1980, 1983). This moral argument is enhanced by anecdotes gathered through concrete experiences. For example, stories about irregularities in custom clearance, difficulties in obtaining licences through official channels, and government officers' vehicles are rife.

Nonetheless the negative assessment cannot go unchallenged. One can argue that similar organizational structures are common in western countries as well. They just do not receive as much attention because the ideological and symbolic reproduction of the official organizational structure is so imposing. Furthermore, an analysis of organizations tends to take its own vocabulary for granted. As Alvesson (1993: 47) says: 'the literature concerned with organizational culture often says more about the culture of the researchers than the researched'.

Analysed from a Tanzanian cultural perspective, diversification and its attendant network interaction acquire positive connotations. High esteem is given to social interaction as can be evidenced from the complex webs of kinship and friendship that knit together individual economic exchanges. Indeed creating social contacts is a Tanzanian cultural imperative. The code of conduct for daily encounters is structured by unwritten rules regarding congeniality, human respect and politeness. All this is replicated in official encounters. Networks with instrumental business aims are commonly softened with affective features while affective networks are combined with instrumental tasks and exchange relations. Economically better-off people are better positioned to orient themselves towards social networks that guarantee their future well-being. However, for both wealthy and poor people, professional competence is merely an official obligation, which is often overshadowed by cultural obligation to maintain and expand their social contacts.

Naturally the relationship between social interaction and instrumental aims is a contested terrain. The compatibility of ego-centred social contacts with the capitalist ethos and associated bureaucratic rules is a century-old debate (Abbott, 1988; Freidson, 1986). They are commonly seen as an uneasy juxtaposition. Several commentators have documented the multiple ways that Tanzanians of different social and ethnic backgrounds navigate through the seeming gap between public and private interests (Trulsson, 1997; Rubin, 1996). Nonetheless it may be misleading to conceptualize these as competing interests. Given the existing material inadequacy of access to daily necessities, work opportunities and social security, the social networks that are an integral feature of 'cultural professionalization' may be better conceptualized as 'enabling' resources. The question is never whether or not to rely on diversification and social networks but how skilfully such activities and networks can be managed. In this respect several commentators have noted that women are far more capable than men of generating trusting and enduring networks which straddle instrumental and affective aims (e.g. Nkhoma-Wamunza, 1992; Rubin, 1996; Swantz 1997, 1998).

It is worth remembering that occupational diversification does not refer to a combination of gainful work with social networks but the combination of two or more gainful activities, which are then facilitated by social networking. It is misleading to reduce diversification to the extraction of resources from work for private consumption. Instead, diversification involved the combination of different resource bases into strategically functional modes of operation. Such combinations are not historically bound. Women seem to have adjusted far more quickly than men by creatively combining new and old informal sector activities with small-scale agriculture and household work. Motivated by the need to support the household under economic duress by any means possible, many women traders have generated innovative strategies. The growth of diversification has been accompanied by a gender bias favouring women. Their small projects and quasi-monetarized networks were previously systematically undermined in formal wage labour. More recent discourses admit that household reliance on the single salary of a male member is past history (Bryceson, 1980). Now the importance of women's income-earning abilities is widely acknowledged.

Hard-core developmentalists have argued for the need to strengthen bureaucratic professionalism through 'good governance' (World Bank, 1995). Basing this argument on western notions of professional competence shows a lack of understanding or intolerance of different ways of organizing work. The call for good governance is based on the assumption that the state administration is inefficient, corrupt and expensive. In their call for reform, the World Bank and other donors give precedence to macroeconomic ideals instead of the microeconomic realities of the work place. Developmentalist discussions of 'good governance', appropriate vocational education and private entrepreneurship should be based on a realistic assessment of labour supply and demand and seriously consider the positive merits of networking and diversifying strategies combined with formal employment. In their absence, Tanzania would have no public schools or hospitals due to the deplorably low levels of official salaries for teaching and medical staff. Fully market-supplied services would inevitably erode the access of lower income households to health and educational facilities. The current employment pattern characterized by low salaries and diversification affords more employment opportunities than a formally restricted but well-paid workforce could offer. Occupational diversification and accompanying social networks offer the only viable middle road.

Conclusion

The development of a system of professions is one of the cornerstones of nation-building, economic development and social change. Professionalization can be analysed broadly from three approaches: state-guided, market-oriented and culturally-conditioned perspectives. Each perspective offers insights. The bureaucratic perspective emphasizes the advantages gained from formal standards while the market perspective is useful for advancing the growth of employment. The debate between the state-guided and market-oriented perspectives is an old one. This chapter has tried to advance a third perspective that takes cultural specificity as its starting point. The cultural analysis of professionalism is constructed around the concept of diversification. Diversification in sideline activities is a common practice in Tanzania and is deeply interwoven in the country's social structure.

Diversification has definite consequences for professionalization. Diversification softens the boundaries between public and private spheres. The moral commitment to an abstract 'professional' ethic is challenged by occupational diversification's instrumental and effective social networks. This culturally counterproductive challenge is ethical in its own right and has important societal consequences. It creates informal organizations within formal organizations and dilutes the external boundaries of formal organizations. The merits of non-professional diversification are seldom acknowledged, because diversification by civil servants is often treated as a form of corruption and rent-seeking. In this chapter, I have argued that there is a distinction between income-enhancing diversification and corruption.

While professionalization has the potential to alienate the elite section of the population from the surrounding material realities, so far Tanzania's egalitarian ideology and close clientage ties of patronage have maintained the elite's concerns with the majority of the population. For example, academic professors maintain links with their rural home areas and highly paid employees provide housing for young relatives seeking education or employment in town.

Formal employment may shape some parts of the economy but, for the majority of Tanzanians, participation in formal employment is a distant dream. Professionalization will develop largely outside state channels, and it remains to be seen what blend of market-oriented and culturally-conditioned values will emerge to shape the work performance of Tanzania's future labour force.

About the author

Pekka Seppälä (PhD University of Sussex) has researched extensively on Tanzania. As an anthropologist, his main topics have been the interface between rural livelihoods and economic policies. Pekka has published the book *Diversification and Accumulation in Rural Tanzania* (Nordiska Afrikainstitutet 1998) and *The Making of a Periphery: Economic Development and Cultural Encounters in Southern Tanzania* (Nordiska Afrikainstitutet 1998 with Bertha Koda). He currently works in the Finnish Ministry for Foreign Affairs with responsibilities for local administration and public sector development cooperation and as a co-head of household with responsibilities for supporting daughter Kim and son Jonas.

Notes

1. Economists tend to analyse bureaucratization through aggregated statistics like the share of public sector recurrent expenditure in gross domestic production. Political scientists have augmented their criticisms with case study material about corruption and mismanagement.
2. Defined as 'currently economically active population 10 years and above' (Tanzania, 2003b).

References

Abbott, A. (1988) *The System of Professions: An Essay on the Division of Expert Labour*, University of Chicago Press, Chicago and London.

Alvesson, M. (1993) *Cultural Perspectives on Organizations*, Cambridge University Press, Cambridge.

Association for the Development of Education in Africa (ADEA) *Statistical Profile of Education in Sub-Saharan Africa* (SPESSA), interactive database. http://www.adeanet.org/adeaPortal/ [last accessed 17 October 2009].

Bagachwa, M.S.D. (1993) 'Impact of adjustment policies on the small-scale enterprise sector in Tanzania', in A.H.J. Helmsing and Th. Kolstee (eds), *Small Enterprises and Changing Policies*, pp. 91–113, Intermediate Technology Publications, London.

Bol, D. (1995) 'Employment and equity issues in Tanzania', in L.A. Msambichaka, A.A.L. Kilindo and G.D. Mjema (eds), *Beyond Structural Adjustment Program in Tanzania; Successes, Failures and New Perspective*, pp. 193–234, University of Dar es Salaam Economic Research Bureau, Dar es Salaam.

Bryceson, D.F. (1980) 'The proletarianisation of women in Tanzania', *Review of African Political Economy* 17: 4–27.

Bryceson, D.F. (1990) *Food Insecurity and the Social Division of Labour in Tanzania, 1919–1985*, Macmillan, Basingstoke, UK.

Bryceson, D.F. (1996) 'De-agrarianization and rural employment generation in Sub-Saharan Africa: process and prospects', *World Development* 42(1): 23–45.

Bryceson, D.F. (1997) 'De-agrarianisation in Sub-Saharan Africa: acknowledging the inevitable', in D.F. Bryceson and V. Jamal (eds), *Farewell to Farms: De-agrarianisation and Employment in Africa*, Ashgate, Aldershot UK.

Center for International Business Research (CIBR) (1995) *Dynamics of Enterprise Development in Tanzania: Final Report on the Round II Survey Data*, Helsinki School of Economics, Helsinki.

Chachage S.L. (1995) 'The meek shall inherit the earth but not the mining rights: the mining industry and accumulation in Tanzania', in P. Gibbon (ed.), *Liberalised Development in Tanzania: Studies on Accumulation Processes and Local Institutions*, pp. 37–108, Nordiska Afrikainstitutet, Uppsala.

Collier, P., Radwan, S., Wangwe, S. and Wagner, A. (1986) *Labour and Poverty in Rural Tanzania: Ujamaa and Rural Development in the United Republic of Tanzania*, Clarendon Press, Oxford.

Freidson, E. (1986) *Professional Powers: A Study of the Institutionalization of Formal Knowledge*, University of Chicago Press, Chicago and London.

Havnevik, K.J. (1993) *Tanzania: The Limits to Development from Above*, Nordiska Afrikainstitutet, Uppsala.

Hazlewood, A., Armitage, J., Berry, A., Knight, J. and Sabot, R. (1989) *Education, Work and Pay in East Africa*, Clarendon Press, Oxford.

Hyden, G. (1980) *Beyond Ujamaa in Tanzania: Underdevelopment and an Uncaptured Peasantry*, Heinemann, London.

Hyden, G. (1983) *No Shortcuts to Progress: African Development in Perspective*, University of California Press, Berkeley.

Lugalla, J. (1993) 'Structural adjustment policy and education in Tanzania', in P. Gibbon (ed.), *Social Change and Economic Reform in Africa*, pp. 184–214, Nordiska Afrikainstitutet, Uppsala.

Maliyamkono, T.L. and Bagachwa, M.S.D. (1990) *The Second Economy in Tanzania*, James Currey, London.

Nkhoma-Wamunza (1992) 'The informal sector: a strategy for survival in Tanzania', in D.R.F. Taylor and F. Mackenzie (eds), *Development from Within: Survival in Africa*, pp. 197–213, Routledge, London and New York.

NORAD (1995) *Civil Service Reform in Tanzania: Consultancy to make Recommendations on a Nordic Initiative for Assistance*, NORAD, Oslo.

Rubin, D.S. (1996), 'Business story is better than love: gender, economic development, and nationalist ideology in Tanzania' in B.F. Williams (ed.), *Women Out of Place: The Gender of Agency and the Race of Nationality*, Routledge, New York and London.

Samoff, J. (1994) 'Financial Crisis, Structural Adjustment, and Education Policy in Tanzania'. Paper presented at the Annual Meeting of the American Educational Research Association, 4–7 April 1994, New Orleans.

Sarris, A.H. and van den Brink, R. (1993) *Economic Policy and Household Welfare during Crisis and Adjustment in Tanzania*, New York University Press, New York and London.

Seppälä, P. (1996) 'The politics of economic diversification: reconceptualizing the rural informal sector in South-east Tanzania', *Development and Change* 27(3): 557–78.

Seppälä, P. (1998) 'Informal sector in Lindi District', in P. Seppälä and B. Koda (eds), *The Making of a Periphery; Economic Development and Cultural Change in Southern Tanzania*, Nordic Africa Institute, Uppsala.

Swantz, M.L. (1997) 'Community and Village-based Provision of Key Social Services: A Case Study of Tanzania', *Research for Action*, no. 41. UNU/WIDER, Helsinki.

Swantz, M.L. (1998) 'Notes on research on women and their strategies for a sustained livelihood in southern Tanzania', in P. Seppälä and B. Koda (eds), *The Making of a Periphery: Economic Development and Cultural Change in Southern Tanzania*, pp. 157–94, Nordic Africa Institute, Uppsala.

TADREG (1997) 'Education, Health and Water. A Baseline Service Delivery Survey for Rural Tanzania', TADREG Working Paper no. 5, Dar es Salaam.

Tanzania, United Republic of (URT) (2003a) *2002 Population and Housing Census: Vol I – Age and Sex Distribution*, National Bureau of Statistics, Dar es Salaam.

Tanzania, United Republic of (URT) (2003b) *Integrated Labour Force Survey 2000/01: Analytical Report*, Dar es Salaam, http://www.nbs.go.tz/labourforce/index.htm [last accessed 17 October 2009].

Therkildsen, O. (1995) 'Civil service reform from below: extreme resource scarcity and unrealistic performance requirements', in L.A. Msambichaka and A.A.L. Kilindo (eds), *Beyond Structural Adjustment Programmes in Tanzania*, pp. 235–52, Economic Research Bureau, Dar es Salaam.

Tripp, A.M. (1996) 'Contesting the right to subsist: the urban informal economy in Tanzania', in M.L. Swantz and A.M. Tripp (eds), *What Went Right in Tanzania: People's Response to Directed Development*, pp. 43–68, Dar es Salaam University Press, Dar es Salaam.

Tripp, A.M. (1997) *Changing the Rules: The Politics of Liberalization and the Urban Informal Economy in Tanzania*, University of California Press, Berkeley.

Trulsson, P. (1997) *Strategies of Entrepreneurship: Understanding Industrial Entrepreneurship and Structural Change in Northwest Tanzania*, Kanaltryckeriet Linköping Studies in Arts and Science 161, Linköping.

World Bank (1995) *World Development Report*, World Bank, Washington DC.

World Bank (1996) *Tanzania: The Challenge of Reforms: Growth, Incomes and Welfare. Volume I: Main Report*, Country Operations Division, Eastern Africa Department, Africa Region.

World Bank (1997) *African Development Indicators*, World Bank, Washington DC.

SECTION V
Conclusion

CHAPTER 14

Between moral economy and civil society: Durkheim revisited*

Deborah Fahy Bryceson

This chapter addresses the moral quandaries accompanying rapid occupational change amidst unfulfilled expectations. Western donor agencies and academic commentators tend to assume the existence of universalized human rights and responsibilities. Using the concepts of the 'moral economy' and 'civil society', analytical focus is placed on the negotiations taking place in everyday life around normative perceptions of rights and responsibilities. Durkheim's classic study of occupational restructuring defines professional ethics as rules of conduct that are intermediary between family and civic morals. Rules, however, presuppose moral authorities and rule setting procedures. The fluidity of African informal sector work over the last three decades has not afforded the permanence and organizational structures necessary for formal rules. Nonetheless, the case studies in this book illustrate how work etiquettes are evolving primarily on the basis of practical work needs, livelihood imperatives and not least good-natured humour and a shared common humanity.

Introduction

Morality is both deeply personal and pervasively public. Current debate on whether people are universally hardwired to be morally judgemental (Hauser, 2006) or culturally pre-disposed to emotional responses that prompt moral judgement (Prinz, 2007) is polarized. However, neither position argues that there is a universal moral ethic. Quite the contrary, cultures throughout the world embody distinct consensual moralities, which encapsulate the shared ethical principles of interaction within their social space. Such moral specificity is reflected in the vocabulary and grammatical structure of any given language.

How do shared cultural values arise? As obvious as it may seem, many theoretical constructs ignore the influence of the material context on moral judgement. Material circumstances and the 'survival margin' ordained by such circumstances will serve as a constraint, motivation or catalyst for weighing moral priorities. An individual's security of livelihood has an enormous bearing on moral judgement. In most agrarian societies, it is relatively easy to see how the moral core of local culture prescribes the socially acceptable form and content of behaviour with respect to production to meet 'basic needs' for food and shelter, reproductive behaviour and sexual relations, as well as the cultural requisites for group acceptance.

Development theory focuses on the achievement of improved living standards and social status associated with expanding material consumption, ownership and changing technology usage. It is generally assumed that rising standards of living and individualism evolve in tandem. As society moves from localized subsistence production to surplus production and exchange, needs are culturally redefined and moral values are reconfigured to reflect more affluent material circumstances and widening social choice. This book's preceding case studies have documented the hardships and uncertainties that African rural and urban dwellers face, which are obstacles to material advance and often impose an unlikely context for the emergence of western liberal values.

This chapter turns to the moral uncertainty accompanying rapid occupational change amidst unfulfilled expectations. The case study findings are considered in light of Durkheim's (1964; 2001) classic study of occupational restructuring in industrializing 19th century Europe. Omitting the assumption of rising affluence, we are left with a scenario in which localized African agrarian moral economy values are eroding and being reformulated under duress, while urban opportunities are far from delivering the promises of modernity embedded in African governments' and donors' development discourse. Western commentators generally assume the existence of universalized human rights and responsibilities. The reality is different. This chapter eschews a universalist position and distinguishes transformative moral negotiations taking place in everyday life from normative views of rights and responsibilities using the concepts of the 'moral economy' and 'civil society'.

Making morality amidst economic upheaval

In his book, *Professional Ethics and Civic Morals*, Durkheim (2001) defined morality as publicly sanctioned rules for the conformity of behavioural conduct. He endeavoured to show how rules were established, sanctioned, and applied within specific societies. Writing at a time of rapid economic change associated with European deagrarianization and industrialization, Durkheim advocated a moral order of rule-based collective discipline rather than the imposition of tyrannical control over the individual. His outlook and aims have resonance in today's African societies and economies. Amidst the upheaval of the past three decades, attempts at adopting identities and devising work etiquettes to facilitate earning a livelihood have proliferated, but there has been little public consensus about work morality. In these contexts, there should be no illusion that a singular moral universe prevails.

Social ethics rest on material foundations and through the course of world history; public morality has melded with the occupational pattern of the dominant productive sector in society. A society-wide moral crisis is virtually inevitable when work in the dominant productive sector experiences sudden diminution or drastic devaluation of its products and services. So too, existing occupationally specific ethical enforcement is likely to crumble as the dominant sector shrinks and new work forms emerge. The next two sections consider the malleability of public morality in relation to African occupational change.

Ethical roots: African moral economy before deagrarianization

Looking at the material and moral transformation of human agency, it is necessary but always hazardous to generalize about African so-called 'traditional' moral values. Like many anthropologists loathe to generalize, Ferguson (2006: 72), in his discussion of 'de-moralizing economies', sketches an African moral discourse and value structure which bears strong resemblance to the concept of moral economy identified in agrarian societies in various parts of the world. A 'moral economy' denotes an agrarian society where the subsistence ethic is primary. As Scott (1976: 6–7) observed amongst Vietnamese peasantries, subsistence is enshrined in these rural settings as the central moral principal underlying work patterns and relationships, designed to minimize risk and ensure the physical survival and security of the group.

African agrarian moral economies, incubated in local economies where food insufficiency was not uncommon and the 'will to live' was primary. The 19th century German philosopher, Schopenhauer, argued that human reason was 'willed' by physical need (Copleston, 1965). At low levels of production where basic subsistence is not continuously assured, a subsistence ethic of social responsibility underlines moral values. African moral economy constructs are illustrative: first, production of wealth and social distribution are inextricably linked. Work is moral when the fruits of labour are socially consumed rather than individually accumulated. The latter is seen as an exploitative transgression of the moral purpose of work. Second, wealth creation is legitimate when it is used to build relational ties. People with more have a responsibility to give to others, generating binding patron–client ties of mutual responsibility. Third, transgression of the distributive responsibilities of wealth creation is censured. Perpetrators of such social disharmony are seen as marked by misfortune and witchcraft.[1]

The pursuit of food security in traditional peasant agrarian settings demanded hard physical exertion during the agricultural season, which contrasted with post-harvest days of feasting and community celebration. While there were hierarchical distinctions between men and women as well as between elders and youth within households and within local communities, there was nonetheless a strong sense of interdependency and responsibility encompassing all ages and both genders (Bryceson, 1990, 1995). In most traditional African religions, morality was primarily guided by responsibility towards other people in the family and community rather than accountability to a higher supernatural being. Sacred and secular worlds were merged (Mbiti, 1975; Opoku, 1978).

The ancestors linked people to one another. They required respect and were expected to intercede in daily life. Concepts of good and evil varied but evil tended not to be assigned to a specific agency. The Yoruba, for example, saw evil as an imperfection or absence of good without attributing causation to individuals (Bewaji, 1998). This contrasts with Christian beliefs positing an opposition between the goodness of God and the evil of the devil, which are embedded in an individual's behaviour depending on the individual's exercise of free will. African conversion to Christianity and Islam has altered religious beliefs, but in many contexts traditional beliefs relating to the intervention of the ancestral and natural spirit world remain prevalent.

Historically, given survival imperatives, African moral responsibility was largely focused on the social collectivity of home-based consumption units rather than the conduct of public work settings. In the context of rapid change, that responsibility is likely to be readily reinterpreted in consonance with the economic experimentation and social restructuring of livelihood necessity. However during this process, the moral beliefs and sanctions of the world's monotheistic religions, notably Christianity and Islam, which have existed as religious veneers in many African peasant societies, often begin to offer more relevant moral underpinnings for those actively involved in economic and social change.

The domination of individualistic values in western societies is often contrasted with the African stress on collective welfare, be it of a family, community or village setting. But this generalization can be misleading. All societies evidence reciprocity in one form or another (Haidt, 2006). Reciprocity *per se* is not a distinguishing feature of African societies. Rather it is the significance of reciprocity in productive systems close to the fine line between basic subsistence and famine, which gives enhanced meaning to the act of reciprocity. Grabbing behaviour in the absence of reciprocity could have fatal consequences in famine situations. Thus moral obligations to reciprocate in African agrarian cultures have been attuned to basic needs attainment in accordance with Schopenhauer's 'will to live' and that will to live has been conceptualized as a collective rather than an individual will in the social context of African agrarian communities. People gained their identity through community membership as opposed to individual pursuit of an occupational career. The foundations of the moral economy were rooted in a shared social identity based on relational ties.

Small-scale rural communities, where everyone knows each other and follows roughly the same way of life cohere as moral economies around a restricted, ascriptive division of labour and the face-to-face accountability of community members. The coherence of the moral economy is challenged not so much by distress circumstances like famines and other production failures, because the moral economy's *raison d'etre* is, after all, to cope with such inevitabilities. Rather, the moral economy begins to unravel as the local division of labour becomes more complex and exchange relations proliferate, extending outwards beyond the boundaries of the local community.

In traditional rural African societies, when boundaries of community-sanctioned behaviour were transgressed, elders and chiefs intervened. Their authority derived from accumulated wisdom or ancestral intercession. Alternatively, witchcraft was called upon to bring various members of the community back in line. But the force of these deterrents increasingly eroded during the colonial period through missionary activity and most recently with the rapid spread of evangelical religious sects. Case studies in this book have explored the interaction of people in new urban, semi-urban or rural social spaces where they share no collectively defined subsistence imperative or common rural roots.

Creating civil society in the African context

Moral economy values, which continue to be felt and expressed despite the loss of their anchorage in African agrarian societies, are less socially enforceable given the geographical mobility and occupational experimentation of the last three decades. In the disjuncture, the transformation of economic and social agency in Africa has been accompanied by the importation of a western civil society discourse. 'Civil society' is a widely used term with a far less clearly delineated meaning than 'moral economy'. It can be traced back to classical thought on democracy and the enlightenment thinking of Thomas Hobbes and John Locke who argued the necessity for a 'social contract' between the state and civil society but differed on the balance between the two. Hobbes saw the need for a strong state as a check on the selfish interests of individuals forming civil society whereas Locke perceived civil society's need to keep the power-seeking state within bounds. Gramsci (1998) reinvigorated the debate in the 20th century, locating civil society between the state and market, as a space within which state power could be challenged. Recognizing that hegemonic states' interests often penetrate civil society organizations, Gramsci argued for building counter-hegemonism, seeing the goal of civil society as self-regulation and the withering away of the coercive state.

The concept of civil society has transmogrified during the 1990s, taking on multiple meanings dependent on context (Mamdani, 1996). In pluralist industrial societies, it denotes autonomous associations and voluntary organizations characterized by participatory, self-governing independence on a non-profit basis whose existence is believed to ensure individual liberty and democracy. In sub-Saharan Africa, civil society is in effect a residual – social relations and institutions that are neither state nor familial in nature. The unfolding meaning of the concept has tended to be instrumentalist and didactic, invoked by international donors to promote democracy as a counterbalance to power concentration in autocratic states (Kasfir, 1998). Civil society organizations are seen to encompass an exceptionally wide spectrum including traditional actors, ethnic groups, political parties, media, democratization movements, and development, gender and non-governmental organizations among many others.

Significantly, civil society activities in sub-Saharan Africa are no longer nationally bound. Non-governmental organizations (NGOs) in African countries are more often than not tied to international NGOs who help fund them and direct their policies. Using Gramsci's concept of hegemony, counter hegemony of African NGOs can be compromised by the international NGOs they are affiliated to, or, alternatively, African NGO personnel's compromised interests when they straddle positions within the African state. In the institutional tangle, the interests and ethics of African civil society are rarely delineated from those of the state and donor agencies. NGOs mask the confusion by projecting simplistic messages about the particular positions they advocate.

Civil society, as it exists in African countries at present, does not provide, let alone enforce, a generalized moral platform upon which people can conduct their daily work lives. Formerly, African nation-states, in their nation-building phase, provided development strategies that were informed by moral economy precepts, casting themselves in the role of the protector of material and social welfare. For example, Nyerere's *ujamaa* philosophy idealized familial relationships in the village setting to didactically promote African socialist values of mutual respect and assistance. His aim was to motivate the work patterns of the national citizenry towards a sense of collective welfare. Nyerere's efforts to involve people in 'imagining the nation' was highly effective. Tanzania is unique amongst East African countries avoiding ethnic tension and violent civil strife. This is an enduring achievement of almost half a century that has outlasted Tanzania's nation-building phase, persisting despite the country's debt-ridden status in the aftermath of the 1979 international oil crisis. Forced to adopt the World Bank's and IMF's structural adjustment and economic liberalization policies, the Tanzanian state was no longer in a position to formulate policies in the interests of 'protecting' the subsistence livelihood of its citizenry (Mbilinyi, Chapter 9). As Ferguson (2006) perceptively observes, neither African civil society nor the state are strictly speaking 'national'. The content and form of their policies are heavily swayed by the agendas of international agencies. Thus, state sovereignty and civil society are not self-determining in Africa as commonly assumed for western democracies.

Western constructs

Imposing universal moral standards

African public life has been heavily criticized in western media and academic critiques for its failure to achieve adequate standards of human rights, bureaucratic impartiality and market efficiency. Lacklustre performance is sometimes portrayed as part of an African cultural persona that cumulatively impedes the continent's development (Chabal and Daloz, 1999). This position is premised on a belief in a universal standard of state and market performance infused with western bias, ignoring that the western professional standards prevailing in developed countries are rooted in a far more stable material foundation and division of labour from that currently prevailing in Africa.

Afro-pessimism has pervaded the Africanist civil society literature (Bryceson, 2000a). Bayart *et al.* (1999: 420), for example, argue that African political power combines with illicit or criminal forms of economic accumulation to form the overall architecture of African society. Adopting an essentialist interpretation of African culture and politics, African power politics and corruption on the part of ruling elites are interpreted as part of an African behavioural repertoire passed down through history.[2] Chabal and Daloz (1999, 2005) depict African political elites as the apex of vast patron–client networks and ethnic ties that engulf the continent. A similar view, equally negative but more technicist in outlook, espoused by the World Bank and other western donors, assumes economically optimizing human behaviour to generally prevail, which is seen to be thwarted in Africa by the aberration of imperfect markets and rent-seeking corruption associated with the intervention of African state officials.

By adopting a market fundamentalist[3] perspective, western commentators ignore the significance of African economic and social contexts and overlook the distinction between the morality of western civil society and African moral economies. The concept of the moral economy denotes agrarian societies with basic age and gender divisions of labour whereas civil society arises in plural societies with diversified divisions of labour where associational ties and norms of public behaviour are non-familial. Individuals interact with one another on a relatively impersonal basis, independent of ties of kinship or locality.

Policies of pretence

Western civil society ideals formed the rationale for donors 'enabling environments and good governance' policies of the 1990s. Tautologically it was assumed that 'civil society', invariably vague and unspecified, would monitor venal African state officials and corrupt governments. The channelling of donor funding away from the state to support a proliferation of NGOs was aimed at providing checks and balances on government. Despite a wide variety of donor-funded support programmes, the implementation of donors' good governance policies has not delivered the expected gains in efficiency and equity. In fact, the outcome is often the opposite from what was intended. The blurring of boundaries between the African state and the donor-supported civil society can serve to extend or entrench the power and corruption of political elites who straddle both realms. At the same time, national law enforcement has weakened as state-directed policy trajectories have been supplanted by the implementation of structural adjustment and economic liberalization policies.

Through donors' support for African NGOs, civil society ethics have been advanced as a universal standard of public behaviour and yardstick for measuring civic performance. In the process, the gap between normative expectations and reality has been accentuated. Levels of public morality are lowered in a downward spiral of material disappointment, without asking if civil society values are realistic in the current context. African states, weakened by years of structural adjustment and economic liberalization policies, can no longer espouse a nation-building ethic nor other forms of generalized morality at the national level. They have little or no scope to do so, confined to policies elaborated externally on a continental basis by international financial institutions and the donor community. The social contract between African nation-states and their citizenries is largely in disarray. Nation-states cannot defend their citizens' rights to livelihood and basic needs and in return their citizenries are not inclined to endorse their leadership.

The negative impact of structural adjustment and economic liberalization policies on African economies led to the eclipse of the 'Washington consensus' with economists blaming Africa's 'market imperfections' and bad governance for the policy failure. The debate on governance widened to include 'social capital', a term borrowed from Bourdieu (1986) albeit omitting his historical contextualization of the concept. What remained was an essentialized notion of the necessity for non-market means of handling market imperfections (Fine, 2001). Social capital was perceived as individually as well as collectively optimizing behaviour built on horizontal associational ties of trust and democratic decision-making. Lumping a welter of social phenomena and processes into one fuzzy concept, social capital theorists attempted to encompass the social dynamics of the state, community and family.

Social capital concepts and good governance policies overlooked several key issues. First, state and market performance are intimately related to the productive capacity of the society. In many African countries, the widespread decline of peasant agriculture, in the absence of economic growth and labour absorption elsewhere in the economy, inevitably triggered insecurity in the national population at large. Under duress, people's survival efforts were unlikely to be pursued with the universal ethics of a 'civil society'. Rather they had to be guided by moral economy sensibilities, the right to a basic livelihood and the necessity of earning income for oneself and one's family and community, which extended to family or ethnic-based businesses *per se* as illustrated in the Guinea Bissau (Lindell, Chapter 8) and Igbo case studies (Chukwuezi and van den Bersselaar, Chapter 2 and Simone, Chapter 5).

Thus, the upheaval in the economic division of labour and trade that has been so pervasive throughout the 1980s and 1990s to the present triggered a disjuncture between moral economy values and social enforcement. Collective monitoring and enforcement mechanisms were destabilized within households and communities. Under these circumstances, subsistence ethics could not conceivably be scaled up to the national level. In fact, they usually ceased operating effectively at the community level and were called into question within individual households, as members' roles in the family division of labour by age and gender underwent radical change (Mbilinyi, Chapter 9).

As material and moral distress deepened, the subsistence ethic of the moral economy lost collective meaning and could be perversely invoked to rationalize individual goals at the expense of the community as a whole.

Occupational consensus: where moral economy and civil society begin to converge

In view of the dysfunction of the moral economy and civil society as originally defined, this section takes a counter tack. The relentless pursuit of work for the sake of family livelihood is the arena in which aspects of moral economy values and civil society rights-based approaches nonetheless provide the templates for priority setting and conflict resolution. While being utilized for these purposes, they are recast in new work contexts and contribute to the evolution of community-based *work etiquettes* that facilitate people's daily livelihood activities. In so doing, the gulf between the exigencies of one's work life and the lack of trust and cooperation amongst people without familial connections can be bridged (Dijkstra, Chapter 3).

Durkheim (2001) defines professional ethics as rules of conduct that are intermediary between family and civic morals. Rules, however, presupposes moral authorities and rule-setting procedures. The fluidity of African informal sector work over the last three decades has not afforded the permanence and organizational structures necessary for rule-setting. However, one can strenuously argue, and indeed our case studies provide ample evidence, that work etiquettes are evolving, on the basis of practical need, shared humanity and good-natured humour. Seppälä (Chapter 13) describes the polite, open-ended behaviour that is considered necessary for good working relations, a blend of congeniality, human respect, and politeness, which paves the way for interpersonal trust in Tanzania.

In the course of trial and error experimentation with diverse work activities, people are designing new forms of cooperation. For individuals, such experimentation entails uncertain outcomes and may meet with undesired as well as desired consequences. However, with everyone taking similar risks, a sense of common identity and collective experimentation can facilitate interpersonal negotiations central to people's economic and social welfare. In the process of negotiation, socially coherent 'communities' start to form.

Communities can be neighbourhoods (spatial), workplaces (economic), religious, or ethnic (social) spaces, which emerge when a sense of collective identity and mutual welfare congeals. Within communities, there is always a tension between the togetherness of 'we' in the community as opposed to disassociation from 'them', i.e. outsiders not sharing community space, identity and mutual interests. Reflexive social interaction within the community deepens the complexity and solidifies the consensual basis of a work etiquette, providing the foundations for the eventual establishment of professional ethics and an authority structure for their enforcement. Bank's (Chapter 10) case study of older women's participation in externally supported NGOs is illustrative. The women acquired a professional mode of behaviour that convinced donors of their funding worthiness much to the chagrin of men in the village traditionally accustomed to being the settlement's spokesmen with the outside world.

As new etiquettes and social alliances coalesce, adverse or complicating consequences for others within the community may arise notably with respect to the egalitarian values, which formerly underpinned the moral economy. Meagher (Chapter 6) notes how rapid class differentiation ensued amongst the Nigerian small-scale industrialists who succeeded in gaining access to state resources at the expense of others who were being edged out of business. Both Mbilinyi (Chapter 9) and Konings (Chapter 12) document the destabilization of the local balance of power between genders as well as age strata. Those on the descent experience feelings of resentment and demoralization.

From work etiquette to professional ethics to civic rights and responsibilities

Durkheim (2001) distinguishes professional ethics from civic morals in several ways. First, he sees them as very diverse corresponding to a wide array of occupations as opposed to more widely recognized ethics associated with a citizenry's relationship to a nation-state. Second, and contingent on the first, professional ethics represent a plurality of particular morals that operate on parallel lines. Third, they are somewhat outside the public consciousness, enforced within the occupation in question and otherwise not attracting general concern or adherence, through what Durkheim (2001: 7) calls 'decentralization of the moral life'. Fourth, professional ethics are lodged between family and civic morals, all representing different spheres of morality. Nonetheless, ultimately professional ethics, like family and civic morals, are subject to the collective power of public opinion, which can act to alter them. Fifth, the strength of professional ethics and their influence depends on the size and stability of occupational groups.

As occupational groups grow in size the need for rule-based interaction becomes imperative. Durkheim (2001) argued strongly for the strengthening and stabilization of professional groups and their development of self-regulation to improve public morality. But professional solidarity and self-regulation of growing numbers, nonetheless, was always vulnerable to impact of the wider economic context. The emergence of a free market industrial boom and bust pattern could lead to the contraction of work availability and social distress. Hence, he argued that regularity of production was important to morale and occupational morality, advocating planning and control to even out fluctuation as well as the provision of forms of subsistence fallback analogous to that traditionally provided by family production units and guilds. In sum, Durkheim saw unregulated free market forces as a barrier to professional stability and a debasing influence on public morality. He viewed the role of the state in labour markets with respect to unemployment benefits, efforts to regularize work availability, and encouragement of workers' professional organization as necessary components of the moral work world and an imperative for social well-being.

Durkheim believed that forming work associational ties set in train a seemingly natural process of moral accountability:

> once the group is formed, nothing can hinder an appropriate moral life from evolving, a life that will carry the mark of the special conditions that brought it into being. For it is not possible for men to live together and have constant dealings without getting a sense of this whole which they create by close association; they cannot help but adhere to this whole, be taken up with it and reckon it in their conduct. (23–4)

A Durkheimian view of cooperation, trust and morality arising during the course of people's daily work life is echoed in the work of contemporary authors (Haidt, 2006; Hauser, 2006; Kohn, 2008). What is generally overlooked is that even Adam Smith, known for his emphasis on capitalist self-interest, acknowledged:

> How selfish soever man may be supposed, there are evidently some principles in his nature, which interest him in the fortunes of others, and render their happiness necessary to him, though he derives nothing from it, except the pleasure of seeing it. (Adam Smith, *Theory of Moral Sentiments* quoted in Wilson (1976: 73)

The writings of Adam Smith and Durkheim were responses to periods of exceptional labour restructuring which have renewed resonance amidst the global economic recession of the early 21st century. At these critical times, occupational and moral choices are consciously deliberated, involving optimizing calculation as well as sentiments of empathy and trust. African work experimentation gives rise to the formation of work etiquettes in localized settings which, given stable conditions, can gradually gain momentum to congeal into shared work identities, professional ethics and organizations that become foundational to long term African material development.

The case studies in this volume provide examples of emergent associational ties of trust and cooperation in the face of uncertainty. Occupational experimentation involves learning by doing, competing with one another as well as establishing mutual trust and cooperation largely on the basis of face-to-face accountability and shared survival imperatives and work exigencies, moving beyond the moral economy but still within its frame of reference. Under conducive circumstances, people piecing together work etiquettes can eventually devise professional ethics suitable to their work environments. In a world of occupational plurality, people's household welfare, work, and professional organization are divided into separate spheres in contrast to the singularity of the agrarian moral economy with its overlap of welfare, work and authority structures in localized familial-based communities.

Our case study material does not provide a great deal of evidence of the development of professional ethics and formal work organization as yet. In fact the opposite has occurred. Professional organizations have folded and workers face increased competitive pressures and labour insecurity. It is worth examining these cases in some detail to discern what is happening.

Konings (Chapter 12) traces how a plantation labourers' trade union eroded within a Cameroonian rural community. A national economic downturn, weakening of the state and the implementation of World Bank enforced structural adjustment policies generated a climate in which the survival of the trade union as an independent agency representing workers' demands vis-à-vis management from 1958 became increasingly untenable. Casual wage labour replaced contractual work conditions and workers' pay declined.

In Nigeria, Meagher (Chapter 6, this volume) analyses the political hijacking of the informal occupational associations that arose in the garment as well as shoe clusters established in the 1980s and 1990s. Both proved incapable of fulfilling their intended purposes of facilitating economic regulation of sector entry, product quality and the encouragement of market schemes, loans and training. Instead they concentrated on lobbying government for assistance, dispute settlement and social welfare with respect to funeral assistance. In so doing, they subverted their aim to be independent civil society agencies and increasingly depended on government. Regional and local government gained leverage over them, extracting political support in return for infrastructural favours.

In Tanzania, the *esprit de corps* of civil servants plummeted during the country's economic crisis of the 1980s. The leadership code was abandoned and civil servants scrambled to diversify their income. Seppälä (Chapter 13) argues that in the process civil service professionalism was forsaken leaving a culturally conditioned politeness and congeniality, a baseline work etiquette in the absence of a professional organization that had the coherence and authority to sanction a professional ethic. Professional bodies of the educated middle class fell in abeyance as their members started moonlighting after their official work hours. Teachers and doctors began offering their services privately and, despite the reluctance of the state to acknowledge their activities, the need to regulate private health clinics for public safety prompted the state to start licensing private health clinics.

Government intervention in this case marked an important step towards re-professionalization. State support was needed to facilitate an enabling environment for development and enforcement of professional codes, but it was not sufficient in the absence of peoples' enduring commitment to specific work spheres. As Durkheim astutely observed:

> [a] society lacking in stability, whose discipline it is easy to escape and whose existence is not always felt, can communicate only a very feeble influence to the precepts it lays down. Accordingly ... professional ethics will be the more developed, and the more advanced in their operation, the greater the stability and the better the organization of the professional groups themselves. (2001: 8)

Table 14.1 Ethical sanctions for work

	Internal to occupational group	Local	National
Gossip	o	o	o
Religious rewards & sanctions		o	o
Media surveillance		o	o
State legal codes		o	o
Professional watchdog agencies		o	o
Professional ethical codes of practice	o	o	o

Outside of professional bodies, there are various channels through which professional ethics or etiquette are sanctioned. Table 14.1 lists these in a rough order of their likelihood of efficacy in situations of relative instability and insecurity. It is interesting to note that sanctions operate within an occupational group at both ends of the sanction spectrum. Gossip is certainly important in the formation of work etiquette whereas professional ethics require a full battery of institutional supports.

Sanction levels depicted above are not evolutionary stages of professionalization. They denote different spheres of social interaction and means of inter-personal influence over work behaviour distinguished from the influence exerted by community members within a localized moral economy and bounded social space who work and consume together on the basis of an inclusive intra-familial moral code. During occupational experimentation, moral influences on behaviour will necessarily become more plural, open-ended and negotiable.

Scaling up to civic morals

Durkheim (2001) argued that the principle duties of civic morals are those of the citizen to the state and the duty of the state to the individual. Civic morals constitute a code of rules that prescribe what the individual should do to avoid damaging collective interests. The state is responsible for the collective good, devising representations and guiding collective goals while safeguarding the rights of the individual and making political space for people of like interests to express themselves. Durkheim was wary, but overall positive, about the role of the state in society, expressing the view that the state had often been a liberator in history and could act to raise levels of production, morality and justice in society. Having already argued that present day African civil society has so far been heavily encrusted with international donor influence which subverts local agenda-setting and democratic justice, are Durkheim's civic morals in any way relevant to the African present or near future?

In sub-Saharan Africa, the nation-state is weak almost everywhere. With the exception of South Africa, mineral-rich Botswana and a number of countries embroiled in civil war, the World Bank and IMF have ventriloquized national economic policies since the 1980s. Citizenries have lost public confidence in their governments' ability to act on their behalf, feeling abandoned or thwarted rather than supported by them. Compensatory African moral agency in these circumstances has necessarily entailed a wide gamut of responses with three main trajectories: first, an effort to seek justice in moral economy terms; second, a spiritual search for moral meaning, and/or third, succumbing to the amorality of a society geared to seizing material advantage regardless of social costs.

The first trajectory, which has continuously surfaced in the case study material of this book and has already been discussed in this chapter, is best termed, 'social etiquette setting'. It is a creative and constructive path charted by people in the course of their daily lives. People venture to cooperate and trust each other on the basis of their common survival imperative. This involves a multitude of risk-taking, morality-forming social encounters every day that coalesces into a moral etiquette rarely structured by government legal codes.

Secondly, a 'spiritual search for moral meaning' has engulfed vast numbers who embrace religious conversion as a modernist break with African traditional morality. Christian Pentecostal churches led by charismatic preachers have attracted enormous followings. Often they play on the economic insecurities of converts by offering a new set of economic values which displace moral economy concerns and kin responsibility with moral adherence and material support to the churches themselves (van Dijk, 2002; Meagher, 2009). So too, Islamic fundamentalist beliefs may become attractive to segments of African society in this context. The adoption of a religiously defined behavioural template more in consonance with the changing work environment and uncertainties of non-agrarian settings can alleviate the uncertainty of one's work life and impart a sense of direction that is collectively endorsed by fellow believers.

Third, people may engage in 'defiant non-compliance or sabotage' of state policies. This can entail pursuing material advantage in contexts where they see the state thwarting rather than facilitating their efforts. Instead of people enjoying government-guaranteed rights and responsibilities of civil society, people's resentment and/or amoral retaliation against government officials' rent-seeking prevails. As Niger-Thomas records (Chapter 11), Cameroonian market women were loath to pay taxes that they believed would be pocketed by state tax collectors. Similarly in Congo, the unproductive rent-seeking of well-placed Kinshasa residents utilizing state positions to access the resources of their mineral-rich economy created a sense of general amorality. The general population outside of state circles sought to gain wealth through pyramid schemes that they believed would let them tap into the otherwise exclusively controlled mineral wealth of the nation (Mohogu, Chapter 4). The Igbo illegal drug and prostitution syndicates in Johannesburg circumvented the state's authority through innovative strategies (Simone, Chapter 5).

Jua (Chapter 7) dissects the descent of youth into disillusionment over their future work lives propelling them towards risk-taking, rebellion and ambition in a 'field of unlimited possibility'. Their dreams of sports stardom and high living using 'body capital' through the proceeds of prostitution, discounts the odds of financial success. The amoral pursuit of unrealistic expectations is in consonance with the state's absence of public accountability. The youth have lost their government bursaries for university education and the possibility of a public sector career path that they would have been availed a decade earlier.

African corruption has been extensively documented and characterized as the 'politics of the belly' (Bayart *et al.*, 1999). Privileged elites' monopolization of resources and returns block the aspirations of those less fortunate who in turn take recourse in extra-legal activities. Political scientists have tended to stress the anarchy of atomistic amorality in Africa, rather than the full spectrum of social behaviour and moral choice of African agency. This has resulted in the unwarranted and indeed distorted Afro-pessimism of much of western press coverage and academic literature.

Finally, there is the possibility of moral revolt or anarchy. African citizenries witness state transgressions in the form of corruption, social discrimination of ethnic or other social groups, and in extreme cases, atrocities against select segments of the citizenry. People's resentment in the first instance is likely to take one of the above forms of moral response, but if levels of abuse rise in the absence of ruling elites' sufficiently calibrating patron–client relations to align strategic clients' vested interests with theirs, public resentment may erupt into civil revolt. Such events can be considered an aberration of traditional African cultural values, which stressed social harmony. They erupt as a molten lava of social tension propelled by occupational upheaval, social identity crisis and rapid class stratification (Bryceson, 2000b; Mamdani 2001). These situations can lead to protracted civil war, as witnessed currently in Somalia and the Congo.

Whatever Africans' moral response is to their continent's deeply felt economic insecurity, the relative lack of occupational identities, professional ethics and generalizable moral codes severely restricts the crystallization of a broadly acceptable amalgam of occupational and social divisions in national society. The alloys for this amalgam are coalescing but they need a far firmer economic base to become pervasive within African national cultures.

Building civic morality

Under these circumstances, most of the literature on African civil society generated by western donors represents wishful thinking. The community and household are assumed to be repositories of altruism while the market is seen as benign or indifferent and the state is almost invariably viewed as the source of undesirable tendencies ranging from inefficiency to malignant corruption.

These caricatures amount to a woefully static and inadequate analytical foundation for promoting development in sub-Saharan Africa.

The continent has witnessed deeply rooted change in its social fabric over the last three decades of economic crisis. Amidst occupational restructuring, production and service provisioning has shifted from localized settings subject to consensual moral economy principles to national arenas of spatially dispersed commerce beyond familial ties and face-to-face encounters where social trust is at issue. Increasingly, under the sway of international financial institutions' policies, the market has dwarfed the state. The paternalism of the African nation-building state exuding moral economy concerns has been replaced with weak, inept states trying to cope with the inequities of market forces at international, national and local levels. Household and community social ethics have necessarily had to realign to embrace the uncertain realities of African state and market dynamics.

Civil society perspectives tend to overlook the institutional interaction of household, community, state and market and above all the influence of material insecurity on the morale and moral etiquette of these institutions. Donor policy is bipolar. On the one hand, market liberalization is advocated despite the uncompetitiveness of so much of African production in the world market and its impoverishing effect on African producers. On the other hand, poverty reduction and, most recently social protection policies, are set as policy goals, largely through household and community targeted 'gesture measures'. Social protection policies are intended to mitigate the economic distress of the marginalized that proliferates as growth maximization strategies are implemented.

International financial institutions operate under the belief that the pursuit of an enabling environment and good governance policies will attract foreign investment and poverty reduction programmes will keep households and communities socially intact. The civil unrest in Kenya that suddenly flared in early January 2008 after national elections is just one of many examples of how inadequate such policies are. National elections inevitably dramatize existing social imbalances alongside considerations of policy and political alliances. Kenya fortunately was steered back from the brink of ethnically-divided civil war but many other countries have not been so lucky.

Inter-institutional dynamics

When the African problematic is approached as a question of political and moral economy, then its resolution necessarily rests on internal consensus-building rather than an externally defined economic growth formula. Furthermore, the road to consensus-building is never simple or neatly sequenced. It cannot be defined as a blanket prescription for all African civil societies. Its solution lies as much in the means as in the ends. Every African society has to evolve its own public morality based on its specific social history, occupational structure and the interlocking dynamics of its household, community, market and state institutions. Policy directions can be suggested to facilitate a harmonious outcome but the outcome and the means to the outcome cannot be pre-defined. External commentators proscribing public morality based on idealized western models of civil society transgress the need for the organic evolution of social trust and in doing so are more likely to create confusion and disillusionment than social cohesion. The transition to a public morality resting on generalizable social trust requires institutional interaction between the household, community, market and state. Each African nation-state needs scope to evolve its own interactive blend of social institutions in line with cultural and occupational configurations. This is quite different to donor conditionality of the last 30 years, which has ignored the operation of households and communities and has constructed the state and market as oppositional forces, privileging the market as the pivot for social change.

Strengthening shaky household and community material foundations

Several of the chapters have shown how the dynamics of the household and community promote or detract from social consensus-building. There has been a long history of adverse consequences of internationally imposed policies that have rebounded on intra-familial relations. Social distrust often begins within the household. Mbilinyi's (Chapter 9) case study of rural women who started earning wages on a nearby sugar estate during economic liberalization illustrates this. Power relations tilted away from male patriarchy. Women resented men's demands on their labour within the household whereas men felt insecure in relation to women's new-found economic autonomy. Rural households' subsistence food production, however, continued to underwrite the material security of the household.

In South Africa, women's initiatives in the area of NGO activities were seen to be usurping men's traditional role in the community. Men felt increasingly marginalized and demotivated as household provisioners. The South African government's experimentation with rural development policies and food security measures had little effect on the long-term declining trend in the rural economy (Bank, Chapter 10). Furthermore, rural households had long passed being reliant on own subsistence food production for daily needs or as an emergency fallback.

Consensus-building, be it in the community or household, requires policies that improve access to basic needs. Subsistence food production continues to be of strategic importance for rural households' material stability in most African countries with the notable exception of South Africa. In addition to prioritizing basic needs, there is a need for development policies to be tailored to the specificities of individual countries with an appreciation of how policies impact on roles and responsibilities within and between households in the community.

Revitalizing the social contract between the African state and its citizenry

Most African states have yet to regain their policy-making initiative from the World Bank despite participatory poverty reduction strategy exercises over the past decade. International financial institutions' neo-liberal agenda has prevailed as the main trajectory of development policy on the continent. It remains to be seen if the proliferation of state intervention measures to salvage western capitalist countries' market implosion, prompted by the 2008 global recession, will reverse the march of monetarist policies (Stein, 2008; Cramer et al., 2009).

African national economies, based primarily on raw material export, have historically been export economies open to world market forces. Market liberalization policies of the 1990s reinforced the openness without measures to enhance the investment necessary to improve African competitiveness in the world market. Thus, African farmers continually lost market share in the world market, their displaced labour finding its way to the service sector, unleashing far-reaching occupational restructuring throughout the continent. Meanwhile, national economies' foreign exchange earnings shrank, making governments unable to generate the revenue to provide the productive and social services necessary for raising national production. Locked in a relentless cycle of fiscal failure, the African state was powerless to stimulate economic recovery.

The informal economy has largely replaced the formal economy in both rural and urban Africa. Simone (Chapter 5) and Lindell (Chapter 8) document the dynamic nature of the informal economy as it expands far outside the state's legal and fiscal reach. Niger-Thomas's (Chapter 11) Cameroonian study dramatizes the distrust that exists between informal sector workers and the state represented by women market traders and male tax collectors. Would female tax collectors have eased the situation? Highly unlikely, given that the dividing line was drawn between state agents as opposed to household provisioners-cum-market traders. The protesting women were not solely taking issue with state taxation. Rather their outrage was targeted at a state which was not ensuring the infrastructure and services generally associated with 'fair tax' payment.

Mbilinyi (Chapter 9) points to the crux of the matter. In local economies where food security is in question, people's acceptance of the supervisory and distributive role of the state is necessarily tied to national governments providing some semblance of infrastructure and social welfare. In the moral economy of the immediate post-independence period, African governments attempted to guarantee basic physical survival through the provision of famine relief when food harvests failed and encouraged peasant agricultural production through commodity pricing policies and input support programmes. The social contract between ruler and ruled in pre-Structural Adjustment Programme African local economies involved an aspirant welfare and developmental state, rather than simply a 'taxing state' of unfulfilled promises.

This chapter has argued that the formation of professional work associations and collectively drawn up codes of conduct for their membership is an important building block in civil society formation and the strengthening of the African state's capacity to efficiently deliver services and facilitate national production. The aim should be to minimize individual and household material insecurity and demonstrate the collective interests involved in occupational specialization and professional standards. But it is necessary to take heed that this is a gradual process. Seppälä (Chapter 13) avoids being judgemental about lack of professionalism when the material basis for such professionalism no longer exists. Building around what exists, the etiquette of social networking for livelihood purposes, is a good start, ultimately serving to build social trust and, over time, the skill base of the economy.

Conclusion: embryonic professionalism and the path to civic morality

The case study chapters in this collection indicate that there have been myriad ways by which local level trust and empathy have been creatively devised in the process of people's everyday work lives despite the open-ended uncertainties of occupational restructuring. However, as yet, this has remained largely restricted to occupationality, as defined in Chapter 1, and has fallen short of occupational professionalism in the Durkheimian sense. New associational ties and community identities are surfacing that extend beyond familial ties. Betwixt and between, people may still rely primarily on face-to-face accountability but not necessarily on the faces of kin.

African livelihoods in rural and urban areas remain fundamentally insecure and unpredictable. The last three decades of western donor-led policy formulation has generally exacerbated rather than enhanced stability for populations undergoing occupational upheaval. Global recession has plunged people into deeper insecurity, where a survival ethic is all that can be clutched at.

Discourse about universal rights and responsibilities in public life and the national economic arena have been diversionary. African culture or corruption cannot be justifiably blamed for the lack of civil society or failings of public life more generally in the face of donor policy indifference to the social repercussions of rapid large-scale labour displacement arising from the SAP and economic liberalization policies that they imposed. Amidst the scramble for alternative work, the material foundations of civil society and public life have yet to take shape and, not surprisingly, there is an overall lack of moral consensus. In the social space between the moral economy and civil society, corrupt officials are the 'fortunate ones' who are likely to escape moral censure if they distribute part of their illicit gains through patron–client networks.

Civil societies are only viable and real in the presence of socially endorsed occupational identities and professional ethics. Bridging the hiatus between moral economy and civil society principles can only be achieved when an occupational order stabilizes and national economies offer a base upon which people can safely move from localized ties of kinship and clientage networks to anchor themselves in a national division of labour underpinned by specialized professional ethics.

Stable occupational identities and the collective enforcement of professional ethics are needed before people can make the leap of faith into trusting an impersonal state and having confidence in market dynamics to enable them to secure reliable livelihoods. In an era of global recession, this need becomes ever greater and ever more difficult to secure.

The spread of economic recession globally hopefully will instil a more profound understanding of the dilemmas of African political economies on the part of western commentators who have overlooked the material context in which the African continent has struggled over the last three decades. Western governments have abandoned neo-liberal market fundamentalist policies and embraced Keynesian policies that involve government subsidizing production, rescuing banks, 'quantitatively easing' money supply and increasing the national debt. When African economies experienced a similarly severe economic shock and recession beginning in the late 1970s, the policy prescription was harsh cutbacks and government non-intervention. Certainly the lessons from the African experience of protracted recession and pervasive labour dislocation testify to the myopia of international financial institutions' insistence on cutbacks on services and investment in Africa during the last two decades.

The comparison between Africa's protracted economic crisis and the 2008 global crisis can be extended to the realm of moral justice. Previously admired for their role in promoting growth and prosperity, western bankers who practiced dodgy derivative investment, sub-prime lending and aggressive take-over deals have been allowed by western governments to retain their over-inflated bonuses and pensions because of legal contractual terms, despite the widespread moral outrage of tax-paying citizenries.[4] They are legally justified but are they more morally justified than corrupt African state officials and businessmen who have similarly looted their respective national economies, but who frequently are obliged to share their takings with family, friends and associational ties under terms of the moral economy?

Durkheim wrote about the transformation of post-agrarian Europe over a century ago. This chapter has applied his concepts of professional ethics and civic morality to deagrarianizing Africa of the present day. It is telling, however, that today's post-industrial west also evidences moral confusion and distrust in the context of the material insecurity of global recession.

In conclusion, occupational change and its accompanying inchoate morality can be disastrous or uplifting to African development. Policies that build producers' confidence and a sense of livelihood security are vital to African recovery, economic development and equitable social transformation. On this foundation, trust within and between occupational groups can be successfully nurtured. Through regularity and security of work, clear occupational identities emerge accompanied by the evolution of professional ethics that occupational groups are willing and able to adhere to. And finally upon these firm material and social foundations, African civil society can thrive. The form it will take will vary from one country to another, but it must be built on the accretion of trust from within the society rather than by government decree or western donor design.

Notes

* I am grateful to Ignacy-Marek Kaminski for his comments on the draft of this chapter.
1. Wolf (1966) stresses the importance of ceremonial affirmation of the community's interdependence within peasant societies worldwide and a common set of do's and don'ts that emphasize regulation of behaviour rather than belief *per se*. Supernatural sanctions are invoked for the sake of maintaining social order within and between household units. Furthermore, conservatism of values and behaviour characterizes the community.
2. This position mutually interacts with western media portrayals of Africa as 'the hopeless continent' as illustrated by headlined feature in *The Economist* (11 May 2000) and 'Africa's despots', (London *Sunday Times* 9 April 2000) as opposed to more recent press coverage revealing hesitant optimism: 'The flicker of a brighter future' (*The Economist* 9 September 2006) and 'Optimism in Africa' (*New York Herald Tribune* 3 October 2006) and 'Africa – There is hope – Despite the persistence of Africa's natural and man-made horrors, the latest trend is cheeringly positive' (*The Economist* 11 October 2008).
3. Market fundamentalism is defined here as a belief in the innate nature of the market as a prime mover or exchange and optimizer of production regardless of the political imbalances and social biases of markets as historical institutions within specific social contexts. While markets are viewed as neutral forums of exchange, states are seen as concentrations of vested interests and power.
4. See 'Anger Management' and 'Bankers: Scapegoat millionaire' (*The Economist* 7 March 2009); 'Greedy bankers still coining it in at our expense' and 'Toxic loans take taxpayers into the unknown', (*Sunday Times* 1 March 2009).

References

Bayart, J-F., Ellis, S. and Hibou, B. (1999) *The Criminalization of the State*, James Currey, London.

Bewaji, J.A.I. (1998) 'Oldumare: God in Yoruba belief and the theistic problem of evil', *African Studies Quarterly: Online Journal for African Studies* 4.

Bourdieu, P. (1986) 'The forms of capital', in J. Richardson (ed.), *Handbook of Theory and Research for the Sociology of Education*, pp. 241–58, Greenwood Press, New York.

Bryceson, D.F. (1990) *Food Insecurity and the Social Division of Labour in Tanzania, 1919–1985*, Macmillan, Basingstoke UK.

Bryceson, D.F. (1995) 'African women hoe cultivators: speculative origins and current enigmas', in D.F. Bryceson (ed.), *Women Wielding the Hoe: Lessons from Rural Africa for Feminist Theory and Development Practice*, pp. 3–22, Berg Publishers, Oxford.

Bryceson, D.F. (2000a) 'Of criminals and clients: African culture and Afropessimism in a globalized world', *Canadian Journal of African Studies* 34(2): 417–42.

Bryceson, D.F. (2000b) 'Disappearing peasantries? Rural labour redundancy in the neo-liberal era and beyond', in D.F. Bryceson, C. Kay and J. Mooij (eds), *Disappearing Peasantries? Rural Labour in Africa, Asia and Latin America*, pp. 299–326, Intermediate Technology Publications, London.

Chabal, P. and Daloz, J-P. (1999) *Africa Works: Disorder as Political Instrument*, James Currey, London.

Chabal, P. and Daloz, J-P. (2005) *Culture Troubles: Politics and the Interpretation of Meaning*, C. Hurst & Co., London.

Copleston, F. (1965) *A History of Philosophy*, Vol 7: *Modern Philosophy*, Part II: *Schopenhauer to Nietzche*, Image Books, New York.

Cramer, C., Johnston, D. and Oya, C. (2009) 'Africa and the credit crunch: from crisis to opportunity?', *African Affairs* 108: 643–54.

Durkheim, E. (1964) [1933], *The Division of Labor in Society*, The Free Press, New York.

Durkheim, E. (2001) [1957], *Professional Ethics and Civic Morals*, Routledge & Kegan Paul, London.

Ferguson, J. (2006) *Global Shadows: Africa in the Neoliberal World Order*, Duke University Press, Durham NC.

Fine, B. (2001) *Social Capital versus Social Theory: Political Economy and Social Science at the Turn of the Millennium*, Routledge, London.

Gramsci, A. with Nowell-Smith, G. and Hoare, Q. (eds) (1998) *Prison Notebooks: Selections*, Lawrence & Wishart Ltd., London.

Haidt, J. (2006) *The Happiness Hypothesis*, Arrow Books, London.

Hauser, M. (2006) *Moral Minds: How Nature Designed Our Universal Sense of Right and Wrong*, Harper Collins, New York.

Kasfir, N. (1998) 'The conventional notion of civil society: a critique', in N. Kasfir, N. (ed.), pp. 1–20, *Civil Society and Democracy in Africa: Critical Perspectives*, Frank Cass and Co., London.

Kohn, M. (2008) *Trust: Self-Interest and the Common Good*, Oxford, Oxford University Press.

Mbiti, J.S. (1975) *Introduction to African Religion*, Praeger, New York.

Mamdani, M. (1996) *Citizen and Subject: Contemporary Africa and the Legacy of Late Colonialism*, James Currey, London.

Mamdani, M. (2001) *When Victims become Killers: Colonialism, Nativism, and the Genocide in Rwanda*, Princeton University Press.

Meagher, K. (2009) 'Trading on faith: religious movements and informal economic governance in Nigeria', *Journal of Modern African Studies* 47(3), 397–423.

Opoku, K.A. (1978) *West African Traditional Religion*, FEP, Accra.

Prinz, J. (2007) *The Emotional Construction of Morals*, Oxford University Press, Oxford.

Scott, J.C. (1976) *The Moral Economy of the Peasant: Rebellion and Subsistence in Southeast Asia*, Yale University Press, New Haven.

Smith, A. (1946) *The Wealth of Nations*, reprinted in Abbott, L.D. (ed.), *Masterworks of Economics*, Doubleday & Company, New York.

Stein, Howard (2008) *Beyond the World Bank Agenda: An Institutional Approach to Development*, University of Chicago Press, Chicago.

van Dijk, R. (2002) 'Religion, reciprocity and restructuring family responsibility in the Ghanaian Pentecostal diaspora', in D.F. Bryceson and U. Vuorela (eds), *The Transnational Family: New European Frontiers and Global Networks*, pp. 173–96, Berg, Oxford.

Wilson, T. 1976, 'Sympathy and self-interest', in T. Wilson and A.S. Skinner (eds), *The Market and the State: Essays in Honour of Adam Smith*, pp. 73–99, Clarendon Press, Oxford.

Wolf, E.R. (1966) *Peasants*, Prentice-Hall, London.

Index